TOURISM AND IDENTITY IN
SCOTLAND, 1770–1914

Erratum

Tourism and Identity in Scotland, 1770–1914
Creating Caledonia
Katherine Haldane Grenier

is Volume Thirty
in the Studies in European Cultural Transition series

General Editors: Martin Stannard and Greg Walker

Tourism and Identity in Scotland, 1770–1914

Creating Caledonia

KATHERINE HALDANE GRENIER
The Citadel

ASHGATE

Published by
Ashgate Publishing Limited
Gower House
Croft Road
Aldershot
Hants GU11 3HR
England

Ashgate Publishing Company
Suite 420
101 Cherry Street
Burlington, VT 05401-4405
USA

Ashgate website: http://www.ashgate.com

British Library Cataloguing in Publication Data
Grenier, Katherine Haldane
    Tourism and identity in Scotland, 1770-1914 : creating Caledonia.—
    (Studies in European cultural transition)
    1.Tourism—Scotland—History 2.Travelers—Scotland—History 3.National
    characteristics, Scottish—History 4.Heritage Tourism—Scotland—
    History
    I.Title
    914.1'1047

Library of Congress Cataloging-in-Publication Data
Grenier, Katherine Haldane.
  Tourism and identity in Scotland, 1770-1914 : creating Caledonia / Katherine
Haldane Grenier.
    p. cm.—(Studies in European cultural transition)
  Includes bibliographical references and index.
  ISBN 0-7546-3694-1 (alk. paper)
  1. Tourism—Scotland—History. 2. Travelers—Scotland—History. 3. National
characteristics, Scottish—History. 4. Heritage tourism—Scotland—History. I.
Title. II. Series.

  DA850.G74 2005
  914.11'5047—dc22

                                                                2005003585

ISBN-10: 0 7546 3694 1

Printed and bound in Great Britain by MPG Books Ltd, Bodmin, Cornwall

Contents

General Editors' Preface

The European dimension of research in the humanities has come into sharp focus over recent years, producing scholarship which ranges across disciplines and national boundaries. Until now there has been no major channel for such work. The series aims to provide one, and to unite the fields of cultural studies and traditional scholarship. It will publish the most exciting new writing in areas such as European history and literature, art history, archaeology, language and translation studies, political, cultural and gay studies, music, psychology, sociology and philosophy. The emphasis will be explicitly European and interdisciplinary, concentrating attention on the relativity of cultural perspectives, with a particular interest in issues of cultural transition.

Martin Stannard
Greg Walker
University of Leicester

Acknowledgements

It is a great joy to thank all those whose emotional, intellectual, and financial assistance enabled me to write this book. I have been fortunate to teach at two colleges which provided generous institutional support. The History Department at the College of Charleston financed a research trip to Scotland in 1992, a remarkable grant to a visiting junior faculty member. The Citadel Foundation, whose work is so vital to the academic mission of The Citadel, funded several research trips, conference presentations, production costs, and a year's sabbatical. Colleagues at both schools were unfailingly helpful, especially those at The Citadel, whose efforts helped make it possible for me to take a leave of absence following the sabbatical. I am grateful to work with such intelligent, kind, and inspirational colleagues.

My research would have been much less thorough without the efforts of numerous interlibrary loan librarians, and I appreciate their abilities to track down obscure Scottish guidebooks, travel accounts, and other sources. Most notable among them is Debbe Causey and her staff at Daniel Library at The Citadel. I also thank the interlibrary loan personnel at the College of Charleston and Alderman Library at the University of Virginia, where this project was begun. I am also grateful to the National Library of Scotland, the Scottish Record Office, Edinburgh Central Library, and the Thomas Cook Archives, especially Jill Hooper. The Citadel Print Shop created camera-ready copy. Victoria Meyer tracked down several illustrations for me at Virginia. Betty Hagglund provided a copy of her transcript of 'A Lady's' 1776 travel account, and of her dissertation on eighteenth-century women travelers in Scotland. Alastair Durie sent me copies of several of his articles on Victorian tourism in Scotland. A special thanks for the delightful tour of Stirling he gave my husband and me! Portions of Chapters 3 and 5 were previously published as journal articles. Thank you to *Nineteenth Century Studies* for permission to republish ' "No Human Foot Comes Here": Victorian Tourists and the Isle of Skye' [10(1996):69-91] and to the *Victorians Institute Journal* for permission to republish 'Tourism and the Idea of the Skye Crofter: Nature, Race, Gender and the Late Nineteenth-Century Highland Identity' [25(1997):105-32].

I have been blessed with many wonderful friends, who critiqued drafts, brainstormed ideas, and raised faltering spirits. I would have had a much more difficult – and less enjoyable – time writing the dissertation which was the genesis of this book without Lynda Coon, Jena Gaines, Ellen Litwicki, and Elisabeth Sommer. Randy Sparks, then at the College of Charleston, helped me to make the transition from graduate student to faculty member, and pushed me to take my work before a wider academic audience. At The Citadel, Keith Knapp, Joelle Neulander, Jeff Pilcher, Kyle Sinisi, and Jennie Speelman are deeply valued critics and highly esteemed friends. Suzanne Ozment offered several helpful ideas about literature and landscape.

I will always be grateful to my parents, Doug and Jean Haldane, for their abiding support of my dreams and efforts, their commitment to my education, and all the many ways they continue to help and encourage me – even providing extra childcare when the workload gets too heavy! I owe particular thanks to my father for introducing me to Scotland, his father's birthplace, and thus planting seeds which led to this topic. My sister, Susan Haldane, is also a constant source of moral support. Dena Haldane and Shona and Tim Edward provided gracious hospitality on many trips to Edinburgh, and spending time with them has been a wonderful benefit to my research. My sons, Ian and Matthew, both born while I was writing this book, are a joyful distraction and I appreciate their patience during the many hours I had to be away from them in order to write. My deepest thanks goes to my husband, Stephen. His faith in my ability to complete this book has sometimes far surpassed my own, and the fact that I did so is in large measure due to his unwavering encouragement, even when he had to call from Afghanistan to express it! This project has often been as much a part of his life as it has mine, and my memories of working on it are inextricably bound up with reminiscences of our years together. I dedicate this book to him, with love and gratitude.

List of Abbreviations

ILN – *Illustrated London News*
NLS – National Library of Scotland
PRO – Public Record Office
SRO – Scottish Record Office

List of Illustrations

Cover: 'Strath Carron, Loch Carron in the Distance.' *Illustrated London News*, August 20, 1870, used by permission of the *Illustrated London News* Picture Library.

Plate section is located between pages 118 and 119

Introduction

'We are in Scotland!', exclaimed Edwin Waugh and his friends as their northbound train crossed the Tweed in 1863. 'A thrill of excitement ran through me, and I looked out eagerly.'[1] Waugh had decided on the spur of the moment to accompany three friends to Scotland, and was exhilarated about the experience that lay before him. 'And there was a touch of adventure about the affair that had its charms. I had never seen any part of Scotland; though its history and literature had been floating about my mind from my earliest years. And now, all that I had read and dreamed of that romantic land came upon me afresh, in one bewildering stream of pleasant anticipation.'[2] Waugh's sense of expectancy reflects the firm hold Scotland exercised on the nineteenth-century popular imagination. An intriguing, mysterious country with a unique culture, Scotland perfectly fulfilled the Romantic ideal. Nature existed there in its most raw and untouched form. Mankind, too, lived close to nature; tourist literature portrayed Scots as hardy, rustic, and unaffected by the sophistication of the outside world. There, many believed, was a deeper sense of the spiritual, which was a comforting sensation for those to whom science seemed to threaten the certainties of religion. Unlike many other nineteenth-century countries, Scotland still seemed connected to the past. Indeed, Scotland came to suggest all the virtues the modern world appeared to have discarded. And, perhaps most intriguing, all this existed within the borders of the leading industrial nation of the nineteenth century.

It is well known that newly positive impressions of Scotland in the late eighteenth and early nineteenth centuries, especially the Highlands, turned the country into a popular tourist attraction. By the Victorian period, Scotland was a favorite destination of members of the English middle and upper classes, Continental and American visitors, as well as Scots eager to learn more about their own country. Thomas Cook, creator of modern package tours, claimed to have taken a total of 40,000 people through Scotland between 1846 and 1861.[3] Tourism was a significant sector of the economy in many parts of Scotland, and its effects filtered to all layers of society other than the poorest.[4]

This study explores English tourists' interest in Scotland in the late eighteenth and nineteenth centuries as a means of examining middle and upper-class popular consciousness. As the pace of economic, social, and political transformations intensified in England in the nineteenth century, English tourists came to envision the north as a place immune to change, and understood journeys there to be antidotes to the uncertainties of modern life. While praised as the home of preindustrial virtues which critics sometimes claimed were disappearing from the more modern south, Scotland was also belittled as unprogressive and backwards. Scotland's role within the Union was to preserve the values which England might have to put aside in order to further the economic greatness of Britain. There was an element of escapism in tourism to Scotland, but visitors were not necessarily seeking to turn their backs on modernity. Instead, they sought confirmation that there were limits to the effects of industrialization. By symbolizing changelessness, the vision of Scotland eased accommodation to the new world of the nineteenth century.

This modern idea of Scotland as a rustic playground was created in the late eighteenth and nineteenth centuries. At that time the Scottish need to refashion a self-image in the wake of political union with England coincided with a new outside curiosity awakened by the Union, as well as the influences of Romanticism, Jacobitism, and the literature of Robert Burns and the mythical Celtic bard Ossian. The eighteenth century also saw simmering tensions between England and Scotland as both sides of the border experienced ambiguity over the Act of Union. Scots struggled with maintaining their own national identity while also desiring to emulate English progress and expansion. Meanwhile, because many in the south resented the transformation of 'England' into 'Great Britain', the Union stirred a developing sense of English nationalism.[5] English nationalists tended to see Scots either as taking away English jobs and favoring their own at English expense, or as 'whingeing ingrate[s]', unwilling to pay their full share of taxes but constantly demanding access to English resources.[6] English resentment was combined with fear. Jacobite attempts to restore the Stuart monarchy in 1715 and 1745 threatened to destroy Britain's political and religious harmony, as well as its commercial prosperity. The 1760s saw a noisy popular Scottophobia in England, stirred in part by John Wilkes' characterizations of Scots as aliens who could never truly be part of the English nation. Worries about Scots' growing influence were not without basis in fact; ambitious, well-educated Scots were involved in the British polity to a degree previously unknown, particularly in the military and the empire.

Those concerns sat side by side with a deep curiosity among English men and women about a long-time, but little-known neighbor, the image of which was being recast by new cultural fashions. Once the Jacobites were no longer a threat and the Highlands were brought under the King's authority, Highlanders' reputed military valor and ingrained loyalty to superiors became assets which could be turned to the service of the crown. Enlightenment notions of the 'noble savage' transformed attitudes towards Highland clansmen. Efforts at the economic improvement of the Highlands gave the region the allure of a culture in the midst of transformation into modernity. Meanwhile, the Scottish Enlightenment earned for Edinburgh and Glasgow reputations as centers of intellectual achievement. Changing styles in landscape appreciation made Scottish scenery newly attractive. Such developments, combined with a growing sense of British patriotism and a fashion for travel, began to prompt inquisitiveness about Scotland and the Scots. Venturesome souls like Richard Pococke, Thomas Pennant, Samuel Johnson, and James Boswell traveled across the Tweed in the 1760s and 70s. The travel accounts which they and others published fed the nascent interest in Scotland, in a period when the wars of the French Revolution and Napoleon soon compelled those interested in travel to avoid the Continent. In the 1790s the foundations of a tourist industry were laid in Scotland, to be expanded in the nineteenth century under the influence of the writings of Sir Walter Scott, the advent of affordable and rapid transportation, the rising affluence of the middle classes, and royal blessings. By the Victorian period, a deeply entrenched tourist vision of Scotland, disseminated by guidebooks, literature, the popular press, and the comments of earlier travelers, was virtually inescapable. So pervasive was this interpretation of Scotland that it even entered political discourse, particularly in questions of public policy regarding poverty and land ownership in the Highlands.

This study is less an examination of the effects of the tourist gaze upon Scotland, although that issue certainly emerges, as it is an exploration of what that gaze reveals about the tourists and their worldview. Many critics have, rightfully, criticized the 'Balmoralization' or 'Tartanization' of nineteenth-century Scotland, the process by which that country's culture was reduced to a few stereotypes which appealed to foreign visitors but reflected little of the reality of Scottish life.[7] Without denying the importance of that analysis, I wish to look at another side of the issue: what did this Balmoralized Scotland mean to those who toured the country or just hoped to? Although a fair amount of work has been done on tourist representations of Scotland and their effects on the host culture, scholars tend to take for granted the appeal of these images to those who consumed them.[8] The tourist clichés of Scotland were so widespread because of the powerful way they spoke to deep-seated concerns and desires of the period, and they therefore repay careful examination. The late eighteenth- and nineteenth-century fascination with Scotland serves here as a window through which to study the middle-class world view, considering such topics as anxieties over industrialization, urbanization, and political change; attitudes towards nature; nostalgia for the past; and racial and gendered constructions of the 'Other'. Scholars of tourism have long argued that participants travel in order to see a predetermined idea of a place, and that their expectations reveal more about themselves than about the sites they visit.[9] By examining the 'markers' which signified 'Scotland' to tourists, I hope to place that country in the context of the popular imagination, and to discover why visitors constructed the kind of gaze they did. The long time span of this study, from the beginnings of modern interest in North Britain to a mature tourist industry in the early twentieth century, allows me to examine ways in which changing cultural needs altered the construction of Scotland. Late eighteenth-century visitors lauded the momentum of modernization there. But in the nineteenth century, as the ongoing experience of industrialization, urbanization, political reform, and intellectual shifts created a sense of a society in transition, Scotland became more valuable as a place rooted in the past. The rhetoric of tourism increasingly froze Scotland in time in the nineteenth century, even though that country was fully a part of the economic, social, and political transformations of the period.

Scholars – and participants, as well – frequently differentiate between 'travel' and 'tourism'.[10] 'Travelers' strike out on their own, seeing themselves as engaging in open-minded explorations of that which is foreign. Tourism, on the other hand, tends to keep the foreign at bay. Often reviled as superficial and perfunctory, 'tourists' stay on the beaten path to see a preestablished canon of famous sites whose meaning is predetermined. This study will occasionally use these terms interchangeably, for lack of synonyms. My topic, however, is tourism and it is the nature of that activity as one whose meaning is preordained by the collective consciousness which most interests me. In company with other scholars in the field, I see tourism as a modern ritual or pilgrimage. Rituals are conventionalized acts through which an individual demonstrates respect towards an object or idea of great value, and expects to be taken beyond the ordinary and the everyday. Though not necessarily religious in nature, rituals promise spiritual and physical regeneration, both through contact with a transcendent reality, and through a break from work and the strains of daily life.[11] Tourism in Scotland was a highly formalized activity, in which visitors' experiences were shaped by a plethora of guidebooks, travelers' accounts, guided tours, and specially designed excursion trips. Those many aids to the process of touring were necessary to sustain the meaning of the journey, for the 'Scotland' sought by tourists was created, not natural, and could be found only if sought with the right attitude. Some areas traversed by visitors were mundane, even unattractive. In the Lowlands, especially, a conscious effort sometimes needed to be made in the nineteenth century to ignore signs of Scotland's thriving industrial economy. The iron foundries of Clydeside cast a permanent orange glow over the horizon. Many of the historic scenes of Edinburgh and Glasgow were essentially slums. The growing commercialization of travel and the crowds with whom visitors had to share the experience also threatened to rob journeys to Scotland of their poetry. If they did not rely on the many 'markers' that signified Scotland, tourists' trips might not serve the intended purpose of providing access to a deeper, richer authenticity. With their dependence on the various travel writings of Scotland, which William Stowe calls the 'quasi-religious texts' of tourism, sightseers ensured that their travels met their expectations.[12] Edwardian travel writer George Eyre-Todd said of the Great Glen, 'For him who has the key to the interests of the region the long day's sail from Inverness to Oban unrolls a panorama of unbroken charm.'[13] The keys were old clan legends, tales of local history, and stories by Walter Scott, conveniently provided in most guidebooks. Without them, Eyre-Todd seemed to suggest, the Great Glen was just another valley. Scotland could not be allowed to become just another country; its cultural significance was too important.

The tourist ritual of Scotland was designed to suit the needs of travelers, but it also exerted a powerful influence upon Scotland. Late eighteenth-century visitors envisioned their role as that of explorers who were getting to know a foreign land and introducing it to their fellow countrymen and women. Their claim of expertise about Scotland was a form of imperial takeover, as was their frequent implication that Scotland needed to be represented by others.[14] Just as travelers to India or Egypt described the landscape in terms which implied the need for the British to domesticate it and make it productive, travelers' frequent suggestions of ways to improve the eighteenth-century Highland economy suggested that it was through English advice that the area would flourish.[15] Throughout the nineteenth century the subjugating gaze of tourism, which reduces a people and a place to attractions which exist for the edification and delight of visitors, tended to downplay Scotland's autonomy and revealed the chauvinism of many visitors. Tourists' discourse about Highlanders defined them to such an extent that crofters' alternative self-understanding had little public power. Tourism's imperialistic tendencies were particularly marked in the Highlands, an area which some scholars claim operated as an internal colony within Scotland.[16] Both Lowland and English tourists could agree that Highlanders were 'the Other' and acted towards them accordingly.

Yet scholars do not concur on whether travel by Europeans within Europe can rightly be considered to have an imperialist function, nor on whether the relationship between England and Scotland (and between the Lowlands and Highlands) was an imperialistic one. Scholars like John Glendening and Charles Withers emphasize Scottish agency in creating their own destiny. The Lowland attitude towards the Highlands, some argue, was far more ambiguous and less universalizing than colonial discourse might suggest.[17] This book maintains that while tourism did often exert imperialist tendencies, the discourse of Scotland was nonetheless a dialogue, not a monologue. Although tourist images of Scotland were powerful and enduring, they were not produced by an external force imposing its own vision upon the country. Scots actively participated in the creation of their country's tourist identity and thereby claimed a role in defining their country. It was they who wrote the early guidebooks which showed visitors how to see Scotland, and it was they who led tourists around, at least until Thomas Cook's tours began in the 1840s. Scots were also tourists in their own country, and wrote several of the most influential travel accounts of the period. Above all, it was a Scotsman,

Sir Walter Scott, who definitively fashioned the Highlands into an irresistible world of romance, in an effort to create a compromise between Scottish distinctiveness and the anglicizing tendencies of the Union. Scottish promoters of tourism needed to present their country in a manner that would attract visitors, but their endeavors did more than merely meet the tastes of outsiders. By identifying Scotland so closely with the Highlands, those in the tourist industry helped to assert a distinctive identity for Scots, while also answering their customers' expectations. In addition to guiding their readers through a storied past and sublime landscape, guidebook authors also sought to acquaint their readers with Scotland's thriving economies and distinguished levels of culture. The fact that such information made little difference to the prevailing discourse of Scotland reminds us of the power of tourist myths. Yet many visitors discovered that they could not control the meaning of Scotland. Rather than allowing Victorians to recapture a pre-industrial oneness with nature, the Scottish landscape might demonstrate just how urbanized and domesticated their own culture had become. Rather than provide a sense of communion with the past, Scotland might show tourists that it, too, was a modern place. Rather than fulfill their expected role as contented rural peasants, Highland crofters might demonstrate a dissatisfaction with their social and economic position nearly as radical as that of some urban workers. Tourism may have rendered Scotland quiet, but not silent, and never uninvolved in the definition of itself.

A study of Britons' travel around their island brings up questions about the nature and extent of Britishness in the eighteenth and nineteenth centuries. Several scholars have recently disputed Linda Colley's analysis that although Britons continued to retain a sense of regional identification, by the 1830s inhabitants of the British Isles had come to think of themselves first and foremost as Britons, rather than as English, Scottish, or Welsh. Scottish historians such as Graeme Morton find a powerful sense of Scottishness in Victorian Scotland, despite the lack of political nationalism.[18] Travel historian Marjorie Morgan uses Victorian travel throughout Britain and the Continent to analyze Britons' identification with Britishness and finds it limited to economic, imperial, and military affairs. By bringing Victorians face to face with the differences between the three countries of Great Britain, she argues, their journeys around the British Isles intensified their association with their home region.[19] This study agrees that English tourists' trips to Scotland confirmed their sense of local identification, but argues further that because visitors found that the image of Scotland contributed usefully to their own sense of the kind of nation they wished to be, journeys north also help remind that Great Britain was a joint project.

Scotland's foreignness was apparent to most English visitors; it was a prime reason for their journey. But some visitors consciously viewed travel to their northern neighbor as an opportunity to improve relations between England and Scotland. This was true of Thomas Cook, who rejoiced in 1846 that 'as science exerts her mighty influence in breaking down the walls of separation betwixt nations and people, the bonds of peace and universal brotherhood are made stronger betwixt England and Caledonia.'[20] Also writing in the 1840s, visitor Herbert Byng Hall hoped that Victoria's prospective visit to the Highlands would 'cement the seal of the Union; erasing nationalities, save in the picturesque garb and romance of other days, from the minds of men, who, as Christians worship one God and as subjects, obey one Sovereign.'[21] Late eighteenth-century visitors, who toured Scotland in a time when the Union was relatively new and relations between Scots and the English sometimes troubled, were particularly motivated to help create a sense of commonality between the two countries. Though they could not help but be struck by English/Scottish diversity, they also emphasized Scotland's many contributions to the Union and rejoiced in the ways Scotland appeared to be becoming more like its southern neighbor. Many saw Scottish distinctiveness as a sign of backwardness, and took for granted that progress necessitated anglicization. But they also assumed that Scots had the ability to rise to English standards, a belief which in their eyes signified respect for Scottish achievements and a hope for a more united kingdom.

Victorians, traveling when the Union was stronger and Britain's world position unrivalled, were more likely to take the fact of a united Britain for granted. But their journeys forced consideration of definitions of 'Britishness', 'Englishness', and 'Scottishness'. They also had to reflect on issues of racial identity when confronted with Highland culture. Elements of Scottish society and culture were puzzling, even offensive to English visitors, and most did not question English superiority, especially to the Highlands. At the same time, they cherished Scottish uniqueness, particularly elements such as the landscape of the Highlands, distinctive forms of dress and ways of life, and tales of Scotland's past. Joseph and Elizabeth Robins Pennell, whose shock at the poverty they saw in the Highlands cast a pall over their 1888 journey, were nonetheless delighted at the Ballachulish Highland Games. They heard only Gaelic, the bagpipes were cheerful, the many tartans made a bright picture: 'We were in a foreign country.'[22] The very purpose of a journey to Scotland was to find foreignness; it was the fact of Scottish distinctiveness which allowed the country to play its role as a counter to the modern world. Scotland, it seemed, possessed characteristics which England might be losing. Because both countries were joined as Great Britain, those qualities could be retained for all. By thus demonstrating the idea of a joint partnership, tours of Scotland affirmed a British identity, even while confirming local allegiances. Meanwhile, by touring their own country, as many did, Scots declared their own uniqueness and sense of national pride, which was not diminished by commitment to a wider Union. Scottish responses to the standard tourist itinerary reveal a strong national patriotism.

A few of the visitors whose reactions to Scotland serve as evidence for my arguments were Americans rather than English or Scots. While American travel to Scotland is not a focus of this study, I did make use of the travel accounts of a few American sightseers, as their responses to the land they toured were so similar to those made by British tourists that they seemed appropriate for inclusion. These American voices also testify to the wide dissemination of the popular vision of Scotland. The Pennells, Americans whose travel account figures prominently in this work, are a slightly different case. Artists who resided in London, the Pennells carved out a niche for themselves in the travel-literature market by consciously arguing against the usual stereotypes of a location, a practice clearly evident in their account of their Scottish tour. As Americans, the Pennells may have had less at stake in the accepted vision of Scotland than did British Victorians. More to the point, their criticism of tourist locations and practices provides a valuable commentary on visitors' expectations.

While tourists appreciated Scottish foreignness, their vision of the country did not represent many of the realities or complexities of Scottish life and culture. By the mid-nineteenth century many of the signs which spoke of Scottishness to tourists were artificially maintained by the tourist industry. It was the numerous souvenir shops selling Scottish kitsch along Edinburgh's Prince's Street, not evidence of a unique society and culture, which told 'Cuthbert Bede' that he was in 'Tartan-Land' in the 1860s.[23] The usefulness to tourists of a particular image of Scotland led to a tendency on their part to appropriate Scottish identity for their own needs. Scotland's image became static, unable to evolve to meet the country's changing needs, because the idea of a place that did not change was so attractive to outsiders. Nor did an appreciation of Scottish uniqueness entail a belief in the possibility of Scottish self-sufficiency. As Murray Pittock argues, '[L]ocal color accentuated the glory of the Empire through stressing how many cultures it contained, and was welcome; nationalist irredentism was quite another matter.'[24] Nonetheless, despite the unchangingness of this public national identity, which many modern critics argue impeded the development of political nationalism, on a more local level it is clear that Scots maintained a vibrant sense of identity which met their own needs. Scots were also undoubtedly more aware than their English visitors of their country's considerable regional diversity. Although I have endeavored to examine tourism all across Scotland, I do follow the interests of most sightseers by paying particular attention to the Highlands and Hebrides. Further research into regional differences and their cultural significance to tourists would surely be profitable, especially in understanding forms of national identification.

Tourism and Identity in Scotland begins with two broadly chronological chapters, which examine the development of Scottish tourism before and after the publication of Walter Scott's *The Lady of the Lake* in 1810. Chapter 1, 'Mapping North Britain, 1770-1810', looks at the first phase of modern travel in Scotland, which was often motivated by enthusiasm for the newly-created British nation. The steady trickle of visitors who began to make their way around Scotland in this period often learned that although in many ways still foreign, Scotland had much to offer the newly created Great Britain. Its most exciting contribution in this period was the idea of North Britain as a dynamic place in the process of modernization, an understanding which made Scotland's image more progressive in the eighteenth century than any time since. The early foundations of the tourist industry in Scotland were being laid by the 1790s as sightseers traveled prescribed routes, often by rote, making use of a slowly evolving network of inns, guidebooks, professional guides, and transportation. However, travel was often difficult in this early period, and visitors frequently thought of themselves as explorers.

The enormous popularity of the works of Walter Scott stimulated a corresponding interest in touring Scotland, and the new technology of transportation soon enabled the middle classes to travel there relatively quickly and easily. Chapter 2 examines the development of mass tourism in Scotland in the nineteenth century. The first cross-border rail lines reached Scotland in the 1840s and steam travel around the Hebridean islands began to take off in that period as well. Other provisions for tourists, such as hotels, guided tours, and a proliferation of guidebooks, also expanded from mid century. Meanwhile, the purpose of the journey also began to shift. Although the romanticization of the Highlands began in the late eighteenth century, visitors of that period were equally impressed by Scotland's Enlightenment reputation as a center of learning and intellectual progress. For many reasons, in the nineteenth century tourists were almost exclusively interested in Scotland as a land of romance. An ever-increasing number of visitors were attracted by the notion of Scotland, particularly the Highlands, as a realm of transcendence and imagination which could revivify the prosaicness of everyday life. But their trips were made possible by the same modernization of nineteenth-century life which they hoped temporarily to avoid. The transportation revolution and the maturation of the tourist industry in Scotland domesticated the experience of travel there, leaving few surprises and endangering the very purpose of the journey. The clichés and stereotypes promulgated by guidebooks, travel accounts, and tour guides enabled sightseers to find the Scotland of their imaginations, a Scotland which had little relevance to the daily lives of most Scots, but which had a profound cultural significance to visitors.

Scotland held out three categories of attractions to tourists: natural ones, such as an outdoor environment which enabled visitors to envision a

world untouched by industrialization; historic ones, which suggested that
the past was uniquely accessible in Scotland; and human ones, particularly
the men and women of the Highlands and Western Isles, who sightseers
believed preserved an ancient way of life in a changing world. Chapter 3,
'Land of the Mountain and the Flood: Tourists and the Natural World',
argues that scenery is a prime example of the tenuousness of the image
which drew tourists north in the nineteenth century. Nature, as manifested
in Scotland, allowed for the expression of a variety of cultural anxieties,
ranging from nostalgia for country life and concern about the effects of
industrialization, to questions about God's dominion over nature. Tourists
were particularly intrigued by the Highlands, where a harsh and bleak
environment provided the opportunity to be both frightened and comforted
by the unaccustomed experience of human insignificance. This perception
of the northwest made the Highlands a compelling challenge to Victorian
men, a suitable sphere in which to put to rest anxieties over the 'crisis of
manhood' resultant from changing concepts of masculinity in the industrial
era. However, the deeper connection with nature which visitors so prized in
Scotland was a fragile one. Their extravagant awe and delighted horror at
the Highlands was often evidence of how far removed from nature their
lives truly were, a distance intensified by the growing use of railways and
steamers as the means by which to view the scenery.

Chapter 4, ' "Free of one's century": Tourism and the Scottish Past',
examines the ways that the past was also an antidote to apprehensions about
the present. Because tourists perceived Scotland as less industrialized and
less modern than England, they believed Scotland provided a stronger link
with history than did the allegedly more urbanized and industrialized England.
The political neutrality of Scottish history as presented by contemporary
historians and the strength of the Union in the nineteenth century enabled
English tourists to develop a vicarious Scottish patriotism while they traveled,
adopting Scottish heroes as their own and appropriating as 'British' the love
of liberty to which Scottish history was believed to testify. So alive did the
past seem to be in Scotland, that visitors often portrayed it as a geographical
location, a place they could visit and in so doing, assert control over the
passage of time. Victorians were also fascinated with Highland dress, which
they understood to be a tradition that had remained unchanged for centuries.
Although kilts and tartans were not as ancient as many tourists believed, nor
were they any longer daily dress for most Scots, they nonetheless provided
evidence of Scotland's alleged rootedness in the past. Tourists' longing for
tangible links with the past led to an overemphasis on Scotland's history, at
the expense of contemporary achievements.

The subject of Chapter 5, ' "A Fountain of Renovating Life": Tourists
and Highlanders', is visitors' curiosity about the people of the Highlands
and Hebrides. Because of the racial and gender constructions with which

nineteenth-century observers perceived Gaels, as well as the belief that they were 'natural' people, most tourists understood crofters as historical artifacts who lived just as their ancestors had. By safeguarding ancient ways of life, nineteenth-century commentators believed, Highlanders and islanders made a valuable contribution to the nation. Rather than laud the coming of 'improvement' to the Highlands, as had travelers of the eighteenth century, those of the Victorian years preferred to emphasize Highlanders' ties to the past. However, in the late nineteenth century, crofters presented an alternative image of themselves through their well-publicized dispute over land control, often known as the Crofters' War. In the process, they challenged the authority of the tourist gaze, although they could not defeat tourism's power to define a people and a place.

The image of Scotland which developed in the late eighteenth and nineteenth centuries was a product of specific cultural needs and anxieties which emerged in both England and Scotland in the beginnings of the industrial era. It quickly came to be regarded as the natural, unchanging essence of Scotland and continues to appeal to large numbers of twenty-first century tourists and would-be tourists.[25] In recent years Scots have worked to counter the tourist myth by presenting a more dynamic, modern impression of their country, and the importance attached to this process testifies to tourism's power of national definition. By situating the tourist vision of Scotland within the context of those cultural aspirations which drove its development, this study aims to uncover the roots of that power.

Notes

[1] Edwin Waugh, *Fourteen Days in Scotland* (Manchester, 1863), pp. 4-5.

[2] Waugh, *Fourteen Days*, pp. 2-3.

[3] Thomas Cook, *Cook's Scottish Tourist Official Directory* (London, 1861), p. 16.

[4] Alastair Durie, *Scotland for the Holidays. Tourism in Scotland c.1780-1939* (East Linton: Tuckwell Press, 2003).

[5] Linda Colley, *Britons. Forging the Nation, 1707-1837* (New Haven: Yale Univ. Press, 1992), pp. 12-13.

[6] Michael Lynch, *Scotland. A New History* (London: Pimlico, 1991), p. 324; Colley, *Britons*, p. 13.

[7] The best known example is Thomas Nairn, *The Break-up of Britain* (London: NLB, 1977). See also David McCrone, Angela Morris, Richard Kiely, *Scotland-The Brand: The Making of Scottish Heritage* (Edinburgh: Edinburgh Univ. Press, 1995), pp. 50-56.

[8] R. W. Butler, 'The Tourist Industry in the Highlands and Islands' (Ph.D. diss., Univ. of Glasgow, 1973); Derek Cooper, *Road to the Isles: Travellers in the Hebrides, 1770-1914* (Boston: Routledge & Kegan Paul, 1979); Durie, *Scotland for the Holidays*; John R. Gold and Margaret M. Gold, *Imagining Scotland. Tradition, Representation and Promotion in Scottish Tourism since 1750*

(Aldershot: Scolar Press, 1995); Mairi MacArthur, 'Blasted Heaths and Hills of Mist. The Highlands and Islands through travellers' eyes', *Scottish Affairs* 3 (Spring 1993), pp. 23-31; Fraser MacDonald, 'St. Kilda and the Sublime', *Ecumene* 2001 8(2), pp. 151-74; Christopher Smout, 'Tours in the Scottish Highlands from the eighteenth to the twentieth centuries', *Northern Scotland* 5(1983), pp. 99-121.

[9]   Dean MacCannell, *The Tourist. A New Theory of the Leisure Class* (New York: Schocken Books, 1976); John Urry, *The Tourist Gaze. Leisure and Travel in Contemporary Societies* (New York: Sage Publications, 1990).

[10]   James Buzard, *The Beaten Track. European Tourism, Literature, and the Ways to Culture, 1800-1918* (New York: Oxford Univ. Press, 1993); Chloe Chard, *Pleasure and Guilt on the Grand Tour. Travel writing and imaginative geography, 1600-1830* (New York: Manchester Univ. Press, 1999).

[11]   See Victor and Edith Turner, *Image and Pilgrimage in Christian Culture* (New York: Columbia Univ. Press, 1978); MacCannell, *The Tourist*; John F. Sears, *Sacred Places. American Tourist Attractions in the Nineteenth Century* (New York: Oxford Univ. Press, 1989); William W. Stowe, *Going Abroad. European Travel in Nineteenth-Century American Culture* (Princeton: Princeton Univ. Press, 1994).

[12]   Stowe, *Going Abroad*, p. 27.

[13]   George Eyre-Todd, *Scotland: Picturesque and Traditional* (New York: Frederick A. Stokes, 1907), p. 275.

[14]   See Susan Morgan, *Place Matters. Gendered Geography in Victorian Women's Travel Books about Southeast Asia* (New Brunswick: Rutgers Univ. Press, 1996).

[15]   See Inderpal Grewal, *Home and Harem. Nation, Gender, Empire and the Cultures of Travel* (Durham, NC: Duke Univ. Press, 1996); Mary Louise Pratt, *Imperial Eyes. Travel Writing and Transculturation* (New York: Routledge, 1992).

[16]   For an example, see Eric Richards, 'Scotland and the uses of the Atlantic Empire', Bernard Bailyn and Philip D. Morgan, eds., *Strangers within the Realm: Cultural Margins of the First British Empire* (Chapel Hill: Univ. of North Carolina Press, 1991), pp. 67-114.

[17]   On the debate over English imperialism in Scotland, see John Glendening, *The High Road. Romantic Tourism, Scotland and Literature, 1720-1820* (New York: St. Martin's Press, 1997); Michael Hecter, *Internal Colonialism: The Celtic Fringe in British National Development 1536-1966* (Berkeley: Univ. of Calif. Press, 1975); Murray G. H. Pittock, *Celtic Identity and the British Image* (New York: Manchester Univ. Press, 1999); Charles W. J. Withers, 'Authorizing landscape: "authority", naming and the Ordnance Survey's mapping of the Scottish Highlands in the nineteenth century', *Journal of Historical Geography* 26, 4(2000), pp. 532-54; and the discussion thread 'Postcolonialism and the Highlands' on Highlands listserv (HIGHLANDS@JISCMAIL.AC.UK), Feb. 2001.

[18]   Graeme Morton, *Unionist Nationalism. Governing Urban Scotland,1830-1860* (East Linton: Tuckwell Press, 1999). See also Pittock, *Celtic Identity.*

19 Marjorie Morgan, *National Identities and Travel in Victorian Britain* (Houndmills: Palgrave, 2001).

20 Thomas Cook, *Handbook of a Trip to Scotland* (Leicester, 1846), p. 93.

21 Herbert Byng Hall, *Highland Sports and Highland Quarters* (London, 1848), pp. 2:247-48.

22 Joseph Pennell and Elizabeth Robins Pennell, *Our Journey to the Hebrides* (New York, 1889), p. 45.

23 Cuthbert Bede [Edward Bradley], *A Tour in Tartan-Land* (London, 1863), pp. 295-97.

24 Pittock, *Celtic Identity*, p. 106.

25 See Celeste Ray, *Highland Heritage. Scottish Americans in the American South* (Chapel Hill: Univ. of North Carolina Press, 2001).

Chapter 1

Mapping North Britain, 1770-1810

We are all Britons from the land's end to the Orkneys, have all the same boasted constitution, the same laws, liberties and Christian religion to defend; and God forbid that names or sounds, affectation, illiberality or prejudice should prevent the natives of Kirkwall and Penzance from regarding each other, as Britons and fellow citizens.[1]

So mused John Lettice during a 1792 trip to Scotland, contemplating a report that 'younger travelers from the south' were ridiculing the Scottish brogue. His sentiments illustrate that although anti-Scottish sentiment continued to be prevalent in the eighteenth and early nineteenth centuries, a sense of pride in a shared British nation was also developing.[2] To Lettice and others like him, trips to North Britain were opportunities to learn more about a region which was both foreign and part of the same nation, and to help put an end to prejudice by promoting a vision of Scots as patriotic contributors to the Union.

The eighteenth century was a crucial period in the development of both British and Scottish national identities after the parliamentary union of 1707. Long two separate, and frequently antagonistic, countries, Scotland and England were to be one nation. As Scots sought ways to define themselves after the loss of political independence, the long series of wars against France, Great Britain's distinctive pattern of commercial development, and the expansion of the overseas empire encouraged the English, Scots, and Welsh to define themselves against 'the Other' overseas.[3] The new fashion for travel in Scotland was a key ingredient in this process of nation building, showing visitors that, although in many ways still foreign, Scotland had much to offer the new nation.[4] Through the now tamed and obedient Highlanders, the lavish country houses, the intriguing antiquities, the sublime and picturesque landscape, and the flourishing industries in the Lowlands, Scotland provided evidence of the benefits of the British constitution, examples of British history, specimens of a domestic landscape that rivaled classical scenery, and proof of the superiority of the British economy and social system. Travel accounts testify that one of Scotland's central attractions in this period was the idea of North Britain as a dynamic place in the process of modernization. In many ways Scotland's image was more progressive in the eighteenth century than anytime since. Even the Highlands, long understood as the very antithesis of Britishness, could be incorporated into this picture of economic and social progress. There, one could witness the transition from a savage, near-feudal, and poor society into a peaceful, loyal, and soon to be productive region.

The growing interest in travel in Scotland also provided a means by which Scots could both retain a sense of native pride, and at the same time promote themselves as enthusiastic citizens of the new nation. John Stoddart, an Englishman who visited Scotland in 1799 and 1800 with an artist friend, observed all across the land an 'anxious desire to recommend the country to the affections of an Englishman.'[5] Scots, too, were sightseers, and energetically publicized their country to themselves and to others by publishing their own travel accounts and writing guidebooks.[6] Scotsman Tobias Smollett's *The Expedition of Humphry Clinker* (1771) used a fictional tour of Scotland to argue against negative stereotypes and to call on South Britons to be more open minded towards their northern neighbors. Robert Heron, a Scot who published two guidebooks of Scotland (one for Scots and one for the English) and an account of his own travels, believed that touring one's native country was a stimulus to patriotism. After viewing the scenery of his or her homeland, examining the character and condition of its inhabitants, and beholding the improvements made by industry, a traveler's national pride was strengthened, and a stronger desire to make a contribution to one's country was evoked.[7] To middle- and upper-class Scots, the promotion of themselves as patriotic Britons and the assertion of their active contributions to a wider political and cultural community was one solution to their quest for a viable self-definition.

Thus, while Scotland had once been considered a place to avoid at all costs, a steady trickle of visitors began to make their way around North Britain in the third quarter of the eighteenth century, often publishing their travel journals or letters, and thereby feeding interest in the northern part of the kingdom. As early as 1759 Lord Breadalbane found that 'It has been the fashion this year to travel into the Highlands.'[8] Bishop Richard Pococke, a well-traveled antiquarian known to contemporaries as 'Pococke the traveler' because of his trip to Egypt and the Holy Land, spent six months examining Scottish ruins and antiquities in 1760. Elizabeth Montague, well-known 'bluestocking' and businesswoman, enjoyed Scottish scenery and society for four weeks in 1766.[9] Thomas Pennant, a naturalist, member of the Royal Academy, and experienced traveler, visited much of the mainland in 1769 and returned to explore the west coast and inner Hebrides in 1772. His 1769 *A Tour in Scotland*, the fullest travel account of Scotland to that point, was a comprehensive discussion of Scotland's scenery, economy, natural history, and local customs. It was a popular success, going through five editions between 1769-1790 and was republished in 1790 with an additional volume based on the second trip.

Pennant was soon followed by Samuel Johnson and James Boswell, who roamed Scotland for three months in 1773 and published accounts of their exploits in 1775 and 1786 respectively. Their numerous adventures and

Johnson's opinionated reflections inspired an open-ended discussion about the merits of Scotland, and motivated many others to follow in their footsteps.[10] Meanwhile William Gilpin assessed Scotland's picturesque qualities in 1776 (though not publishing until 1789), and John Knox toured under the auspices of the British Society for Extending the Fisheries in 1786. By the time Lettice reached Scotland in the 1790s, enough men and women were making the trek to speak of the foundations of a tourist industry: prescribed routes sometimes followed by rote, designated sights marked off by viewing platforms, guidebooks, and a slowly evolving industry of inns, professional guides, boat and coach rental.[11]

Many motives lured Englishmen and women across the border: an interest in Scotland's scenery and history, the desire to participate in what was becoming a fashionable trend, the fact that the Continent was closed to travel during the 1790s and early 1800s. Mingled with these aspirations lay a deep curiosity about their northern neighbors. As they traveled, most felt a sense of pride in the spread of British civilization and the British constitution, finding commonalties as well as differences across the border. National prejudices and superstitions were daily wearing out, said Lettice, noticing as did others that Highland dress was giving way to 'British dress'.[12] The author of *Scotland Delineated* rejoiced that intolerance was gradually losing ground on both sides: 'In short, the happy era seems not so very distant, when the ENGLISH and SCOTS shall be, in every sense of the word, ONE NATION'.[13]

Getting to know Scotland was an act of British patriotism for eighteenth- and early nineteenth-century travelers and tourists, many of whom seemed chagrined to know so little of a place that was now part of their own nation. Often travel accounts were as much geography texts as remembrances of one's experiences. A botanical expert and an authority on Highland customs accompanied Pennant on his second trip. Travel writers discoursed on the topography, history, economy, demography, customs, urban environment, and social structure of Scotland. Concerned to provide as accurate information as possible, many writers supplemented their observations with other research, such as Sir John Sinclair's *Statistical Account of Scotland*.[14] However, this 'British' patriotism did not exclude an Anglocentric bias. English visitors, and many Lowlanders, tended to naturalize the centrality of union with England in Scotland's development. Many travelers and tourists conflated 'British' with 'English' pride, implying that Scotland's role in the Union was to become more like England. By portraying themselves as 'explorers' and 'discoverers', non-native visitors belittled Scots' ability to represent themselves or their nation.

By the early nineteenth century Scotland was no longer unknown territory. A host of travel writers and tourists had mapped the country, both physically and imaginatively. As early as 1786, Boswell found it unnecessary to describe Loch Lomond, as it was so familiar through others' descriptions. In 1809 the

Quarterly Review panned John Carr's *Caledonian Sketches* as a 'hackneyed subject' treated in a 'hackneyed manner'. So common were travel accounts of Scotland now, said the reviewer, that one could adequately satisfy one's curiosity without stirring from home.[15] To the eighteenth-century visitor, this loss of foreignness was a necessary, if sometimes melancholy, feature of the creation of Great Britain. It was left to later generations of tourists, prompted by different cultural urges, to decide if the vision of Scotland was more valuable as North Britain or as a pre-modern foreign land.

Scotland's Contributions to the Union

John Carr's 1809 account of his trip to Scotland began with a grateful acknowledgment that Britain was 'favored by Heaven and fortified by nature against the political storms that rage around us.'[16] Not least among the contributions Scotland could make to the developing sense of nationalism was evidence of the strength and vitality of the British constitution. The mere ability to travel peacefully throughout the British Isles, especially when contrasted with the turmoil on the Continent, was a sign of the nation's political and social stability. Visitors to the Highlands were especially cognizant of this blessing. Only a few decades earlier the Highland-based Jacobite rising of 1745 had threatened the peacefulness of the Hanoverian succession. Travel writers in the second half of the century titallatingly assured their readers that clans had committed brutal and atrocious acts against one another in fairly recent times. 'The turbulent spirit of the old times continued even to the present age' said Pennant.[17] But as the very presence of travelers in the Highlands testified, this once lawless region, understood as an inverted image of the constitution,[18] was by the late eighteenth century well within the jurisdiction of that same constitution. The Union with England, said an anonymous female visitor in the 1770s, put an end to the 'inhospitable bickerings' of the clans and provided 'a proper proportion of liberty to the commonality'.[19] Because of the peace brought by the British government, it seemed, visitors could roam the country at will, without the slightest danger from the natives.

The blessings of the British constitution were also elucidated by the fashion for visiting stately homes and gardens, a practice as central to eighteenth-century tours of Scotland as it was of England. Country houses, as Ian Ousby points out, were built to be shown. Not only were they the museums of the era, housing fine collections of art and showcasing the best of Britain's architecture, but the display of great estates to the public was a sign of the opening of the elite. Faced with competition from the newly prosperous and influential middle-class commercial interests, the aristocracy carved out a role for themselves as models of taste and refinement, providing examples of how to use one's wealth. Middle-class visitors in turn demonstrated respect for their social superiors, and by expecting entry into the homes of the upper classes, celebrated their own rising power.[20]

Favorites in Scotland were Blair Castle at Blair Atholl, popular for its fine landscaped grounds; Hamilton House, renowned for its collection of paintings including Reuben's *Daniel in the Lion's Den*; Hopetoun House, rebuilt and enlarged by William and Robert Adam; Taymouth, the seat of Lord Breadalbane; and the Duke of Argyll's estate at Inverary. The eagerness with which visitors tramped though these properties was a recognition that Scotland's nobility was now on a cultural par with England's – a strong statement given that Highland nobles had fairly recently been regarded as uncouth feudal potentates. Lettice was pleased at the manner in which the Duke of Argyll's plantations had been improved since the last century: 'But how wonderful the change which has taken place with the progress of time!'[21] Thomas Newte (a pseudonym for visitor William Thomson) rejoiced that the castle on Loch Awe which once belonged to the Earl of Breadalbane, 'from which [his clansmen] issued forth...like those of all uncivilized times and countries to commit occasional depredations on their neighbors', was falling into ruins. This he interpreted as a sign of the new, more civilized age in Scotland.[22]

Country houses evinced modern British greatness; antiquarians found Scotland a fertile place to uncover some of the glories of Britain's past. Between 1750-1850, as Sam Smiles shows, the study of ancient Britain was transformed. Enlightenment and Romantic notions of the noble savage made primitive peoples worth paying attention to, the apparent survival of the ancient British tongue in Gaelic-speaking communities provided a tantalizing link with the remote past, new methodologies, such as archeology, made the study of the prehistoric past more feasible, and the growing interest in developing a national history made it patriotic.[23] Scotland proved to have numerous antique sights worth exploring: Druidic, Roman, and medieval. Men like Charles Cordiner, Francis Grose, and Richard Pococke traversed Scotland primarily to catalogue the area's antiquities, and many others joined in the endeavor, describing and drawing the vitrified fort Craig Phadrick near Inverness, Roman camps at Callendar and Ardoch, and other Danish forts, Druidical temples, standing stones, and Pictish cairns.

Such sites had a multitude of meanings to the eighteenth-century mind. To some, prehistoric antiquities were problematic, for they suggested an identification with 'primitive' people too close for comfort in the Age of Enlightenment.[24] To others, the exploration of Britain's antiquity offered the beginnings of a national history. While Anglo-Saxonism would eventually become the dominant strand in English nationalism, that was not clear in the eighteenth century, and Celtism also offered an attractive civic myth. British ancient history was popularly understood as the story of a sturdy and hardy people who resisted Roman rule and thus demonstrated their instinct for freedom and independence.[25] Scotland, never fully occupied by the Romans, could be an important part of that story. An 1821 guidebook described the 'innate...love of liberty' manifested as Caledonians skirmished against the Romans, burning with the desire for revenge, eager to recover their independence.[26] At the same time, Roman ruins were also regarded as evidence that the great age of Augustus had lived on British soil – implicitly transferring some of that splendor to Britain.[27] William Stukeley, a well known antiquarian, particularly delighted in Roman artifacts: 'I hold myself obliged to preserve as well as I can the memory of such things as I saw; which, added to what future time will discover, will revive the Roman glory among us, and may serve to invite noble minds to endeavour at that merit and public-spiritedness which shine through all their actions.'[28] Meanwhile, for Scots, the study of native antiquities could be an act of nationalism, as Scottish patriots sought to investigate and preserve their indigenous culture in the face of English assimilation.[29] Some eighteenth-century Scots saw in ancient Rome parallels to the fate of their own nation, and found in classical literature an opportunity for coded anti-unionism. Scotland, like Rome, was overthrown through weakness and the abandonment of traditional ideals.[30] To them, exploring Scotland's classical sites may have been an exercise in Scottish nationalism, not British unionism. While traveling from Glasgow to Stirling, Robert Heron reflected happily that he was traversing on the very scenes where the Romans shone at arms and where the battles celebrated by Ossian were fought.[31]

Through its people, too, could Scotland contribute knowledge about Britain's past. Travelers evinced a profound interest in the ways of life of rural Scots, especially of the Highlanders, engaging in what was essentially early ethnological work by investigating and exploring Gaelic culture. Nearly every travel account of this period contained ruminations on the character of Highlanders and discussed their customs, traditions, and ways of life. Because conditions were changing quickly, many visitors believed theirs was the final opportunity to examine and record genuine Highland folkways. Visitors described the 'singular customs' they encountered: forms of dress, types of homes, farming methods, funeral traditions, dialect, local superstitions and customs. Those of a literary bent collected Gaelic songs and legends. Some took advantage of the chance to research the truth of the Ossian poems – generally with conflicting conclusions. Thomas Pennant was a particularly copious collector of folk culture, describing in detail the diverse local habits and beliefs, variations in the costumes of the natives, types of agriculture, even the different types of weapons formerly used.

This interest was part of a European-wide fascination with 'the folk' in the eighteenth century, which posited the study of rural society as the uncovering of the true nation. Because of the belief in the four-stage development of human societies, late eighteenth-century enlightened thought in Scotland rejected the notion that Highland culture possessed any specific national or ethnic importance. Yet both Scottish and English travelers were nonetheless intrigued with the idea that Highlanders could be living members of an earlier stage in British development.[32] To the author of the 1803 *Gazeteer of Scotland*, Highlanders were a branch of the ancient Celtae, descendents of the first inhabitants of Britain.[33] Isolation had secluded the Highlanders, the 'Indians of Scotland', keeping them an 'unaltered' race who provided an idea of 'that primeval state when man and beast were joint tenants of the plain'.[34] Although many travelers were shocked and amazed at the 'backwardness' of Gaels, their findings generally reached the encouraging conclusions that while the people were poverty-stricken, superstitious, and ignorant, they were also instinctively virtuous, an idea that dates at least from late seventeenth-century accounts of the Hebrides.[35] Highlanders, it seemed, possessed an innate loyalty, independence, and love of liberty, qualities considered central to the British character. They showed respect for their 'superiors' not through learned behavior, but through a natural courtesy and loyalty. This naturalization of the social hierarchy was an attractive conservative myth in a revolutionary age and offered more evidence of British superiority over their continental neighbors.[36] Even clan violence and the Jacobite rebellions were viewed positively in this construction, as evidence of Highlanders' inborn loyalty. The 'feudalism' which so many improvers disparaged could be rewritten as benevolent paternalism not unlike that of an English country squire, as when Pennant described the inhabitants of the Loch Tay area as 'happy under a humane chieftain'.[37]

North Britain's landscape, too, helped further belief in a distinctive British culture. Interest in nature was almost a patriotic duty to some. It was described by John Aikin in 1790 as equivalent to those innately British characteristics of a love of liberty and truth.[38] The new theories of the sublime and the picturesque refashioned Scotland's environment from barren, unattractive, and difficult, to alluring, exotic, and attractive. Scottish scenery was increasingly the region's most compelling lure to visitors. It was the ideal fulfillment of the new landscape aesthetics of the eighteenth century, even if the crowds ignored the precise definitions of 'sublime', 'beautiful', and 'picturesque' as delineated by specialists.

As discussed by Joseph Addison in 1712 and popularized by Edmund Burke in 1756, the sublime was a state of mind awakened by the great and energetic aspects of nature. According to Burke, pain and danger were the strongest emotions one could feel, so the sublime was best evoked by that with an implied threat; scenes that were dark, obscure, vast, gloomy, large.[39] The picturesque, by contrast, as defined by William Gilpin and Uvedale Price in the last quarter of the century, emphasized seeing over feeling. Picturesque composition required natural scenes which made appealing pictures, calling for intricacy: ruggedness, diversity of shapes and sizes, fragmented outlines. Gilpin applied these qualifications to the Scottish landscape on his 1776 visit and found them most appropriate. Scotland's mountains appeared in every possible shape, making good backgrounds for pictures. Although not as heavily vegetated nor as colorful as they might be, the lakes were as varied as the mountains. The rivers were beautiful, with frequent cascades: 'true classical rivers'. The estuaries were just the right size.[40] By the 1790s standardized 'picturesque tours' of Scotland were well known,[41] as were the scenes which best evoked the 'agreeable horror' of the sublime: the falls of Clyde near Glasgow, the Fall of Foyers in the Highlands, the tiny island of Staffa rocked by the waves of the Atlantic, the steep and barren valley of Glencoe.

Malcolm Andrews connects the new landscape aesthetics to a self-conscious promotion of British, not European, cultural standards. By stressing the viewer's immediate individual response to place, both the sublime and the picturesque challenged the cultural authority of the classics (at least by the second half of the eighteenth century), and consequently of the elite. Although sublime and picturesque tours were often formulaic and predictable, there were no absolute standards of taste and no classical education was necessary. All an individual needed to appreciate a scene was his or her emotions and the natural genius of the place. This subjective and informal approach to landscape was a reflection of the widening of the social elite, and of the freedoms secured by an enlightened political system.[42] The application of these ideas of landscape to Scotland indicated the area's Britishness, while in applying these philosophies, tourists demonstrated their cultural nationalism.

Both the association between the Highlands and the sublime and the link between the landscape and British chauvinism were strengthened by the enormous popularity of James Macpherson's Ossian poems, first published in 1760. Allegedly translations of poems by a third-century Gaelic bard, the epics were highly emotional and full of scenes of melancholy grandeur – mist, mountains, waterfalls, and an atmosphere of loss, grief, and decay – which were well calculated to meet the requirements of the sublime. Although the authenticity of these works was highly controversial, raising contentious questions about Scotland's cultural capabilities, their effect was electric. Ossian's spell was firmly cast over the Highlands.[43] Particularly appealing to fans in the new British nation was the fact that these were works of a native-born poet. The Highlands had produced a Celtic Homer, a Briton equal if not superior to the classical genius, who wrote magnificent works in a time when most Europeans were savages.[44]

Much of the new interest in scenery was a conservative effort, an attempt to 'rediscover landscapes where there are not only no traces of contemporary industrialization, land enclosure and estate improvement, but where the georgic idyll in all its forms is lost and where the terrifying "levelling" influences from across the Channel can never come.'[45] This could have deep moral consequences; coding the empty prospect as evidence of nature's terrible and awesome power drew attention away from the manner in which landowning policies were transforming Highland ways of life. Yet in Scotland, attraction to the natural environment was combined with a fascination with the promise of 'improvement' held out by economic development. One of the appeals of a visit to Scotland was the opportunity to witness this process. Between 1746-1820 agricultural, commercial, and industrial development took off in the Lowlands, and the Highlands became the specific target of forced economic and social change. An effect in part of the new opportunities available with the Union, southern economic development was mainly centered in the central Lowland valley, anchored by Glasgow. As in England, the key sectors of the economy were agriculture, textiles, and iron. New agricultural techniques began to be introduced on a large scale, transportation was improved, the linen industry expanded, and establishments like the Carron Iron Works took advantage of Scotland's vast coal fields. In the 1780s and 1790s machinery was introduced and work was reorganized into factories.[46]

The rapid development of commercialism and industrialism in Scotland became another of the country's lures to fellow Britons, who evinced patriotic pride at the spread of commercial values to the north. Enterprises such as the mining village of Leadhills, textile manufacturing in Paisley, the cotton mills of New Lanark, the shipping industry and associated commercial ventures of Glasgow and the Clyde, the Caledonian Canal, the Carron Iron Works, and numerous other coal mines, forges, textile mills, and bleaching fields were regular stops on most tours of Scotland, described even by tour books. John Lettice, a particularly indefatigable industrial tourist, stopped at virtually every commercial and manufacturing concern he encountered, and was disappointed to be turned away from the steel forge at Erskine Ferry and the Paisley textile mills. Such interest was not restricted to those whose business was commerce and improvement. John Leyden, a man of letters who was actively engaged in tracing the authenticity of the Ossian poems, toured the slate quarries at Easdale, visited an experimental farm near Taynish, viewed a large water-wheel at Blair Drummond, and observed the Duke of Argyle's modern drying barn. Although interest in industrial tourism is most common in travel accounts written by men, women, too, toured the Carron Iron Works and New Lanark.[47]

The detail with which travelers described the particulars of Scottish economic development suggests that this was a topic of great interest to them and one which they felt their readers should know about. The Scottish economy testified to the patriotism of North Britons, counteracting the stereotypes of beggarly Scots moving south to take away English jobs. It illustrated the strength of the Union and the benefits of the British constitution, and allowed the English to feel a paternal pride in Scotland's growth to social maturity. Linda Colley observes that commercial activity and patriotism were one and the same to eighteenth-century Britons. Investment in the economy both demonstrated and encouraged loyalty, and the expansion of trade was proof of Britain's status as the freest and most distinctively Protestant of nations.[48] Furthermore, eighteenth-century culture understood the commercialization of society as the birth of an explicitly modern order.[49] Members of commercial societies were regarded as industrious, moral, and virtuous, using all their natural talents and abilities to civilized ends. Scots, it seemed, at least in the Lowlands, had passed through the earlier stages of social and economic development (hunting, pasturage, and agriculture) and were joining the English at the highest level: commerce. In fact, Thomas Newte argued that Scotland was a more fertile ground for economic growth than was England. Just as lime or marl works faster on new than old ground, he asserted, so new inventions and institutions are introduced more smoothly in countries not pre-occupied by habits and customs than in those convinced they are already improved.[50]

Lettice's ceaseless interest in industrial tourism was therefore central to his desire to promote an integrated Union. He emphasized that North Britain had 'for some time' taken a 'brilliant' role in its expansion.[51] Others described David Dale, owner of New Lanark, as 'patriotic'.[52] The Carron Works were 'a great service to the country', 'giving bread to many hundreds', evidence of the great power man had gained over nature.[53] Pennant thought the busy manufacturing town of Paisley must be an agreeable sight to 'every man who wishes well to his country.'[54] He was similarly pleased with the sight of a hundred boats laying their nets in the isolated Loch Jurn:

> So unexpected a prospect of the busy haunt of men and ships in this wild and romantic tract, afforded this agreeable reflection: that there is no part of our dominions so remote, so inhospitable and so unprofitable, as to deny employ and livelihood to thousands; and that there are no parts so polished, so improved and so fertile, but which must stoop to receive advantage from the dreary spots they so affectedly despise; and must be obliged to acknowledge the mutual dependence of part on part, howsoever remotely placed and howsoever different in modes or manner of living.[55]

Several tourists contrasted scenes of industry with the struggles and conflicts of earlier periods of history. Joseph Mawman, a visitor from London in the early nineteenth century, toured New Lanark en route to the Falls of Clyde:

> We blessed ourselves, that we lived in an age when those banks, which were once the hiding-place of the patriot Wallace, struggling for the liberties of his

country, had become the busy scene of useful mechanics; and instead of echoing with the sounds of bugles, or ringing with the clash of arms and the shrieks of death, were cheered with the habitations of plenty, piety and peace.[56]

Similarly, Pennant found the sight of a formerly unused tract of land which had been converted into meadows, linen fields, and textile manufacturings 'far more agreeable' than a nearby battlefield.[57] The author of a 1798 guidebook exulted that the Antonine Wall near Stirling, 'that barrier of Roman usurpation', was almost entirely demolished by the plowshare, rejoicing that unfettered commerce occupied the seat of imperious usurpation.[58]

It was clear to all observers that industry was of great benefit to Scotland, although Carr thought the cotton mills must be unpleasant for child laborers.[59] Several travelers stressed the large numbers of people employed by various enterprises, for the industrious productivity of a substantial population was seen as a sign of the health of the nation.[60] Leadhills employed 500 miners when Pennant visited in 1769, T. Garnett found 700 at a cotton mill in the village of Doune near Stirling and 1,000 people at another mill in Fintry near Callendar.[61] The Carron Works provided jobs for another thousand at the turn of the century.[62] Garnett, an English physician who lived in Glasgow for several years and toured Scotland before moving to London, praised New Lanark: 'What ground for exultation this must afford to the worthy owner! What a number of people are here made happy and comfortable, who would, many of them, have been cut off by disease, or, wallowing in dirt, been ruined by indolence.'[63] Likewise the iron foundry at Bunawe 'has been found highly beneficial to the poor natives, who find constant employment, humane treatment, and good wages in its various departments.'[64]

Scotland's towns and cities were oft-visited by tourists and travelers, and the eighteenth-century absorption with economic progress is shown in visitors' attraction to evidence of municipal commercial and intellectual development as well as scenes of historic significance. Because eighteenth-century culture understood towns as signs of civilization and order, Scotland's urban growth was a further indication that the region was well in the mainstream of modernization, defined as following in English footsteps.[65] Perth, Inverness, Aberdeen, and Dundee were all characterized as 'well-built', 'populous', 'busy', 'flourishing', and their thriving economies were particularly praised. Libraries, schools, hospitals, and industrial and commercial ventures were popular attractions across the country. Glasgow, 'the most improving place in Britain', the 'greatest commercial town in the kingdom', impressed tourists with its 'general appearance of flourishing commerce, and increasing opulence'.[66] There, travelers visited the University, where Lettice raved about the 'splendid collection', distinguished faculty, and impressive facilities, especially for the study of science.[67] They stopped by the glassworks and ironworks. They observed the flourishing trade and manufacturing region along the Clyde, pointing out the new canals, bridges, and roads, all evidence

of the 'spirited exertions of an active and thriving people' and 'that might
[sic] Genius of Commerce'.[68] The spacious streets and elegant new buildings
spoke to the refinement and taste of Glaswegians, as did the subscription
coffee room which held half the newspapers of London and numerous
provincial and continental journals.[69]

Similarly, while Edinburgh's historic Old Town with the Castle, Holyrood
House, the Parliamentary buildings, and the University was an obligatory
sight, the New Town attracted the most attention and interest, although this
can be partly attributed to the smells, dirt, and infamously unsanitary
conditions of the crowded medieval city. In the New Town, visitors commented
on the wide, handsome streets, the elegant buildings, the magnificent houses,
the many public buildings, the numerous charitable institutions, the new
ballroom, 'which will, perhaps, surpass in elegant magnificence any one in
Britain',[70] and the intellectual excitement of the Scottish Enlightenment. John
Knox asserted that the city would soon vie with the 'most elegant cities in
Europe.'[71] Designed by James Craig in 1766, the New Town was intended to
symbolize a common British culture in which Scotland played a leading role
in promoting the values of progress and improvement. Edinburgh would bring
to life the ideal of the perfect free and prosperous city, thus demonstrating to
the rest of the world – especially London – that Scotland was as fashionable
and progressive as any European capital. Such a large building campaign
made evident Scotland's wealth, the combination of Scottish and English
names attached to streets and squares illustrated pride in the Union, the grand
Robert Adam Register House showed Scottish patriotism.[72]

Nonetheless, while Scotland's Britishness was abundantly evident in the
thriving towns and cities, busy industries, and usefully employed workers, it
was equally clear to the eighteenth-century traveler that North Britain was
still a work in progress. Some visitors were unimpressed by Edinburgh's
implicit claims to Scottish cultural leadership in the Union. John Stoddart
felt there were not enough shops, the society was less lively than it could be,
and noted that grass grew in most of the streets.[73] Newte noticed that Glasgow
had many elegant houses – but they were only half finished. The window
shutters and doors were unpainted, many of the walls were bare plaster.[74] No
observer failed to note that considerable poverty was visible all over Scotland,
most obviously in the Highlands. There, destitution and indigence
demonstrated the absence – and thus the necessity – of British government
and commercial growth. The very distinctiveness of the Highlands appeared
to prevent the region from being a productive, contributing part of the realm.[75]
English and Lowland visitors were scandalized by the 'miserable', 'wretched'
huts made of dirt, mud, or loose stones, the 'lean, withered, dusky and smoke-
dried' inhabitants turned yellow with peat smoke, the 'fare that may rather be
called a permission to exist, than a support of vigorous life'.[76] Said Newte,
'No Kamskataka hut can be worse than a Highlander's.'[77] John Lane Buchanan

compared the treatment of Hebridean tenants to beasts of burden.[78] The waves of emigration following the turn of the century Highland clearances seemed a danger to the health of the country, and indicated the need for commercial development. That the effects of poverty were most severe for women was further evidence of the need for modernization. Women and children, even in the Lowlands, commonly were shoeless and the sight of a barefoot woman came to be one of the indications of arrival in Scotland. Travelers credited Scots with total disregard of the 'delacacy of the female sex'; Scotswomen were short and brawny, had poor complexions, and were compelled to toil much harder than females of a comparable class in England.[79]

Although Pennant spoke at one point of 'unblameable poverty'[80] it was clear to visitors that these conditions existed because many Scots, especially Highlanders, had not yet learned the essential commercial and industrial values. They were 'slothful', 'indolent', 'lazy', 'stupid', 'idle'. They were unwilling to do anything to provide for themselves until famine pinched.[81] At the same time, there was little doubt that, as Philip Homer put it, with the proper encouragement Gaels could become active and industrious.[82] Highlanders could develop energy and diligence, the land could be fertile and productive. More towns, more commercial enterprises, more transportation facilities, more efforts to 'excite the industry of the people' and the Highlands 'will soon become one of the most valuable districts of the British Isles.'[83] Thus, throughout the eighteenth century but especially after the '45, Gaelic Scotland was the target of a concerted effort to bring the benefits of the British constitution north. This endeavor, as is well known, was fuelled by concerns that in their political, social, and economic character, the Highlands were barely under the authority of the Crown. As A. J. Youngson points out, the objective of the several economic development schemes was to use the region to increase the national wealth and to make the people more industrious.[84] The perceived problem was not that Gaels were poor, for eighteenth-century economists thought in terms of the welfare of the state rather than of individuals, but that they were indolent. Under the auspices of the government and of private organizations like the British Fisheries Society, roads and canals were built, towns were founded, the herring fishing business was developed, and linen manufactures were begun.

Much of the excitement of a trip to the Highlands lay in the opportunity to see – and even participate in – the transformation of the Highlands into a contributing sector of the British nation. The idea that the region was in the midst of the progression into civilization quickly became an essential piece of the construction of the Highlands. An ancient way of life, it seemed, was being rapidly transformed. 'There is not an instance of any country having made so sudden a change in its morals as this I have just visited....Security and civilization possess every part, yet thirty years have not elapsed since the whole was a den of thieves, of the most extraordinary kind.'[85] The undertaking was understood as a patriotic *national* endeavor. Newte emphasized the advantages to the entire nation of expanding Highland fisheries – chiefly the increased employment.[86] Carr observed that the Caledonian Canal was important to Britain as a whole.[87]

Many of the visitors whose writings helped create the tourist map of Scotland were either active agents of the improvement process (Edward Burt, a member of General Wade's road-building expedition; Buchanan, a missionary for the SSPCK; John Knox of the British Society for Extending the Fisheries) or sympathizers with it (Pennant, Newte). Viewing Scotland through the lens of what Margaret Hunt calls the 'commercial gaze', these and other visitors carefully observed the possibilities for economic development in the Highlands and made numerous suggestions.[88] Better farming methods and equipment might well improve the level of production; the agriculture of lower Lorn was 'susceptible of very great improvement'.[89] Timber might be grown for considerable profit, large enclosures might make the ground more profitable.[90] Oban, (then a tiny Highland village) could be turned into a royal dock and arsenal.[91] Canals would bring more traffic, commercial intercourse, and employment.[92] Developing the fishing industry was the most frequent recommendation, and the possible means and certain benefits of such an endeavor were the subject of extensive discussion. Fisheries, said Garnett, were an 'inexhaustible fund of wealth'. 'This is the true source of wealth to these parts of the kingdom, and if attended to as its importance calls for, will fill all the indented shores of North Britain with population, wealth and every comfort and convenience of life.'[93] Newte thought the government could supply some old fifty-gun ships, with officers and seamen accustomed to fishing. Highland boys, organized in clan groups, could be apprenticed to work on the ships, thus learning how to fish, realizing the benefits of industry, and becoming acquainted with the art of seamanship should they be needed at war.[94]

While they might seem like opposite tendencies, the twin fascinations with the possibilities of economic improvement in Scotland and with the landscape as a place beyond the bounds of civilization operated together in the eighteenth and early nineteenth centuries.[95] The tendency of visitors to give advice on economic development hinted at Scotland's need for outside help, positing the Highlands in particular as a region ripe for outsiders' economic domination. At the same time, the new landscape aesthetics also rendered Scotland the passive object of others' efforts. Although picturesque tourists rejected overt signs of humans' alteration of the land, the picturesque also had the effect of appropriating the land by subjecting it to a series of rules and manipulations. To many, the delightful horror of the sublime was mingled with improvers' distaste at unproductive land. And only with the roads and forts brought by the improvers could seekers of the sublime and picturesque view the wild with relative complacency. [96]

Whether they were scenic tourists, improvers, or antiquarians, those who introduced Scotland to the English public also defined Scotland. The role of the many travel accounts, diaries, letters, and sketches produced by visitors was not just to make Scotland known, but to interpret, to make sense of the place. This role placed tourists and travelers in a position of authority. To a certain extent, their texts naturalized conquest in much the same way Mary Louise Pratt understands the travelers' accounts of Africa and Latin America.[97] Visitors' definitions of Scotland included a clear implication of cultural inferiority, for to most, England's superiority was self-evident.[98] While travelers from both sides of the Tweed lauded Scots as active and patriotic Britons, they also presented England as the standard Scotland needed to reach, and portrayed North Britain as the recipient of outsiders' efforts. Scotland's economic contribution to the Union lay in the fact that it was finally catching up to English standards. The 'British' pride evoked by travel in Scotland often seemed to conflate 'English' with 'British'. According to 'a Lady', traveling probably in the 1770s,

> The Scotch for some ages past have been insensible of what degree of improvement their country was capable; but they have now opened their eyes to conviction and I dare say a hundred years hence, our posterity shall behold them with a spirit of emulation making large strides to equal us.[99]

John Knox noted that the verdant fields near Loch Etive were clear evidence that Englishmen must live there.[100] Garnett considered the spread of English cloth and English styles of dress a sign of progress.[101]

Such attitudes can be found in travel accounts written by both English and Scottish travelers, for middle- and upper-class Scots frequently shared the implicit sense of Scottish provincialism manifested in travel literature, especially regarding the Highlands.[102] To many Scots, however, the travel industry was an opportunity to counteract that sense of inferiority by claiming their right to help shape their country's image. Scots were active participants in tourism, both as sightseers and as promoters, and in so doing, they put forward their own definition of Scotland. Certainly there were many ways in which late eighteenth- and early nineteenth-century travel and tourism in Scotland could exert an appropriative power. Those who observed and researched Highland culture rendered Gaels subjects for study rather than autonomous individuals. By describing, drawing, measuring, and cataloguing the antique artifacts of Scotland, tourists represented themselves as the preservers of Scotland's past. When Thomas Pennant visited the ruins of St. Columba's sixth-century monastery on Iona, the reputed burial place of Scotland's earliest kings, the nunnery was being used to stable cattle and tombstones were covered with dung.[103] Sarah Murray, who toured Scotland in 1796, found the grounds of the cathedral planted with potatoes and vegetables.[104] Both considered such desecration to be clear evidence of the islanders' lack of civilization, and visitors of the 1780s and 1790s began to fear the imminent decay of the remaining monuments. Fifty years later, however, John Macculloch, a geologist, found the ruins in much better shape, natives no longer 'allowed' to appropriate them for stables. He attributed the change to the descriptions published by earlier visitors.[105] Travelers were the indispensable caretakers of Scotland's past.

Travelers also constructed themselves as necessary agents in bringing to light the values of North Britain's scenery. According to visitors, many Scots were unaware of the aesthetic worth of the land which surrounded them. 'Only lately', said Pennant, 'have the North Britons become sensible of the beauties of their country.'[106] Thus, armed with an understanding of the sublime and the picturesque, collecting views with their paintbrushes and Claude glasses, it was travelers and tourists who gave the land its meaning. Visitors frequently presented themselves as 'explorers' and 'discoverers' who located unknown scenes – even if they were guided to these sights by local residents. Sarah Murray credited herself with discovering the beauty of the Trossachs, and led other tourists to 'Murray Point' at Loch Katrine.[107] Macculloch attributed Loch Scavaig and Loch Coruisk on Skye to himself. Joseph Banks was widely referred to as the discoverer of the island of Staffa.[108] In fact, Loch Katrine was recommended to Murray as a romantic site.[109] Residents of Skye advised Macculloch to go to Loch Scavaig, knowing the geologist would find there the specimen he sought. Banks was led to Staffa by a guide who took his party around the island. Staffa was home to two families and their cattle in Banks' day; he pitched his tent next to a house on the island. But those who had gone before Banks to Staffa were not travelers 'of taste'.[110] Aesthetic encounters with the land functioned as near-colonial confrontations; those without the proper cultural lenses were written out, and the land was claimed by those who could appreciate it properly.[111] Pennant asserted that Staffa was indeed unknown in the Highlands; he met two gentlemen from the nearby island of Mull who seemed to know nothing of the place, 'at least they never mentioned it as any thing wonderful.'[112] Preparing to go to Loch Scavaig, Macculloch dreamed of finding scenery 'which as it appeared to have been utterly neglected by the only two persons who had ever opened their eyes on it would crown me with the laurels of a discoverer.'[113] Only when traversed by travelers and tourists was Scotland's value truly appreciated.

Nonetheless, tourism's colonial implications must be qualified in a couple of ways. If tourism was a form of taking possession, both English and Scottish tourists and travelers claimed the land in the name of Great Britain, a nation of which Scots were a part. Meanwhile, travelers – English or Lowland – could not always impose the meaning they wished Scotland to have. As John Glendening argues, Scotland talked back, and visitors were transformed by their experiences in a number of ways.[114] Indeed, for many, transformation was a key purpose of travel to North Britain; negative stereotypes should be contradicted, unfair generalizations should be undermined. One female visitor found that, because of 'wrong representations', her original opinion of Scots had been ill-founded. Although she continued to have some criticisms, by the end of her trip she was a staunch defender of 'our mountainous neighbors.'[115] One of John Carr's preparations for his trip to Scotland was to 'purif[y] my mind from the prejudices which ill-humored or sarcastic representations had at various times impressed upon it.'[116]

Nor did tourism and travel silence local forms of self expression. Katie Trumpener examines the early nineteenth-century genre of 'national tales' in Scotland and Ireland, seeing them in part as anti-colonial tracts endeavoring to describe the land 'as it really is', in opposition to outsiders' travel accounts.[117] Although Gaelic voices were not heard in the touristic conversation about the definition of Scotland, in part because of Enlightenment Scotland's rejection of Gaelic culture as a viable element of Scottish identity, Highlanders continued to express their opinions about the social changes they faced.[118] They, too, made use of tourism where they could. It was not Joseph Banks who named Fingal's Cave on Staffa; according to Bank's own narrative the local guide told him that the cave was named for 'Fhinn MacCoul'.[119]

Many tourists read this story as evidence of the authenticity of the Ossian poems; it may also demonstrate that Hebrideans recognized the potential in an Ossianic connection.[120] Although Scottish travelers and tourists shared many attitudes with their English cohorts, Scots who toured their own country asserted a Scottish patriotism. The newly developing travel industry was thus both a means for Scots to affirm their own sense of national identity as well as to demonstrate that Scotland was an active partner in the Union.

The Adventure of Travel

To this age full of curiosity about the world, when readers reveled in tales of the exploration of faraway places, the discussions of intriguing landscapes and unusual customs combined with the challenges of travel to construct Scotland as a place where adventures could be had.[121] Scotland seemed almost virgin territory, where exciting exploration was being done. The fact that, as Samuel Johnson observed, parts of one's own nation were as unknown as Borneo or Sumatra was an enticing opportunity.[122] In Scotland, ordinary British citizens, without even leaving their own national state, could know the thrill of stepping into an unknown region, an experience previously restricted only to those able to venture far from home. Yet as these adventurers explored Scotland, creating what would become the country's nineteenth-century tourist map, they also began to tame it by explaining, interpreting, and characterizing North Britain.

Eighteenth- and early nineteenth-century visitors to Scotland were both male and female, and tended to be members of the educated and professional classes. As many tourists and travelers brought servants with them, experiences of Scotland filtered further down the socio-economic ladder. Many visitors were literary figures, such as William and Dorothy Wordsworth, Samuel Coleridge, John Keats, and John Leyden. Garnett was a doctor who had taught at the University of Glasgow. Joseph Banks and Thomas Pennant were natural historians, Sarah Murray was the widow of a Scottish military officer. They were English and Lowland Scots. Anyone who traveled in this period took uncomfortable conditions for granted, but, perhaps especially for these scholars and professionals, trips to Scotland required stamina, resourcefulness, flexibility, a sense of adventure, and sometimes even courage – especially if one planned to venture to the Highlands. These were not trips to be undertaken lightly, and they required careful preparation. Murray advised prospective visitors to secure a strong, roomy carriage with well-corded springs. They should carry powerful chains, linch pins, shackles, turn screws, a hammer, and some straps. Food, wine, tea, sugar, salt, napkins, a knife and fork, bed linens and towels should be brought with them.[123]

As this advice suggests, there was little public transportation in Scotland during this period and strangers needed either to provide their own or to be flexible enough to adjust to unconventional methods of travel. Most travelers rented some type of coach, but these were of varying quality and were not always suitable for rough terrain. Coach passengers often had to walk up the steepest roads, as horses could not pull both them and the carriage. Murray traversed Glencoe on a peat cart with a board fitted across it for a seat. The Wordsworths and Coleridge, who were trying to travel inexpensively, rented what was known as a 'Jaunting car'. It had back to back hanging seats, with room for three people on each side, and a hollow in the middle for luggage. Passengers' feet were about a foot off the ground. There was no roof.[124] When Garnett wished to take a ferry across Loch Lomond two teenage boys hoisted him and his traveling companion on their backs and carried them out to the boat.[125] The Wordsworths called a ferry at Loch Awe by lighting a small fire atop a certain hill.[126]

The north of Scotland was more accessible than ever before in the second half of the eighteenth century, thanks to the network of roads and bridges built as the government endeavored to subdue the Highlands after the Jacobite risings of the first half of the century. But tours were far from easy. Once reaching the Highlands travelers rode horseback, discovering that many roads were impassable by carriage. Johnson was glad he and Boswell had divested themselves of much luggage after leaving Inverness; it was hard to carry many belongings when 'climbing crags and treading bogs and winding through narrow and obstructed passages.'[127] John Knox advised that Sutherland was 'a country where no man, who cannot climb like a goat, and jump like a grasshopper, should attempt to travel, especially in the month of October.'[128]

Those who attempted to visit the Western Isles rented small boats. They frequently characterized the sailors as ignorant, unskilled, and unsure of how to get to their destination. When Stoddart attempted to visit Staffa in 1800, he encountered a violent gale at the Sound of Ulva, and grew concerned that they would not be able to reach the island. The guides agreed that 'assuredly' they could not get to Staffa. They only left land, they said, because Stoddart asked them to.[129] Travel conditions were worsened by language barriers. Although English was making substantial inroads into the Highlands in the late eighteenth century, especially in border regions,[130] one could easily find oneself in a squall on the open sea in a shallow boat with seamen who spoke barely a word of English, as happened to John Leyden. (He, fortunately and unusually, spoke a little Gaelic.)[131] Many visitors hired guides, who were valuable both as translators and for advice on the best routes and places to spend the night.[132] The weather could magnify any difficulties. The ability to visit Highland sights was almost always weather dependent. Boswell and Johnson were doubtless not the only Hebridean travelers stranded for long periods by the rain; in fact, John Carr advised that while in ideal conditions a journey to Mull, Staffa, and Iona could be done in two to three days, the same trip might become an arduous undertaking of ten to fourteen days if the weather was bad.[133] Coleridge shortened his visit rather than endanger his weak health by journeying in an open cart in the rain.

Lodgings were of uneven quality and could be a challenge to find. This was more true of the Highlands than the Lowlands, which were fairly well supplied with inns. Murray located only two inns in Inverness in the 1790s,[134] although enterprising aristocrats such as Lord Breadalbane quickly began to establish more in tourist-prone locales. Even in the Lowlands, however, poor weather could easily strand a traveler in an isolated region where the lack of public accommodation placed him or her at the mercy of local hospitality. Often this was a pleasant experience. Even in the Hebrides travelers were treated royally by Scots of the gentle classes, especially when they came armed with suitable letters of introduction. Johnson and Boswell 'found nothing but civility, elegance, and plenty' at the home of Malcolm Macleod, proprietor of Raasay, Rona, Fladda, and extensive holdings on Skye.[135] Those who encountered Scots of the humbler classes, too, recounted the kindness and generosity of strangers who shared meager amounts of food, dried wet clothing, and provided lodgings as comfortable as their living standards allowed. Travelers generally interpreted such graciousness as an example of

Scots' natural and uncorrupted goodness. John Bristed, on the other hand, alleged that such treatment was pure capitalism. He and a friend traversed Scotland in the early nineteenth century dressed as common sailors, in order to 'see and investigate the manners of the great body of the people' without being treated 'artificially'.[136] They were initially turned away from virtually every inn they went to, only getting lodging after convincing innkeepers they were really gentlemen under the rough clothes. When they ran out of money towards the end of the trip no one would give them food, gentlemen or not. However, he claimed that people were much more generous in the Highlands than in the Lowlands, a conclusion which prevented Bristed's account from fully refuting the commonplaces about Scottish hospitality.

Even when travelers did easily find accommodations, arrangements could be bleak. In 1803 Coleridge and the Wordsworths spent one night at a ferryman's house at Loch Katrine, a home which was probably of a higher standard than many. A small hut of unplastered stone, it consisted of three compartments: the cowhouse, the kitchen and living area, and the bedroom. The areas were divided only up to the riggings, permitting free passage of light and smells from one area to another. Smoke from the fire filled the room. Hens roosted above them in rafters which were crusted over with smoke. William, Coleridge, and another traveler they met on the road (a man from Edinburgh on a walking tour to John O'Groats) slept in the barn. Dorothy slept on a hard but clean bed of chaff.[137] Travel accounts abounded with horror stories. Leyden claimed to have fasted for 29 hours when the inns and huts he found near Glen Roy had no food.[138] Murray's lodging at Hawick was uncomfortable, loud, and so dirty she could not bear to eat breakfast.[139] Garnett had plenty of company on Iona: 'Besides the light infantry etc., in the beds, we had several chickens, a tame lamb, two or three pigs, a dog and some cats, which last went and came at pleasure through a hole in the roof.' Rain came through the roof, too.[140] Travelers complained frequently about unclean conditions, slow service, and high prices. Many people told of waiting hours in the morning for breakfast after specifically ordering an early meal so they could get on the road.

Touring Scotland was not just troublesome and arduous; sojourners also portrayed it as potentially hazardous, especially in the Highlands. The danger was sometimes more rhetorical than real, but people were concerned about more than the discourse of the sublime. Traveling to the Western Isles in small boats could indeed be risky. Murray described a perilous trip between the islands of Skye and Raasay (a fairly short distance) on rough seas, during which both she and her servant expected to die.[141] She was again in serious danger rowing back from Corryvrekan, a large whirlpool between the islands of Scarba and Jura.[142] Boswell, too, had moments sailing around the Hebrides when he feared his life was over. Traversing the land was not as treacherous, but travelers did not always feel secure there either. There were regions where even horses had a difficult time. Pennant called the road into Glen Tilt, a rugged path so narrow the horses had to cross their legs to pick out a secure route, 'the most dangerous and the most horrible I ever traveled.'[143]

Notwithstanding all the strenuous and irritating aspects of an excursion in Scotland, more and more people began to go there around the turn of the century, activating the rudiments of a tourist industry. The closing of the Continent because of the wars of the French Revolution and Napoleon partly – but only partly – explains the growing interest in the north of the Tweed. Given all the unfavorable characteristics of Scotland, few people would go there simply because they could go nowhere else. Rather, the challenge posed by North Britain was one of the attractions. Poor roads, impassable mountains, and dangerous passes had long prevented travelers from venturing north, but in the late eighteenth century those conditions became one of the reasons for the trip. Those who experienced danger frequently seemed rather pleased to have done so, as when Boswell reflected on a terrifying storm he encountered between the islands of Skye and Mull: 'I now saw what I never saw before, a prodigious sea, with immense billows coming upon a vessel, so as that it seemed hardly possible to escape. There was something grandly horrible in the sight. I am glad I have seen it once.'[144] Both Pennant and Murray were disappointed when scenes they expected to be hazardous were actually calm and safe.[145]

If Scotland's reputation for adventure and excitement was one of the lures of a visit there, growing numbers and the concomitant realization of tourism's commercial possibilities began to chip away at some of the need for intrepidity. This was particularly, though not exclusively, true of the Lowlands. In 1800 Garnett could still claim he did not meet a single traveler on foot or horseback in the three weeks of his Highland tour,[146] but in the south encounters with fellow excursionists became increasingly common. Ben Lomond was much frequented by visitors 'from every quarter of the island', as well as foreigners.[147] The Wordsworths met a party of English tourists at the Falls of Clyde, busily stuffing bundles of heather into their carriage.[148] Competition for limited accommodations intensified; when Homer and his companion approached Cairndow they met a 'large' party – four women, two men – and quickly realized that one group would have to travel on to Inverary.[149] The Highlands were not immune to the consequences of tourism; Stoddart claimed that a number of visitors' names were carved on a column in Fingal's Cave on Staffa.[150]

These groups were not striking out on their own. By the 1790s sightseers usually followed suggested short and long tours of Scotland, which allowed them to visit those sites considered most vital. These were not formal tours; they appear to have developed organically as word spread of the best routes to see the scenes most worth seeing. Individual trips varied, depending upon interest, time, travel conditions, and weather. Yet the very existence of recommended circuits indicates the extent to which Scotland was coming to be known, even by those who had not yet been there. Already in 1771, Smollett led his band of tourists in *Humphry Clinker* along what came to be known as the Short Tour. Both the Long and Short Tours began in Edinburgh or Glasgow, generally Edinburgh. After spending a few days there, admiring the picturesqueness of the Old Town and the Castle and enjoying the prosperity and beauty of the New Town, an eighteenth- or early nineteenth-century tourist probably stopped at the Falls of Clyde. These were a series of three waterfalls near Lanark: Cora Lin, Bonnington, and Stonebyres. A favorite subject for artists of the period, the falls were well known as ideal evocations of the sublime.[151] Indeed, for those not venturing to the Highlands, the Falls of Clyde were one of the best representations of Scotland's wild and terrific characteristics, and were a highlight of many tours.[152]

Glasgow was the usual next stop, followed by the bonny banks of Loch Lomond, staying perhaps at Arrochar. The most common route continued up a steep road through the bleak mountains of Glencroe, to Inverary and Loch Awe, a stretch considered dreary and hideous by some, awefully desolate and sublime by others. Alternatively, many tourists headed to Perth and continued on to visit Ossian's Hall near Dunkeld, a trip which could be combined with the Duke of Atholl's carefully laid out pleasure grounds at Blair Atholl. Situated on the Duke's land forty feet above an impressive cataract on the river Bruar, the Hermitage was built in 1757 as a summer retreat. In 1783 the fourth Duke transformed the structure into 'Ossian's Hall', commissioning the painter George Steuart to provide a painting of the blind bard singing to a group of maidens. Guides led visitors to the structure by a titillating route which allowed them to hear but not see the roaring falls. When they entered the building, they saw at first only the Steuart painting, which suddenly split apart and slid into the walls, creating an entrance to the viewing room. This chamber was almost completely covered with mirrors on the walls and ceiling, reflecting the waterfall and multiplying the image around the spectators. Water appeared to be pouring in all directions as the sound of the falls echoed around. Most visitors were overwhelmed by the experience, although some found it distastefully artificial.[153]

Such was the extent of the Short Tour. Those with stricter time constraints concentrated on Edinburgh, Glasgow, the Falls of Clyde, and Loch Lomond. Because this tour excluded the highest and wildest of the mountains and the difficulties of roaming the Hebrides, it was a feasible way to obtain an idea of Scotland. But as Womack points out, this was a domesticated version of North Britain which concentrated on places where large-scale estate management was most evident.[154] The Short Tour appealed to the taste for improvement as well as the fascination with the sublime, allowing those who followed it to see numerous examples of modern industry and commerce, great houses with planned gardens, with glimpses of wild nature at the Falls of Clyde and Loch Lomond.

Improvement was a theme on the Long Tour, too, as visitors investigated social and economic conditions in the Highlands and considered the benefits of the British constitution as manifested by the 'newly civilized' clans. But they also experienced a fuller immersion into the sublime, and traversed areas much less touched by commercial development. The Long Tour led strangers deeper into the Highlands. Some followed Johnson and Boswell's route up the east coast to Aberdeen, across to Inverness, then to the Western Isles. Others kept to the west, following the Great Glen to Fort William, Fort Augustus, and Inverness. In either case, those on the Long Tour made every effort to include Staffa and Iona. The site of a monastery established in the sixth century by St. Columba, Iona was a must-see sight, usually visited in conjunction with Staffa. Reputed to be the burial ground of the earliest kings of Scotland and of the Lords of the Isles, Iona's ruins were a treasure trove for antiquarians, but were also popular with other tourists. The tiny island's popularity owed something to the period's taste for melancholy ruins and graveyards, but St. Columba's efforts to bring enlightenment to the Scots may have served as an inspiration to these earnest improvers. Johnson's reflections, the lens through which most later travelers understood the island, had a contemporary relevance: 'We were now treading that illustrious island, which was once the luminary of the Caledonian regions, whence savage clans and roving barbarians derived the benefits of knowledge, and the blessings of religion.'[155]

Staffa, although actually visited by only the most hardy pilgrim, was the ultimate destination of eighteenth-century Highland tours. A diminutive isle composed of basaltic rock, from a distance Staffa appeared to be a large flat-topped rock with perpendicular sides. Regularly shaped pillars fifty to sixty feet high along the sides of the island appeared to be holding it up. Spectacular caves dotted the sides. The most famous of them, Fingal's Cave, was covered inside with majestic pillars, and was accessible only by boat and only in favorable weather. Joseph Banks first drew the island to popular attention after a fellow English traveler on Mull told him of an island 'where he believed no one even in the Highlands had been'.[156] Banks' ecstatic description was appended to Thomas Pennant's *Tour*, and quickly seized the imagination of the reading public. Banks' admiration of this display of nature's powers, his excitement at finding a new wonder, and the enigma of the tiny island resisting the heavy Atlantic waves made Staffa irresistible. The island was mysterious, unusual, isolated, awe-inspiring, difficult if not dangerous to reach, and associated with Ossian. Fingal's Cave, 'grand almost beyond imagination',[157] was the highlight of an excursion to Staffa. Boats heaved and rolled on the waves while visitors fired their guns and allowed the echoes to add to the magnificence of the cave, or thrilled to the sound of bagpipes resounding along with the roar of the waves. Some tourists brought bagpipers along specifically for that purpose.[158] Small vessels, the only ones which could enter the cave, were reportedly easily smashed by waves against the sides of the caverns. His guide told J. E. Bowman in 1825 that 'many' limbs had been crushed.[159]

The amount of time spent in Scotland obviously varied. Johnson and Boswell's journey lasted about two and a half months, not counting the time at Boswell's home. John Leyden accompanied two young foreigners who had been studying in Edinburgh on a Highland trip which took place between mid-July and October, 1800. William Gilpin squeezed most of the Short Tour into a fortnight, while Joseph Mawman was able to take a month for his version. In 1803 Philip Homer managed to take in most of the Long Tour, excluding Staffa and Iona, in a month.

As the early 'exploration' of Scotland began to settle into defined routes, identifiers developed which marked the essential sites. In addition to Ossian's Hall, the Duke of Atholl built gravel walks on both sides of the Bruar, and bridges where the falls were most remarkable.[160] As early as 1708 seats and a viewing platform helped people appreciate Cora Lin at the Falls of Clyde.[161] By 1798 two wicker huts sat at the foot of Loch Katrine to provide shelter for strangers who might wish to relax and enjoy refreshments they brought with them.[162] By 1800 visitors could rent boats at Loch Lomond in order to fish or to visit the loch's many islands (at what John Stoddart considered an extravagant price).[163] At every location favored by tourists local residents offered their services as guides. In smoothing the path for tourists, such 'markers' also domesticated the scenes they came to see, in much the same way that the picturesque made nature an attraction rather than an indomitable force.[164] Even in the Highlands the sublime could be made a bit easier to see; an arch was built at the Fall of Foyers for the convenience of those wishing to view one of the Highlands' best examples of nature's awesome power.[165]

Textual guides were available, too, helping to provide tourists with a sense of mastery over Scotland. Most visitors relied on the travel accounts of those who had gone before them for advice on where to go, what to do, and how to get there. Many visitors (Johnson and Boswell, for instance) carried with them a copy of Martin Martin's 1695 *Description of the Western Islands*. Pennant's *A Tour in Scotland* was regarded by many as an indispensable handbook. Johnson and Boswell were also widely read. Many travel accounts, such as Sarah Murray's, were designed to serve as guidebooks as well as tales of their author's adventures. The ancestor of modern guidebooks or tourist handbooks also began to appear in this period, as Scots began to take advantage of both the financial possibilities offered by the interest in their country, and the opportunity to present their land to others. Among the earliest was Charles Burlington's *The Modern Universal British Traveler,* published in 1779.[166] *The Traveller's Guide or, a Topographical Description of Scotland*, was published in Edinburgh in 1798. It was a general description of Scotland, organized regionally, with information on the major industries, demography, and attractions of each region. It was particularly useful for the extensive directions: maps, listings of the major roads, and the best routes to most destinations. The *Traveller's Guide* made little effort at selectivity; rather than picking a few routes that tourists might prefer, as later became the practice, the book was an extensive description of things to see in Scotland. Robert Heron's *Scotland Delineated* (1799) was organized in a similar fashion, describing the attractions in each county that might interest English visitors. His *Scotland Described* (1797) was intended for Scots, designed to inform them about their country. In *Scotland Delineated* Heron informed his English audience of attractive scenery and contextualized his descriptions with quotes from previous well-known travelers like Thomas Pennant and Samuel Johnson. He told his Scottish readers less about their country's scenic properties, and more about its industry, agriculture, and topography. He also enumerated the many benefits brought by the Union. Localized works also appeared, such as Charles Ross' *The Traveller's Guide to Lochlomond, and its Environs* (1792) and the anonymous *A Sketch of the Most Remarkable Scenery near Callander of Monteath*, in its fourth edition by 1808.[167] James Denholm's 1798 edition of *The History of the City of Glasgow* included directions for tours of Loch Lomond and the Falls of Clyde.[168] The series known as *Duncan's Itinerary*, consisting of pocket-sized volumes containing a map indicating the most important sights and information presented road by road, began in 1805.[169]

Able to follow in the footsteps of earlier travelers and aided by an embryonic tourist industry, visitors of the 1790s and later were unlikely to complain, as Boswell did, of missing an ancient chapel in St. Andrews because no one told him it was there.[170] Unlike Gilpin, turn of the century tourists could not be unaware of the existence of the Falls of Clyde.[171] Yet some of the sense of discovery was gone. Johnson, Boswell, Gilpin, Pennant, et al. had mapped Scotland, and in the process told their later followers how to see the country. Guidebooks, suggested tours, and benches and bridges at scenic views made later sightseers more passive. They reacted to expectations already created for them rather than to a fresh and unseen place. They were tourists, not explorers. Nonetheless, in the late eighteenth and early nineteenth centuries, travel in Scotland was still an adventure, and that adventure attracted visitors. Roads were yet rough, seas perilous, inns of uncertain existence. There were in this period no complaints that journeys had become too easy, or that growing numbers were destroying the experience.

Yet fears about the possible perils of tourism for Scotland, especially the Highlands, are also evident. Parallel to the hymns to the values of improvement in eighteenth-century travel literature of Scotland ran a counter strain which Peter Womack calls a latent anti-imperialist myth.[172] In this vision, a product of the eighteenth century's undercurrent of ambivalence about commercialism, the isolation of the Highlands was a protection from the sordid values of commercialism, and contact with the Highlands and their residents could enrich and purify those at a more 'advanced' stage of social development. In *The Expedition of Humphry Clinker* Scotland (not just the Highlands) is seen as the locale of spiritual and physical health, a contrast to the dissipation and degeneracy of Bath and London.[173]

Contemporaries were divided over the consequences of travel upon North Britain. On the one hand, many visitors believed travel, especially journeys from England, would foster improvement. Garnett argued that the many visitors to the Highlands provided an example of gentler and more polished manners, and thus helped in the extirpation of 'feudalism'.[174] The poor service encountered in Scotland – inattention to time schedules, bad food, dirty facilities – was read as evidence that many in Scotland did not yet possess commercial and industrial values. But others were loath to see tourism bring commercialism in its wake. The opportunity to make money seemed to be tainting those who lived in tourist-prone regions. John Macculloch once forced, over protests, a young shepherd boy to take a shilling after they had companionably climbed Ben Lawers together. He later regretted his actions, fearing that he had taught the boy to sell the civility he was accustomed to give. Just so, he said, Englishmen assist in corrupting the Highlanders with an ostentatious display of wealth.[175]

Writing of his 1829 journey to Scotland, Beriah Botfield cautioned his readers not to lament that the Highlands were losing their distinctiveness, for that was to bemoan the progress of civilization.[176] John Lettice assured readers that the decline in manners and morals detected by some observers as Scotland grew more prosperous was part of an inevitable cycle.[177] Most eighteenth-century philosophers agreed that that some sort of fundamental decay eventually accompanied social progress. To many, this was a necessary evil, leading to the greater advancement of society.[178] One effect, however, was that in the process of becoming 'British', Scotland could lose some of the very features that made it so compelling. Hence the urgency and excitement of travel in eighteenth and early nineteenth-century Scotland; one could witness the Highlands before they became fully modern, and could be present at North Britain's transition to constitutional liberty and economic progress. The majority were willing to see old customs and lifestyles go, in favor of the greater good of advancement and improvement. Their Victorian descendants, filled with deeper doubts about the real meaning of 'progress', would be much less open to change in Scotland.

Notes

[1] John Lettice, *Letters on a Tour through various parts of Scotland in the year 1792* (London, 1794), pp. 35-6.

[2] On anti-Scottish sentiment, see Linda Colley, *Britons. Forging the Nation 1707-1837* (New Haven: Yale University Press, 1992), pp. 101-32; Daniel Green,

'Introduction', in William Cobbett, *Cobbett's Tour in Scotland*, Daniel Green, ed., (Aberdeen: Aberdeen University Press, 1984); Paul Langford, *A Polite and Commercial People* (New York: Oxford University Press, 1992), pp. 323-29; Peter Womack, *Improvement and Romance. Constructing the Myth of the Highlands* (London: MacMillan Press, 1989).

3   Colley, *Britons*; Christopher Harvie, *Scotland and Nationalism. Scottish Society and Politics 1707-1994* (New York: Routledge, 1994); Gerald Newman, *The Rise of English Nationalism* (New York: St. Martin's Press, 1987); Murray G. H. Pittock, *The Invention of Scotland. The Stuart Myth and the Scottish Identity, 1638 to the Present* (New York: Routledge, 1991).

4   On tourism and English identity in the eighteenth century see Ian Ousby, *The Englishman's England: Taste, travel and the rise of tourism* (New York: Cambridge University Press, 1990).

5   John Stoddart, *Remarks on Local Scenery & Manners in Scotland during the Years 1799 and 1800* (London, 1801), p. 61.

6   *The Traveller's Guide or, a Topographical Description of Scotland* (Edinburgh, 1798 and 1814); *The Gazeteer of Scotland* (Dundee, 1803); *Scotland Delineated, or a Geographical Description of every shire in Scotland* (Edinburgh, 1791). This last example was essentially a geography book intended for use by 'the young reader'.

7   Robert Heron, *Observations made in a Journey through the Western Counties of Scotland in the autumn of 1792* (Perth, 1793), p. 1:5.

8   Cited in Peter Levi, 'Introduction', in Samuel Johnson and James Boswell, *A Journey to the Western Islands of Scotland* and *The Journal of a Tour to the Hebrides*, Peter Levi, ed., (New York: Penguin, 1984), p. 12.

9   Ian Ross, 'A Bluestocking Over the Border: Mrs. Elizabeth Montagu's Aesthetic Adventures in Scotland, 1766', *Huntington Library Quarterly: A Journal for the History and Interpretation of English and American Civilization* 28(1965), pp. 213-33.

10   Johnson and Boswell's trip became a tourist attraction itself; later generations of visitors considered areas Johnson had visited 'classic ground', and following their path was a favorite activity. For an example of one of Johnson's critics, see 'A Lady', 'A Journey to the Highlands of Scotland with Occasional Remarks on Dr. Johnson's Tour', (London, 1776). The author ridiculed Johnson's account as a 'volume of vacancy' (Letter VI) full of obvious points and unnecessary criticism of Scots. This source has often been attributed to Mary Ann Hanway but some scholars dispute that claim. See Elizabeth Hagglund, 'Tourists and Travellers: Women's Non-Fictional Writing about Scotland, 1770-1830' (Ph.D. diss., University of Birmingham, 2000), pp. 39-41.

11   See Alastair Durie, *Scotland for the Holidays. Tourism in Scotland c. 1780-1939* (East Linton: Tuckwell Press, 2003).

12   Lettice, *Letters*, pp. 265-66.

13   *Scotland Delineated*, p. 22.

14   See T. Garnett, *Observations on a Tour through the Highlands and Part of the Western Isles of Scotland* (London, 1800).

15   'Carr's Caledonian Sketches', *Quarterly Review* I (February 1809), pp. 182-83.

[16] Sir John Carr, *Caledonian Sketches or a Tour through Scotland in 1807* (London, 1809), p. 18.

[17] Thomas Pennant, *A Tour in Scotland MDCCLXIX* (London, 1790), p. 2:241.

[18] Womack, *Improvement and Romance*, p. 15.

[19] 'Journey to the Highlands', Letter XIII (b).

[20] Ousby, *Englishman's England*, pp. 58-65. See also David Cannadine, *Decline and Fall of the British Aristocracy* (New Haven: Yale University Press, 1990); Carole Fabricant, 'The Literature of Domestic Tourism and the Public Consumption of Private Property' in Felicity Nussbaum and Laura Brown, eds., *The New Eighteenth Century. Theory, Politics, English Literature* (New York: Methuen, 1987), pp. 254-75; Mark Girouard, *Life in the English Country House* (New Haven: Yale University Press, 1978); Adrian Tinniswood, *A History of Country House Visiting. Five Centuries of Tourism and Taste* (Cambridge: Basil Blackwell and the National Trust, 1989).

[21] Lettice, *Letters*, 239.

[22] Thomas Newte [William Thomson], *A Tour in England and Scotland in 1785* (London, 1788), p. 125.

[23] Sam Smiles, *The Image of Antiquity. Ancient Britain and the Romantic Imagination* (New Haven: Yale University Press, 1994). See also Esther Moir, *The Discovery of Britain: The English Tourist* (London: Routledge & Kegan Paul, 1964), pp. 47-57; Ousby, *Englishman's England*; Stuart Piggott, *Ancient Britons and the Antiquarian Imagination* (New York: Thames and Hudson, 1989).

[24] Smiles, *Image of Antiquity*, p. 15.

[25] Smiles, *Image of Antiquity*, pp. 39-44.

[26] *An Account of the Principal Pleasure Tours in Scotland* (Edinburgh, 1821), pp. 113-15.

[27] Ousby, *Englishman's England*, p. 99.

[28] Moir, *Discovery of Britain*, p. 53.

[29] Katie Trumpener, *Bardic Nationalism. The Romantic Novel and the British Empire* (Princeton: Princeton University Press, 1997), pp. 3-34.

[30] Pittock, *Invention of Scotland*, pp. 35-8.

[31] Heron, *Observations*, pp. 2:436-37.

[32] Colin Kidd, 'Gaelic Antiquity and National Identity in Enlightenment Ireland and Scotland', *English Historical Review* 109: 434 (Nov. 1994), pp. 1197-214.

[33] *Gazeteer*, 'The Highlands', n.p.

[34] John Leyden, *Journal of a Tour in the Highlands and Western Islands of Scotland in 1800* J. Sinton, ed. (Edinburgh: Wm. Blackwood & Sons, 1903), p. 252; Johnson, *Journey*, (Levi, ed.), p. 66; William Gilpin, *Observations on the Highlands of Scotland* (London, 1789; reprint with an introduction by Sutherland Lyall, Richmond, England: The Richmond Pub. Co., 1973), pp. 2:135-36.

[35] See Martin Martin, *A Description of the Western Islands of Scotland* (London, 1716; reprint, Edinburgh: Mercat Press, 1970).

[36] Womack, *Improvement and Romance*, pp. 137-38.

[37] Pennant *Tour*, p. 3:22.

[38] Quoted by Malcolm Andrews, *The Search for the Picturesque. Landscape Aesthetics and Tourism in Britain, 1760-1800* (Stanford: Stanford University

Press, 1989), p.10.

[39] Edmund Burke, 'A Philosophical Enquiry into the Origin of our ideas of the Sublime and the Beautiful', *The Works of the Right Honorable Edmund Burke* vol. 1 (London, 1801). See also Samuel H. Monk, *The Sublime* (Ann Arbor: University of Michigan Press, 1960); Marjorie Hope Nicholson, *Mountain Gloom, Mountain Glory: The Development of the Aesthetics of the Infinite* (Ithaca: Cornell University Press, 1959).

[40] Gilpin, *Observations*, pp. 2:127-33.

[41] See Andrews, *Search for the Picturesque*.

[42] Andrews, *Search for the Picturesque*, pp. 3-66.

[43] See Paul Baines, 'Ossianic Geographies: Fingalian Figures on the Scottish Tour, 1760-1830', *Scotlands* 4.1(1997), pp. 44-61.

[44] Ossian was supposedly the son of Fingal, king of a legendary race of giants who once roamed the Highlands. In his old age, Ossian celebrated the achievements of this ancient warrior breed, and his poems allegedly were passed down through oral tradition until Macpherson collected and translated them. The immediate popularity of the epics led to more collections in 1761 and 1763. Scholars now agree that Macpherson's works were not the direct translation of an ancient bard, but much of the basis of 'Fingal' does appear to be genuine Gaelic ballads, collected by Macpherson from oral tradition. The later works, especially 'Temora', were more clearly written directly by Macpherson. See Andrews, *Search for the Picturesque*, pp. 203-304; Howard Gaskill, ed., *Ossian Revisited* (Edinburgh: Edinburgh Univ. Press, 1991).

[45] Andrews, *Search for the Picturesque*, p. 66; John Barrell, *The Idea of Landscape and the Sense of Place* (Cambridge: Cambridge Univ. Press, 1972) p. 79.

[46] Rosalind Mitchison, *A History of Scotland* (New York: Routledge, 1982), pp. 357-78.

[47] 'A Journey to Scotland' (1790) MS. 15905, NLS, Sept. 10, Sept. 20; C. S. Stewart, *Sketches of Society in Great Britain and Ireland* (Philadelphia, 1834), p. 2:125; Elizabeth Selwyn, *Journal of Excursions Through the most interesting parts of England, Wales and Scotland* (London, 1823), pp. 142-47. The Carron Iron Works exercised some control over whom they admitted. Durie, *Scotland for the Holidays*, p. 27.

[48] Colley, *Britons*, pp. 55-100.

[49] Drew R. McCoy, *The Elusive Republic. Political Economy in Jeffersonian America* (Chapel Hill: Univ. of North Carolina Press, for the Institute of Early American History and Culture, Williamsburg, VA, 1980), pp. 13-47.

[50] Newte, *Tour*, p. 277.

[51] Lettice, *Letters*, p. 491.

[52] *Traveller's Guide* (1798), p. 92.

[53] Pennant, *Tour*, p. 1:263; *Travellers' Guide* (1798), pp. 155-56; Lettice, p. 491.

[54] Pennant, *Tour*, p. 2:166

[55] Pennant, *Tour*, p. 2:399.

[56] Joseph Mawman, *An Excursion to the Highlands of Scotland and the English Lakes* (London, 1805), p. 188.

[57] Pennant, *Tour*, p. 1:93.

[58] *Travellers' Guide* (1798), pp. 155-56.

59   Carr, *Caledonian Sketches*, p. 316.
60   A. J. Youngson, *After the '45* (Edinburgh: Edinburgh Univ. Press, 1973), pp. 54-60.
61   Pennant, *Tour*, p. 2:129; Garnett, *Observations*, pp. 2:169, 2:177-78.
62   Newte, *Tour*, p. 252-54.
63   Garnett, *Observations*, p. 2:236.
64   Garnett, *Observations*, p. 1:130.
65   Youngson, *After the '45*, p. 37.
66   Garnett, *Observations*, p. 2:185; 'Journey to the Highlands', Letter III; F. C. Spencer, *Journal*, p. 57.
67   Lettice, *Letters*, pp. 60-62.
68   Mawman, *Excursion*, p. 115.
69   Lettice, *Letters*, pp. 59-60.
70   Newte, *Tour*, p. 263.
71   John Knox, *A Tour Through the Highlands of Scotland and the Hebride Islands in 1786* (London, 1787; reprint, Edinburgh: James Thin, 1975), p. 8.
72   David Daiches, *The Paradox of Scottish Culture: The Eighteenth-Century Experience* (London: Oxford University Press, 1964), pp. 68-97; A. J. Youngson, *The Making of Classical Edinburgh* (Edinburgh: Edinburgh Univ. Press, 1966).
73   John Stoddart, *Remarks on Local Scenery & Manners in Scotland during the Years 1799 and 1800* (London, 1801), p. 1: 79.
74   Newte, *Tour*, pp. 98-9.
75   Womack, *Improvement and Romance*, pp. 6, 22.
76   Newte, *Tour*, p. 93; Pennant, *Tour*, p. 2:262.
77   Newte, *Tour*, p. 141.
78   John Lane Buchanan, *Travels in the Western Hebrides* (London, 1793), p. 144.
79   Mawman, *Excursion*, pp. 93-4.
80   Pennant, *Tour*, p. 3:279.
81   Pennant, *Tour*, p. 2:366.
82   Philip B. Homer, *Observations on a Short Tour Made in the Summer of 1803 to the Western Highlands of Scotland* (London, 1804), pp. 198-89.
83   John Macculloch, *The Highlands and Western Isles of Scotland* (London, 1824), p. 4:240; *Gazeteer* (1803), n.p.
84   A. J. Youngson, *After the '45*, pp. 47-66; See also T. M. Devine, *Clanship to Crofters' War. The social transformation of the Scottish Highlands* (New York: Manchester Univ. Press, 1994); Womack, *Improvement and Romance*.
85   Pennant, *Tour*, p. 2:400.
86   Newte, *Tour*, pp. 115-19.
87   Carr, *Caledonian Sketches*, pp. 221-22.
88   Margaret Hunt, 'Racism, Imperialism, and the Traveler's Gaze in Eighteenth-Century England', *Journal of British Studies* 32:4 (October 1993), pp. 333-57.
89   Leyden, *Journal*, pp. 271-72.
90   Newte, *Tour*, pp. 138-40.
91   Garnett, *Observations*, pp. 1:141-43.
92   Newte, *Tour*, p. 152; Garnett, *Observations*, pp. 1:330-34.
93   Garnett, *Observations*, p. 1:97.

[94] Newte, *Tour*, pp. 115-19.

[95] Womack, *Improvement and Romance.*

[96] On landscape as appropriation, see Andrews, *Search for the Picturesque*; Barrell, *Idea of Landscape*; Womack, *Improvement and Romance.*

[97] Mary Louise Pratt, *Imperial Eyes. Travel Writing and Transculturation* (New York: Routledge, 1992).

[98] However, Thomas Newte enumerated a series of disadvantages the Union brought to Scotland; such as subjecting the Scottish economy to customs duties in England before it was prepared for such costs, checking commerce on the east coast and nearly dismantling a series of towns there, drawing the nobility and gentry to London, and depriving Scots of 'not a little' of their national character, such as the 'ardor inspired by the presence of the sovereign' and exclusive control over their own affairs. *Tour*, pp. 286-88.

[99] 'Journey to the Highlands', Letter XVII.

[100] Knox, *Tour*, p. 18.

[101] Garnett, *Observations*, pp. 2:280-84.

[102] See Marinell Ash, *The Strange Death of Scottish History* (Edinburgh: The Ramsay Head Press, 1980); David Daiches, *The Paradox of Scottish Culture: The Eighteenth-Century Experience* (New York: Oxford Univ. Press, 1964); Harvie, *Scotland and Nationalism*; Colin Kidd, *Subverting Scotland's Past. Scottish whig historians and the creation of an Anglo-British identity, 1689-c.1830* (New York: Cambridge Univ. Press, 1993); Eric Richards, 'Scotland and the Uses of the Atlantic Empire' in Bernard Bailyn and Philip D. Morgan, eds. *Strangers Within the Realm: Cultural Margins of the First British Empire* (Chapel Hill: Univ. of North Carolina Press, 1991), pp. 67-114.

[103] Pennant, *Tour*, p. 2:283.

[104] Sarah Murray, *A Companion and Useful Guide to the Beauties of Scotland*, William F. Laughlan, ed., (Hawick: Byways Books, 1982), p. 151.

[105] Macculloch, *Highlands and Western Isles*, p. 4:148.

[106] Pennant *Tour*, p. 3:59.

[107] Murray, *Companion*, pp. 35-7; Leyden, *Journal*, pp. 15-16.

[108] Murray, *Companion*, pp. 35-7; Macculloch, *Highlands and Western Isles*, pp. 3:465-84; Sir Joseph Banks, 'Account of Staffa' in Pennant, *Tour*, pp. 2:300-10.

[109] Elizabeth Spence argued that a minister, 'Dr. R_ of Callander' published the first account of the Trossachs in 1790, four years before Murray's, in his *Statistical Account of Callander*. Elizabeth Isabella Spence, *Sketches of the Present Manners, Customs, and Scenery of Scotland* (London, 1811), p. 1:200.

[110] Garnett, *Observations*, p. 1:226.

[111] Womack, *Improvement and Romance*, p. 85; Barrell, *Idea of Landscape*, p. 62.

[112] Pennant, *Tour*, p. 2:301.

[113] Macculloch, *Highlands and Western Isles*, p. 3:466.

[114] John Glendening, *The High Road. Romantic Tourism, Scotland, and Literature, 1720-1820* (New York: St. Martin's, 1997).

[115] 'Journey to the Highlands', Letter XIV, Letter XVII.

[116] Carr, *Caledonian Sketches*, p. 3.

[117] Trumpener, *Bardic Nationalism*, pp. 128-57.
[118] See James Hunter, *On the Other Side of Sorrow. Nature and People in the Scottish Highlands* (Edinburgh: Mainstream Publishing, 1995).
[119] Pennant, *Tour*, p. 2:303.
[120] There were other late eighteenth-century traditions about the naming of Fingal's Cave; see Baines, 'Ossianic Geographies', pp. 47-8. For more on the naming of the Highlands, see Charles W. J. Withers, 'Authorizing Landscape: "authority", naming and the Ordnance Survey's mapping of the Scottish Highlands in the nineteenth century', *Journal of Historical Geography* 26:4 (2000), pp. 532-54.
[121] On the eighteenth-century fascination with travel, see Barbara Maria Stafford, *Voyage Into Substance: Art, Science, Nature and the Illustrated Travel Account, 1760-1840* (Cambridge, MA: MIT Press, 1984).
[122] Samuel Johnson, *A Journey to the Western Islands of Scotland*, Alan Wendt, ed., (Boston: Houghton Mifflin, 1965), p. 66.
[123] Murray, *Companion*, pp. 11-13.
[124] Donald E. Hayden, *Wordsworth's Travels in Scotland* (Tulsa, OK: Univ. of Tulsa Press, 1985), p.11.
[125] Garnett, *Observations*, p. 1:53.
[126] Dorothy Wordsworth, *Recollections of a Tour Made in Scotland*, J. C. Shairp, ed., (Edinburgh, 1874; reprint, New York: AMS Press, 1973), p. 136.
[127] Johnson, *Journey*, (Levi, ed.), p. 52.
[128] Knox, *Tour*, p. 255.
[129] Stoddart, *Remarks*, pp. 298-99.
[130] Charles W. J. Withers, *Gaelic in Scotland 1689-1981. The Geographical History of a Language* (Edinburgh: John Donald, 1984).
[131] Leyden, *Journal*, pp. 103-4.
[132] John R. Gold and Margaret M. Gold, *Imagining Scotland. Tradition, Representation and Promotion in Scottish Tourism since 1750* (Aldershot: Scolar Press, 1995), p. 44.
[133] Carr, *Caledonian Sketches*, p. 277.
[134] Murray, *Companion*, p. 65.
[135] Johnson, *Journey*, (Levi, ed.), p. 74.
[136] John Bristed, *Anthzplanomenoz, or a Pedestrian Tour through part of the Highlands of Scotland in 1801* (London, 1803), p. v.
[137] Wordsworth, *Recollections*, pp. 102-5.
[138] Leyden, *Journal*, pp. 194-96.
[139] Murray, *Companion*, p. 18.
[140] Garnett, *Observations*, p. 1:244.
[141] Murray, *Companion*, p. 189.
[142] Murray, *Companion*, pp. 169-72.
[143] Pennant, *Tour*, p. 1:123.
[144] Boswell, *Journal*, p. 331.
[145] Pennant, *Tour*, pp. 2:417-8; Murray, *Companion*, pp. 84-8.
[146] Garnett, *Observations*, p. 1:109.
[147] Garnett, *Observations*, p. 1:59.
[148] Wordsworth, *Recollections*, p. 39.
[149] Homer, *Observations*, p. 53.

[150] Stoddart, *Remarks*, p. 307.

[151] On artists' views of the Falls of Clyde, see James Holloway and Lindsay Errington, *The Discovery of Scotland. The Appreciation of Scottish Scenery through Two Centuries of Painting* (Edinburgh: National Gallery of Scotland, 1978).

[152] David Irwin, 'Three Foaming Cataracts: The Falls of Clyde', *Country Life* 187 (Nov. 1974), pp. 1166-1168.

[153] David Irwin, 'A "Picturesque" Experience: The Hermitage at Dunkeld', *The Connoisseur*, 187(Nov. 1974), pp. 196-202.

[154] Womack, *Improvement and Romance*, pp. 62-3.

[155] Johnson, *Journey*, Levi, ed., pp. 140-41.

[156] Pennant, *Tour*, p. 2:301.

[157] Leyden, *Journal*, p. 40.

[158] On the role of sound in sublime tourism, see William H. A. Williams, 'Blow, Bugle, Blow: Romantic Tourism and the Echoes of Killarney', in S. Henriquez, ed., *Travel Essentials. Collected Essays on Travel Writing* (Las Palmas de Gran Canaria: Chandlon Inn Press, 1998), pp. 133-47.

[159] J. E. Bowman, *The Highlands and Islands: A 19th Century Tour*, introduction by Elaine M. E. Barry, (New York: Hippocreme Books, 1986), p. 110.

[160] Leyden, *Journal*, p. 257.

[161] Irwin, 'Three Foaming Cataracts', p. 1166.

[162] Garnett, *Observations*, p. 2:175.

[163] Stoddart, *Remarks*, p. 228.

[164] See Chloe Chard, *Pleasure and Guilt on the Grand Tour. Travel writing and imaginative geography, 1600-1830* (New York: Manchester Univ. Press, St. Martin's Press, 1999) on the ways tourism serves to keep danger and destabilization at a distance. On the ways in which 'markers' and 'signifiers' set off tourist attractions, see Dean MacCannell, *The Tourist* (New York: Schoken Books, 1976).

[165] Garnett, *Observations*, p. 1: 322.

[166] Womack, *Improvement and Romance*, p. 36.

[167] Ross is cited in Womack, *Improvement and Romance*, p. 64; *A Sketch of the Most Remarkable Scenery near Callander of Monteath* (Stirling, 1808).

[168] James Denholm, *The History of the City of Glasgow. To which is added a sketch of a Tour to Loch Lomond and the Falls of the Clyde* (Glasgow, 1798).

[169] Gold, *Imagining Scotland*, p. 50.

[170] Boswell, *Journal*, p. 189.

[171] Gilpin, *Observations*, p. 2:71.

[172] Womack, *Improvement and Romance*, pp. 84-6.

[173] See Glendening, *High Road*, pp. 157-94.

[174] Garnett, *Observations*, pp. 1:313-14.

[175] Macculloch, *Highlands and Western Isles*, pp. 1:113-14.

[176] Beriah Botfield, *Journal of a Tour through the Highlands of Scotland* (Edinburgh, 1830), p. xiv.

[177] Lettice, *Letters*, pp. 527-35.

[178] McCoy, *Elusive Republic*, pp. 13-47.

Chapter 2

The Development of Mass Tourism, 1810-1914

'Johnson's Tour to the Hebrides' commenced in August, and was completed in November, occupying fully three months, and though it might be far more romantic and instructive than a tour under present arrangements, it would hardly be endured by the present race of Tourists to be cast upon the long and apparently flat and uninteresting island of Coll, on the way to Staffa, for a fortnight. Why, in a fortnight we now travel as far as Johnson and his friend Boswell travelled in their three month's tour![1]

Writing in 1861, Thomas Cook, who was himself instrumental in the development of Scotland's tourist industry, summed up the changes in the nearly one hundred years since the curious began trekking to North Britain. While visitors of the eighteenth century saw themselves as exploring and introducing a relatively unknown part of the kingdom, Scotland was familiar to later generations of visitors. They knew what they wished to see, and how it should be experienced. Neither weather, terrain, nor distance ought to hold them back. 'Uninteresting' sights should be dispensed with. These expectations were met by a smoothly running tourist industry which developed over the course of the nineteenth century, enabling an ever-increasing number of visitors to make Scottish tours. Christopher Smout estimates that in the early nineteenth century there might have been a score of travelers to the Highlands, by the late century, 10,000 a year.[2]

The evolution of large-scale tourism was in many respects the logical extension of foundations laid in the late eighteenth century as a map of the favored sights developed, visitors increasingly followed that route by rote, and an infrastructure emerged to meet their needs. Already in 1810 Walter Scott complained that 'Every London citizen makes Loch Lomond his washpot and throws his shoe over Ben Nevis.'[3] The unique development of the nineteenth century was the changing role Scotland played in the imaginations of tourists and non-tourists alike. Scotland came to be seen as a place of 'culture'; a space separate from ordinary social life which offered a counter to the negative consequences of the modern industrial world.[4] Journeys to Scotland were rituals; liminal experiences which offered spiritual renewal and even physical regeneration through contact with a transcendent reality.[5] Although aspects of that interpretation could be seen in eighteenth-century travelers' reactions to Scotland, especially to the Highlands, the romanticization of Scotland came to fruition in the early nineteenth century.[6] As the once-despised Highlands came to represent the whole, and as industrialization and urbanization became increasingly problematic and worrisome, Scotland was no longer seen as 'North Britain', a land of learning and fledging industry. Rather, Scotland symbolized the preservation of 'traditional' values and ways of life.

The simultaneous evolutions of an organized infrastructure geared towards affordable and easy middle-class travel to Scotland, and the new purpose such journeys played in the imaginations of visitors gave rise to a fundamental tension between the means and the objectives of the trip. Although Scotland was coming to represent the stability, unchangeableness, and 'poetry' that seemed elusive in industrial society, that same industrialization was a crucial component of Victorian tours. Tourism, Victorians knew, could not help but alter the places it encroached upon, even while it promoted their imperviousness to change. Thomas Cook admitted that 'romance' was lost with the rise of tourism, but he, in his role as a promoter of that industry, could quickly discount that loss. Others could not, for to most nineteenth-century visitors Scotland was the very definition of romance. The interpretation of Scotland which lured tourists was a fragile one, which was endangered both by the processes of tourism and by the various transformations of the nineteenth-century economy and society. However, tourism also enabled individual sightseers to maintain in their imaginations the romantic Scotland they came to see. Though often denigrated as preventing sightseers from genuinely looking around them, tourism showed those who came north how to perform the ritual of Scotland in such a way that it fulfilled its desired purpose.

A Nation of Highlanders

While the idea of a progressive, modernizing North Britain was a key factor in the creation of British nationalism and patriotism in the eighteenth century, a competing vision of Scotland developed at the same time, often from the same roots. In the nineteenth century Scotland's Enlightenment reputation as a center of learning and intellectual progress was superseded by fame as a land of romance. As such, Scotland was a contrast to the utilitarian world, a realm of transcendence and imagination which could revivify prosaic, arid, everyday life. Yet this characterization also made Scotland somehow ephemeral – an unchanging, unreal land without permanent consequences or impact upon the outside world (or the outside world upon it). Tourists' tendency to concentrate on the romance of Scotland – more specifically of the Highlands – had the effect of overlooking and downplaying the intellectual and economic vitality of much of the country. This practice exerted a powerful sway upon Scottish culture and national identity throughout the nineteenth and twentieth centuries, and its consequences have been frequently and justly criticized. Andrew Hooks notes, however, that in their historical context the romanticization and 'celtification' of Scotland constituted an imaginative response to the realities of the early nineteenth-century Scottish experience.[7]

The notion of Scotland as romance focused chiefly on the Highlands, which accordingly came to be seen as the true heart of Scotland, representing the nation at large. The association of Scotland with the Highlands was a new development. As late as the mid eighteenth century, few if any Lowlanders regarded Highlanders as 'true' Scots. Rather, they were a separate and culturally inferior people: lawless, irreligious, and uncivilized. However, once the arm of the government well and truly reached the Highlands in the second half of the eighteenth century and their inhabitants could be considered safely 'tamed', a variety of cultural influences combined to refashion the idea of the Highlands and their place in Scottish culture. Highlanders had long been objects of curiosity and once no longer a threat they could be invested with the exotic allure of a dying culture. Romantic and Enlightenment ideas of the virtues of the 'noble savage' made a positive trait of Highlanders' 'primitiveness'. The Enlightenment theories of social development which posited Gaels as examples of an early stage of society rather than members of a wholly independent culture not only validated efforts at 'improvement', they allowed the Highlands to be incorporated into Scotland. To patriotic Scots the attribution of a Highland heritage to all of Scotland offered a uniqueness and distinctiveness that 'North Britain' did not have, a form of Scottishness that was particularly appealing as contact with England intensified and differences between the Lowlands and England grew less marked.[8]

While they continued to assert themselves as loyal subjects who actively contributed to the Union, around the turn of the century Lowland aristocrats and members of the bourgeoisie adopted Highland heritage as their own. Even as the transformation of patterns of landownership and occupation destroyed old social structures in the Highlands, organizations like the Highland Society of London (founded 1778) and the Celtic Society of Edinburgh (1820) attempted to preserve the dress, music, and martial heritage of Gaels, by organizing piping and Gaelic poetry competitions and working to re-legalize Highland dress. The kilt, actually an early eighteenth-century invention worn by Highland peasants, was affected by the aristocracy as a symbol of Scottish ancestry and asserted as the authentic traditional national dress. Cloth manufacturers, especially William Wilson & Son of Bannockburn, standardized the sett (pattern) of tartans and began assigning them to individual clans, more or less arbitrarily. By the 1820s a fictionalized

Highland culture which ignored genuine Gaelic poetry, music, and customs in favor of Ossianic fakery was widely accepted by both Scots and foreigners.

A key element of the creation of 'Highlandism' was the remaking of Jacobitism and of the Highland warrior. In spite of the fierce hatred directed at Charles Edward Stuart and his followers during their invasion of England, there was also a certain glamour to his undertaking, and that glamour flourished once the cause was definitively defeated. The failure of the rebellion and the strength of the Union made the '45 a safe symbol of Scottish patriotism, and a non-threatening adventure tale to the English. The story of the '45 was a dramatic tale ripe for retelling by the popular imagination: the poor but noble clansmen fired up with devotion to their long-awaited king, the brave and dashing figure of 'Bonnie Prince Charlie', the Jacobites' triumphant and unexpected entry into Edinburgh, the questionable decision to turn back from Derby, the devastating defeat at Culloden, and Charles' months of hiding in the Highlands, aided by the heroic Flora MacDonald and protected by loyal Gaels who cared more for his safety than the sizeable reward on his head.

This tale reconfigured Highlanders, whose alleged steadfast devotion to the Stuarts was written as an innate loyalty to their superiors. This understanding was soon fostered by the harnessing of Highlanders' fabled martial prowess in the service of the state rather than against it. Between 1757-1760 William Pitt turned to the Highlands to raise troops to fight France, and over the course of the eighteenth century over 50 battalions of Highland troops were organized, distinguishing themselves in combat around the world.[9] The intentional similarities between Highland regiments and clan structure nourished the belief that Gaels' military talent was 'natural', the product of clan culture and the Gaelic character. The tartan kilt was the uniform of Highland regiments; until the proscription on Highland dress was lifted in 1782 theirs was the only legal wearing of the 'traditional' costume. The assignment of individual tartans to each regiment contributed to popular credence in tartans as markers of clan solidarity. The frequent commanding of Highland regiments by members of the families of clan chiefs further associated regiments and clans.

Meanwhile, the Romantic movement cast a spell over Scotland, both Highlands and Lowlands. The Highland landscape was wild and sublime, a place where deep emotions could be evoked. The Lowlands possessed soft, mild, pastoral scenes. Scotland's very location was romantic; northern latitudes were considered the natural home of romantic sensibilities. Scottish literature by Allan Ramsay, James Macpherson, Robert Burns and others taught British, European, and American readers that Lowland peasants were a simple, dignified, loyal people with a strong sense of traditional communal values; that the Ossianic Highlands were remote, exotic, and melancholy; that the unsophisticated Scots were natural poets in a way that members of more 'civilized' societies could not be; and that Scotland's history was appealingly tragic and heroic. 'Scottish scenery, Scottish Highlanders and Lowland peasants, Scottish folk-song and poetry, Scottish history, all of these were coming together at the close of the eighteenth century to make Scotland into perhaps the most romantic country in Europe.'[10] Scotland's growing popularity with vacationers also fostered this conception, for it was also in the early nineteenth century that leisure travel was reconfigured as a 'holiday', a temporary escape from the stresses and strains of modern social life.[11]

In the first decades of the nineteenth century there was more than one way to imagine Scotland, but not for long. The progressive, intellectual vision of Enlightenment Scotland quickly gave way to the romanticized, celtified vision because the second more closely met the needs of tourists from an ever more industrialized and urbanized society, and because of the influence of Walter Scott. Scott fashioned Scotland as the definitive romantic country, making inescapable and irresistible a construction which was already widespread. Under his pen the Highlands evoked energy and liberation from the restraints of society.[12] By becoming Scotland's foremost tourist guide, Scott showed readers how to appropriate this place which seemed at once so near and so distant from everyday life. Tours in Scotland seemed a 'hackneyed' subject to the *Quarterly Review* in 1809.[13] But in 1810 the publication of Scott's narrative poem *The Lady of the Lake*, released just at the beginning of the tourist season, revitalized interest in Caledonia. Every house and inn in the Trossachs region was soon crowded with visitors. Elizabeth Spence, who traveled to Scotland in 1810, advised those planning to stop at Loch Katrine to hire a carriage in advance. Already in August of that year 500 carriages had been through the area. William Pearson, a friend of the Wordsworths, noted in 1822 that the inn near Loch Katrine had become a 'great resort'; visitors had come from Italy, Spain, the United States, the West and East Indies, and China.[14]

The most popular writer of his day, Scott's view of Scotland had a wide circulation. Although his reputation faltered among contemporary literary critics around the 1860s, the 'Wizard of the North', the 'Bard of Abbotsford', was generally regarded from 1814 until 1900 as the greatest British novelist and was regularly compared to Shakespeare. Not even Charles Dickens was the object of more personal affection and hero-worship from his Victorian audience and Scott was equally popular in Europe.[15] Walter Scott was a deeply patriotic Scotsman whose passion for the history and traditions of his homeland were strongly colored by the sentimental Jacobitism he developed as a boy, but which did not impede him from a conviction that Scotland's future lay with the Union.[16] A Tory with ambitions towards landed society and an avid and knowledgeable antiquarian, to Scott the past was the source of continuity, heritage, and the forces which had shaped Scottish character and institutions. His central objectives as a poet and historical novelist were to preserve Scotland's history before memories faded and distinctive characteristics dissolved into English ways, to invoke in Scots pride and respect for their native land, and to interpret Scotland to his fellow Britons so they could understand this part of the kingdom more clearly and sympathetically. His recurrent theme was the conflict between the lost heroic past to which he responded with deep nostalgia, and the inevitable and necessary changes which offered such promise for Scotland.[17] Scott saw this tension as a struggle between opposing systems of values, rendered often as Highlands vs. Lowlands, Jacobitism vs. Union. Because Scott often used the Highlands as his symbol of Scotland's past, the effect of the past/present dichotomy offered in his work was to render Gaeldom ever more definitively as a place apart from the modern world. His protagonists, when presented with a choice between the forces of the present and reality, and those of history and romance, must choose the former. Yet it is the choice Scott asks his characters – and readers – to reject that he invests with passion, fascination, and enchantment.

This tension can be seen in *The Lady of the Lake's* seminal vision of the Highlands. Roderick Dhu, the symbol of past lawlessness and resistance to change, is a far more compelling figure than James V, emblem of a united, prosperous, lawful Scotland. Roderick's death, his pride and power symbolically outmatched by James' skillful sword handling,[18] makes clear the direction in which Scotland must go. But Roderick has the readers' sympathy and respect, and his death is a cause for grief. Scott's characterization of Loch Katrine as an 'inviolate sanctuary of peaceful beauty, a self-contained "enchanted land" protected from the real outer world by "sentinel mountains"'[19] likewise undercuts his verdict against Highland ways. Though he may suggest with Roderick's death that the future lies inevitably with a Scotland more linked to civilization, his Loch Katrine is regenerative and life giving. It was the image of the exiled Douglas and his daughter Ellen living an idyllic, innocent, simple life where the rules of ordinary living were suspended, real identities shed, and ancient quarrels healed which so appealed to his readers and drew them to the Trossachs by the hundred.

With a point that can be extended to other of Scott's Highland novels, James Buzard argues that the lesson of *Waverley* is 'not that romance must be rejected or outlived in favor of "reality" but that it must be strictly sequestered as "culture"'.[20] Although Scott's first novel undercuts its central character's predilection for romanticizing the Highlands, *Waverley* also fully satisfies the reader's demand for romance. Scott makes clear that the Highlands *are* romantic. His Highland Line is 'a psychological construct, the barrier between the mundane and the romantic, safety and danger, present and past.'[21] It is also the barrier between real and unreal. The Highlands promise heightened experience, excitement, and adventure, but because those promises stand in contrast to everyday life, they define the Highlands as temporary. One goes on holiday there, has adventures, and then goes back to real life. While Enlightenment theorists saw the Highlands as a stage in social evolution, in Scott's fiction the Highlands do not evolve. They remain a magical, but sequestered world unto themselves, releasing a sentimental 'afterglow of romance'.[22]

At this moment when early nineteenth-century tourists were learning to define leisure travel as a temporary release from the stresses and strains of daily living, Scott underscored this present/past, real/unreal contrast by explicitly comparing *Waverley* to a Highland tour. The story, he says, is 'a humble English post-chaise' which can conduct the reader 'as soon as possible to a more picturesque and romantic country', a reminder that romance is indeed a legitimate goal of a trip to the Highlands.[23] Waverley is essentially a tourist led by the narrator/tour guide on a Highland tour, and the reader vicariously travels with him. Passively, compliantly, Waverley is guided through 'a picturesque and romantic country' where his imagination and emotions can be freely exercised. Watching rather than participating, submitting to the interests of the plot and of other characters much as a tourist submits to guides and schedules, Waverley is led safely through a quest for romance and then back to reality, refreshed by his experiences.[24] In a similar but less overt fashion, many of Scott's protagonists are temporarily but never completely caught up in a world of adventure and imagination. The reference to tourism reminds us why this is only temporary. The Highlands are a holiday land: what happens there is only play.

For Scott and many others of his time, the packaging and isolating of Scotland's past as 'romance' was a means of creating a balance between assimilation and Scottish cultural distinctiveness. Scott asks his readers to be open to romance, but within reason.[25] Christopher Harvie argues that by 1819 Scott's vision turned bleaker, his optimism about the Union and the established government less certain. His later works, like 'The Highland Widow', suggest that the attempt to bridge the gap between the former Highland ways and modern civilization may be destructive, a vision Harvie sees as Scott's metaphor for Scotland as a whole. But Scott's financial troubles tied him to 'the treadmill of profitable romanticism', and he chose not to overtly confront his growing pessimism in his fiction.[26] Thus there was little to prevent his readers, living in a rapidly changing society and increasingly aware of the utilitarianism of modern life, from seizing upon the exoticism and otherness of the Scotland he created. Scott's thesis that the romance of the past ultimately must give way to the possibilities of Union had less effect upon the evolving image of Scotland than did the exoticism with which he clothed the Highlands.

The difficulties inherent in Scott's project of ennobling the past yet asking Scots to move on to the future are manifest in his arrangements for George IV's visit to Edinburgh in 1822. This, the first visit to Scotland of a Hanoverian monarch, was designed as a 'peace-giving occasion',[27] symbolizing the strength of the Union, royal recognition of Scotland as an integral but separate part of the kingdom, and official forgiveness for the Jacobite rebellions. Scott hoped thereby to call attention to a nostalgic blending of Scotland's past and present as well as Scotland's cultural independence. Scott staged a series of extravagant pageants, all with a Highland theme. He encouraged clan chiefs to bring suitably dressed followers to Edinburgh to parade before the king. The climax of George's two week visit was a procession from Holyrood House to Edinburgh Castle when Scotland's crown, scepter, and sword of state – recently 'found' by Scott – were paraded before the monarch, escorted by the once-outlawed Clan Gregor. Yet as critics even then argued, by presenting Scotland as a tartanized 'nation of Highlanders' Scott made it nearly impossible for observers to see any sign of the progressive, intellectual, industrial element that had once been central to Scotland's developing identity. The occasion solidified the importance of the new traditions that expressed Scotland's alleged Highland heritage. George's wearing of a kilt in Royal Stewart tartan set the fashionable seal of approval on those once seditious garments, and confirmed their new meaning as symbols of Scottish ancestry. J. M. W. Turner's dreamlike paintings of processions of red-kilted Highlanders marching to Edinburgh Castle glamorized a sight which would once have been terrifying to denizens of Scotland's capital.[28]

If George IV's visit cemented the celtification of Scotland, Victoria's numerous trips symbolized the meaning of that refashioning to middle-class tourists. She first visited the northern portion of her kingdom on an official state visit – during tourist season – in 1842. Like George IV, Victoria and Albert were greeted by an extravagantly and artificially tartanized Scotland, with all the expected trappings: scenery, kilted clansmen, the military. The royal couple was hailed at Taymouth Castle, home of the Marquis of Breadalbane, by a splendid gathering of the marquis' employees and dependants in full Highland dress. A huge festival was held in the evening, with lavish illuminations and Highland dancing by torchlight. To Victoria, 'it seemed as if a great chieftain, in olden feudal times, was receiving his sovereign.'[29] At Dunkeld, Her Majesty was met by an imposing collection of the Atholl Highlanders complete with claymores and battleaxes:

> The magnificent trees and the grey ruins of the cathedral…added highly to the effect. Then there was the encampment of the Highlanders to the right, peeping from the glades and alleys green, and the warlike lines of the sons of the mountain, of whom nearly 15,000 assembled in the garb of the Gael. Many of them were men of gigantic stature, especially the battleaxe phalanx and those who were equipped with bucklers.[30]

In Crieff 100 of the local tenants, dressed in tartan, some with Lochaber axes or other arms, toasted Victoria and Albert. Although not members of the military, the men had been 'zealously drilled' for several days by officers of the local regiment.[31]

This Highland grandeur could be enjoyed at home through the press. The *Illustrated London News*, which would become a chief organ of middle-class Victorian culture, had just begun publication in 1842 and the queen's journey was the perfect occasion to present their 'most splendid' issue.[32] The paper provided detailed accounts of Victoria and Albert's every move and educated their readers by including background information about the sights the royal couple visited. Numerous illustrations of Scotland's scenery and of the events of the tour publicized Scotland's attractions and furthered the process of 'celtification'. Reports on the royal excursion were accompanied by excerpts from *Black's Picturesque Tourist*, a popular Scottish guidebook which had itself only begun publication in 1840. Such articles implicitly reminded readers that they, too, could visit this compelling location which so enchanted the Queen. Press coverage continued for several weeks after the visitors came home and a series on the history and proper wearing of Highland dress gave more attention to Scotland the following month.

George IV paid one reluctant two-week visit to Scotland; Victoria and Albert were so delighted that they decided to return annually. These yearly trips to Scotland, often well-covered by the press, and the publication of two volumes of Victoria's Highland diaries, *Leaves from the Journal of our Life in the Highlands* (1868) modeled for her subjects the meaning of Scotland as culture. It was a place immune to the stresses, strains, and social problems of nineteenth century life. Scotland was to Victoria the imaginary domain of freedom depicted by Scott, of whose works she was an avid reader. According to the *ILN* she went there in search of 'privacy, quiet, seclusion'.[33] Balmoral, the royal family's private home in Scotland, seemed a place apart from real life. There, she said, 'All seemed to breathe freedom and peace, and to make one forget the world and its sad turmoils.'[34] She was the 'simple lady of the manor', who walked in the country and visited neighbors. She watched the sheep clipping and went salmon leistering (spearing). Albert developed a passion for hunting. They made boat tours around the west coast in 1847, just like other tourists, and twice made short trips incognito, staying at local inns and sightseeing. When riding or hiking she dressed simply in a plain shepherd's plaid, 'equipped like a Highland gude wife.'[35] She wore tartan dresses and Albert ordered a full dress of tartan for shooting. They affected Highland customs: eating bannock, Atholl brose, oatcakes, and even haggis.[36] Albert studied Gaelic.[37]

These sojourns, like those of other tourists, were exercises in 'staged authenticity',[38] highly selective and always colored by the status of the royal family. They also perfectly encapsulated the vision of Scotland which tourists would seek for the remainder of the century, completing the popularization of Scotland's new image just as the railway system was about to make Scotland more accessible than ever. The first Anglo-Scottish rail line was finished in 1848, the year Victoria and Albert purchased Balmoral. Thereafter railroads, guided tours, and all the equipment of tourism would allow Victoria's English subjects to follow her northwards in ever growing numbers. Scotland's much acclaimed seclusion would become ever more elusive.[39]

The Nuts and Bolts of Tourism

The refashioning of Scotland into 'culture' and 'romance' coincided with the transportation revolution of the nineteenth century and the rising standard of living of the middle classes. It became both attractive and feasible for middle-class Britons to tour Scotland, and thousands did so. Alastair Durie sees the 1850s, when crossborder rail lines were newly completed, as the turning point in the tourist boom.[40] By the turn of the century Edinburgh train stations were annually inundated with visitors from the south. Newspaper accounts spoke of trains being run in four or five portions, of 'hundreds' of people arriving from nearly every town on the Northeast and Midland line, of 'extraordinary' crowds.[41] In the early twentieth century so many people converged on the small Highland resort of Oban that its usual population of 5,000 trebled in holiday time.[42] By mid-century, an interconnected network of institutions that operated the tourist industry smoothed the path for these pilgrims. Most visitors' experiences were contained within a coordinated system of railways, steamboats, guidebooks, and guided tours which led them through the ritual of Scotland, working in conjunction with the expectations participants brought with them. An institutionalized and often predetermined format for travel made Scotland available to many – but was also somewhat at odds with the purpose of the trip.

Central to the infrastructure of tourism were the railroads, which substantially reduced the amount of time required to journey to and around Scotland. The first cross-border line, run by the Caledonian Railway, opened in 1848. Their express train took only 12 ½ hours to travel between London, Edinburgh, and Glasgow, a journey of 43 hours by coach.[43] So popular was the Caledonian's service that the company ran three trains a day even before the line was completed, taking passengers by coach over the unfinished portions.[44] The North British Railway (NBR) opened a second rail route in 1850. Since 1846 they, too, had ferried passengers part way by coach. A third line, the Midland Route, opened in 1876. By the turn of the century these three companies all ran between six and nine daily trains to Scotland in the summer, and a trip from London to Edinburgh or Glasgow took only eight hours. Inverness was then 13 hours' distance from London; Aberdeen only 11 hours and 15 minutes.[45] As one guidebook boasted in 1895, 'In these days of luxurious locomotion the traveler is carried from London into the very heart of the Western Highlands with almost as little exertion as if he were going from the city to his suburban home.'[46] In 1901 when the Fort William to Mallaig line opened, travelers could make a through booking from London to Stornoway, on the distant island of Lewis, a 24 hour trip.

Within Scotland, rail links of use to tourists developed fairly quickly in the industrializing Lowlands, but more slowly in the less populated northwest. A Glasgow to Edinburgh route opened in 1842.[47] In the 1850s and 1860s the NBR established branch lines to some of the highlights of what was known as 'Scott Country': Kelso (1851), Jedburgh (1856), Hawthornden and Roslin (1866).[48] The opening of the Caledonian & Dumbartonshire Railway in 1850 facilitated travel to Loch Lomond. Although Aberdeen was accessible by rail by 1850 and Inverness in 1863, it was only in the third quarter of the century that trains could carry tourists to many Highland attractions. The Dingwall to Skye Railway reached Strome Ferry in 1870, where steamships carried passengers on to the Hebridean island of Skye. However, only by 1880 could one travel by train to Oban, the favorite jumping off point for travel to the Western Isles. Given the lack of industrialization in the northwest, there was little incentive to build rail lines, and as important as tourists were to the rail companies of the Highlands, even late in the century tourist traffic alone would not support the cost of operating a line. In 1883 when promoters first proposed a Glasgow and North Western Railway which would reach Inverness via the popular tourist sites of Loch Lomond, Glencoe, Ballachulish, travelling along Loch Leven, Loch Linnhe, and Loch Ness, they predicted that their customers would be fish, sheep, and tourists, in that order. Parliament ruled there was not enough traffic to warrant the line. A modified version of the proposal was approved six years later, as part of an effort to stimulate the region's economy and reduce its isolation in the wake of the land dispute that had recently swept across the Highlands and islands. Although the route, which opened in 1894 as the West Highland Railway, meandered through some of the most spectacular scenery in the west and was even more popular with tourists than promoters expected, as late as 1907 it did not make a profit.[49] Nonetheless, tourists were one of the railways' most important customer bases. Promotional material for those lines which traversed the Highlands advertised train travel as not just a means to an end, but an exciting and worthwhile object in itself. A guide to the Fort William to Mallaig line claimed it had been built 'as if on purpose' to provide the best views for tourists.[50]

Steamboats filled some of the gaps left by railways; in fact several steamboat companies were affiliated with rail lines. Much of northwest Scotland was accessible by water, thanks to the many lochs and rivers, the indented coastline, and two major canal systems: the Crinan Canal to Fort William (1801) and the Caledonian Canal, running southwest to northeast across the Great Glen connecting the Irish Sea with the North Sea (opened to traffic in 1822, completed in 1847). Europe's first commercial steamboat, Henry Bell's *Comet*, began navigating the river Clyde between Glasgow and the nearby fashionable watering place of Helensburgh in 1812. The Clyde quickly became the center of Scotland's steamer business. By 1825 weekly sailings were available from Glasgow to the Hebrides on the *Maid of Islay*, a small boat with two cabins and fourteen beds which sailed to Islay, Oronsay, Iona, and Staffa.[51] Visitors could tour Loch Lomond by steam as early as 1820; by 1825 two rival companies plied the loch.[52] In 1845 guidebooks assured travelers that there was scarcely a spot of the smallest interest in the Western Highlands or islands, approachable by water, that could not be visited during the summer at a trifling expense.[53]

The passenger steamer trade reached its peak in the last quarter of the nineteenth and the early twentieth centuries. In 1906 over 50 steamers served the Clyde and Loch Lomond.[54] In 1885 the official guidebook to MacBrayne's steamers listed 90 ports of call; in 1896 there were 147 possible destinations along the Clyde and the west coast, providing travel to virtually anywhere one could wish to go, including quite remote places. These boats served more than just the tourist market; steamers were the only form of trade, travel, and communication between the mainland and residents of the Hebrides. They were also a favorite form of recreation for Glasgow workers, for whom a trip 'doon the watter' was a popular day's outing. But tourism was a key component of the business. Clyde steamboat companies targeted southerners through advertisements in the London *Times* and in Scottish papers. The Glasgow and Caledonian Canal Steamboat Company, which traveled to the Western Isles and Inverness, recommended in 1825 that: 'Ladies, Gentlemen, and Families from the South desirous of visiting the sublime scenery of the Highlands will find these vessels admirably suited for the purpose. They are amply provided with every accommodation and the utmost attention has been paid to the convenience and comfort of passengers.'[55]

Turn of the century steamers were large and luxurious. In the Edwardian years it was popular to have strolling fiddlers or German bands on board. In one case the Berlin Philharmonic performed a concert of sacred music on a Sunday cruise in an effort to demonstrate the respectability of Sunday steamers.[56] Certain boats, particularly the MacBrayne Company's *Lord of the Isles* and *Columba*, were famous even outside of Scotland. Those two vessels, built in the 1870s, introduced a new standard of luxury to the Clyde steamers, possibly in an effort to compete with the rail networks which were then were beginning to move north. Intended to cater to wealthy tourists, not Glasgow workers on a day off, they were known as boats in which the 'best people' sailed. Both ships were remodeled and enlarged at the turn of the century; the new *Columba* was capable of holding 2,000 people and possessed a hairdressing saloon, a bookstall, a fruit stall, and a post office which handled 270,000 letters a month.[57]

Despite the proliferation of railways and steamers, coaches were still an essential means of travel and one with which Scotland was well provided by mid century. There were excursions to virtually every popular scenic spot, often in connection with trains and steamers. Coach routes were often established by the proprietors of inns in popular tourist districts, as an effort to encourage customers to stay at their inn.[58] Even in the more populated Lowlands coaches remained a chief means of transportation once tourists arrived in Scotland. As late as the 1880s, when rail travel was widespread in the Lowlands, crowded vehicles took tourists through 'Scott Country', to the Falls of Clyde, and to the Trossachs.[59] Tourist 'Cuthbert Bede', a pseudonym for Edward Bradley who in 1863 published a composite account of two trips to Scotland with his wife, described carriages at Loch Lomond especially designed for the viewing of scenery: they were a sort of long luggage box with rows of seats on top. The luggage went inside, the people outside. There was no roof, however, should it rain.[60]

The extensive provision for travel offered in Scotland in the mid and late Victorian period did not always lead to smooth and relaxing trips. Visitors fussed about the crowds, the long waits for boats and trains, the frequent delays while cargoes bound for Hebridean residents were loaded and unloaded, the effects of the weather on the comfort of a sail. Alexander Smith, who traveled frequently to Skye in the mid-nineteenth century, warned that the steamer to Oban from the south was rarely on time, and when it did finally arrive, two-thirds of the passengers were invariably seasick.[61] Those who visited out of the way places still occasionally felt themselves to be in considerable peril. Catherine Sinclair, daughter of a Highland nobleman who wrote of travels probably made in the 1850s along the west coast and the far north, considered Banavie 'precipitous country' and believed there were places where she would have been killed on the spot had the carriage overturned. The road to Loch Awe she called 'dangerous' – the more so as her driver kept falling asleep.[62] Frances Murray, who spent a summer on Oronsay in 1886, described several distressing sea trips in rough weather, including occasions when she had to sleep all night on a small boat when the weather was too stormy to risk landing.[63]

Nonetheless, with trains and steamers Victorian and Edwardian tourists could travel in relative comfort to areas which a hundred years earlier often seemed unattainably remote. In 1804 Philip Homer was crushingly disappointed when he had to give up a trip to Staffa because he could find nowhere at Oban to leave his horse during the trip.[64] In his attempt to reach Staffa in 1800, T. Garnett took a ferry from Oban to the island of Kerrera, then another to Mull, spent the night at Achnacraig, crossed Mull by land, and finally got a boat to Staffa from Torlisk, after waiting two days for the weather to clear.[65] But by 1885 MacBrayne's Steamship Company offered a daily excursion to Staffa and Iona from Oban. The trip took nine to ten hours, including an hour's stop on each island. Pilgrims could enter Fingal's Cave in lifeboats that seated 30 to 40 people, and their way was eased by handrails of wire rope inside the cave and a stairway to the top of island. At Iona, a guide met the boat, which in calm weather could land at a small partly-artificial stone pier, whisked visitors through the ruins, gave them enough time to buy a few necklaces of shells, and got them quickly back on board. The total cost was between five to 15 shillings.[66]

Just as forms of travel changed, so too did lodging facilities. Gone were the days when Garnett shared his bed with an army of insects and animals while rain dripped through the ceiling. Tourists continued to complain about the expense, crowdedness, and sometimes the scarcity of hotels and inns, yet by the turn of the century Scotland was liberally covered by reputable and often quite luxurious accommodations which offered a variety of amenities. True, there were times and places when finding a room could still be challenging, especially early in the century. In 1843 there were still few inns in the Trossachs region, according to *Black's*. Those that existed were usually crowded and the guidebook noted dryly that the 'usual effects of monopoly' were exhibited, with the civilities proportioned to the amount of money a tourist appeared to have.[67] Even later in the century the most popular destinations might be short of beds during the busy summer months. In their caustic account of touring the Hebrides in the 1880s, Joseph and Elizabeth Robins Pennell, American artists who lived in London, alleged that they slept in the schoolhouse on Iona because the three inns were all full.[68] They could only find lodging in a drawing room at the Sligachan Inn on Skye.[69] During the shooting season, hotels in Inverness retained rooms in private homes for overflow customers.[70]

On the other hand, in 1861 Thomas Cook assured potential visitors that Oban had plentiful accommodations; he had been there when the town was occupied by at least 500 tourists, yet had room for plenty more at moderate charges.[71] And indeed, the quantity and quality of Scottish hotels steadily improved from the 1840s, in proportion to the number of visitors. New hotels in places like Lanark, Edinburgh, Glasgow, Inverness, and Loch Lomond were advertised in Scottish papers in the 1850s and 60s, calling attention to their convenience for tourists, the attractive scenery in the vicinity, the availability of horses and carriages for those touring the surrounding countryside, and coaches which would meet arriving trains or boats. An 1866 visitor praised the Trossachs Hotel: 'To get iced seltzer water with your sherry and a perfect French omelette in the middle of a Highland pass, miles from any inhabited house is a rare luxury, but you can get it at the Trossachs Hotel.'[72] The opening of a new railway was usually followed by a spate of hotel construction. A 1903 guidebook observed that because of the railway, Fort William became a popular resort with 14 inns 'in a marvellously short space of time'.[73] Oban had ten hotels by then.[74] Skye, which had earlier been notorious for its lack of accommodations, reportedly had hotels all over the island in 1891.[75] By 1910 these included a health resort at Kyleakin which advertised facilities for boating, bathing, fishing, and motoring. There was long an inn at Glen Sligachan, a spot on Skye famed for its desolation and isolation. Although late-century travelers to Mull found very few inns in the interior of the island,[76] the small coastal town of Tobermory on the island had three hotels and was a popular summer resort.[77] By at least 1895 an inn sat at the mouth of Glencoe. A small temperance hotel perched on top of Ben Nevis, popular among those who wished to spend the night and watch the sunrise on Britain's highest mountain.

Grand luxury hotels appeared in Scotland around the turn of the century. Often built by railway companies and located centrally near major train stations, these establishments offered electric lights, elevators, garages, athletic facilities, and places to fish or hunt. Scotland's first rail hotel was the Station Hotel in Inverness, opened in 1878 and owned by the Highland Railway. It was followed the next year by Glasgow's St. Enoch Station Hotel, which occupied more ground than any in the kingdom and had 200 guest rooms and 80 rooms for servants. It could accommodate the third largest number of guests in the country.[78] Rail companies also built well-appointed golf resorts overlooking the sea: Cruden Bay (1896), Turnberry (1906), Gleneagles (1914). In the 1880s, hydropathics and other health resorts accounted for half or more of all advertised lodging. (Hydropathics were large temperance hotels and health establishments, popular for family vacations, which offered water cures, exercise, and healthy eating.[79]) Ads for these resorts boasted pure air, lovely scenery, excellent cuisine, as well as all the latest treatments for rheumatism and gout, facilities for tennis, croquet, bowling, golf, fishing, and eventually, car rental and daily motor tours. The better Scottish hotels were said to be very like their American counterparts: spacious and comfortable with many public rooms.[80] They had a cosmopolitan flavor; guests were mostly English or foreign tourists, the staff frequently German or English. In 1915 the *Glasgow Herald* reminisced about the pre-war days in Oban: '... when yachts crowded the Bay and all Mayfair seemed concentrated on the Oban promenade, the Teuton servitors in shining linen buzzing about hotel doorways...'[81] John Reid, an artist who roamed Scotland in the 1870s, had a 'Cockney' waiter at a Loch Leven hotel, who worked in Oxford during the year and in the Highlands in the summer.[82]

The continuous extension of the transportation networks and the ongoing addition of inns and hotels did not in themselves smooth the way for tourism. There was initially little coordination among the many companies seeking to provide for tourists, and in the first half of the nineteenth century, Scotland seemed to offer only a bewildering and disconnected maze of steamships, railways, coaches, and inns. Guided tours, as invented by Thomas Cook, were the crucial ingredient in making Scotland a viable destination for inexperienced travelers. By shepherding his clients to Scotland's most popular sites at the least expensive rate and taking care of their transportation, lodging, and board, Cook was instrumental in effecting an interdependent network of tourist facilities. He thereby popularized leisure travel among the middle classes. A one-time itinerant Baptist preacher and active member of the Temperance movement, Cook began by organizing excursions to temperance rallies and operating alcohol-free pleasure trips for workers. A successful 1845 trip for 350 people from Leicester, Nottingham, and Derby to Liverpool and back, with opportunities to visit Caernarvon and to climb Mount Snowdon, inspired Cook to attempt a trip to Scotland. Rail lines to Scotland were not yet complete, so the 350 excursionists whom Cook led north in 1846 traveled by rail from Leicester to Fleetwood, then to Ardrossan by steamer, and rail again to Edinburgh and Glasgow. Although the voyage itself was decidedly unpleasant – the train lacked bathrooms or food, the steamer did not have enough cabins – they were met with great fanfare. A band greeted the excursionists at the station in Glasgow, a salute was fired, and a grand soiree took place at the City Hall. The group, the largest single assemblage of visitors to tour Scotland to that point, met a similar reception in Edinburgh. There they were addressed by the publisher William Chambers and each member of the party was given a commemorative volume, *The Strangers' Visit to Edinburgh*. The group then journeyed to Stirling, Loch Lomond, and Ayrshire.[83]

The next year Cook led two more groups to Scotland, making his first tour of the Highlands. Between 1848 and 1863 (with the exception of 1851, when he was busy with tour groups to the Great Exhibition) Cook spent two months every summer conducting four tours to Scotland, a total of 5,000 visitors per season. A special 'juvenile trip' attracted nearly 2,000 people in 1854.[84] Although Cook's business became synonymous with large guided excursions, his customers were not required to spend all their time in Scotland with the tour group. The usual practice was for clients to be conveyed to Edinburgh in a specially chartered train, after which they had a fortnight to take advantage of the cheap train tickets Cook offered to the key attractions, including the 'Scott country', Loch Lomond, Perth, Aberdeen, and the western Highlands and islands. They could travel singly or in groups, and could take as many or as few of the tours as they chose. However, many preferred the security of traveling with Cook himself. He usually accompanied the train, then went on to supervise the tours to the Highlands, leading several himself every summer.

Journeys with Cook could be strictly regimented affairs; Cook was sometimes referred to as the 'Field Marshall'. He expected his participants to rise early. Large parties were divided into groups of 50, with a 'captain' appointed for each company. But he took good care of his clients, investigating new routes ahead of time and writing special guidebooks which described the itinerary and the sights to be seen. Those who lacked the confidence to travel by themselves, or those like single women for whom traveling alone was not socially acceptable, could feel completely comfortable under Cook's care. Women were often a majority of his customers, sometimes with friends or family, sometimes alone. His tours cost less than individual touring, as Cook's tourists could take advantage of group rates everywhere from trains to restaurants. Indeed, Cook believed that a central part of his work was to allow ordinary people to enrich themselves through the cultural expansion of travel. A testimonial article in *Cook's Excursionist* in 1856 praised the inexpensive excursion trains. '…I am heartily thankful that the wants of the million are cared for and that Bobson, Dickson and Tomson (and of course with Mistresses Bobson, Dickson and Tomson) can o'erleap the bounds of their own narrow circle, rub off rust and prejudice by contact with others, and expand their souls and invigorate their bodies by an exploration of some of Nature's finest scenes.'[85] However, the fact that Cook did not generally offer third class accommodations on his tours qualifies his claims of equalitarianism.[86]

Cook's success put him in competition with Scottish rail companies, who were eager to carve out for themselves a bigger share of the tourist business and save the cost of Cook's agency. In mid-century rail companies began providing 'circular tours' to favorite locations on their lines, and in 1863 refused to allow Cook's Tours the use of rail lines for his Scottish tours, effectively banning his business from Scotland. He made up for this loss by offering trips to the Continent, and was allowed back in Scotland in a more limited fashion by the early 1870s. By then he had much more competition; by 1873 the NBR, in addition to daily outings to Loch Lomond, offered a 'Grand Circular Tour' from Glasgow to Inverness via Oban, Fort William, and the Caledonian Canal. In 1882 the Caledonian Railway Company alone had 62 tours by rail, steamer, and coach.[87] In 1860 the London and Northwestern Railway, which booked passengers to Scotland in conjunction with the Caledonian line, began issuing tourist fares to Scotland between May 1 and October 31. Originally such tickets were good only for 28 days, but in 1876 they were extended to two months. Tickets were available in both first and third class. Passengers could stop anywhere along the line and stay as long as desired, just so the trip was finished in the specified period. (In the early 1860s, at least, such arrangements were issued only in England, and were not available for Scots wishing to travel south.[88]) Cook began offering a similar system in 1861, continuing when his company was able to return to Scotland. His 'tourist tickets' or 'circular tickets' allowed customers to take advantage of Cook's prices and recommendations, yet travel on their own and at their own pace. The tickets were sold in renewable two week blocks, and covered the cost of all the transportation, lodging, and board on nearly 50 combinations of tours, whose itineraries were laid out by Cook.

Those who traveled independently also sought guidance about how to see Scotland, and found it in the nineteenth century's abundant proliferation of guidebooks. Guidebooks or 'handbooks' were a new genre of travel literature in the nineteenth century. Their development has been attributed to the London-based House of Murray and the German publisher Karl Baedeker and Sons, who in the 1830s began supplementing the subjective and impressionistic 'travel accounts' of the eighteenth century with what were intended as systematic, impersonal, and accurate descriptions of what travelers could expect on their journeys.[89] The format devised by Murray and Baedeker was actually anticipated in Scotland. Morison's *New Picture of Scotland*, published in 1807, divided Scotland into 'tours' which plotted the most manageable and interesting means by which to see those sights most peculiar to an area. The author described interesting attractions along the roads and in every town on the route, and informed readers about local government, industries, and history. Tours in *New Picture of Scotland* extended as far north as the Orkney Islands and west to the Hebridean island of Lewis.[90] Other short, portable books which led readers on a series of tours emerged in the 1820s. Examples include *Lumsden & Son's Steam Boat Companion, or Strangers' Guide to the Western Isles and Highlands of Scotland* (1820) and *Scottish Tourist and Itinerary* (1825), both of which described in some detail routes through what the *Scottish Tourist* called 'the most romantic regions of Scotland'.[91] Interesting alternative circuits were explained in footnotes, which allowed some flexibility and choice for travelers. *Lumsden & Sons*, a little book measuring only three and a half by eight inches, actually included several itineraries on land as well as water, advising visitors where to catch the boat, the distance of each tour and how long it might take, which road was the best to take, and where a stranger could get food for his horse – or whisky for himself. The authors recounted the history of each area visitors would pass through, and characterized attractive scenery or interesting natural features.

By the 1840s there was a wide variety of guidebooks, maps, and 'pictorial handbooks'. William Rhind sold *The Scottish Tourists' Portable Guide to the Great Highland Tour* in six pocket-sized installments, enabling tourists to buy only the tours they wished to follow. In 1861 Thomas Cook claimed to know of at least 50 guides to Scotland, of various sizes and devoted to assorted districts, and the numbers were to grow in the following decades.[92] Among the most popular and respected of them were those by George and Peter Anderson, and Adam and Charles Black, works which occupied in Scotland Murray and Baedeker's roles as accountable and recognizable individual authorities. The Andersons were a father and son team of Inverness improvers who spent ten years preparing the first edition of *Guide to the Highlands and Islands*, published in 1834. They visited every site they described and submitted the manuscript to other local residents for review. This was a careful and exhaustive work, initially consisting of six routes around the Highlands from Inverness. It was designed to educate as well as to lead tourists to the best sights.[93] The Andersons discoursed on local natural history, the economy, commercial resources, history, religion, and education in the Highlands. They provided directions to most points of interest, and often included more than one route to a given attraction, even those on which they admitted few tourists traveled. Not prone to sentiment or exaggeration, they candidly admitted that the mid-century steamer to Skye was slow and tedious, that visiting the island's key attractions 'involves a good deal of personal exertion and fatigue', and that 'the uncertainties of the climate frequently expose the tourist to pitiless rains, and to possible disappointment in the object of his visit.'[94] *Anderson's* guidebook was periodically revised and updated, and later editions were reorganized on a more practical plan with tours starting in the south. Active promoters of railways in the north, the Andersons also wrote handbooks for the Highland Railway.

Adam and Charles Black were Edinburgh publishers who first produced *Black's Picturesque Guide to Scotland* in 1840. New editions, as well as guides to various specific localities, were published annually throughout the nineteenth century.[95] Like the Andersons, the Blacks emphasized the accuracy of their information, pointing out to readers that the discussions of Edinburgh and Glasgow were written entirely by natives. They included a good measure of practical advice: which road would be the most interesting to take, which views to pay special attention to, where the good inns were, whether a specific landscape was best seen in calm or stormy weather, if a suggested hike was strenuous or not, how long a route might take to walk, where prices would be particularly expensive. Footnotes recommended interesting diversions along the main routes. At the end of the volume was a detailed 'itinerary' with specific directions.

In laying out specific tours to travel and directing the interpretation of the sights, guidebook authors were crucial to the evolution of the tourist understanding of Scotland. Because Scots wrote and published the great majority of the guidebooks of the first half of the century, they were able to assert a powerful role in determining how their country was to be seen and imagined. Robert Chambers' motive for publishing his 1827 guidebook, *The Picture of Scotland*, he said, was his long-standing desire to help preserve 'what was dearest to Scotland': the memory of ancient manners, the celebration of Scottish wit and humor, familiarity with Scotland's 'wonderful, beautiful, glorious past.'[96] By the time more sources began to be published in England, the defining characteristics of the tourist image of Scotland were already well established. Although the authors of *Anderson's*, *Black's*, and numerous other guidebooks throughout the century prided themselves on providing visitors with useful and up-to-date information, most were generally as concerned with directing gazes and showing how to imagine Scotland as with providing practical advice. Many of these authors betrayed an ambivalence about how best to represent Scotland. On the one hand, the image of a vital, progressive, and modern Scotland continued into the promotional literature of the nineteenth century. Guidebook producers continually called attention to the strong economies and flourishing industries of towns and cities on their itineraries, thereby reminding contemporaries of Scots' numerous contributions to the British nation and empire. In 1843 the Blacks emphasized improvement in living standards; Scots, they said, had advanced more rapidly than the English or Irish in wealth and the 'necessaries and conveniences of life'.[97] Their account of Edinburgh stressed cultural attainments: 'It would be difficult to name a place which unites so many social advantages, and where a person of cultivated mind and moderate fortune could pass his time more agreeably.'[98] George Meason's 1859 *Official Guide to the North Western Railway* included a lengthy discussion of Glasgow's commercial district, describing the type of work done in several factories and recommending a visit to the Crawford Street Chemical Works and J. and R. Tennant's Wellpark Brewery.[99] Guidebook publisher Thomas Murray introduced readers to the extent of manufacturing that took place in Scotland, citing the number of cotton, flax, and wool factories, paper mills, distilleries of spirits and malt liquor, iron furnaces, and the Clyde ship building.[100] He lingered over the thread production at Paisley, and praised the four great sea docks at Dundee and the employment provided to 50,000 inhabitants by the jute and linen factories.[101]

On the whole, however, characterizations of Scotland in nineteenth-century guidebooks were weighted decisively towards 'romance' rather than industry and commerce. Scotland's industrial accomplishments were greatly overshadowed by impressions of a rural, traditional country infused by poetry and history. Most manuals devoted considerable space to excited and sensational accounts of the scenery. Guidebook authors also favored what *Black's* described in 1840 as 'traditional, literary, and historical illustration': poetry, especially that of Scott and Wordsworth; tales and legends of interesting events connected with the particular scene under discussion; historical accounts of the area; other visitors' impressions of an attraction. Such contextualization was intended to fix the scenery 'more permanently' in tourists' minds.[102] Illustrations usually depicted castles, large rugged mountains, cozy Highland villages, events from Scottish history, or waterfalls with trees hanging picturesquely over the sides.

In the 1880s travel writers Joseph and Elizabeth Robins Pennell found *Black's* a better guide to the romance and history of Scotland than to its roads. It is a poor comfort, they said, to be given a quotation when you ask for a good route.[103] However, the continual popularity of this series and many others modeled upon it suggests that a guide to romance and history was just what many visitors wanted. The influence of tourist handbooks lay in their role as reflections of the aspirations and expectations tourists brought with them, as well as the desire of authors to promote a distinctive, original identity for Scotland which would distinguish it from the rest of Great Britain. If, as the stereotype asserted, sightseers paid too close attention to their guidebooks, it was because those texts helped ensure that they would have the sort of experience of Scotland which they sought. Reflecting the tastes of their readers, guidebooks were one layer of the many markers which illustrated the role of individual sites in the encounter with 'culture' which Scotland was expected to provide. As the tourist path grew more and more beaten in the second half of the century, directions on where to find steamboats or which road to take to the next town likely were more widely available, and a good quotation to contextualize the scene and divert tourists' attention from the crowds may have been more important.

Guidebooks also helped canonize particular routes and sites. The better guidebooks allowed for considerable diversity in tours by suggesting more than one route to a given attraction and providing a comprehensive overview of Scotland rather than only describing the most popular attractions. There were always individual travelers anxious to explore the more distant areas. However, the vast majority of visitors found that the routes mapped by their eighteenth-century predecessors, altered a bit to suit new inclinations and to take advantage of new technology, best fulfilled their desire for a manageable tour of the romantic. Most nineteenth-century tours began in Edinburgh. 'Tweed-clad tourists are everywhere' was one Lowlander's description of Edinburgh in the summer in 1865.[104] Reactions to Edinburgh reflect the shifts in what tourists valued in Scotland. No longer did Edinburgh, through the fashionable New Town, prompt reflections on Scotland's economic, intellectual, and cultural contributions to a flourishing Union. Instead, tourists' attention focused on the Old Town, where they 're-lived' the thrills and intrigues of Scotland's past. A guidebook of 1912 found the New Town of Edinburgh 'rather formal and gaunt', but the Old Town was 'a thing apart', a place full of history and reminiscence.[105] A writer for *The Leisure Hour*, which published a serial on 'The Tourist in Scotland' in the summer and fall of 1860, 'felt as if entering deeper into the shadowy realms of history' when approaching Edinburgh.[106] Led by guidebooks such as *Murray's Scottish Tourist*, which recommended seeing the view of the city from Calton Hill and visiting the magnificent neo-classical National Gallery, visitors to Edinburgh did usually include a visit to the New Town on their itinerary. Historic monuments such as the Castle, Holyrood Palace, and the Canongate were of greater interest, however.[107] Visitor Chauncy Townshend wrote to his wife in the early 1830s that while the New Town was very 'goodly', one did not go to Edinburgh to see a repetition of Bath or London.[108]

Guidebooks recommended a week's stay in the 'Athens of the North', suggesting that tourists also visit the surrounding countryside, especially

'Scott Country'.[109] Walter Scott's beloved home, Abbotsford, was the highlight of this circuit round the Borders, which included the nearby ruins of Melrose Abbey, immortalized in Scott's *Lay of the Last Minstrel*; Dryburgh Abbey, where Scott was buried; Roslin Castle; Hawthornden Castle, the home of the poet and historian William Drummond and the site of several caves cut into the rock below the house which were occasionally used as hiding places during border wars; and the Ettrick and Yarrow rivers. Tourists began making pilgrimages to Abbotsford during Scott's lifetime, and by the late 1830s over 2,000 visitors came yearly to see the house, inspect his library and study, and examine his collection of antiquarian relics. The annual number of visitors rose to 7,000 by the turn of the century.[110]

In the first four decades of the nineteenth century, tourists commonly headed north from Edinburgh up the east coast, on a route popularized in the eighteenth century. They visited Perth, Stirling, and perhaps the Duke of Atholl's country house and pleasure gardens at Blair Atholl, before turning southwest to tour Loch Katrine and Loch Lomond, winding up at Glasgow, or orienting westwards towards Inverary and the western islands. As the train and steamboat facilities expanded in the 1850s it became more common for tourists to set out from Edinburgh directly to Glasgow, visit surrounding areas, and then alight for the Highlands and islands. Glasgow was a somewhat problematic attraction. Victorian tourists in Scotland evinced much less interest in industrial tourism than their eighteenth-century predecessors. Now bigger, dirtier, and less novel than it had been in the eighteenth century, industry was the antithesis of the usual expectation of Scotland – and Glasgow was a rapidly growing industrial and commercial city. Although the cotton and chemical industries declined over the course of the century, shipbuilding, engineering, and ironmaking took their place. Glasgow was a leading railway and overseas shipping center, serving much of the retail trade of Scotland. The population jumped from 274,000 in 1831 to 511,000 in 1881 and 761,000 in 1901, when Glasgow was the 'second city of the British Empire'. Similar growth took place throughout what became the Clydeside conurbation; by 1901 the West Central Scotland region contained nearly two millions of Scotland's four and one half million inhabitants.[111] Consequently, Glasgow was to some an unappealing place to visit, the more so as it offered few of the historic sites prized by Victorian tourists. *Black's* admitted that modern growth had 'quite smothered' the traces of the early city.[112] The University, libraries, and coffeehouses that had so impressed Enlightenment-era men of letters attracted little attention from middle-class Victorian families. A teenage girl whose 1863 travel journal included a sketch of 'Our first impression of Glasgow' depicted only a crowded skyline of smokestacks and black smog. Her comments about the city concentrated on black alleys and slums, and factory girls 'with shawls over their heads and their bare feet sludging along in the mud and wet'.[113] Another description from the 1860s spoke of 'the ceaseless din of hammers in hundreds of dockyards and foundries, beating with a sort of rhythmic clangour in orderly pulsations; the steam-blast and railway shriek seem perpetually to echo amid the seething smoke from factory stalks.'[114]

Yet even if Glasgow was an atypical stop on the tour of Scotland, many people did stop there. Glasgow's busy harbor, flourishing factories, and elegant suburbs and parks were potent symbols of Britain's wealth and productivity, just as they had been in the late eighteenth century. William Winter, an American visiting the homeland of his dead wife in the early twentieth century, believed that to see Glasgow's busy streets and 'sumptuous' public buildings and monuments, and to hear the 'clatter of the hammer' in the Clyde shipyards 'is to know the restless puissant, victorious spirit of the present day and to feel that Scotland is the land of deeds as well as dreams.'[115] The family of the teenager mentioned above spent a few days there, touring the wharves, the Cathedral, Necropolis, and the fashionable Kelvingrove Park. Many other tourists did the same, describing it as a 'fine city' and a 'little London', and comparing it favorably to English cities.[116] The potteries and glassworks were also popular attractions.[117] A guidebook of 1906 admitted that Glasgow was not an ideal tourist resort, but it was a well-built city and an excellent center for excursions to the western Highlands.[118]

Murray's suggested week in Glasgow allowed one day to see the city, then sent tourists away to the Trossachs, Arran, the 'Land of Burns', and seaside resorts.[119] The trip from Glasgow to the Trossachs was a favorite. Typically one took an early morning steamer to Dumbarton, ate breakfast, and proceeded to the loch by a train which was met by a steamer for those who wished to cruise the large loch. Many spent the night at Tarbet and arose early the next morning to climb Ben Lomond. Loch Katrine could be reached by coach or by a short hike from Inversnaid. A trip to Lochs Katrine and Lomond and the Trossachs was a minimum requirement if one desired a 'Highland tour'.[120] In 1887 *Baedeker's* called the jaunt from Glasgow to Loch Lomond, Loch Katrine, Stirling and then to Edinburgh, one of the most delightful tours in the UK.[121]

The Trossachs might be the minimum Highland Tour, but most strangers wished to see more. The proliferation of railways and steamers meant that more people than ever could do so – but also ensured that they saw Highlands which had been tamed by mechanization. In the early nineteenth century when geologist John Macculloch stumbled upon Loch Scavaig and Loch Coruisk on the island of Skye it was a scene 'which seemed never before to have been violated by the presence of man.'[122] In the late nineteenth century, tourists in search of this 'gloomy', 'savage', and 'fearful' locale could take a tour on one of MacBrayne's steamships, available three times a week. When Sarah Murray sought a good view of the Falls of Foyers in 1796, she climbed rocks and clung to trees to get to a small ledge deemed 'impossible' to reach by her guide. She had to lay down to keep from falling off the ledge, but, soaked with spray, occasionally shutting her eyes and gulping, Murray was able 'to admire and I might say, almost adore.'[123] Victorians, by contrast, made a hurried walk of three-quarters of a mile to the falls while the steamboat waited in the Caledonian Canal, paid a pier toll of four pence, glanced around quickly and scurried back to the boat. *Punch* joked that tourists could see just as good a waterfall at the Colosseum at Regent's Park, with the advantage that there they could sit in chairs and look as long as they liked, without being rushed by sailors from the steamer.[124]

Nonetheless, nineteenth-century trips to the Highlands were rich with meaning for those who made them, and it is perhaps unfair to compare the Victorians to their predecessors, who might have preferred more comfortable modes of travel. Highland scenery represented the unvanquished might of nature and opportunities for human (especially male) daring and strength: hiking, mountain climbing, and deer stalking. By the 1870s Skye, with its magnificent scenery, its famed solitude, and its many Jacobite associations came to be seen as a highlight of a Highland tour, occupying nearly the same position Staffa had once held. While many only saw as much of the island as the MacBrayne's steamer showed them, travelers with a little more time spent a few days on the island, possibly using Portree as a base and making the rounds of the Storr and the Quiraing (large rock formations on the coast), and perhaps the Spar Cave. Such scenes allowed the Highlands to represent a microcosm of the uncivilized world, in a period of growing concern over the negative consequences of modernization. These were also Highlands cleansed of any troubling social or political issues; the emphasis on the magnificence of the empty landscape diverted attention from the reasons that the land was uninhabited.

Because the Highlands seemed a place untouched by time, history was close at hand. Wandering through Glencoe or Culloden Moor, both considered 'must-see' sights, many visitors felt a closeness to the past which seemed elusive in the more rootless industrial society. At Glencoe tourists reveled in the 'gloomy grandeur' of the valley and let themselves be titillated by gazing upon the scene 'where one of the most inhumane acts ever perpetuated took place.'[125] One could find tangible links with the past; the site of the 1692 massacre was occasionally pointed out at a spot with some ruined huts and green patches.[126] Similarly, as late as 1900 the trenches of Culloden were allegedly still green over the bodies of those who had fallen there in 1746.[127] Although eighteenth-century improvers tended to understand the battle of Culloden as a victory for progress, by the late nineteenth-century the battlefield had taken on an 'elegiac quality'.[128]

By mid-century, Highland tours usually began with a steamer journey to Oban either via the Crinan Canal or the coast, part of what MacBrayne's Steamboat Company called the 'Royal Route' between Glasgow and Inverness through the Caledonian Canal. Even when the west Highlands were accessible by rail, this remained a popular journey. Oban was the 'Charing Cross of the Highlands', the headquarters for steamer trips to the Hebrides (such as a day's outing to Staffa and Iona or Skye) or for continuing further up the coast. Having developed for the most part concurrently with the rise of tourism, Oban was a town of hotels and photograph shops, into which it seemed trains were forever emptying excursionists and carrying them away again.[129] 'Everyone' went there, but only on the way to somewhere else. Though guidebook authors portrayed it as bustling and vital, visitors often found the town crowded and frenzied, as multitudes of tourists searched for hotel rooms or anxiously awaited their steamer. Alexander Smith, a popular Lowland poet whose composite account of annual trips to Skye to visit his wife's family, *A Summer in Skye*, was one of the most popular Hebridean texts of the period, described the scene in the 1860s:

> Every variety of pleasure-seeker is to be found there, and every variety of costume. Reading parties from Oxford lounge, smoke, stare into small shop windows, and consult 'Black's Guide'. Beauty, in light attire, perambulates the principal street and taciturn valour in mufti accompanies her. Sportsmen in knickerbockers stand in groups at the hotel doors; Frenchmen chatter and shrug their shoulders; stolid Germans smoke curiously-carved meerschaum pipes; and individuals who have not a drop of Highland blood in their veins flutter about in the garb of the Gael.[130]

Once the railway reached Fort William in 1894 that little town on Loch Linnhe also became a favorite spot to spend a few days enjoying the scenery and climbing Ben Nevis, Britain's highest mountain.[131] It was a strenuous but not a forbidding hike and after 1883 one could reward oneself by visiting the refreshment room adjacent to an observatory atop the peak. Others traveled on to Inverness where a few days' stay might be in order, seeing the nearby sights, including Tomnahurich Hill, an unusually shaped hill reputed to be the home of fairies; Culloden Moor; Craig Phadrig, a vitrified fort; Cawdor Castle, fourteenth-century home of the Thanes of Cawdor; and the ancient stone monuments of Clava. While many, perhaps most, tourists returned south on the west coast steamers, some wandered back to Edinburgh via Braemar, Deeside, and Perthshire, perhaps visiting Blair Atholl and the Pass of Killiecrankie along the way.

With rail and steam, the essentials of the above itinerary could be covered in two to four weeks, which appears to be the length of the average Victorian tour. Cook sold his tourist tickets in two-week blocks, and *Baedeker's* 1887 example of a typical tour lasted three to four weeks. In 1860 a family of five made a tour up the east coast from Edinburgh to Aberdeen, across to Inverness, then down the west coast by steamer, hitting all the major attractions except the Hebrides, in just under a month.[132] For those with less time to spare, guidebooks gave advice on cramming as many sights as possible into a week. Even the month-long visits were hurried trips. Attempting to see as much of the country as they could, most tourists spent little time in one place. The peak season for travel was late July and August, although summer tourist promotions usually began in early June.

The expansion of the tourist infrastructure put such tours well within the price range of middle-class families, who evidently made up the largest proportion of tourists. There is little, if any, evidence of complaints over transportation costs. *Baedeker's* guidebook commented in 1887 that the competition of the many steamboat and rail companies and the extensive development of the system of circular tours made transportation expenses very moderate.[133] Competition among travel agencies, which expanded in the Edwardian era, also kept prices low. In the early twentieth century a number of travel agencies offered package tours at a variety of prices, appealing to different income levels and possibly making Scotland accessible even to the upper working classes. By contrast, the high cost of Scottish hotels was notorious enough to be satirized by *Punch*:

Those Scotch hotels! Those Scotch hotels
Are fit for princes and for swells;
But their high charges don't agree
With humbler travellers like me...[134]

Nonetheless, although the increasing sophistication of hotels tended to inflate lodging costs in some areas, a money-conscious traveler could find an inexpensive temperance hotel in most major cities. *Baedeker* maintained in 1887 that some of the hotels in the Highlands which still had a monopoly of the trade probably deserved their expensive reputation, but prices elsewhere had improved recently and cost no more than average English establishments.[135]

Towards the turn of the century a shift in the tenor of Scottish tourism can be detected, as many visitors increasingly came in pursuit of health and recreation, rather than to make the rounds of the famed historic and literary attractions. Sportsmen of various stripes had long been drawn to the Highlands, but in this period tourist areas across Scotland sought to lure less specialized enthusiasts with the possibility of quiet and luxurious surroundings where they could stay for a while and combine sightseeing with recreational sports. Whereas Beriah Botfield considered it necessary to explain the game of golf to his readers in the 1830s, by the early twentieth century it seemed that every town, no matter how small, deemed a golf course a necessary enticement to vacationers.[136] Grand luxury hotels in the countryside were perfect spots for such vacations, which suggests an effort on the part of the wealthy to differentiate themselves from middle-class tourists who rushed from sight to sight. The string of coastal resorts along the Clyde and the east coast that had attracted middle-class Scottish families for much of the century also began to attract a growing proportion of summer residents from England by the 1880s.[137] Promotional material suggests a heightened effort to interest visitors in these communities. *Scottish Western Holiday Haunts* for instance, called attention to the summer resort communities of the west coast, acquainting potential visitors with the history and traditions of the area, its sea and shore, the 'mild and salubrious climate', and the bustle and stir of the piers and promenades.[138] The North British Railway attempted to appeal to a new generation of potential tourists with an advertisement thinly disguised as a travel account: *The Epistles of Peggy.* 'Peggy' was a modern young woman, full of spunk and slang, writing letters to friends about her Scottish vacation with her 'Pater'. Her 'letters' described an athletic and healthy holiday. She reported to friends that she was toned up and brown as a fillet, aglow with ruddy health. Although the characters did some touring, visiting Edinburgh, Stirling, Fort William, and Glencoe, Peggy and her father spent most of their time playing golf and tennis, fishing, swimming, and hiking up Ben Nevis.[139]

Late Victorian tourists found that turn of the century Scotland was no longer an unknown country to which one traveled with trepidation. It was a land of romance, with historical associations, quaint people, both fictional and real, and spectacular scenery that contrasted with the transformations and social tensions which troubled late Victorian and Edwardian society. It was also a convenient and familiar vacationland, filled with most of the comforts of home. But to some visitors a nagging question remained; could the continual expansion of tourism be detrimental to the cultural significance that made travel to Scotland so valued an experience?

Preserving the Vision of Scotland

'The tourist comes and poetry flies before him as the red man flies before the white. His Tweeds will make the secret top of Sinai commonplace one day.'[140] 'Mr. M'Ian', a character in Alexander Smith's *A Summer in Skye* loosely based on Smith's father-in-law, expressed the threat posed by the expansion of the facilities of tourism. More and more people could see Scotland – but the commercialization, the crowds, the hustle and bustle of trains and steamers, and above all, the mechanistic and superficial attitudes of tourists endangered the journey's purpose as a trip to a place outside ordinary experience. One of the central criticisms leveled against tourists has long been their lack of originality. Like automatons, they follow each other, nose in guidebooks, repeating the same clichés, never truly seeing what is around them, mainly interested in checking attractions off a list.

This stereotype developed concurrently with the rise of tourism; James Buzard sees the formation of modern tourism and the belittling of tourists as a single phenomenon. As travel was democratized and institutionalized, the denigration of 'tourists' became a means of understanding one's own experiences to be authentic and original. By condemning tourists, one showed oneself to be a 'traveler' who journeyed with an open mind, sensitive to the truth of the places he or she visited. These mythic figures were determined by, and helped determine, the ways nations represented culture and acculturation to themselves. The 'traveler' could successfully understand and make use of objects of culture; the 'tourist' could not.[141]

Both individual visitors and the tourist industry itself developed a variety of strategies to guard against the 'touristification' of Scotland. These included critiques of tourists and the infrastructure of tourism, the ostentatious adoption of alternative ways to travel, and the use of Scotland's literature as an entryway into a more 'real' experience. The objective of these efforts was the preservation of the magic and poetry that drew visitors north and gave Scotland meaning. If Scotland were to become ordinary and commonplace, it would no longer offer the experience of the transcendent which is the purpose of ritual. The strategies of 'anti-tourism' worked in conjunction with the guidebooks and other elements of the infrastructure of tourism to ensure that Scotland's role as a place of 'culture' would be maintained.

Tourism had its defenders. Observers were well aware of its practical benefits. Alexander Nicholson, a scholar and sometime sheriff from the Hebrides, thought a grand hotel at the entrance to isolated Loch Coruisk was a good idea; while it was a shame to disturb the 'sacred solitude of Nature's great scenes', people ought to be able to see those sights and they might as well do it in comfort.[142] To Thomas Cook, tourism was an expression of a more open society and an outgrowth of Victorians' technological and industrial achievements. Critics, on the other hand, were doubtful that all those who took advantage of Scotland's new accessibility appreciated it properly, or that technology necessarily improved the experience. Cook's Tours were singled out for particular denunciation for covering too much ground too rapidly and superficially, in too regimented a fashion. Tourists seemed to only care about 'doing' the key attractions. John Reid observed that they were too busy to admire the scenery, intent only on the accomplishment of a certain mileage in a given time.[143] The Pennells wondered why most of their fellow passengers on the steamer from Skye had even bothered to come; the women read novels, the men slept, no one looked at the scenery. 'But they had done their duty – they had been to Scotland for the holidays.'[144]

Tourism led to a transformation of the old rhetoric of invasion; this time, the English were invading Scotland. As early as 1824 John Macculloch characterized Birnam Pass as 'the gate and portal whence bold highland caterans once issued in dirked and plaided hostility, sweeping our flocks and herds, and where (such are the changes of fashion) their Saxon foes now enter in peace, driving their barouches and gigs, and brandishing the pencil and the memorandum book.'[145] They may have come in peace, but to many observers, this was a dangerous invasion. Tourists not only failed to suitably value Scotland, their indifference spoiled the experience for others. As Buzard notes, tourists were denigrated alternately as 'superficial surface-skimmers and the blundering agents of profound (and lamentable) social and cultural change.'[146] They left broken bottles atop Ben Cruachan and whisky bottles and sandwich tins at MacLeod's tomb on Skye.[147] The smoke from their torches and their tendency to chip pieces off the rock destroyed the glory of Skye's Spar Cave.[148] Cuthbert Bede was annoyed at the requirement that a guide take him around Melrose Abbey, but hearing of the predilection of many tourists to carve their names on tombs or picnic at the high altar he understood that it was necessary. 'The ancient iconoclasts are matched by the modern destructives.'[149] By bringing commercialization in their wake tourists trivialized Scotland. 'Holyrood is charming – so charming, so thorough, so real, as to enable you almost to forget the horribly practical and business-like manner in which it is exhibited. Fancy paying your entrance money at the gate of Mary Stuart's Palace, and receiving in exchange a cardboard ticket, which has just been impressed with the ordinary railway date-stamping machine.'[150] William Pearson found 'something mean and *commercial*' in the exhibition of Ossian's Hall and the Duke of Atholl's house 'for pecuniary consideration.'[151] James Wilson, who traveled around the Scottish coasts in the company of a friend on official business with the Board of Fisheries in the early 1840s, was pestered by 'keen-eyed greedy guides' anxious to show him around Iona and Staffa. Such attendants, he said, 'poison tourists' life in many solemn places.'[152]

Worse, perhaps, the coaches, trains, and steamers that carted tourists around disturbed the poetic atmosphere. In 1843 Henry Cockburn, a Scottish lawyer and politician, lamented the sound of the coach horn in the Trossachs:

Alas, alas! it has been heard all this summer. A romantic tourist pinched for time can now be hurried from Fort William to Edinburgh in one not long day. A coach left Fort William all this season at about six in the morning, and after blowing away to Ballachulish, up Glencoe to Kingshouse, and from thence to Tyndrum, and down Glenfalloch to Tarbet, which it reached about two, its passengers could get into a steamer there and reach Glasgow in time for the five o'clock train which landed them at Edinburgh about seven. Spirits of Fingal and of Rob Roy! what say ye to this?[153]

The *genius loci* of Oban was exorcised by steam whistles and the mob of knickerbockered and waterproofed tourists comparing notes about their *tables d'hôte*.[154] The spirit of the Trossachs, too, grew elusive: 'Do you think any poetry can withstand the pandemonium into which, just as you have begun to enter into the beauty of the loch, and to recollect what you have read about it, you are suddenly plunged by that horrible landing; and the necessity of finding a place somewhere, and flying on through mud and din to the *table d'hôte* at the hotel.'[155] There was, observed J. A. MacCulloch, who lived for several years on Skye in the late nineteenth century, 'nothing romantic' about the MacBrayne's Steamship Company's tourist excursion to Loch Coruisk on Skye.[156] Another visitor found that it was difficult to truly appreciate the atmosphere of St. Columba's ruined abbey on Iona with 'the crush of tourists talking, joking and sentimentalizing.'[157]

The plentiful complaints about trains, steamers, and the tourists who rode them allowed other visitors to establish their own difference from 'tourists'. *They* were truly travelers, explorers, desirous of really 'knowing' Scotland. Many demonstrated their status as what Buzard calls 'anti-tourists' by eschewing the tourist industry altogether. Some spent the night on Iona, rather than allow guides to hurry them through the ruins, or yachted around Skye to see the islands' more out-of-the-way attractions. Others canoed and camped on Loch Katrine the better to dine on Ellen's Isle and hear the old minstrel lay echoing on the calm water, or rented a private boat to Staffa rather cope with excursionists who howled and hooted and disturbed the solemn echoes.[158] Hiking through Scotland rather than taking the train or steamer became a symbol of genuine traveling: no man knows a country till he has walked through it, said Alexander Smith.[159] Occasionally even guidebooks recommended walking or hiking, the better to appreciate a particular area.[160] As an indication of their own status as pure 'travelers', the Pennells said they walked for seven weeks and scarcely met even a tramp. They claimed that although there was much talk of walking tours of the Highlands, few were actually made.[161]

Renting a yacht or a private boat was obviously more expensive than taking the beaten path, and hiking and camping across Scotland may have required more leisure than some visitors could afford. Criticism of tourists grew partly from class biases, from the assumption that the 'Bobsons, Dicksons, and Tomsons' that Cook was so proud to bring to Scotland were not appropriate visitors. However, issues of class seem to have been less volatile among travelers to Scotland than on the Continent, where Buzard found that much of the invective against tourists in the early nineteenth century was linked to contemporary fears of the mob and the social 'leveling' that was destroying the aristocracy's exclusive access to the Grand Tour.[162] Scotland did not have the Continent's long history of aristocratic touring, and was not the symbol of 'high' culture that Europe was, so middle and lower class travel seemed less threatening. And because deer stalking remained an aristocratic preserve well into the late nineteenth century, an element of social exclusivity remained. Although an offended traveler once told Thomas Cook that tours of the Highlands should be reserved for the 'first classes of society', Cook assured prospective clients in 1861 that this was a rare reaction and that aristocratic travelers were often delighted that so many others were able to travel.[163] Ultimately, being a 'genuine' traveler depended not on class but upon one's enthusiasm and sensitivity to one's surroundings.

Those who decried the shallowness of tourists or lamented the coming of the railways were not attempting to challenge the pervasive image of Scotland. They sought to uphold it. For all that they claimed to know Scotland better, anti-tourists were drawn by the same mythology of Scotland that lured everyone else, and their reactions were little different from those suggested by guidebooks. Most of those who claimed to know the 'real' Scotland did not assert they had cast aside the widespread commonplaces, they had simply been able to delve deeper into the stereotypes. J. A. MacCulloch argued that the tourist 'is too much engaged in scampering from hotel to hotel' to understand Skye's 'rare charm' or to discover even a tenth of the island's beauty. To really appreciate Skye, one must live there, as he did for seven years. His description of a visit to Loch Coruisk, Skye's premier tourist attraction, reads much like an intensified version of the themes found in the guidebook published by the MacBrayne's Steamship Company.[164] Anti-touristic rhetoric served to ensure that the essential components of the vision of Scotland were not swallowed by commercialization, modern technology, and allegedly uncaring crowds. Scotland should not be taken for granted.

Guidebooks, in keeping with their role as signposts to the ritual which gave Scotland meaning, helped preserve the desired vision of Scotland by providing detailed characterizations of scenery, often walking readers through the expected emotional responses to a famous scene. They recounted attractive views, often in copious detail, and continually advised readers that sights were 'romantic', 'picturesque', 'awe-inspiring'. In this manner, promotional literature endeavored to draw tourists' attention from noisy crowds, distracting machines, and other signs of modernization and focus it on the object of their journeys. The guidebook designed for passengers on the MacBrayne's steamship tour of Skye directed those who chose to be rowed ashore at Loch Scavaig that 'A few minutes' walk brings us with beating hearts in full view of Loch Coruisk – the solitude only intensified by the plaintive sough of the wind and the ceaseless gurgle of the mountain torrents.'[165] The manual went on to follow this paraphrase of James Wilson's 'truthful' description of his response to Coruisk with a lengthy quote from his canonical rendition of the scene, thus encouraging excursionists to emulate his reactions.

Literary traveling proved to be one of the most effective means of sustaining the vision of Scotland as 'culture', especially for those who, by choice or necessity, stuck with the well-trodden tourist itinerary. By the second half of the nineteenth century those who toured Scotland had few opportunities for originality. There was little left to explore and the most famous sites were already thoroughly delineated by others. The steamer route from Oban to Staffa and Iona had been described to death, said Reid in 1878.[166] As Buzard shows, however, in his study of travel to the Continent, by positing originality in the inner life of the individual rather than in new actions, Romanticism enabled even the participant on the most standardized tour to see him/herself as an uniquely 'authentic' traveler. The key to true traveling, taught early nineteenth century works like *Corinne* and *Childe Harold*, was the sensitivity and enthusiasm of the traveler. Anyone who demonstrated the proper emotional intensity, regardless of how he or she journeyed, could claim to be a 'traveler' and not merely a 'tourist'.[167] As William Winter pointed out, 'every track is beaten, in these days of systematic touring and all-conquering steam, and, as to the results of observation, everything is dependent on the eyes that see.'[168] While visitors to the Continent modeled themselves on a sanitized and depolitized Byron in order to demonstrate their passion and their departure from ordinary life, those who roamed Scotland enacted Walter Scott, and to a lesser extent other of Scotland's writers, as a means of playing an insider's role.

Because Scott's fiction was so intrinsically tied to place, it was remarkably well suited to the needs of tourists, who considered his poems and novels the best possible guidebooks.[169] The tourist industry encouraged this notion. According to the 1827 *Scottish Tourist and Itinerary* the route to the Trossachs was a walk into a scene from *The Lady of the Lake*:

> On turning, we see every dingle, bush and fern start into armed men, at the whistle of Roderick Dhu. We have never read anything so finely descriptive of the manners of ancient Highland warfare as this account in the *Lady of the Lake*. It is so true to nature, so vivid, we are as much astonished as Fitz-James, and almost expect to see the nodding of bonnets, the waving of tartans, and the heath bristling into claymores.[170]

Visitors who were well acquainted with Scott's works could claim to be travelling in a place where they were already at home. Guidebooks throughout the century assured them that the landscape, especially in the Trossachs, would be well known to readers of Scott. While leading readers to Callander, the *Scottish Tourist* commented, 'Need we remind the tourist that we are now upon classic ground, and that the characteristic features of almost every object will be recognized by the stranger who is familiar with *The Lady of the Lake*.'[171] Intimacy in this case did not exclude exoticism. The tourist at Loch Katrine entered a realm of poetry and magic, but the 'stranger' was not an outsider. He/she belonged in this special realm. Said J. E. Bowman, 'Though the scenery is new and enchanting, we recognize it at every turn.'[172] Although it was her first visit, a female tourist in 1869 was already conversant with the Trossachs: 'It was a route I had often travelled with Fitz-James for company, and I almost expected to come upon either himself or the remains of his 'gallant grey' as we passed through the Trossachs.'[173]

Because they believed Scott's works to be so true to life, those who enacted his novels and poems illustrated that they could see beyond the trappings of tourism into the 'real' Scotland. W. H. Maxwell, a former soldier who published his account of travels in Scotland in 1852, visited the abbey of Lindisfarne with *Marmion* in hand, and 'could not see the abbey as it was, but as it had been.'[174] Pilgrims were aided in this process by the very agents of the superficialities of tourism: tour guides and guidebooks, which helped readers invoke Scott and thus to claim status as 'genuine' travelers. Guidebooks provided sightseers with the Scott associations of any given sight or attraction, often quoted the relevant poem or description so as to evoke the proper atmosphere, and assured readers that Scott's portrayals were accurate and true to life. Tour guides at Loch Katrine led visitors to scenes from *The Lady of the Lake* as if the poem were documented truth. 'There is the glen in which the grey hunter fell; yonder is the rock on which the prince was challenged by Roderic [sic] Dhu.' Listening to this, C. S. Stewart, an American who toured Britain in the 1830s, 'forgot that every object thus associated with the scene had its origins only in the genius of the poet, and in the fruitfulness of his imagination, and mused and felt, in gazing upon them, as if all were the truths of history.'[175] Coach drivers in the Trossachs also helped passengers by reciting lines from *The Lady of the Lake* as they reached the pertinent spots.[176] Before the negligence of some tea-making tourists burned it down in 1837, sightseers at Loch Katrine could visit a small hut on 'Ellen's Isle' meant to emulate the fictional home of Ellen and her father, Douglas. Walls were covered with animal skins and antlers, chairs were made of tree branches, tables displayed Highland weapons and armor.[177]

The avalanche of Scott associations which was heaped upon visitors to Loch Katrine allowed them to express their status as 'real' travelers in a variety of ways. Some were bemused that local residents seemed to believe so strongly in the truth of the fictional events created by Scott.[178] To others, the need to rely on guidebooks and tour guides to invoke Scott's presence rather than direct knowledge could mark someone as a 'mere' tourist. 'The tourist who would enjoy aright these scenes should not be contented with the meagre quotations in the guidebooks, or only read in the poem the little bit referring to a particular scene, but drink in the whole poem; thus every spot will suggest associations that will greatly enliven the landscape and often give him a key to understand the people.'[179] The A & C Black publishing company of Edinburgh sold pocket-sized 'Tourist Editions' of *The Lay of the Last Minstrel*, *Marmion*, *The Lady of the Lake*, *Rokeby*, and *The Lord of the Isles*, so travelers could conveniently refer to them while touring.[180] Thomas Cook provided a reading list so his clients could properly prepare themselves for their trips.[181] Chauncy Townshend was disdainful of those who reached Loch Katrine but did not bother to seek out the associations it was famous for – 'For what on earth do such people travel?'[182]

Because Scott associations could be found throughout the country, Scotland was suffused with a poetic aura, which counteracted the encroachments of tourism and provided plentiful opportunities for visitors to exercise their sensitivity. At the sound of Mull, said Alexander Smith, *The Lord of the Isles* comes to mind, just as *The Lady of the Lake* does at Loch Katrine. 'All the scenes of the noble poem rise in vision before you.'[183] It was not uncommon for pilgrims to seek the ruins of Melrose Abbey by moonlight, to read aloud *The Lay of the Last Minstrel*.[184] A trip to Loch Muich reminded Queen Victoria of lines from *The Lady of the Lake*.[185] An 1868 description of the route from Glasgow to Carlisle mentioned a Scott association at virtually every turn.[186] The spirit of Scott was said to haunt Edinburgh: in the house where he lived, on the street in which 'such and such incident suggested such and such passage',[187] along his favorite walk around the Salisbury Crags. The Trossachs, of course, was the setting of both *The Lady of the Lake* and *Rob Roy*. *Rob Roy* was also set partly in Glasgow. Arran was the site of many episodes of *The Lord of the Isles*, as were Loch Shiel, Oban, and Loch Scavaig on Skye. Lee House, near the Falls of Clyde, was the home of the original Lee Penny, from *The Talisman*. Glen Urquhart possessed scenes from *The Legend of Montrose*. Tantallon Castle in North Berwick was described in *Marmion*. Ettrick and Yarrow provided the site of *The Lay of the Last Minstrel*. Arbroath was cast in *The Antiquary*.

While Walter Scott was the favorite and most evocative literary portal into the 'real' Scotland, he was not the only one. Cook's suggested reading list included *Kidnapped* by Robert Louis Stevenson, and several selections from a then-popular Victorian novelist, William Black. Other travelers would add Robert Burns and even Samuel Johnson. In fact, the variety of literary associations in Scotland was nearly endless. The varied interests and approaches of these authors enabled even those on standardized tours to assert individuality through the authors by whom they claimed familiarity with Scotland. Because Johnson toured in the early days of leisure travel to Scotland, reenacting his trip by recalling his famous ruminations on Iona, his meeting with Flora MacDonald, and his delightful visit to Raasay allowed tourists to cast themselves in the role of 'explorers'. Readers admired William Black, a Glasgow-born novelist whose most popular works included *A Princess of Thule* (1873), *MacLeod of Dare* (1878), and *In Far Lochaber* (1888), for his 'Turneresque' depictions of scenery, especially sunsets, and his contrast of the simplicity of Highland life with the garishness of society and fashion.[188]

Robert Burns was the second most popular literary guide to Scotland. Nineteenth-century readers understood Robert Burns and his characters as honest representations of Lowland peasants. References to his poetry and visits to the 'Land o' Burns' were therefore believed to operate as routes to the experience of everyday Scottish life.[189] As they did for Scott, guidebooks and other promotional material encouraged this notion, promising tourists, for instance, that 'Tam o' Shanter's Inn' had changed little since Burns' day.[190] Early nineteenth-century visitors were sometimes able to meet Burns' widow. Later ones went to his birthplace, where by mid century the woodwork in one room was completely covered with tourists' names and initials.[191] There they might, like Edwin Waugh, sit and look around, trying to imagine daily life when the poet was a child. They could also see the spot outside where whitewash was chipped away on one of the walls to reveal the original clay structure reared by Burn's father.[192] They visited the cottage where Burns later lived, which was converted into a public house early in the nineteenth century but purchased by Burn's Monument Trustees in 1880. They went to 'Tam o'Shanter's Inn', where they could allegedly see the identical cup Tam drained and the very chair he sat in before his haunted ride. Some picked grass from Burns' grave for souvenirs.[193] Burns was particularly popular with emigrants from Scotland, among whom his poetry evoked a sentimental nostalgia about the Scotland their ancestors left behind, with Scots, to whom he was an icon of Scottish nationalism, and with poets, who idolized his 'natural genius'.[194]

The continual evocations of Scott, Burns, Johnson, Black, and others inevitably became stereotypes in themselves, the more so as the practice was well contained in the structures of tourism. Malcolm Ferguson, a Scot who wrote of a trip to Skye in the 1880s, said he had never been more disappointed with a scene than with Loch Coruisk, famously characterized by Scott in *The Lord of the Isles* and praised by tourists ever since. In Ferguson's opinion, the loch did not deserve half the glowing and exaggerated descriptions that had been written about it – nor did other scenes that acquired fame through association with Scotland's poets and authors.[195] But rare was the tourist willing to cast doubt on the essential truthfulness of Scott or other of Scotland's bards. They might gently chide the 'Wizard of the North' for having 'gloried and exhausted' the Trossachs, making it impossible to for later arrivals to admire them.[196] They might further inflate an attraction's reputation as Elizabeth Spence did by declaring the Trossachs so extraordinary that no one – not even Scott – could truly depict their sublimity.[197] They might attempt to deflate the myth by pointing out that Loch Katrine's famed 'Ellen's Isle' had really been inhabited 'not by a gentle girl and her aged harper, but by a desperate gang of outlaws of the clan Gregor.'[198] Some mocked the effusions of guidebooks and the exaggerations of tour guides, therefore establishing their own uniqueness as travelers. By doubting the truthfulness of a guide in Stirling Castle who with great seriousness pointed out Roderick Dhu's cell, a sightseer of 1869 showed that she could not be taken in.[199] A teenager at Glencoe made fun of *Black's* embellishments:

> Arriving at the entrance of Glencoe, we found ourselves in want of the 'strange and awful fears' which, according to Black, ought now to have 'begun to press'

but which we had found too inconvenient to bring with us. However, we did our best with the 'gloomy raptures' and listened with all our ears for 'the Eagles' Cry' which was to mingle its echo with those of the 'thousand streams' that 'rush down the cliff.'[200]

Challenging the core of the received romantic vision of Scotland, however, was risky business. Artists and travel writers Joseph and Elizabeth Robins Pennell undertook a tour of Scotland in the late 1880s. They hated it. Their trip, they said, was the most miserable they had ever made. They disliked Scott and had no affinity for the trappings of touristic Scotland. The weather was vile, although they claimed it was considered a crime to say so. Though Scotland possessed a beautiful countryside, it was 'the most abominable to travel through' and its people suffered dire poverty. The Pennells' travel account, published first in *Harper's* and later in book form, was an indignant outcry against the misery of Highland crofters, whose 'bondage', they said, was more cruel than that of the slaves of the United States or the serfs of Russia. They bitterly castigated unseeing tourists who either ignored the people or appreciated them as picturesque.

The Pennells' observations were harshly criticized as 'sentimental' and 'nonsensical' misrepresentations of the plight of Highlanders. The couple commented angrily in the preface to the book-length account of their travels that critics did not want to know what really happened to travelers on their journeys. 'We were taken to task for not discovering in Scotland and the Scotch what has been made the fashion to find there – for not giving second-hand descriptions, which are the stock in trade of Scotch guide-books, whether romantic or real; in a word, for not staying at home and manufacturing our journey in the British Museum.'[201] The Pennells' anti-tourism went too far. Those who lamented crowds and superficiality implied that there was indeed something worth preserving about the image of Scotland. Theirs was an effort to sustain the desired vision of Scotland rather than to deconstruct it. By focusing on the difficult issues of poverty and aristocratic power, and by confronting the falsity of tourists' images of Scotland and the harm they wrought, the Pennells endeavored to tear down the myth – and they met a strong reaction. The tourist image of Scotland, so carefully preserved by the rhetoric of tourism, had a powerful resonance in Victorian popular culture. Whereas in the eighteenth and early nineteenth centuries Scotland served as a locus for nationalist pride through demonstrations of the virtues of being British, a society facing the troubles and insecurities of industrialism found a more romanticized Scotland to be a welcome counter to the new cultural anxieties. Without even leaving Great Britain, one could encounter a place that was apparently immune to modernization. In Raymond William's words, Scotland was 'the court of appeal in which real values were determined, usually in opposition to the "fractitious" values thrown up by the market and similar operations of society'.[202] As the Pennells found, no matter how distorted this role might be as an image of Scottish life and society, it was one the mid and late Victorians were eager to retain.

Notes

1   Thomas Cook, *Cook's Scottish Tourist Official Directory* (London, 1861), p. 27.
2   Christopher Smout, 'Tours in the Scottish Highlands from the eighteenth to the twentieth centuries,' *Northern Scotland* 5 (2) 1983, p. 120.
3   Quoted in James Holloway and Lindsay Errington, *The Discovery of Scotland: The Appreciation of Scottish Scenery through Two Centuries of Painting* (Edinburgh: National Gallery of Scotland, 1978), p. 103.
4   On definitions of 'culture' see Raymond Williams, *Culture & Society:1780-1950* (New York: Columbia Univ. Press, 1983) and James Buzard, *The Beaten Track: European Tourism, Literature, and the Ways to 'Culture' 1800-1918* (Oxford: Clarendon Press, 1993), pp. 1-17.
5   On rituals, see Victor and Edith Turner, *Image and Pilgrimage in Christian Culture* (New York: Columbia Univ. Press, 1978); Dean MacCannell, *The Tourist. A New Theory of the Leisure Class* (New York: Schocken Books, 1976); John F. Sears, *Sacred Places. American Tourist Attractions in the Nineteenth Century* (New York: Oxford Univ. Press, 1989), p. 6.
6   On Romanticism in eighteenth-century tourism in Scotland, see John Glendening, *The High Road. Romantic Tourism, Scotland, and Literature, 1720-1820* (New York: St. Martin's Press, 1997).
7   Andrew Hook, 'Scotland and Romanticism: The International Scene' in Andrew Hook, ed., *The History of Scottish Literature vol. 2* (Aberdeen: Aberdeen Univ. Press, 1987), pp. 307-21. I've borrowed the term 'celtification' from Robert Clyde, *From Rebel to Hero. The Image of the Highlander, 1745-1830* (East Linton: Tuckwell Press, 1995).
8   On the transformation of ideas of the Highlands, see Clyde, *From Rebel to Hero*; T. M. Devine, *Clanship to Crofters' War. The social transformation of the Scottish Highlands* (New York: Manchester Univ. Press, 1994); Sharon MacDonald, *Reimagining Culture. Histories, Identities and the Gaelic Renaissance* (New York: Berg, 1997); Hugh Trevor-Roper, 'The Invention of Tradition: The Highland Tradition of Scotland', in Eric Hobsbawm and Terence Ranger, eds., *The Invention of Tradition* (New York: Cambridge Univ. Press, 1983), pp. 15-41; Charles Withers, 'The Historical Creation of the Scottish Highlands' in Ian Donnachie and Christopher Whatley, eds., *The Manufacture of Scottish History* (Edinburgh: Polygon, 1992), pp. 143-56.
9   Devine, *Clanship to Crofters' War*, pp. 91-2.
10 Hook, 'Scotland and Romanticism', p. 318.
11 Buzard, *The Beaten Track*, pp. 101-7.
12 Holloway and Errington, *The Discovery of Scotland*, p. 129.
13 'Carr's Caledonian Sketches', *Quarterly Review* I (February, 1809), pp. 182-83.
14 Elizabeth Isabella Spence, *Sketches of the Present Manners, Customs, and Scenery of Scotland* (London, 1811), p. 1:199; William Pearson, *Papers, Letters & Journal of William Pearson* ed. by his wife (London, 1863), p. 268.

15   See John O. Hayden, ed., *Scott, the Critical Heritage* (London: Routledge & Kegan Paul, 1970); James Hillhouse, *The Waverley Novels and their Critics* (New York: Octagon Books, 1970); Hook, 'Scotland and Romanticism'.

16   As Christopher Harvie points out, this was far from a contradictory or diluted form of nationalism in this era of 'semi-independence' under the political management of Henry Dundas and his successors, who until 1832 ensured that Scotland's legal, clerical, and political institutions were run in Scotland by Scots. Christopher Harvie, 'Scott and the image of Scotland' in Raphael Samuel, ed., *Patriotism: The Making and Unmaking of British National Identity* vol. II *Minorities and Outsiders* (New York: Routledge, 1989), p. 175. On 'semi-independence', see Bruce Lenman, *Integration, Enlightenment, and Industrialization: Scotland 1746-1832* (London: Edward Arnold, 1981).

17   Edgar Johnson, *Sir Walter Scott: The Great Unknown* (New York: Macmillan, 1970); Glendening, *The High Road*; Maurice Lindsay, *History of Scottish Literature* (London: Robert Hale, 1992). On Scott, see also David Brown, *Walter Scott and the Historical Imagination* (Boston: Routledge & Kegan Paul, 1979); Francis Russell Hart, *The Scottish Novel: From Smollett to Spark* (Cambridge, MA: Harvard Univ. Press, 1978); Edwin Muir, *Scott and Scotland: The Predicament of the Scottish Writer* (Edinburgh: Polygon Books, 1982); Eric G. Walker, *Scott's Fiction and the Picturesque* (Salzburg: Institute fur Anglistik & Amerikinsitk, Universitat Salzburg, 1982).

18   Johnson, *The Great Unknown*, p. 1:354.

19   Holloway and Errington, *Discovery of Scotland*, p. 109.

20   Buzard, *Beaten Track*, p. 51.

21   Glendening, *The High Road*, p. 185.

22   Glendening, *The High Road*, p. 174.

23   Walter Scott, *Waverley* (New York: Oxford Univ. Press, 1986), p. 24.

24   On Waverley as a tourist, see James Buzard, 'Translation and Tourism: Scott's *Waverley* and the Rendering of Culture', *Yale Journal of Criticism. Interpretation in the Humanities* 8 (2): Fall, 1995, pp. 31-59. See also Glendening, *The High Road*, pp. 173-94.

25   Glendening, *The High Road*, p. 178.

26   Harvie, 'Scott and the image of Scotland'.

27   *Times* of London, Aug. 15, 1822.

28   See Devine, *Clanship to Crofters' War*, pp. 87-8; Gerald Finley, *Turner and George IV in Edinburgh* (Edinburgh: Tate Gallery in association with Edinburgh Univ. Press, 1981); James N. M. Maclean and Basil Skinner, *The Royal Visit of 1822* (Edinburgh: Univ. of Edinburgh Press, 1972).

29   Victoria, Queen of Great Britain, *Victoria in the Highlands: The Personal Journal of Her Majesty Queen Victoria* David Duff, ed. (London: Muller, 1968), p. 39.

30   *ILN*, September 3, 1842.

31   *ILN*, September 17, 1842.

32   *ILN*, August 20, 1842.

33   *ILN*, September 21, 1844.

34   Victoria, Queen of Great Britain, *Leaves from the Journal of Our Life in the Highlands. 1848-1861* Arthur Helps, ed. (London, 1868), pp. 65-6.

35   *ILN*, September 28, 1844.

[36] *ILN*, September 21, 1844.

[37] Glendening, *The High Road*, p. 231.

[38] See MacCannell, *The Tourist*.

[39] Glendening, *The High Road*, pp. 229-34.

[40] Alastair Durie, 'Tourism in Victorian Scotland: The Case of Abbotsford', *Scottish Economic & Social History* 12:1992. See also R. W. Butler, 'Evolution of Tourism in the Scottish Highlands', *Annals of Tourism Research* vol. 12 (1985), pp. 371-91; Alastair Durie, *Scotland for the Holidays. Tourism in Scotland c. 1789-1939* (East Linton: Tuckwell Press, 2003); Smout, 'Tours in the Scottish Highlands'.

[41] *Times* of London, August 12, 1908; *The Scotsman*, August 7, 1899; *Daily Mail*, August 1, 1908.

[42] *'Bonnie Scotland': A Comprehensive Guide and Reference Book to Scotland* (London: The Photocrom Co., Ltd., 1916), p. 96.

[43] John Thomas, *A Regional History of the Railways of Great Britain. Vol. VI Scotland: The Lowlands and the Borders*, revised and enlarged by Alan J. S. Paterson (Newton Abbot: David & Charles, 1984), p. 144; Michael Lynch, *Scotland. A New History* (London: Pimlico, 1991), p. 410.

[44] *The Scotsman*, June 12, 1847.

[45] London and Northwestern Co., pub., *Where to Spend the Holidays* (London, 1906), n.p.

[46] *"Mountain, Moor and Loch"*. Illustrated by Pen and Pencil on the route of the West Highland Railway (London, 1895), pp. 14-15.

[47] C. J. A. Robertson, *The Origins of the Scottish Railway System 1772-1844* (Edinburgh: John Donald, 1983), pp. 309-10.

[48] Thomas, *Regional History*, pp. 97-100.

[49] John Thomas, *The West Highland Railway*, extra material by Alan J. S. Paterson (Newton Abbot: David & Charles, 1984), pp. 32-83.

[50] North British Railway Co, pub., *Fort William to Mallaig* (1901), p. 32.

[51] London *Times*, July 29, 1825.

[52] *Glasgow Herald*, August 26, 1825; September 2, 1825.

[53] William Rhind, *The Scottish Tourist's Portable Guide to the Great Highland Tour* (Edinburgh, n.d.), p. 9.

[54] Thomas, *Regional History*, p. 310.

[55] *Glasgow Herald*, June 3, 1825.

[56] Alan J. S. Paterson, *The Golden Years of the Clyde Steamers* (Newton Abbot: David & Charles, 1969), pp. 228-29.

[57] Smout, 'Tours in the Scottish Highlands', p. 112.

[58] 'A Journal of a few days from Home in the summer of 1856 with selected poetry and songs.' (1856) MS. 9233, NLS, n.p.

[59] F. M. L. Thompson argues that the railway stimulated the greater use of horse transportation. See 'Victorian England: The Horse-Drawn Society' in Richard M. Golden, ed., *Social History of Western Civilization Volume II* (New York: St. Martin's, 1992), pp. 159-70.

[60] Cuthbert Bede [Edward Bradley], *A Tour in Tartan-Land* (London, 1863), p. 200.

[61] Alexander Smith, *A Summer in Skye* (Boston, 1865), pp. 51-2.

62   Catherine Sinclair, *Sketches and Stories of Scotland and the Scotch and Shetland and the Shetlanders* (London, n.d.), pp. 101; 65.

63   Frances Murray, *Summer in the Hebrides* (Glasgow, 1887).

64   Philip B. Homer, *Observations on a Short Tour Made in the Summer of 1803 to the Western Highlands of Scotland* (London, 1804), pp. 75-6.

65   T. Garnett, *Observations on a Tour through the Highlands* (London, 1800), p. 1:144.

66   David MacBrayne's Royal Mail Steamers, pub., *Summer Tours in Scotland* (Glasgow, 1885), p. 54; Karl Baedeker, *Great Britain* (London, 1887), p. 492; George Eyre-Todd, *Scotland, Picturesque and Traditional* (New York: Frederick A. Stokes, 1907), p. 310.

67   Adam and Charles Black, pub., *Black's Picturesque Tourist of Scotland* (London, 1843), p. 188.

68   Joseph Pennell and Elizabeth Robins Pennell, *Our Journey to the Hebrides* (New York, 1889), p. 84.

69   Pennell, *Our Journey to the Hebrides*, p. 160.

70   George Anderson and Peter Anderson, *Handbook to the Highland Railway System from Perth to Forres, Keith, Inverness, and Bonar Bridge* (Edinburgh, 1865), p. 61.

71   Cook, *Cook's Official Directory*, p. 95.

72   Edmund Yates, 'Letters to Joseph, No. II' *Temple Bar*, vol. 18 (November 1866), pp. 422-23.

73   Donald Macintyre, *Guide to Prince Charlie's Country* (Fort William, n.d.), p. 21.

74   Macintyre, *Prince Charlie's Country*, p. 120.

75   Highland Railway Timetables and Tourist Program (1891) BR/TT(S)/60/11, SRO, n.p.

76   Pennell, *Our Journey to the Hebrides*, p. 52.

77   Macintyre, *Prince Charlie's Country*, p. 128.

78   *Glasgow Herald*, July 1, 1879. See also Jack Simmons, 'Railways, Hotels, and Tourism in Great Britain 1839-1914', *Journal of Contemporary History* vol. 19 (1984), pp. 201-22.

79   Smout, 'Tours in the Scottish Highlands', p. 115.

80   W. W. Nevin, *Vignettes of Travel* (Philadelphia, 1881), p. 237.

81   *Glasgow Herald*, June 5, 1915.

82   John Reid, *Art Rambles in the Highlands and Islands of Scotland* (New York, 1878), p. 81.

83   See Thomas Cook, *Handbook of a Trip to Scotland* (Leicester, 1846). On Thomas Cook, see Buzard, *The Beaten Track*, pp. 48-65; Piers Brendon, *Thomas Cook. 150 Years of Popular Tourism* (London: Secker & Warburg, 1991); John Pudney, *The Thomas Cook Story* (London: Michael Joseph, 1953); Edmund Swinglehurst, *Cook's Tours: The Story of Popular Travel* (Poole, Dorset: Blandford Press, 1982); John R. Gold and Margaret M. Gold, *Imagining Scotland. Tradition, Representation and Promotion in Scottish Tourism since 1750* (Aldershot: Scolar Press, 1995), pp. 101-4; Lynne Withey, *Grand Tours and Cook's Tours* (New York: William Morrow, 1997), pp. 135-66.

84   *Cook's Excursion Advertiser*, June 1856.

85 *Cook's Excursion Advertiser*, June 1856.

86 Buzard, *The Beaten Track*, p. 50.

87 *The Scotsman*, June 8, 1882.

88 *The Scotsman*, June 5, 1862.

89 Buzard, *Beaten Track*, pp. 65-77. See also Withey, *Grand Tours*, pp. 68-74. Gold, *Imagining Scotland*, pp. 86-115, briefly discusses Scottish guidebooks. For general discussions of the rhetoric of nineteenth-century guidebooks, see Inderpal Grewal, *Home and Harem. Nation, Gender, Empire, and the Cultures of Travel* (Durham, NC: Duke Univ. Press, 1996), pp. 85-133; William W. Stowe, *Going Abroad. European Travel in Nineteenth-Century American Culture* (Princeton: Princeton Univ. Press, 1994), pp. 29-54.

90 R. W. Butler, 'Evolution of Tourism in the Scottish Highlands', p. 375; *The New Picture of Scotland* 2 vols. (Perth, 1807).

91 *Scottish Tourist and Itinerary, or A Guide to the Scenery and Antiquities of Scotland and the Western Islands* (Edinburgh, 1834), p. xi.

92 Cook, *Cook's Scottish Tourist*, p. 41.

93 The six main routes were: Inverness to Perth by the Highland Road; Inverness to Glasgow by way of the Great Glen and Fort William; Stirling to Fort William via Callender and Glencoe; Inverness to Wick, Thurso, and John O'Groats. Descriptions of Skye, the Long Island, and the Orkney and Shetland Islands were also included.

94 George Anderson and Peter Anderson, *Guide to the Highlands and Islands of Scotland* (Edinburgh, 1863), pp. 215, 216.

95 For example, *Black's Economical Tourist* (1840), *Black's Tourists & Sportsman's Companion to the Counties of Scotland* (1847), *Black's Guide to the Trossachs, Loch Catrine, Loch Lomond and Central Touring District of Scotland* (1853), *Black's Guide to Staffa, Iona, Glencoe and the Caledonian Canal* (1854), *Black's Guide to Skye, Wester Ross-shire and the Hebrides* (1873).

96 Robert Chambers, *The Picture of Scotland* (Edinburgh, 1827).

97 Black, *Black's Picturesque Tourist* (1843), p. 13.

98 Black, *Black's Picturesque Tourist* (1843), p. 21.

99 George Meason, *The Official Guide to the North Western Railway* (London, 1859).

100 Thomas Murray & Son, pub., *Murray's Scottish Tourist* (Glasgow, 1868), p. 7.

101 Murray, *Murray's Scottish Tourist*, pp. 34; 116-17.

102 Adam Black and Charles Black, pub., *Black's Picturesque Tourist of Scotland* (Edinburgh, 1840), pp. iii-iv.

103 Pennell, *Our Journey to the Hebrides*, p. 10.

104 Smith, *A Summer in Skye*, p. 50.

105 Charles G. Harper, *Motoring in Scotland* (London: Royal Automobile Club, 1912), pp. 34-6.

106 'The Tourist in Scotland: Days in Edinburgh', *The Leisure Hour* 9 (448): July 26, 1860, p. 470.

107 Murray, *Murray's Scottish Tourist*, pp. 46-60. Also see *Over the Border: or a Rossendale Lady's Impressions of Scotland* (Haslingden, 1869), pp. 16-17.

108 Chauncy Hare Townshend, *A Descriptive Tour in Scotland* (Brussels, 1840), p. 371.

[109]   See Murray, *Murray's Scottish Tourist*, pp. 46-60.

[110]   Durie, 'Tourism in Victorian Scotland'.

[111]   David Daiches, *Glasgow* (New York: Granada, 1982); Olive Checkland and Sydney Checkland, *Industry and Ethos: Scotland 1832-1914* (Edinburgh: Edinburgh Univ. Press, 1984), pp. 38-42.

[112]   Adam Black and Charles Black, pub., *Black's Picturesque Tourist of Scotland* (Edinburgh, 1881), pp. 390-91.

[113]   Miss Parker, *A Tour in Scotland in 1863* (London: The Roxburghe Club, 1984), n.p.

[114]   'The Tourist in Scotland. A Bird's-eye View of Glasgow', *The Leisure Hour* 9 (455): September 13, 1860, p. 581.

[115]   William Winter, *Over the Border* (New York: Moffat, Yard and Co., 1911), p. 220.

[116]   *Over the Border*, pp. 8-9; Spence, *Sketches of the Present Manners*, pp. 1:83-84, see also pp. 1:84-95.

[117]   'The Tourist in Scotland: A Bird's Eye View of Glasgow', p. 582.

[118]   *Where to Spend the Holidays*, pp. 57-8.

[119]   Murray, *Murray's Scottish Tourist*, pp. 61-75.

[120]   A. R. H. Moncrieff, *Bonnie Scotland* (London: A & C Black,1904; reprint, London: A & C Black, 1912), p. 196.

[121]   Baedeker, *Great Britain* (1887), p. 486.

[122]   John Macculloch, *The Highlands and Western Isles of Scotland* (London, 1824), pp. 3:473; 3:476.

[123]   Sarah Murray, *A Companion and Useful Guide to the Beauties of Scotland* William F. Langhlan, ed., (Hawick: Byways Books, 1982), pp. 73-4.

[124]   Charles Keene, John Leech, George Du Maurier, et al., *Mr. Punch in the Highlands* (London: Educational Book Co., Ltd, 1907), pp. 28-30.

[125]   Macintyre, *Guide to Prince Charlie's Country*, p. 43. Thirty-eight members of the MacDonald clan were killed by government troops in the valley of Glencoe in 1692 when their leader failed to take an oath of allegiance to William III in a timely manner.

[126]   Black, *Black's Picturesque Tourist* (1881), p. 500.

[127]   George Anderson and Peter Anderson, *Guide to the Highland Railway and the Sutherland Railway* (Edinburgh: John Menzies, 1900), p. 73.

[128]   David McCrone, Angela Morris and Richard Kiely, *Scotland – the Brand. The Making of Scottish Heritage* (Edinburgh: Edinburgh Univ. Press, 1995), p. 192.

[129]   Pennell, *Our Journey to the Hebrides*, p. 46.

[130]   Smith, *A Summer in Skye*, p. 50.

[131]   According to Macintyre, *Guide to Prince Charlie's Country*, 'the shrill whistle of the steam engine awoke [Fort William] to newness of life' p. 21.

[132]   *A Tour in Scotland in 1863.*

[133]   Baedeker, *Great Britain* (1887), p. 457.

[134]   Keene, Leech, Du Maurier, et al., *Mr. Punch in the Highlands,* pp. 190-92.

[135]   Baedeker, *Great Britain,* (1887), p. 457.

[136]   Beriah Botfield, *Journal of a Tour through the Highlands of Scotland* (Norton Hall, 1830), p. 52; Moncrieff, *Bonnie Scotland*, p. 23. On the expansion of interest in golf in the late nineteenth century, see Alistair Durie, *Scotland for the Holidays*, pp. 123-28; James Winter, *Secure from Rash Assault: Sustaining the*

Victorian Environment (Berkeley: U. of California Press, 1999),
pp. 224-30.

[137] Alastair Durie, ' "From Agreeable to Fashionable"; the Development of Coastal
Tourism in Nineteenth Century East Lothian', article manuscript supplied by
the author, p. 13.

[138] T. C. F. Brotchie, *Scottish Western Holiday Haunts* (Edinburgh: John Menzies,
1911), pp. 39; 10-18.

[139] *The Epistles of Peggy Written from Scotland* (n.p., n.d.). This book has no
publication information, but internal evidence suggests that it was published
on behalf of the North British Railway Co.

[140] Smith, *Summer in Skye*, pp. 149-50.

[141] Buzard, *The Beaten Track*, pp. 1-17.

[142] Alexander Nicholson, 'The Isle of Skye', *Good Words* 16 (1875), p. 387.

[143] Reid, *Art Rambles*, p. 29.

[144] Pennell, *Our Journey to the Hebrides*, p. 162.

[145] John Macculloch, *The Highlands and Western Islands*, p. 1:16.

[146] Buzard, *The Beaten Track*, p. 12.

[147] Philip Gilbert Hamerton, *A Painter's Camp* (Boston, 1879), p. 177; Pennell,
Our Journey to the Hebrides, p. 156.

[148] Botfield, *Journal of a Tour*, p. 253; William Keddie, *Maclure & MacDonald's
Illustrated Guides to the Highlands* (Glasgow, n.d.), p. 16.

[149] Bede, *Tour in Tartan-Land*, p. 341.

[150] Yates, 'Letters to Joseph', p. 419.

[151] Pearson, *Papers, Letters, & Journal*, p. 256.

[152] James Wilson, *A Voyage Round the Coasts of Scotland and the Isles* (Edinburgh,
1842), pp. 128, 116.

[153] Henry Cockburn, *Circuit Journeys* (Edinburgh, 1889), p. 206.

[154] A. R. H. Moncrieff, *Highlands & Islands of Scotland* (London: A & C
Black, 1906; reprint, London: A & C Black, 1925), p. 56.

[155] 'Among the Lochs: Being a Narrative of Some Passages in the Archdeacon's
Holiday', *Blackwood's Magazine* 90 (October, 1861), p. 489.

[156] J. A. MacCulloch, *The Misty Isle of Skye* (Edinburgh: Oliphant, Anderson &
Ferrier, 1905), p. 135.

[157] Edmund Gosse, 'Journal in Scotland' (1876) MS. 2562, NLS, n.p.

[158] Nevin, *Vignettes of Travel*, pp. 248-9; Robert Buchanan, *The Land of Lorne*
(London, 1871), pp. 2:147-274; T. H. Holding, *Cruise of the Ospray: Canoe
and Camp Life in Scotland* (Newcastle-on-tyne, 1878), pp. 42-3; Gordon-
Cumming, *In the Hebrides*, pp. 103-4.

[159] Smith, *Summer in Skye*, p. 5.

[160] Thomas Cook, *Cook's Tourist Handbook of Scotland* (London, 1895), p. 63;
Brotchie, *Scottish Western Holiday Haunts*.

[161] Pennell, *Our Journey to the Hebrides*, p. 19.

[162] Buzard, *The Beaten Track*, pp. 80-97.

[163] Cook, *Cook's Official Directory*, pp. 29-30.

[164] J. A. MacCulloch, *The Misty Isle of Skye*, pp. 9-10; 131-48.

[165] David MacBrayne's Royal Mail Steamers, pub., *Summer Tours in Scotland*
(Glasgow, 1885), p. 65.

[166] Reid, *Art Rambles*, p. 72.

[167]   Buzard, *The Beaten Track*, pp. 107-30.
[168]   Winter, *Over the Border*, p. 172.
[169]   Baedeker, *Great Britain*, (1887), p. 488; Smith, *Summer on Skye*, p. 4.
[170]   *Scottish Tourist and Itinerary or A Guide to the Scenery and Antiquities of Scotland and the Western Islands* (Edinburgh, 1827), p. 68.
[171]   *Scottish Tourist and Itinerary* (1827), p. 66.
[172]   J. E. Bowman, *The Highlands and Islands: A 19th Century Tour*, introduction by Elaine M. E. Barry (New York: Hippocreme Books, 1986), p. 81.
[173]   *Over the Border*, p. 11.
[174]   W. H. Maxwell, *Wanderings in the Highlands & Islands* (London, 1852), p. 2:180.
[175]   C. S. Stewart, *Sketches of Society in Great Britain and Ireland* (Philadelphia, 1834), p. 2:151.
[176]   'The Tourist in Scotland. A Group of Scottish Lochs', *The Leisure Hour* 9 (456): September 20, 1860, p. 597.
[177]   Bede, *Tour in Tartan Land*, pp. 226-27; Townshend, *Descriptive Tour of Scotland*, p. 36.
[178]   'Journal of a few days from home', n.p.; Townshend, *Descriptive Tour of Scotland*, p. 39.
[179]   Reid, *Art Rambles*, p. 30.
[180]   Advertised in George Anderson and Peter Anderson, *Guide to the Highlands and Islands of Scotland* (Edinburgh, 1851).
[181]   Cook, *Cook's Tourist Handbook of Scotland*, p. 14.
[182]   Townshend, *Descriptive Tour of Scotland*, p. 42.
[183]   Smith, *Summer in Skye*, p. 361.
[184]   Botfield, *Journal of a Tour*, p. 8.
[185]   Victoria, *Victoria in the Highlands*, pp. 122-23.
[186]   T. Murray, *Murray's Scottish Tourist*.
[187]   Yates, 'Letters to Joseph', pp. 414-23.
[188]   Hart, *The Scottish Novel*, pp. 336-40.
[189]   MacCannell, *The Tourist*, pp. 91-107.
[190]   Brotchie, *Scottish Western Holiday Haunts*, p. 105.
[191]   *Over the Border*, pp. 5-6.
[192]   Edwin Waugh, *Fourteen Days in Scotland* (Manchester, 1863), pp. 96-7.
[193]   Richard Ayton and William Daniell, *A Voyage Round Great Britain* (London, 1814-1825; reprint, London: Tate Gallery, 1978), p. 2:188.
[194]   See Glendening, *The High Road*, pp. 195-219 on Keats' visit to the scenes of Burn's life.
[195]   Malcolm Ferguson, *Rambles in Skye* (Glasgow, 1885), p. 84.
[196]   'Among the Lochs', p. 493.
[197]   Spence, *Sketches of the Present Manners*, pp. 1:203-4.
[198]   'The Tourist in Scotland. A Group of Scottish Lochs', p. 598.
[199]   *Over the Border*, p. 11.
[200]   Parker, *A Tour in Scotland in 1863*, n.p.
[201]   Pennell, *Our Journey to the Hebrides*, p.v.
[202]   Williams, *Culture & Society*, p. 34.

Chapter 3

Land of the Mountain and the Flood: Tourists and the Natural World

Prevented from traveling to the Continent by the Franco-Prussian War in 1870, Edmund Gosse, who later became a well-known poet and critic, toured Scotland in the company of a friend. He calculated that he was further away from London aboard the steamer to the island of Lewis than if he had been in south Italy or Turkey. He could reach London more quickly from Belgrade, he decided, than from the Hebrides. Consequently, 'It was impossible but that all the hurry and anxiety of life should seem gone and quite dead.'[1] Crossing the border to Scotland took English visitors farther away from home than the miles might suggest. In traveling to Scotland, they believed, they headed for a place of peace and stillness that contrasted with the busyness and crowdedness of industrial life. It was an empty land where humans were strangers and nature exercised a fierce and untamable power. There one's health was restored, and one's contact with the spiritual was revived. There one could escape the strife, divisions, and prosaicness of industrialized society, and retreat into a rural paradise where it was still possible to believe in fairies.

Tourists' reflections on nature in Scotland include many such visions of the countryside as a contemporary Arcadia. Scenery was Scotland's most compelling lure to visitors. A desire to see the allegedly untouched mountains, waterfalls, lochs, and glens of the Highlands and Lowlands was the chief reason most tourists gave for their journeys. Scotland's best known tourist attractions were natural ones: Loch Lomond, Loch Katrine, the Cuillin mountains and Lochs Scavaig and Coruisk on Skye, the Falls of Clyde, the Falls of Foyers, and the valley of Glencoe. Most travel journals, diaries, and guidebooks are full of lengthy and often very detailed descriptions of the scenery encountered in Scotland. Tourists were struck by the variety of landscapes in Scotland. Augustus Tipple, an Englishman who spent several weeks visiting a friend in Scotland in the 1840s, commented that the scenery was so diverse that there was never a sameness or dullness about it.[2] Tourist literature alleged that Scotland embodied – and surpassed – the best qualities of scenery from around the world. Visitors made comparisons with the Alps, the Rhine, the cataracts of Norway, the Italian lakes, and even Homerian Ithaca and the River Styx. Several spots in the Highlands seemed fit playgrounds for Pan, Diana, and their favorite nymphs.

That tourists considered Scotland's scenery at all attractive is testimony to changing fashions in landscape in the eighteenth and nineteenth centuries. Travelers had long judged the rugged and bleak Highlands, like other mountainous areas, as repulsive impediments to travel rather than objects to be sought and admired. Edward Burt, writing from General Wade's road building expedition in the 1720s, found the terrain far from appealing; 'there is such a sameness in the parts of the hill, that the description of one rugged way, bog, ford, etc. will serve pretty well to give you a notion of the rest.'[3] To Samuel Johnson, 'An eye accustomed to flowery pastures and waving harvests is astonished and repelled by this wide extent of hopeless sterility.'[4] By the middle to late eighteenth century, however, more and more visitors looked at Scotland through the eyes of the sublime and the picturesque. They saw the landscape as an example of what Marjorie Hope Nicholson terms the 'aesthetics of the infinite', wherein the contemplation of space elated the human soul, releasing it from finite limitations. Romantics began to find Scotland an ideal place to evoke the emotional power of the natural world. Painters like Paul Sandby, J.M.W. Turner, and the illustrators of early travel accounts helped cast the scenery in an attractive light.[5]

'Landscape', in this chapter, will be considered a cultural construct, defined as travelers' perceptions of the outdoor environment. As historian Marjorie Morgan puts it, 'What people saw or noticed, what they ignored, and the meaning they invested when they cast an eye over and described an outdoor scene are assumed to provide important insights into their identity and values.'[6] The Victorians increasingly located the authentic heart of the nation in rural areas, and they came to see Scotland as a place where one could encounter 'real' life: perfect rest and peace, an increasingly elusive spirituality, the unvanquished might of nature, and the opportunity for the exertion of human daring and strength. Scotland's landscape was the perfect remedy for the elusiveness, rootlessness, meaninglessness, and poetrylessness attributed to the modern industrial world. In reality, the deeper connection with nature which visitors so treasured in Scotland was a tenuous one. Their desire to describe, sketch, and categorize the scenery was a form of domesticating and civilizing the wild. Their extravagant awe and delighted horror at the Highlands was in many cases evidence of how far removed from nature their lives truly were, a distance intensified by the growing use of railways and steamers as the means by which to view the scenery. Scotland's landscape was not untouched by human hands and it was far from paradise for many of those who tried to make a living there. The very emptiness of the Highlands might have spoken of deep social divisions and distress, although to most sightseers it did not. Their interpretation of the scenery was an ideological one, which was not without effects upon the population of the Highlands, a topic which will be explored more fully in a later chapter. Nonetheless, Scottish scenery had a powerful resonance to visitors. Because nature still appeared to exist there in its pristine state, in spite of humans' many encroachments upon the natural world, Scotland's countryside played an integral role in the Victorian adjustment to an industrial economy and society.

Landscape and 'Scottishness'

In 1805 the 'very beautiful' Clyde valley, enriched with gentlemen's seats, 'excellently' cultivated and richly clothed with fine trees, reminded Joseph Mawman of England.[7] Seventy-one years later Edmund Gosse lay in the long grass under a 'pastoral' beech tree near the Lowland town of Linlithgow, and reflected that the area was 'very charming in a quiet, unobtrusive English way.'[8] Quite early in the nineteenth century, as Elizabeth Helsinger shows, landscape depictions of 'Englishness' came to be associated with fertility, beauty, and productivity. At the same time as verbal and visual depictions of cultivated land became increasingly important as metaphors of 'Englishness' in the post-1815 period, they were also sites of a struggle for the definition of the nation as competing groups claimed their right of representation in the creation of the English self image.[9] In the last quarter of the century the link between English national identity and landscape grew regionally specific, tied to the rural south's geography of rolling hills, hedgerows, and villages with half-timbered houses and neat greens.

The fact that commentators often characterized scenes of fertile countryside in Scotland as 'English' shows how deeply engrained was the link between landscape and national identity. 'England' was gentle and domesticated; 'Scotland' was untamed and unbroken. The beauty and peacefulness of the 'English' countryside spoke of the British capability to control their environment. Inderpal Grewal argues that by describing the Indian countryside as rich, verdant, and 'beautiful', nineteenth-century British travelers implicitly recommended that their nation needed to civilize that land.[10] By contrast, with their emphasis on the vastness of the natural world in Scotland, visitors imagined that nature there was too powerful for humans to control. Such a vision was a provocative statement of human limitations which allowed nature in Scotland to meet a variety of cultural anxieties, ranging from nostalgia for the country and concern over the consequences of industrialization, to questions about God's role in the creation and the preservation of the spiritual in an utilitarian world. As an image which reflected the psychological and emotional needs of tourists more than the reality of life for rural Scots, this understanding of the Scottish countryside was no less imperialistic than that promoted by visitors to India, but thoughtful tourists also found that they could not completely control the meaning of the Scottish landscape.

Understood as a country less urbanized and industrialized than England, Scotland was the consummate target of Victorians' idealization of the countryside which contrasted the truth and purity of rural areas with the artificiality and inauthenticity of the city. No longer did scenes of economic production, perhaps small cotton mills, 'enliven' the scenery as they did to eighteenth-century travelers. Rather, as the consequences of humans' primacy over the environment became increasingly evident, nineteenth-century tourists in both the Lowlands and the Highlands sought to evade signs of humans' encroachment upon the natural world. Virtually all tourists agreed that the journey to Scotland allowed them to retreat from modernity and immerse themselves in the creation. In stressing that in Scotland one was surrounded by 'another world', remote from the 'goings on of civilized life', visitors like Chauncy Hare Townshend cemented the link between 'England' and productivity.[11] Augustus Tipple found himself 'buried right away from the busy bustling world: Nature held her undisputed and solitary sway.'[12] The realm of nature was the site of a deeper and truer reality than was accessible in the 'vulgar world.'[13] The scenery of Loch Lomond 'is grand indeed, and well calculated to raise the mind above the monotony of every day life.'[14] One might lose his or her taste for the petty concerns of daily life.[15] 'So pervading and complete is the lovely spirit of [Glenfinnan], that when, to enhance our present quiet, I cast a glance back upon the goings on of civilized life, I declare that its visitings, dinnerings, plays, concerts, exhibitions, parties, etc. seemed but as far off dreams. I was already gone an age deep in solitude.'[16]

Eighteenth- and nineteenth-century landscape descriptions frequently set the ostensible timelessness and purity of the Scottish countryside (and its inhabitants) against the various forms of fallenness attributed to the industrial world. A view of a barefoot Highland girl standing on a crag while horses grazed and a dog collected the sheep, was declared 'a perfect Eden' by a steamship passenger en route to Inverary in 1856.[17] Any fertile, moderately populated, but isolated locale was likely to be termed 'Arcadian', 'Edenic', or a 'Paradise'. To Alexander Nicholson, Talisker was 'the very picture of a Happy Valley, sequestered from all the world, the home of innocence and peace.'[18] Although these characterizations called attention to the fecundity of the environment, they de-emphasized the human exertion needed to make the land productive. As 'Edenic' locales, fruitfulness was part of their natural essence, a description in keeping with the idea that 'Scottish' scenery was untouched by humans. What mattered to tourists about nature in Scotland was not its ability to support the men and women who lived and worked on it, but its offer of healing, both spiritual and physical, from the various troubles of modern life. A guidebook to the West Highlands suggested that it was worth breaking the Sabbath in order to visit the valley of Glenfinnan 'if the tourist could enter into the spirit of the scene and carry with him to the unrest and turmoil of his city life, a vision of the peace and beauty of the glen.'[19] In the midst of Scotland's scenery, as the Romantics taught, those gripped by sadness and pain might find solace. A visitor of 1829 composed a poem at the Falls of Bruar, confessing her reluctance to return from the roar of the falls to 'a wretched world where grief and pain/Await our every step.'[20] To William Winter, Loch Awe was 'a place so beautiful and so fraught with the means of happiness that time stands still in it, and even "the ceaseless vulture" of care and regret ceases for awhile to vex the spirit with remembrance of anything that is sad.'[21]

Tourist literature did not discuss the benefits of a vacation in the country for those who toiled long hours in factories and lived in urban slums. It was for members of the middle classes, adversely affected by the hustle and bustle of modern life, the strains of work, the unhealthiness of the city, or a multitude of private sorrows, that Scotland's natural environment held out a near sacramental power. 'The rude hand of health whose established dwelling place is in the hills and glens of Scotland' was key to the country's lure to tourists.[22] Victorians were deeply concerned on both private and public levels about the state of national health. Recurrent waves of epidemics, revelations of poor hygiene in working-class areas, investigations into the numerous occupational diseases which accompanied industrialization, and the conviction that stress and overwork weakened both the body and the mind seemed clear proof that the country was healthier than the city.[23] Interest in Scotland's healthful qualities centered specifically on the 'fresh' and 'health-giving' air, for most experts attributed disease to a noxious invisible gas or miasma.[24] 'The freshest and most invigorating airs one could wish for blow here [in Douglas dale], and the glorious wine of life runs free for the wayfarer.'[25] Victoria and Albert, said the *Illustrated London News*, 'have derived considerable benefit from the pure and bracing air of the Highlands.'[26] The long life spans of residents of parts of the Highlands and islands also testified to the benefits of the climate.[27] Chauncy Townshend, who like many traveled to Scotland hoping to improve his health, was infused with a sense of strength and vitality by the refreshing air of Braemar: 'One feels oneself inhaling longevity as one inspires it....Oh! Let me take another breath, and still a deeper, down to the bottom of my lungs, till, tipsy with the fine spirit, I leap and shout, and forget that there are such things as fatigue and sorrow, disease and death in the glorious world!'[28] The many hydropathics built in Scotland in the second half of the nineteenth century contributed to the belief that the country was a place where one's health could be improved.

Scotland was not the only place in the British Isles where one could withdraw from the 'world' to reap the emotional and physical benefits of nature, although nature's offerings seemed more bountiful there. What was unique to Scotland was the 'unconquered and untamable wildernesses of the

northern Highlands', and it was they which most intrigued tourists and
which best encapsulated the definition of 'Scottish' scenery as immune to
the transforming hand of humanity.[29] Sparsely populated and often
cultivated only with great difficulty, the barren and windswept mountains
of the Highlands were a striking contrast with the domesticated landscape
associated with England. The Highlands' scarcity of inhabitants, which
was central to nineteenth-century readings of the area, was actually of fairly
recent origin. With the lack of success of most of the eighteenth-century
attempts at the economic development of the Highlands, most landowners
turned to sheep farming, forcing tenants onto small plots of land near the
coast or encouraging to them emigrate. The resulting depopulation of vast
tracts of the interior of the Highlands allowed the region to be read as
antagonistic to human powers.[30]

One way to uncover Victorian understandings of the Highland landscape
is to examine responses to a locale then considered to epitomize the area:
Loch Scavaig and Loch Coruisk on the island of Skye. Such an investigation
also illustrates the importance of literary and touristic texts in defining the
meaning of Scotland's natural attractions. Loch Scavaig and Loch Coruisk
are located in the Cuillin mountain range on the southwest coast of Skye, an
island which was a highlight of any mid to late Victorian tour of Scotland.
Tourist literature made it clear that if one was to see anything on the island, it
should be these two lochs. Skye without the Cuillins, said J. A. MacCulloch,
would be like *Hamlet* without the prince.[31] Indeed, many did see little else
on the island; the MacBrayne's steamship tour merely stopped in Loch
Scavaig, allowed a quick walk to Coruisk, sailed once around the island,
then whisked tourists back to the mainland.

Victorian observers described Loch Coruisk as a loch with jet black, still
waters, lying in an oval-shaped valley, roughly three miles long and one-
half to one mile wide. A stream connected it to nearby Loch Scavaig, actually
an ocean bay. Little vegetation grew in the region. The lochs were
'discovered' by the geologist, John Macculloch, who traveled the Highlands
and islands extensively between 1811-1821, becoming something of an
authority on the region. He published two influential books, *A Description
of the Western Islands of Scotland* (1819), a geological survey, and *The
Highlands and Western Islands of Scotland* (1824), which was both a
delineation of the physical environment of the region and a controversial
assessment of the character and manners of the Highlanders. As he recounted
in *The Highlands and Western Islands of Scotland*, Macculloch was advised
on a geologic trip to Skye that at Loch Scavaig he 'should find rocks enough.'
His informant alleged that the spot was 'as far from bonny as possible,' but
it sounded promising to Macculloch.

> Of course, I dreamed of nothing but Loch Scavig [sic]; embodying all sorts of
> impossible rocks into all sorts of impossible shapes…satisfying myself that…I
> should at least see…scenery, which, as it appeared to have been utterly

neglected by the only two persons who had ever opened their eyes on it, would crown me with the laurels of a discoverer.[32]

After a prolonged journey, caused by what Macculloch portrayed as the typical incompetence of Highlanders, he reached Scavaig. The bay, he said, was surrounded by high mountains, 'dark, uncertain, and mysterious,' inaccessible by land except to well-trained shepherds. Likewise, sailing could be dangerous; unexpected squalls might easily overturn a boat. He entered the bay at dusk, finding it a 'scene of stillness and gloom.' Although he admitted to later visiting Scavaig with a busy fishing fleet, the dominant idea of Macculloch's account was of 'the deep gloom of that which seemed never before to have been violated by the presence of man.' Even the bustle and noise of the later expedition was swallowed up by the 'solemnity' and 'magnitude' of the surroundings.[33]

Exploring further, Macculloch followed a cascade, the only object enlivening the landscape. Suddenly 'a valley burst on my view, which, in a moment, obliterated Loch Scavig [sic], together with all the records of all the valleys that had ever left their traces on the table of my brain.' He had found Loch Coruisk. So extraordinary was the sight 'that I felt as if transported by some magician into the enchanted wilds of an Arabian tale.' The scene 'want[ed] every thing…that, in a better climate, might have rendered it the delight, as well as the wonder and admiration, of the world,' yet Macculloch was fascinated. 'Not an atom of vegetation [was] anywhere discernible' aside from the grassy islands in the loch. So high and steep were the mountains that 'the sun rarely reaches into the valley, which thus seems lost in a sort of perpetual twilight.' 'It appeared as if all living beings had abandoned this spot to the spirit of solitude. I held my breath to listen for a sound, but every thing was hushed. Neither motion nor sound was there, and I almost startled at that of my own footsteps'.[34]

The Highlands and Western Islands was written in the form of letters to Walter Scott, and Macculloch concluded this section of his narrative with a comment to his friend that besides the two of them, knowledge of the region was still only shared by half a dozen people.[35] That changed in 1815 when Scott published *The Lord of the Isles*, which contains the first widely-read description of the region. Scott had toured the coast of Skye in 1814, and his perceptions were likely influenced by Macculloch:

Seems that primeval earthquake's sway
Hath rent a strange and shattered way
    Through the rude bosom of the hill,
And that each naked precipice,
Sable ravine, and dark abyss,
    Tells of the outrage still.
The wildest glen but this can show

Some touch of Nature's genial glow…
But here, – above, around, below,
     On mountain or in glen,
Nor tree, nor shrub, nor plant, nor flower,
Nor aught of vegetative power
     The weary eye can ken.[36]

By speaking of an 'outrage' against nature, Scott introduced a post-lapsarian theme while retaining Macculloch's interpretation of Coruisk as a valley where in Scott's words, 'No human foot comes'.[37] In this manner, Macculloch and Scott defined the discourse of the region for the remainder of the century. Nearly every nineteenth-century description of Lochs Scavaig and Coruisk, whether in a guidebook or a personal account, owed something to Macculloch and Scott. A profusion of visual representations also flooded the market, among them J. M. W. Turner's *Loch Coruskin* which effectively captured the aura depicted by Scott. This rendition of the Highland landscape permeated popular culture to such a degree that it became difficult to see Skye in any other way. Few tourists could have come to the island without some idea of what it was supposed to look – and feel – like.

The tenacity of this vision of Scavaig and Coruisk is testimony to its attractiveness. The lochs were examples of the sublime: vast, dark, and obscure, evoking fear and terror. The total desolation of the scene captivated visitors. Descriptions characterized the area as 'gloomy', 'savage', 'fearful', 'sterile', 'lonely', even 'grisly'. So horrific was the setting that visitors often claimed to be terrified. 'We came almost with beating hearts upon Corruisken, a deep, dark, solemn piece of still water, of a peculiar leaden hue, and surrounded by such grisly terrors that one is really at first afraid to look at them.' said James Wilson in 1842.[38] At a nearby spot, John Macculloch found that 'silence and solitude seem for ever to reign amid the fearful stillness and the absolute vacuity around: at every moment the spectator is inclined to hush his footsteps and suspend his breath to listen for some sound which may recall the idea of life or of motion.'[39] Richard Ayton alleged in 1820 that Loch Scavaig was so frightful that some people could not force themselves to approach the spot; he met a man who was so affected by the somber atmosphere of the loch that he feared he was growing suicidal, and hastened to turn back.[40]

The source of the terror inspired by these lochs was the complete lack of human associations. According to Henry Cockburn, writing in 1841, 'The peculiarity of the interest in Scavaig arose from the total absence of all human interference. The scene would have been the same had man not existed.'[41] Later visitors agreed. The Cuillins often seemed to be not only untouched by humanity, but untouchable. People who ventured there were overpowered. John Macculloch 'felt like an insect amidst the gigantic scenery'; over fifty years later Robert Buchanan 'felt dwarfed to the utter significance of a pygmy'.[42] Not only humans were rendered insignificant there. Visitors portrayed Coruisk as abandoned since the dawn of time; indeed it seemed that time stood still. 'You seem to stand in nature's primeval workshop; here are the very bones of the old earth.'[43] Life, vitality, even God himself were cast aside by the forbidding and sterile gloom. James Wilson's 1842 depiction of the scene, the salient points of which were often repeated by guidebooks and other visitors, helped codify this understanding: 'The dead dull lake lay beneath, the ruins as it were of a former world were scattered on all sides....There was nothing within the vast diurnal sphere that breathed the breath of life, – no sound, nor sight of any moving thing – nothing but a dead and stony, seemingly a God-forsaken world.'[44]

Loch Scavaig and Loch Coruisk were one of the Highlands' most desolate locales, but far from the only one. Comments about scenes without a trace of human habitation were commonplace. Despite the growing popularity of the Trossachs, an early-rising tourist of 1851could claim to find no indication that the foot of man had ever invaded the silent sanctuary.[45] Near Callander, 'There was a solitariness which spread an awe over the spirits amounting almost to fear. We passed through an avenue of trees which look'd as tho' they had shed their leaves and renew'd them for centuries without a human eye to observe or a voice to make a remark thereon.'[46] It was evidently possible, even in the late nineteenth century, to believe that parts of the Highlands had seldom been seen by humans. As late as 1905 J. A. MacCulloch could perceive no sign of life at the Storr, an unusual rock formation on Skye: 'in all that wide landscape you might be the sole survivor; silence and immensity fill the soul, and the still small voice speaks and holds you spellbound.'[47]

According to Marjorie Morgan, such scenery embodied everything that made English tourists uncomfortable in outdoor settings. Accustomed to their own less dramatic hills and mountains, the English often tended to be ill at ease among towering mountain peaks, whose height and impassability made them feel confined and oppressed. English tourists also preferred views with some signs of human habitation. The horror evoked by the Cuillins, therefore, was not just the rhetoric of the sublime, it reflected the disquiet experienced by visitors to a foreign and 'un-English' landscape.[48] Nonetheless, the popularity of the Highlands, especially uninhabited areas like Loch Scavaig and Loch Coruisk, shows that English travelers were also intrigued by places where nature was believed to be impervious to human might. The primary attraction of the Highlands lay in the opportunity to observe at close range the horrifying powers of the creation and to be overpowered by them. While some visitors were disappointed once they got there, the Highlands' reputation for gloom, desolation, and solitude was one of the chief lures which initially drew them north. It was a draw similar to that exerted on the Victorian imagination by the Arctic, another place imagined as boundless, inhuman, and inorganic, which became a stage for allegories of the contest between man's strength and courage, and the harshness and inscrutability of nature.[49] With the aid of the theory of the sublime, the Highlands, like the Far North, reminded humans of the vastness of their own souls as they responded to nature, and of their own smallness in the universe.

The theory of the sublime, of course, had already recast the Highland landscape before the nineteenth century, but Victorians responded with a new urgency to this framework for looking at nature. In such places a culture with considerable evidence of humans' ability to dominate and control nature saw a different picture. Alexander Smith alleged that at certain spots in the Hebrides, man saw nature at its worst. He suggested that the reason modern progress had made no headway there was not that the islands were behind the times; rather, human-made technology, great though it was, could not compete with the even greater forces of nature in the Hebrides. 'Even man, the miracle worker, who transforms everything he touches, who has rescued a fertile Holland from the waves, who has reared a marble Venice out of salt lagoon and marsh, was defeated there.'[50] Man is not at home in that world, said Smith. Nature is too strong; it rebukes and crushes him. Dozens of other commentators agreed. Jabez Marrat, a Protestant minister who toured Scotland in the 1870s, alleged that 'Human skill and industry can tame the shaggy wilderness, and can turn the brown moor into a scene of smiling meadows and cornfields; but Glencoe is abandoned to everlasting sterility.'[51] William Winter was repeatedly 'rebuked and humbled by the final, effectual lesson of man's insignificance – a lesson severely taught by the implacable vitality of these eternal hills.'[52] In contrast with the solitary hills and the gloomy ocean of the north of Scotland, 'man and all his works dwindle to insignificance and seem no more than the dying echo of a wave that is spent.'[53] Nature, he realized, was 'austerely indifferent to the life of Man.'[54]

Comments about the terrible power of nature in the Highlands were sometimes more rhetorical than real, and the Highland sublime was almost puny in comparison to the Arctic, or even perhaps the Alps. But the Arctic was out of reach for most Britons – Lochs Scavaig and Coruisk were not. There members of the middle classes could experience the sublime for themselves, and realize, without risking the danger associated with the Far North or the Alps, that even within Great Britain the environment still posed a challenge to humans. The Highlands were 'the only part of these islands where man has practically made no mark upon the landscape, and where the land itself seems too large for its people.'[55] They offered the novel possibility of being mastered by nature, a potentiality which lay at the root of the cultural significance of the Highlands. Even those who never went there knew of their power.

Challenges to the sovereignty of nature were many, however, and the advance of scientific knowledge was perhaps the most potent. The Highlands' rebuke of man's sense of authority over the environment did not necessarily invoke the biblical God as the source of this power and might. The desolation and emptiness described by virtually every visitor to the Cuillins suggested to some a physical world formed not by the guiding hand of a benevolent creator, but by undirected and uncaring elemental forces. In the 1840s James Wilson picked up on the post-lapsarian, even post-apocalyptic, impression introduced by Scott, rendering Coruisk as 'God-forsaken', the 'ruins...of a former world.' Wilson argued elsewhere in his text that the study of the mysteries and grandeur of nature as evinced in places like Staffa would teach of the 'Great Creator['s]' character and would therefore guard the student against 'the entangling mazes of a false and feeble, because a godless philosophy.'[56] His account of Coruisk, however, published a few years after Charles Lyell's *Principles of Geology* (1835), allowed readers to interpret the loch in the light of Lyell's suggestion that changes in the earth's surface were not contingent upon the needs of humans. Wilson's was one of the most widely available renditions of Loch Coruisk, excerpted in guidebooks throughout the century. As science increasingly pointed towards a universe which was the result of the blind operation of laws of nature, Wilson's description could be agitating. His assertion that a rock from one of the mountains could crush to pieces any man-made cathedral could be read both as a statement of man's humility before the creation and as a comment on the ability of indifferent nature to destroy faith.[57]

Looking back, one could see that the emotion-laden topic of science was present in the construction of Lochs Scavaig and Coruisk from its beginnings. John Macculloch was, after all, a scientist, and he was both preceded and followed to the Highlands by numerous geologists, mineralogists, and botanists, both amateur and professional.[58] Investigations into the natural history of the Highlands were a favorite pastime among visitors, and curiosity about the formation of the unusual surroundings was part of the rhetoric of Scottish travel writing. Some amateur naturalists found they could not be certain of a traditional Christian God who created the Highlands. Robert Buchanan, a sportsman who in 1871 published an account of a yachting and hunting trip around the Highlands and Hebridies, could admit to no 'perfect religious confidence', while spending the night beside Loch Coruisk, only a feeling of 'awful communication with the unseen Intelligence.'[59] On his first visit to Coruisk, Alexander Nicholson, who was born on Skye, was caught in a thunderstorm which sounded like the voice of God – but only because he was 'young and undisturbed by any scientific views'. The most he could be certain of when older was that the sight of the 'silent majestic' Cuillins seemed proof that they must have been created by 'the exercise of Will'.[60] Not only did science call into question Biblically-based beliefs about the age and creation of the earth, science was a form of intellectual mastery and thus a threat to the sense of mystery and solace of nature. If one could explain the forces which made the Highlands so awe-inspiring, then the sublime had been conquered.

To many others, however, rather than casting doubt on God's power, science pointed to a deeper, fuller knowledge of him. Even Robert Buchanan considered geology a 'sublime Muse' through whom the light of God could be seen.[61] Hugh Miller, a well-known Scottish geologist and a devout Christian, argued that although geology postulated an older earth than did the Bible, a less finite conception of creation only evoked a greater God.[62] Across the Highlands, tourists found that contemplation of the scenery directed their thoughts involuntarily to God as the creator. The insignificance of man evinced there was a reminder not only of the greatness and power of nature, but also of the greatness and power of the Almighty. After discussing geology and the terrifying force of the elements, J. A. MacCulloch concluded that the very enormity of the mountains (the vastness of 'mere matter') led one's thoughts 'from the work to the Worker.' He summed up with Psalm 121: 'My help cometh even from the Lord, who hath made heaven and earth.'[63]

Such assertions helped to defend the Highlands' symbolic value of imperviousness to the contemporary world. None of the published descriptions of lochs and glens were explicitly anti-Biblical, and any spiritual apprehension was always implicit. In fact, while Highland scenery may have prodded visitors to consider some disturbing ideas, tourists countered by imagining a place where magic and mystery dominated at the expense of the rational. Yet modernity in the form of skepticism and religious doubt continued to sneak past the sentinel mountains. A reading of the Highlands as the domicile of the irrational could actually serve to highlight the disbelief of tourists. While numerous observers asserted that Skye, for instance, was an unearthly place, and visitors sometimes portrayed islanders as exemplary Christians, the aspect of the supernatural most associated with the Cuillins was not traditional Christianity, but a vague, often unspecified, otherworldliness. Foreigners had long considered Scotland a half mythical country, where strange things might happen which one would not look for closer to home. Tales of the 'second sight' reinforced that notion.[64] The Highlands were 'eerie', a place of 'magic'. Tourists frequently characterized Scottish scenes as 'fairy-like'. Visitors said they would not be surprised to meet 'the fabulous creatures of the Celtic mythology'[65]: monsters, demons, fairies, mermaids. The Quirang (a rock formation on the Skye coast) was an appropriate locale to communicate with angels or fairies.[66] Skye was a 'weird and uncanny' island where even at the turn of the century one could detect 'trace[s] of that primitive pagan element'.[67] Coruisk was the 'Home of Mystery,' the 'chosen home of Spirit-Giants,' and the setting for several ghost stories and legends.[68] A 'grisly shape' was said to frequent the 'lonely' Coire-nan-Uraisg, also on Skye.[69] At the Cave of the Ghost near Coruisk the 'taisch [spirit] o' a shepherd has been seen...sitting cross-leggit, and branding a bluidy sheep'.[70]

The idea that Scotland was the abode of spirits and ghosts established that the mystical still held local power. Carole G. Silver argues that a fascination with 'the secret kingdom of the fairies' was a hallmark of the Victorian period, one which expressed a reaction against utilitarianism and offered a protection against 'sterile rationality'. For those troubled by religious doubt, belief in fairies offered an imaginative alternative or supplement to Christianity, in much the same manner as did spiritualism.[71] As manifested among tourists, however, interest in the spirit world provided only a vicarious connection with the irrational, for they generally did not participate in this supernatural world. They could only assert that it existed for natives. John Macculloch made this point clear in the tale of his first trip to the Cuillins. Highlanders, said Macculloch, considered Coruisk the 'haunt of the Water Demons.' To the men of Skye, these spirits were not to be trifled with. Macculloch himself perceived an almost magical aura at Coruisk and was not surprised that natives considered it haunted. He, too, was unnerved by the vastness, the emptiness, and the bleakness of the scene. But his emotions were closer to an intellectual awe; he did not feel personally threatened. His boatmen, it seems, did. Macculloch portrayed them as almost paralyzed with the fear of meeting 'spirits'. The men were under 'considerable alarm' as Macculloch wandered Coruisk alone. Later, 'As we rowed back to our vessel, I observed an unusual silence and air of mystery among the men; while they pulled as if an enemy had been behind them, looking about at every moment, and then at each other, till as we gained the opener sea, their terrors seemed to disappear.'[72]

This section of Macculloch's narrative draws a clear distinction between his own boldness at venturing to such a remote spot and the Gaels' contrasting lack of bravery.[73] His rational and scientific mind, he suggested, stood him in better stead in the Highlands than the outdated and quaint superstitions of those who lived there. Macculloch recognized the appeal of the mysterious and confessed to a melancholy grief that 'we have, in these latter days, been philosophized out of half our pleasures.'[74] But he also relegated faith in fairies to 'the follies that belong to the childhood of nations, to an age of barbarism', out of which Highlanders were inevitably growing.[75] Mid to late Victorians, on the other hand, prized the beliefs of the islanders as a positive sign of their rootedness in the pre-modern world. These later observers were more likely to regret that Gaels were losing their faith in the spirit world. 'The march of education and the School Board system have deprived the world of much of the romantic.'[76] The tourists who followed John Macculloch by fifty years or so seemed to prefer to walk not in his footsteps, but in those of his Highland crew, although they also conceded the backwardness of a superstitious worldview. They enjoyed pretending that they, too, gained a closer contact with the other world. Consider J. A. MacCulloch's depiction of Harta Corrie: 'You shudder as you pause by the stone; in fancy the glen rings with fierce shouts of the clansmen and the shrieks of the dying...and you hurry away lest some shape of dread should confront you.'[77]

Neither MacCulloch evinced much credence in supernatural beings. Canon J. A. (John Arnott) MacCulloch was an amateur anthropologist, whose *The Childhood of Fiction* (1905) elaborated on theories that fairies and folk tales were remnants of 'savage' beliefs and customs.[78] Yet while he, like John Macculloch, implied that credence in the spirits belonged to former times and to unenlightened cultures, he clearly wished to see a ghost. He could not, however, for they were present only 'in fancy'. Robert Buchanan allowed for the possibility that the ghost stories of Coruisk were true. But by placing the tales in the mouth of his Celtic companion Hamish Shaw, he identified the ability to experience the supernatural as a Celtic trait.[79] A Highlander, so tourists suggested, could actually perceive what outsiders could only imagine. Nevertheless, even if they, as temporary visitors from a more rational and skeptical world, could not believe in the old ghosts, demons, and fairies, the idea that at least some of the men and women of the Highlands could kept the immaterial alive in an increasingly logical world. At the very least, by refusing to dismiss such superstitions out of hand, Victorian tourists forbade modern skepticism from banishing premodern creditability. They thus allowed nature to retain the sense of the inexplicable sought in an ever-more explicable universe, and demonstrated a wistful yearning for a place where spirituality was simple and unthreatened.

'Manly Pastimes'

'When I first trod these glorious hills [of the Highlands], and breathed this pure air, I almost seemed to be entering upon a new state of existence. I felt an ardour and a sense of freedom that made me look back with something like contempt upon the tame and hedgebound country of the south.'[80] The comments by William Scrope, author of the 1838 *The Art of Deer Stalking*, demonstrate that the reading of the English countryside as gentle and cultivated also cast it as devitalized, a contrast to the potency of the Highlands. The understanding of the north as a place where modernity could not make inroads preserved the area as a testing ground for humans against the primeval world. Scrope's association of the Highlands with independence and the south with confinement was echoed by many other men who represented their trips to Scotland as necessary flights from the world of urbanization, industrialization, and domesticity in order to rejuvenate a threatened masculinity. T. H. Holding set off on a canoe and camping trip in Scotland in the 1870s because '[F]rom bricks, feather beds, carpets, starched linen, and even female society, I had a desire to fly, as most of these of a sudden assumed, more or less, a state of life from which independent manhood might for a time, however brief, break away.'[81] In the second half of the nineteenth century especially, the Highlands were a compelling challenge to Victorian men, a suitable sphere for the exercise and cultivation of a physical masculinity the health of which prompted considerable anxiety in the period. What better way to overcome the seeming inertia, passivity, and effeminacy of industrial life than to conquer an environment like the Highlands where humans could be seen as impotent?

The social and economic changes of the nineteenth century prompted what James Eli Adams refers to as a 'crisis of manhood', as industrialization challenged traditional concepts of masculinity. The identity of the new middle class of the late eighteenth and early nineteenth centuries was intimately linked to new gender roles, as men broke away from older notions of manhood to a different self understanding. But this transition was not without anxiety, and definitions of masculinity continued to alter throughout the Victorian period. The separation of work and home transformed fatherhood, distanced fathers from sons, and called on men to develop new forms of authority in the family. Property became a less common and less secure source of male power and index of maturity and independence. New types of jobs and opportunities for social advancement strained relations between generations. The necessity of delayed marriage to secure middle-class status weakened associations between manhood and sexual prowess. The growth of business and professional jobs heightened issues of self definition in occupations which had not earlier been integrated into traditional understandings of maleness.[82]

The new middle-class male identity claimed self-discipline as a pivotal masculine attribute, the quality which fitted men for economic life. Belief in their ability to control emotions, rein in desires, and triumph over circumstances created a powerful sense of autonomy. Yet the roles as businessmen and professionals for which this characteristic suited men also induced considerable stress. Health treatises warned of the nervous strains posed by overwork which induced physical and mental disease.[83] The new bourgeois careers, it seemed, might be weakening men. Such anxieties about the viability of the new manliness were compounded by fears that Great Britain was becoming a 'wealthy but unmanly society.' The series of foreign policy crises at mid-century, including the Crimean War, the Indian Mutiny, and the Second Opium War shook confidence in British vigor.[84] Later, turn of the century revelations of the physical weakness of recruits during the Boer War prompted widespread fear of racial degeneration. In the second half of the century, as notions of masculinity increasingly emphasized the 'ascetic' regimen of renunciation, the suspicion grew that manhood could not be sustained by the feminine ease of the home.[85] This concern called into question a central tenant of the cult of domesticity; the premise that women's spirituality and purity, manifested in the home, imparted moral health to their husbands who spent so much time in the competitive and amoral world. MacKenzie argues that a 'cultural frontier thesis' of masculinity developed in late Victorian and Edwardian Britain, a thesis which identified as essential masculine attributes those qualities necessary for survival on the imperial frontier: courage, endurance, individualism, sportsmanship, resourcefulness, and close knowledge of nature.[86] Scotland, of course, was not the frontier, but as a place where a man could meet nature in its allegedly rawest form, the Highlands presented many of the same opportunities for the development and affirmation of manliness, with the advantage of easier access and affordability. This notion was present even earlier in the century; in the 1850s W. H. Maxwell found the Highlands to be just the place for 'rougher specimen of mankind', who had spent Christmas in the Bay of Biscay or had made hurried Peninsular marches in bad weather with the Iron Duke.[87]

To be sure, there was more than one possible gender construction of the Highlands. As several scholars have identified, the popular understanding of the area portrayed it as a domestic enclave whose society fostered feminine virtues – naturalness, sentimentality, spirituality, emotionality, the innocence of childhood – while the Lowlands and England were rational, sophisticated, and intellectual.[88] In the Highlands, a 'feminine nature constructed at the margins of society, separated from civilization and unmediated by modernity' called out for male domination.[89] Yet the Highlands were also a masculine realm: a rugged land peopled by hardy and robust warriors. This conception of the northwest of Scotland drew on an alternative, and specifically male, vision of the environment than as the source of spiritual renewal. John M. MacKenzie reminds us that a vision of nature as violent and needing to be forcefully dominated continued to exist in the nineteenth century. Victorian culture manifested a concurrent fascination with cruelty and death in the natural world, a fascination which invited men to appropriate the violence of the creation in an attempt to control it.[90]

Scotland's outdoor environment spoke to nineteenth-century middle-class male anxieties in two particular ways, drawing on alternative visions of nature. The natural world's offer of spiritual and physical refreshment had special relevance to men. The fresh air and simple food of the Scottish countryside was believed to strengthen the physique, and consequently regenerate the intellects, of 'brain-weary' men. There, 'the jaded city man may have rest of mind and change of scene'.[91] William Douglas, who spent a few weeks hill-walking and fishing in Sutherland in 1888, noted an inn which seemed the 'beau-ideal of a summer resort for a busy man who required rest for the mind as well as body, away from the cares and worries of everyday life.'[92] Memories of the lochs and peaks of Skye, said Edmund Gosse, would act to a man with any sort of an 'inner eye' 'like cool waters to his spirit, jaded with the daily monotony of labor.'[93] Even more than mental and physical health, nature offered the 'dreams of unreflecting abandon' that Adams argues lay at the heart of masculine discipline.[94] Trips to Scotland were opportunities to cast off their personas as middle-class professionals and family men. One hunter admitted that if at night some 'fair blue eyes' away in the south were veiled in sorrow at his absence, his were closed in sound slumber as he dreamed of deer, grouse, and hares.[95] A significant number of men who wrote of their vacations in Scotland created pseudonyms for themselves and their companions, thereby differentiating this adventure from their real lives. An unpublished account of a hunting party in North Uist in 1908 assigned nicknames to each of the five members of the party: 'the Stoutest of Captains', 'The Chronicler', the 'U.P. (Universal Provider)'.[96] The refusal to use real names suggested that one's identity in the domestic or the business world had no value in the wilderness. Anonymity allowed the participant to detach himself from his home and professional life, immersing himself the more fully in this all-male realm where his physical abilities were his most important qualities, not his education, his wealth, or his family background, all of which were indicated by his name.

In temporarily abandoning their usual identities, men also threw off the need for constant self regulation. More than one writer referred to Tennyson's 'The Lotus Eaters' in which Ulysses' mariners chose no longer to strive for home, but to 'live and lie reclined' in a place 'in which it seemed always seemed afternoon.'[97] Visiting the Orkney Islands after taking his degree at Oxford, Menzies Fergusson 'felt inclined to believe oneself in some fairy country where work was needless, and dreaming the only thing to be enjoyed.'[98] In *A Painter's Camp* (1879), Philip Gilbert Hamerton described a summer spent camping and painting on an island in the middle of Loch Awe. It was a 'Crusoe life' (complete with a servant named 'Thursday'), composed of lazy afternoons sailing serenely down the loch with friends, smoking pipes, and talking. 'The splendid lake, from shore to shore, lies hushed in a long, deep trance of calm, that has lasted I know not how many burning days. I count the days no more. They have been still, and burning, and blue like today, now for I know not how long. Why should I count the days? Some body else will count them, far away in the stifling towns.'[99] Alexander Smith lived alone in a Skye bothy for a time, using a notched stick to keep track of the days.[100]

Such fantasies of liberation from the burdens of professions and family illustrate the ambivalence with which many middle-class men viewed the role they carved out for themselves. Their interest in the possibility of a life of leisure, one spent daydreaming, or hunting, or meditating on the landscape, was in part an audition of alternative definitions of masculinity, that of the noble proprietor of land or the uncivilized 'savage'. Many visitors to Scotland were attracted to the idea that time, that tyrant of the middle class to which aristocrats paid no attention and of which savages had no need, meant nothing in the Highlands. T. H. Holding rarely thought about the time while on a canoe trip through the Scottish lochs and rivers. 'The happiness of knowing no regulations, limits, or calls, was so delightful, that to think of the rush in twenty minutes time down in that station, for an express train, was hateful.'[101] The temptation to renounce a life of work and discipline, says Adams, 'bears witness to the possibility that one might surrender to desire, and thereby unsettle the triumphant masculine conquest of self and circumstance'.[102]

In many other ways, however, male experiences in Scotland reinforced ideals of masculine self discipline. In the end, though they may have heaved a sign of regret as they did so, Victorian men went home. Unlike Tennyson's mariners, these travelers only temporarily answered the call of the land of the Lotos-Eaters. Indeed, as Hamerton admitted, the lotos (the plant which, when eaten, rendered the sailors unwilling to return home) did not grow in Scotland. The best he could do was to smoke his pipe in the cool shadow of his tent, enjoy the dream of unreality which was his life on Loch Awe, 'and envy those lotos-eating Greeks no more.'[103] Hamerton thus implied his ultimate choice of the life of work, political economy, and the many responsibilities of the Victorian middle-class male. The possibility offered by Scotland of abandoning those duties ultimately served as an exercise in reasserting self mastery. In deciding to go back to their lives and work, despite the lure of other possibilities, Victorian men demonstrated the strength of their will power. They confirmed that, for them, sovereignty over desires was a central tenant of masculinity.

While vacations in Scotland allowed men to put aside for a time the burden of obligations required by their social and familial positions, many embraced other forms of discipline designed not to make them better businessmen or professionals, but to cultivate the physical aspects of maleness which sometimes seemed overlooked in daily life. Victorian men participated in a range of what Maxwell termed 'manly pastimes' in the Highlands: hunting, fishing, hiking, camping, climbing mountains.[104] Renditions of parts of the Highlands, such as the Cuillins, as 'desolate', 'sterile', and 'inaccessible' implicitly elevated the achievements of those who went there. If by climbing, hiking, or hunting one conquered so terrible an environment, then one demonstrated a strength equal to that of the elements.[105] The north's reputation as a harsher environment than England's intensified the challenge and rewards of Highland activities. The *Illustrated London News* argued that fishing in Scotland was a much more physical sport than in England.[106] The rough seas, fierce wind, and rocky shores made yachting potentially treacherous, as Robert Buchanan realized when sailing a small vessel to the northern Hebrides. The 'exacting' Cuillin mountains, parts of which could only be attained by hand to hand climbing, were a fit place for climbers to exercise the British aptitude for exploration and conquest which their sport demonstrated.[107] It was true that the highest of the Cuillin peaks had already been summitted in the 1830s, and they did not therefore offer the same challenge as the Alps or the Caucasus. They were worth taking seriously, nonetheless. Several writers relayed stories of climbers, both experienced and novice, who fell to their deaths, their 'mangled bodies' later discovered at the foot of the precipices.[108]

In emphasizing that danger was an inherent aspect of the Highland environment, men laid claim to the northwest of Scotland as a place suited only to the brave and the strong. The pleasurable fear associated with the sublime became in many male adventure accounts a threat originating not in aesthetic approaches to landscape, but in perilous surroundings. Alexander Smith observed a curious hostility, a lack of trust, between man and his environment in the Western Isles. The Hebridean 'rubs clothes with death as he would with an acquaintance.'[109] Nearly all descriptions of male exploits in Scotland included at least one passage where the narrator's life seemed to be in jeopardy. Some survived storms at night on the open seas, others faced down wounded stags. Holding experienced real fear for the first time in his life when it seemed his canoe might capsize in the Forth on the first leg of his journey.[110] When Robert Buchanan sailed into Loch Sligachan (another loch in the Cuillins), he described for readers the 'danger above and danger under': rocks, squalls, and treacherous shoals.[111] Even though he admitted that no real problems were anticipated, the possibility was lodged in readers' minds.

The sport most associated with Scotland, and the one that most spectacularly demonstrated the subjection of nature, was hunting. Interest in hunting increased steadily throughout the century, first among the aristocracy and later among other classes, reaching its peak between 1880-1910. A variety of game roamed the Highlands: grouse, hare, snipe, woodcock. Avid hunters even went after seals and whales. In the late nineteenth century the days preceding the opening of the grouse season on August 12 were the busiest period in Scotland's tourist season as crowds of shooters with their families, dogs, and luggage descended on Waverley Station in Edinburgh before heading further north. The greatest prize was deer, especially the red deer of the Highlands. In 1883 there were 1.9 million acres of deer forest in Scotland; by 1906 there were 3.5 million, a development which reflects not only a growing demand, but the collapse of the price of mutton and wool in that period. Land that had been converted from mixed farming usage to sheep pastures in the late eighteenth-century Clearances was consequently reconverted to deer parks in the late nineteenth century.[112]

Hunting, especially deer stalking, was an elite activity, restricted through the private ownership of deer parks to the aristocracy, the very wealthy, and their friends. Yet the sport was influential on a masculine reading of the Highlands even for those who never took part in it, and the culture of hunting was intimately linked with nineteenth-century images of Scotland. The royal family's fondness for Scotland was instrumental in that regard. Prince Albert was an avid sportsman, although he never became a very good shot or a very discriminating stalker. Hunting represented to Albert a sense of freedom and primitiveness, as it did for so many other upper-class men. Although the sport was well established by mid-century when the Prince Consort's passion was at its height, his enthusiasm was widely publicized and helped to cement hunting's status as a fashionable upper-class activity. The widely accessible images found in the art of Sir Edwin Landseer, especially his deer hunting scenes, evoked 'the sense of untamed freedom, the communion with nature in its most sublime mood, the exhilaration of wild and solitary places'.[113] Landseer epitomized – and disseminated – the position of hunting and stalking in nineteenth-century culture, a position which made the sport a key element in the vision of nature which drew people to the Highlands.

The challenge of deerstalking lay both in the animal itself, and in the terrain he roamed. Stags were worthy opponents for even the most virile hunter; they were noble and powerful with 'acute' reasoning. They were also dangerous, especially when wounded and cornered. Had deer recognized their power, one writer believed, an attack by two or three could be deadly.[114] All a stalker's powers of body and mind were needed to catch a stag, and if they were not properly exercised a 'clever' animal could defeat him.[115] A deerstalker needed muscles of marble and sinews of steel. He should be able to run like an antelope, possibly for miles at a time, and breathe like the trade winds. He should have strong, flexible ankles, and be capable of scrambling swiftly down precipices with sharp stones. He should have a steady hand and require little sleep. He could expect to wade through torrents (but must keep his powder dry) or 'glid[e] down a burn like an eel.' To get a good shot, he had to be willing to spread himself out like a frog and wriggle through a burn, covered with water, moss, and black mud, then to lie still for a couple of hours, perhaps with a keen north-wester' blowing, or midges attacking. He needed to be wary and circumspect, carefully surveying the ground and calculating his chances of success. He had to be calm in moments of stress and danger. If, after hours of strenuous stalking and patient waiting, he missed the shot, he should be stoic enough to accept disappointment and try again. Late nineteenth-century commentators also required good sportsmanship; the true test of a day's sport was not the number of head secured but the amount of pluck and skill requisite to secure it.[116]

By shooting, stalking, fishing, and other outdoor activities Victorian gentlemen tested their wills against their bodies, and their bodies against the environment, thereby strengthening their discipline, improving bodily and emotional health, and affirming that masculine identity demanded the physical and mental strength to conquer nature and one's own weaknesses. The antlered head that a successful stalker could hang on his wall was a tangible symbol of his manliness.[117] Equally important, after a month of spending his days by the 'wild burnsides' and on 'moors of heather and bog myrtle' a man 'will be bronzed as a Druid and have muscles of iron, and there will have been breathed into him a new understanding of the inner spirit and instinct of the dwellers among the hills.'[118] Even a solitary hiker or climber who kept moving when he longed to rest could see himself as engaged in a battle of will over fleshly limitations. Such exertions, historian Bruce Haley notes, were a relief from the mental struggle with intellectual uncertainties which wracked so many Victorians. Battling against a lofty mountain, a large salmon, or a powerful stag was a simpler and more certain fight, with a more definite outcome, than endless pondering over issues like the validity of faith in the modern age.[119]

Such activities were closely linked with a love of nature, and reminiscences of Highland adventures often included lyrical descriptions of the scenery in which they took place. Sportsman Herbert Byng Hall alleged that shooting 'combined the pleasure, – indeed, the endless delight, to be found in Nature's picture gallery, so variedly and so beautifully set before us.'[120] The best sportsman was 'the true and genial lover of one of God's greatest gifts – the beauties of the wilderness, and being allowed to roam unmolested through them.'[121] The ability to be at ease while immersed in nature signified that one was not weakened by urban life.

> Here, everything bears the original impress of nature untouched by the hand of man since its creation....In such a place as this, the wild Indian might fancy himself on his hunting grounds. Traverse all this desolate tract, and you shall find no dwelling, nor sheep, nor cow, nor horse, nor anything that can remind you of domestic life; you shall hear no sound but the rushing of the torrent, or the notes of the wild animals.[122]

A successful hunter, fisher, or climber needed to be able to read nature's signs, just like Native Americans or mountain shepherds did, and could thus imagine himself taking on the roles of earlier, more primitive males. In so doing, the 'spineless bourgeois' of the Lowlands and England appropriated some of the vitality attributed to men of less civilized societies, including that of the Highlands.[123] Hunters frequently equated their abilities with those of Native Americans, sometimes jokingly, as when a shooter in 1908 successfully caught a goose after putting into effect 'all the wiles of the Indian and artifices of other famous hunters.'[124] Comparisons to classical heroes also exalted sportsmen's achievements. According to Scrope, a young hunter who had killed his first stag might see himself as one in a line of ancient champions: he was 'a king – a hero – a demigod! Hercules was a pretty fellow; so was Theseus; so was Pirithous; but although they subdued various monsters, they probably never killed so fine a stag in all their lives.'[125]

Demonstrations of power over a nature seemingly unviolated since the creation was a form of staking a claim, an affirmation of the imperial project.[126] Many hunters called to mind the Ossianic heroes, thus reminding that physical prowess and dominance over the environment was part of their national heritage. By taking part in the sport they re-established that birthright. Hunting, said Hall, was an ancient British legacy: '[T]he love of rural sports then engendered in the hearts of Britons, has, from age to age, been handed down from generation to generation, and the passion burns in the breasts of Englishmen with an ardour undiminished.'[127] Participants believed that outdoor adventures, especially hunting and mountaineering, illustrated the superiority of the British character. Britons, for instance, dominated Alpine mountain climbing because of 'the pre-eminence of our own countrymen over all others in matters requiring determination, intrepidity, and skill'.[128] The insistence that parts of the Highlands remained unseen by humans made the region a suitable challenge for the British mandate of exploration which was so popular in the age of expeditions to Africa and the Arctic.[129] A group of tourists who climbed Scuir nan Gillean in 1860 recognized that their achievement was not as noteworthy as climbing Mont Blanc, but since the mountain had been considered unattainable until twenty-five years earlier, they still took pride in the accomplishment.[130]

The links between nationalism and Highland sports can be understood in part as endeavors to strengthen British manhood so as to prepare men for the work to be undertaken in the empire. Many proponents of empire considered hunting, which required some of the same abilities needed for warfare, to be a useful skill which separated ineffective from effective imperialist nations.[131] On another level, sports in the Highlands can be read as assertions of proprietorship over a still uncivilized Gaelic territory, a reading which is fortified by the controversy over land use which raged throughout the area for much of the eighteenth and nineteenth centuries. The large tracks of land on which aristocrats and their visitors stalked deer and shot grouse was often the same property to which local crofters believed they had an ancestral right for use as pasture. Highland landscapes were often empty for specific reasons, not simply because humans had been unable to venture there for centuries. Many areas were unfertile and there was little reason for local residents, who needed to make a living from the land, to go there. Other areas were systematically emptied of inhabitants to make way for sheep farms and deer parks in the Clearances of the late eighteenth and early nineteenth centuries. Reading such locales as scenes where nature's potency reigned supreme, and exalting those hunters, hikers, explorers, and scientists who wandered there, effectively naturalized English and Lowland superiority over Highlanders and islanders. English and Lowland commentators frequently feminized Gaels, characterizing them as simple and childish. Their poverty could be (although it was not always) attributed to laziness and an unwise use of resources. This judgement of the differences between Gaels and outsiders could easily be interpreted as ethnic and gender distinctions appropriate to an imperial context. Gaels, it seemed, could not face the fierce powers of nature manifest in the Highlands – but others could. Such a reading was implied in Macculloch's rendition of his solitary exploration of Coruisk while his Highland boatmen cowered in fear. He triumphed because he was intelligent and rational; they were not. Highlanders did not always play the role assigned to them by such narratives. Periodically during the century, and especially in the 1880s and 1890s, considerable tension emerged between the owners and gamekeepers of sporting estates and Highland crofters (small tenant farmers). Late in the century resentment against owners sparked the occupation of several parks by crofters who attempted to kill as many deer as possible, thus reminding sportsmen that the Highlands were not simply an empty space on which male visitors could enact dominance. Other people were present, who problemmatized the construction of the Highlands as a sphere where middle and upper class men rejuvenated their masculinity.[132]

Despite the assumptions of racial and gender superiority on the part of most English and Lowland male adventurers, they were often dependent on Highland ghillies or guides. Many of those who headed north in response to 'some stirring of the primeval instinct to forsake beaten ways'[133] were not 'rougher specimen of mankind'. Robert Buchanan's yachting excursion around the Hebrides depended upon the sailing abilities of a Highland captain. Short-term visitors did not know the terrain or where animals might be found, sometimes they did not know much about shooting. Deer drives, in which gamekeepers flushed a large herd towards a group of waiting shooters, sometimes took the place of stalking. Without a guide mountain climbers might easily get lost in the mist and walk off a cliff. The ghillie's deeper knowledge of nature, greater strength, and better skill at hunting potentially undercut both the heroic ideal of the individual going out to battle nature alone and the racial superiority of Anglo-Saxons. The alleged 'primitiveness' of the Highlander ensured that he retained some of the vitality, energy, and virility seemingly lacking in modern society. Numerous images, often more obvious than those which feminized the Gael, masculinized him and his surroundings.[134] Male Highlanders were consistently described as 'manly', 'hardy', and 'robust'. Their physical stamina testified to the extent to which British middle-class men were devitalized by modernization, as suggested by the not infrequent jokes about English sportsmen who could not keep up with their energetic Highland guides. 'Christopher North', a popular Scottish poet, novelist, and essayist, described the 'small, puny, piteous, windpipes' who criticized Scots, yet were themselves 'feeble and fearful creatures [who] would crawl on their hands and knees, faint and giddy, and shrieking out for help to the heather stalks, if forced to face one of thy [Scotland's] cliffs, and foot its flinty bosom!'[135] The periodic criticism of those hunters who took part in none of the painstaking preliminary work of stalking, only arriving to shoot when and where their ghillie ordered, was an implicit caution against letting one's Highland assistant call into question one's masculine prowess. The fact that these guides were hired labor whose importance lay in the extent to which their abilities helped the hunter served to contain their possibly more vital masculinity and impart it instead to their employers. Yet they remained unsettling figures in masculine readings of the Highlands. Ghillies, for instance, sometimes carried sportsmen on their backs to help them ford rivers.[136] Such a demonstration of humility, strength, and immunity to the elements indicated the Highlander's subservient status – but was also a disconcerting reminder of an innate kind of physical masculinity that visitors often could only hope to temporarily recapture.

Women traveled in the Highlands too, and their presence was both an essential component of the construction of the region as a male sphere, and a challenge to it. The gender components of the tourist/traveler distinction of the nineteenth century rendered women as 'tourists', men as 'travelers'. Because women required the protective structures of tourism, they could not easily approach the *genius loci* of a site.[137] Men could therefore claim to see a more 'authentic' Scotland than did feminized tourists. This was especially true of men who engaged in sporting activities. Because men were more free to roam they had access to the environment on a deeper level than did women, for whom opportunities to camp, hunt, or climb were more rare for much of the century. T. H. Holding believed he had a truer experience of Loch Katrine on his canoe and camping trip than did the hurried mob of steamship passengers on the guided tour of the loch.[138] The practical advice frequently offered in guidebooks on how women could best traverse difficult Highland territory reminded that they could enter this male realm only with special provisions. If traveling to Skye, for instance, women should rent ponies for the excursion to the Cuillins.[139] So difficult was it to investigate Fingal's Cave on Staffa, said a writer in 1834, that he thought it impossible for female tourists to go more than halfway in without considerable risk.[140] Women were emotionally as well as physically unfit for the power of the Highland landscape, suggested some. A man who wrote a rather jocular account (in verse) of an 1857 Scottish tour described a young bride made nervous by the scenery on the coach trip to Fort William. 'She was so trembling, so timid, frightened as a hare, And seemed too fragile, the ills of life to bear.'[141]

Many women (like many men) did take advantage of organized tours which limited their exposure to nature to views from the deck of a steamship or the window of a railway carriage. Some were apprehensive while climbing steep mountains or crossing narrow bridges. Yet Scotland's environment posed a challenge to women as well as men, and many accepted it eagerly, finding a sense of freedom from the restraints of civilization similar to that found by their male counterparts. In the 1790s Sarah Murray proudly constructed herself as an explorer, and believed she was the first woman to see several sublime attractions. She fearlessly crossed the steep mountain pass Corryarrack in a carriage, even though a young Oxford student's conviction that this was impossible caused five Edinburgh gentlemen to turn back.[142] Returning from the Fall of Foyers, at that point a difficult trek, she passed four male travelers, who while slipping and tumbling down the banks of the falls, stared as if they wondered how she got there.[143] A summer in the Highlands showed young Isabella Bird the challenge and possibilities of travel.[144] Constance Gordon Cumming, a Highland woman who traveled to India, Fiji, and Hawaii, spent six months on Skye in the 1870s living a life seemingly as unencumbered as that of any male traveler. She was apparently accompanied by her brother, but her own representations of her journey depict her as a lone woman traveling independently.[145]

Just as the Highlands were a tamer challenge for men than was Africa or the Arctic, so was it a less radical statement for a woman to tour the Hebrides than the Rockies or North Africa.[146] Yet even those who journeyed with family groups and strayed little from the beaten track found themselves facing physical obstacles which demanded they place their fears and bodies under the control of their wills. Climbing Ben Lomond with her family during their Scottish tour of 1862, Mrs. John Gower was quite nervous as she approached the top of the mountain. But 'summoning resolution I commenced the ascent.'[147] When a group of four friends decided to hike up Ben Venue in 1836, it seemed to one of the women among them a 'herculean task to reach the summit of so steep a mountain'. She determined nonetheless to make the attempt, and reached the halfway point. 'Success quickened my energies and hope with perseverance enabled me to accomplish more than I had anticipated was practicable.'[148] Other women hiked, fished, and hunted, although only a few stalked deer.[149] Herbert Byng Hall commented in the 1840s that ladies 'and delicate ones, too' rode up the steep sides of Ben Lawers with no difficulty.[150] Around the turn of the century Constantia and Kathleen Warden took a three month cycling tour of the Highlands, often biking twenty to thirty miles a day and hiking another ten. They met several other female cyclists, traveling either with husbands or with large parties of mixed company.[151] When wandering the Quirang Edmund Gosse met two women who had climbed in the Alps and the Pyrenees – but they assured him that a trek through the Quirang was not a trifling excursion.[152]

As it became more socially acceptable late in the nineteenth century for women to engage in physical activity, promoters of tourism endeavored to draw Scotland to the attention of young women attracted to the active outdoors life. The North British Railway's late-century promotional booklet *Epistles of Peggy* is one example. As the creation of a railway company, 'Peggy' symbolized tourism, rather than path-breaking exploration and her adventures had little in common with those men who sailed around the rough waters of Hebrides in a small boat, or spent a day chasing a deer. While she might model to young women the attractions of a Scottish vacation, she also pointed to the taming of the Highlands. Women were symbols of the paraphernalia of tourism that threatened the security of the region as a male testing ground. Steamboats and railroads allowed even the least hardy tourist, one who perhaps made the short hike to the edge of Loch Coruisk after being set ashore by the steamer, to claim participation in a struggle against the wilderness. Even hunting was no longer a genuinely challenging pursuit at mid-century, according to visitor Jacob Abbott:

> Every wild and sequestered ravine is within reach of a hunting-lodge, from which the moors around are filled with English sportsmen, who shoot grouse to send in boxes to their southern friends. Instead of having to carry their means of protection and subsistence on their backs, they are followed by servants and ponies to relieve them of every burden. Thus everything is changed. The summits of the mountains are scaled in safety by ladies from every quarter of the globe, whose genteel attendants carry spy-glasses, and sandwiches and wine from the inn, instead of dirks and guns.[153]

The emphasis on the Highlands as a manly region was in part an effort to prevent that despoliation. Such seems to be the purpose of Robert Buchanan's description of a night spent near Loch Coruisk. Referring to himself as 'the Wanderer,' Buchanan depicted his escapades as fit for those who, like him, would be unfazed by sleeping under overhanging rocks in a storm and bathing in the cold and 'eerie' loch. It was not a location for females. His party was accompanied to the edge of Coruisk by a woman identified only as 'the lady', probably Buchanan's wife. After a 'good night's kiss' she and most of the other men turned back, leaving Buchanan alone with his dog and his Highland companion for the real adventure.[154] Similarly, a group of men who climbed Ben Lomond in 1856 were initially impressed with the bravery of a honeymooning bride mounted on horseback whom they passed along the way. She seemed indifferent to the rather dangerous path, and remained on horseback throughout the excursion. Traveling further, the men grew concerned for their own safety and felt more secure walking than riding. They then became convinced that the bride, earlier described as a 'brick', was not brave; she was merely ignorant of horsemanship and of the true dangers of the situation.[155] Thus did they endeavor to guard the mountain's status as a test of male stamina and courage.

Nature and the Encroachments of Technology

Late in the nineteenth century tourists began to complain that the Fall of Foyers, once deemed Britain's finest waterfall, was ruined by a nearby aluminum factory.[156] This was an unusual lament in the Highlands, where there was little industry throughout the nineteenth century. Nonetheless, when

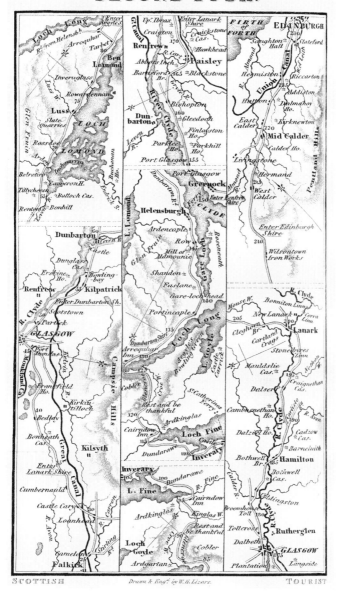

Fig. 1 Map showing a suggested tour from Edinburgh to Glasgow, Dumbarton, Loch Lomond, Inverary, Loch Long, Hamilton, Lanark and the falls of Clyde. *The Scottish Tourist and Itinerary or A Guide to the Scenery and Antiquaries of Scotland and the Western Islands*, Edinburgh, 1834.

Fig. 2 The Dingwall and Skye Railway: Auchnashellach. *Illustrated London News*, August 20, 1870, used by permission of the *Illustrated London News* Picture Library.

Fig. 3 J.M.W. Turner. 'Loch Coruisk.' National Gallery of Scotland, used by permission.

Fig. 4 'Entrance to Loch Scavaig, Skye.' Adam Black and Charles Black, *Black's Picturesque Tourist of Scotland*, Edinburgh, 1881.

Fig. 5 Fingal's Cave.' Adam Black and Charles Black, *Black's Picturesque Tourist of Scotland, Edinburgh*, 1865, p.451.

Fig. 6 'Iona.' Adam Black and Charles Black, *Black's Picturesque Tourist of Scotland*, Edinburgh, 1865, p.453.

Fig. 7   'Ben Lomond.' Adam Black and Charles Black, *Black's Pictureque Tourist of Scotland*, Edinburgh, 1865, p.223

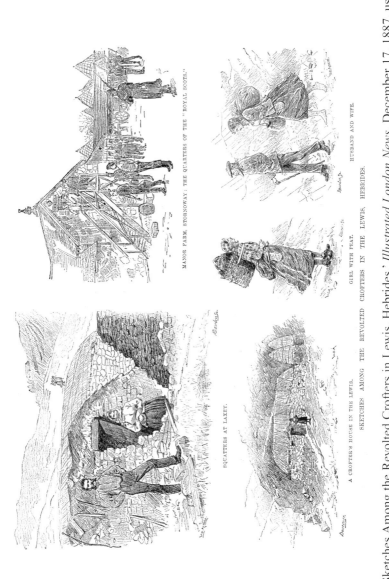

MANOR FARM, STORNOWAY: THE QUARTERS OF THE "ROYAL SCOTS."

HUSBAND AND WIFE.

GIRL WITH PEAT.

SQUATTERS AT LAXEY.

A CROFTER'S HOUSE IN THE LEWIS.

SKETCHES AMONG THE REVOLTED CROFTERS IN THE LEWIS, HEBRIDES.

Fig. 8 'Sketches Among the Revolted Crofters in Lewis, Hebrides.' *Illustrated London News*, December 17, 1887, used by permission of the *Illustrated London News* Picture Library.

combined with the ever larger crowds of sightseers, the expanding network of trains and steamboats, and the ease by which tourists could visit locales once considered almost inaccessible, such an establishment symbolized the breaching of the sentinel mountains which were to guard the Highlands against modernization. Although imagined as a place where nature was stronger than humans, Scotland was very much a part of Great Britain's industrial economy. Nature was not truly immune to human dominance there, a fact made clear to tourists by their use of trains and steamboats as platforms from which to view the scenery. Yet although individual tourists frequently expressed concern over the encroachment of modern technology into the Scottish landscape, most were not deeply troubled. The rituals of tourism discussed in the previous chapter are partly responsible for tourists' lack of unease about visible signs of modernity. They saw a pristine landscape because that is what they most wished to see, and the tourist industry guided them to that vision. Just as importantly, however, visitors to Scotland were not put off by signs of technology because their search for a nature untouched by human hands was not a rejection of industrialism per se, it was an effort to place industry and its accompanying transformations into context.

Concerns about industrialization's possible harm to the beauties of Scottish scenery were evident throughout the century, particularly when tourists noticed the scarring of a once-idyllic scene. As early as the 1820s the vale of Leven, covered with manufactories and bleaching fields, was no more the pastoral stream of which Smollett sang.[157] In the 1840s James Wilson lamented the news that a bobbin factory was to be established near Loch Sunart. 'It is a melancholy and fantastic thought to dwell on, that these fair woods, cut into pieces of a few square inches, are so soon to be set whirling amid the ceaseless din and flocky atmosphere of a cotton mill in Glasgow.'[158] Several species of native Highland animals and birds began to die out by the first half of the nineteenth century, doomed by outside market demands and a rising population.[159] As a result of becoming Glasgow's reservoir, from which 50 million gallons of water were carried daily along 35 miles of tunneling and aqueducts, the water level of Loch Katrine was raised, and Scott's 'silver strand' was partly submerged.[160] In the 1880s the Gareloch was considered too dirty for swimming and Loch Long was covered with 'stinking slime'.[161] Pollution began to destroy the fishing in some of Scotland's famed rivers.[162] Early in the twentieth century A. R. Hope Moncrieff bemoaned the changes to the river Clyde, 'once romantic shore/Where Nature's face is banished and estranged,/And Heaven reflected in thy wave no more'. When he wrote, it was encircled by 'sooty exhalations', 'unsightly brick-lanes', and 'clanking engines.'[163] Indeed, guidebooks often advised tourists to travel downstream from Glasgow before catching steamers to the Highlands and islands, in order to avoid the river's smell. 'Never in the foulest corners of London', said Gosse, who did not exercise that option, 'were my nostrils tortured as on the highly respectable Clyde.'[164]

Because they interjected a machine between humans and the natural world, railways could be a particularly troubling issue to many tourists and travel writers of Scotland. Railways passed over or through obstacles, erased the distinction between night and day, and defied existing conventions of land speed. Through trains, Victorians became as powerful as the sorcerers of old, having forged a 'second' or 'produced' nature. The rail traveler was not part of nature, as stagecoach passengers could perceive themselves to be; the landscape was but a distant panorama presented to the passive viewer.[165] Rail and steam were profound signs of humans' ability to conquer the environment and make use of the earth's resources, and thus ran counter to the construction of 'Scottish' landscape as immune to human authority. Several commentators considered the idea of trains cutting through the wild Highlands to be a travesty. In 1861 Thomas Cook was indignant at a rumor that 'the goths of science have got an Act of Parliament for a railway right through the Pass of Killiecrankie!' While he believed that much was owed to the railways, a line through 'this remarkable Pass' seemed out of place.[166] Another writer lamented the possibility of a route through Glen Lyon: 'It seems taking a most unwarrantable liberty to cut a railway along the base of a mountain about which Ossian raved.'[167] In the 1840s tourists protested plans to establish a steamboat on Loch Katrine, regarding it as an indignity to nature and poetical sentiment. (By 1846, however, a steamer did run on the loch.)[168] Constance Gordon Cumming bemoaned the coming of railways to the west Highlands: 'Just imagine the snorting iron horses having found their way to these wilds (solitudes no longer) and making those grand misty summits echo back their hideous shriek and whistle.'[169] The insistence of the authors of guidebooks that the railway was not a blemish on the Scottish countryside implies that many people believed otherwise.[170]

Complaints about unsightly factories or lengthening rail lines were not signs of what would today be called ecology, belief in the need for caution when exploiting or controlling natural forces.[171] Victorians did evince a deep conviction that nature's sacred places should be protected from desecration, and an organized preservation movement began to make itself heard in England from the 1860s onwards. However, this movement had little impact in Scotland, where there were no efforts similar to the unsuccessful campaign in the 1870s to prevent the Manchester City Corporation from turning Lake Thirlwell in the Lake District into a reservoir.[172] Travel writers were chiefly worried about the ways in which the intrusion of machines – trains or industry – could destroy the sense of purity and isolation so essential to the meaning attached to 'Scottish' landscape. This concern implicitly privileged visitors' craving for pristine scenery over the practical and economic needs of local residents. A bleachmill seemed too 'prosaic' for the 'poetic waters of [the river] Esk' in the heart of Scott Country in 1860. 'Valuable as the establishment undoubtedly is, we wished that it had utilized any less distinguished stream!'[173]

Nonetheless, tourists did not generally wish to ban modern technology from the Highlands, much less the rest of Scotland. Gordon Cumming admitted that a luxurious railway carriage made traveling easier and more comfortable than did a crowded coach. Chauncy Townshend conceded that while the Loch Lomond steamer was 'an abomination in the eye of Poetry and Romance, it is a great and practical convenience in the sober judgment of common sense.'[174] Other visitors went further than these reluctant admissions of the necessity of modernization, and reveled in the display of Britain's industrial and technological capacities in Scotland. Cuthbert Bede considered the Loch Katrine waterworks to be one of the most gigantic engineering works of modern times, surpassing the aqueducts that fed Rome. To a 'thoroughly practical man', he wrote, the entrance tunnel to the waterworks possessed an attraction 'that will outweigh the charms of the most picturesque landscape.'[175] Such comments point to the fact that industrial advances evoked at once pride in human abilities and anxiety about the consequences of those advances. The sight of huge machines tearing into the earth and rearranging the topography of Great Britain fascinated Victorians, and railroad construction sites were sightseeing attractions throughout the century.[176] The erection of railways in the Highlands were spectacular engineering feats, which made them tourist attractions in their own right. Guidebooks called passengers' attention to some of the more remarkable accomplishments, such as the 'magnificent' stone viaduct that crossed the River Ness outside Inverness on the Highland Railway, or the bridge which took the Fort William to Mallaig line across Glenfinnan, described as 'one of the engineering triumphs of the line', or a 120 foot long tunnel halfway between Pitlochry and Blair Atholl which required ten dry arches, 500 feet of masonry, and 35,000 cubic yards of rock cutting.[177] According to promoters, riding on the West Highland Railway was in itself part of many tourists' itineraries. Likewise the Forth Rail Bridge, completed in 1890 and described as the 'greatest construction of the world', was an attraction worth seeing.[178] In advertising their trips between London and Scotland, the Carron Steamship Line made a point of emphasizing that theirs was the only route to provide a 'perfect view' of the Forth Bridge.[179] W. A. Stephenson, a young man who came to Scotland with the Polytechnic in 1890 chiefly to visit an industrial exposition in Edinburgh, was thrilled to cross the bridge, which he called 'the great engineering feat of the age'.[180] Proponents of railways in the Highlands also noted the promise they held out of economic improvement in isolated areas. A long *Illustrated London News* article upon the occasion of the opening of the Dingwall and Skye Railway in 1870 noted the expected economic benefits for the Highlands, commenting that, 'at the very first, the railway began to contribute to the material prosperity of the country.'[181]

That same article is an example of the way tourist literature endeavored to mediate any tension travelers might feel between their need for – and interest in – modern technology, and its possible disruptive effects upon the expected experience of Scotland. The anonymous author began by emphasizing the convenience of the new rail line, an offshoot of the Highland Railway which stretched east to west and operated in conjunction with steamers to Skye and Lewis. It was now practicable, without changing carriages, to 'dine late in London to-day and to-morrow sup in full view of the Hebrides'. This assertion encouraged readers to be impressed with the technological and industrial achievements which enabled them to journey with ease and speed to a once remote area. The writer occasionally noted the gradient of the line's ascent up a mountain or referred to the navvies who built it, thus reminding readers of the engineering skill and human muscle required to construct the route. In case the image of rapid rail travel to the mystical Hebrides threatened the romance of a voyage to Skye, however, the remainder of the article situated the journey within the established commonplaces of Highland landscapes. The route was chiefly described in terms of the views which would surround passengers and the history they would encounter. The body of the article characterized the scenery visible from the train, claiming it 'will be like a revelation' to many tourists. It was country 'in which the strength of the system of clanship endured longest in the Highlands', parts of which 'were, as they still are substantially, occupied by the clans Munro and Ross'. By detailing the imperviousness of clans in that region to governmental authority until well into the eighteenth century, the writer encouraged potential passengers to see the area in terms of an heroic past, and to forget that the train visibly brought the nineteenth century. Views from the train were 'eminently picturesque' and 'glorious'. The route traversed a variety of landscapes: steep mountain passes, marshy plains, attractive lochs. It culminated with a view of the Cuillins. Nor was the train an alien feature in that environment. Nature, it seemed, had absorbed this new addition to the landscape. 'It is curious how soon the country adapts itself to any change of circumstances.' Bothies built to house construction workers were covered with a rich coating of fresh grass growing on the turf of which they were made. The accompanying illustrations called attention to the majestic scenery of the area and downplayed rail's impact on the views. In one, a miniature train with a puff of clean white smoke was barely visible below huge, looming, barren mountains at Auchnashellach. In another depiction the train chugged along a mere scratch in the earth beside Loch Carron, as rugged mountains towered above, the curving lines of the track emphasizing its harmony with nature.[182] The vastness of the Scottish environment completely dwarfed this wee human creation.

This account of the Dingwall and Skye railway was in keeping with the tendencies of railway literature throughout Great Britain, which put a positive interpretation on the new visual experience brought by the railways by overlooking the noise, soot, and smoke of trains and instead calling travelers' attention to the views outside their windows. Train passengers, asserted guidebooks, would experience something new in history. Comfortably seated in a sealed compartment and protected from the rigors of the climate and the environment, they would enjoy an ever changing panorama.[183] Railway literature suggested that the train was the best way to genuinely experience nature in Scotland, suggesting that rail travel did not distance passengers from the environment. Trains, promoters argued, provided access to the landscape. The West Highland Railway, said 'Peggy', was one of the most glorious journeys imaginable; those who had not traveled on it lacked true intimacy with Scotland at its best.[184] Rail passengers saw some of Scotland's most spectacular and distinctive scenery; another source claimed the Dingwall and Skye Railway passed 'gigantic mountains', 'boiling cauldrons' of the river Beauly, and high rocky banks crowned with birch and pine.[185] Promotional material constantly emphasized the beauty of rail lines and the splendid sights tourists could see without having to get out of their seats. The West Highland Railway '...never for one moment meets the prosaic: the panorama of landscape that passes before the carriage windows changing almost every minute, into more and more bewitching visions of infinite variety.'[186] The Highland Railway was 'one of the most beautiful lines in the three kingdoms', reportedly as popular for its scenic qualities as it was for its practical value as a route to Inverness.[187]

By characterizing trains and steamboats simply as part of Scotland's scenery, history, and poetry, promoters of tourism sought to make tourists comfortable with the idea of machines carving their way through the Scottish landscape. Yet their comments often contained mixed messages which at once eased and manifested fears of mechanization. While defending the railroad, the guide to the West Highland Railway actually reminded travelers that there were critics of mechanization. 'Never was there a railway that less disfigured the country through which it passed. Like a mere scratch on the mountain slopes, it glides from valley to valley, unobtrusive as a sheep path, and not even John Ruskin would respond to it as a desecration of the Highland solitudes.'[188] The frequently-made observation that new railroads 'opened up' previously unknown territory is suggestive of the Victorian ambivalence about the machine. The rhetoric encouraged late nineteenth-century passengers on the line to visualize themselves as entering virgin territory and charting a path for others, just as British explorers did across the globe. The route of the West Highland Railway, '...throws open to the public wide and interesting tracts of country which have been almost as much unknown to the ordinary tourist hitherto as Central Asia was ten years ago to the geographer.'[189] Yet the action was performed by the train, not an intrepid individual, and the looked-for result was that a greater number of tourists would come. An illustrated guide to the West Highland Railway quoted Christopher North's description of Rannoch Moor: 'a prodigious wilderness, with which perhaps no man alive is conversant, and in which you may travel for days without seeing any symptoms of human life….few have been far in the interior, and we never knew anybody who had crossed it from south to north, from east to west.' That unexplored spot was now crossed by the West Highland Railway and the guidebook proudly proclaimed that 'the most frail invalid may inspect, at his ease, this prodigious wilderness.'[190] Similarly, the *ILN's* illustrations of the Dingwall and Skye Railway, by emphasizing differences in scale between trains and the surrounding scenery, had the effect of elevating the human achievement in bringing rails to so hostile a countryside. Thus did the Victorians domesticate the environment even as they exalted its imperviousness to humans.

Arguing that modern technology was an aid to the enjoyment of nature, rather than an instrument which might rob it of its significance was a means by which Scottish authors of guidebooks could call attention to their country's technological and engineering accomplishments while continuing to promote the vision of nature sought by tourists. The apparent effectiveness of such an argument is a counter to those scholars who have seen an aversion to technological development in late nineteenth- and early twentieth-century English culture.[191] Tourists were eager to construct the Scottish landscape as one which humbled human abilities, sometimes in the face of contrary evidence, because that interpretation fulfilled a variety of cultural anxieties. In doing so, they were not rejecting industrialism. Rather they sought the knowledge that there were limits to its consequences. The belief that rail and steam could penetrate the Highlands, yet the landscape appear to be untouched by human hands was powerful testimony that industry was not pervasive, that its effects were contained. Pride in industrial achievements thus did not contradict the thrill of seeing pure nature. It may well have been the intersection of technology and nature, more than nature itself, which did the most to enable the Scottish landscape to meet tourists' cultural needs. Indeed, the sight of a railway amidst the hostile Highland environment may have brought relief to English visitors who found themselves ill at ease in such landscapes.

That hypothethical sense of relief may then have reminded travelers that they were indeed members of an industrial society. By the middle of the nineteenth century Great Britain was demographically an urban country. No longer was rural life a shared experience and reference point for the middle classes, rather it was increasingly the object of specialized study or an attraction to be visited. Nature was unfamiliar in any form other than the domesticated suburbs.[192] Historians may have overstated the extent of rural nostalgia prevalent in late nineteenth-century England, a society which was in Peter Mandler's words 'aggressively urban and materialist'.[193] Nonetheless, many of Victoria's subjects were apprehensive about the economic, social, and political transformations of the nineteenth century. A central purpose of a trip to Scotland was to, at least temporarily, re-establish a closeness with the natural world, and therefore to ease some of that anxiety. Most visitors, strongly motivated to find particular visions of nature and aided by the tourist industry, did so. The texts of tourism, however, could not completely control what tourists might discover in Scotland. The very novelty of those places that appeared to have been left alone since they were created disclosed to middle-class tourists just how urbanized and domesticated their culture now was. Nature might reveal skepticism, not spirituality. Rather than discover a natural world which humans could not tame, tourists sometimes saw in Scotland just how thoroughly their society controlled the environment. Men who attempted to exercise their more physical and primitive selves might realize just how civilized they actually were.

Some Scottish travel writers laid claim to a closer communion with nature than that of tourists, by asserting that outsiders' reactions to the Highland landscape resulted from their own unfamiliarity with the natural world. Robert Buchanan, for instance, stressed that the 'weird and silent' landscape in the Cuillins evoked contentment, not apprehension. 'The eye is satisfied at every step, the shadows and the silence only deepen the beauty, and the mood awakened is one, not of shapeless, shuddering awe, but of brooding mystic joy.' Buchanan was not immune to the magnetism of the Cuillins and described it with the same rhetoric as did others. The difference was that as one allegedly more accustomed to the wilder aspects of the environment, he was not fearful or repulsed. It was the men who 'live in cities and read Thackeray' who were uncomfortable in these surroundings.[194] One of those men, Alexander Smith, claimed he might go mad if he spent the night in Coruisk; his companion, an inhabitant of the island, thought Smith was talking 'nonsense'.[195] Alexander Nicholson, another resident of Skye, claimed that the silence of the barren mountains was not oppressive to the 'born mountaineer'.[196]

With such comments, Scots played into the popular stereotypes of themselves as a 'natural' folk, and used them to remind tourists that brief visits to the Highlands did not constitute genuine intimacy with nature. With the story of a young London couple who planned to spend a few days in the Highlands, *Punch* made a similar point around the turn of the century. The couple were initially excited about their rustic surroundings: 'To cross the edge of civilization had for months past been our heart's desire; and to have achieved a jumping-off place only approachable by a burn exceeded our wildest ambitions.' They were disconcerted to realize that what they thought was the cowhouse was actually their lodging, but pluckily interpreted the hens on the bed as 'fresh proof of rusticity.' Their enthusiasm faded as they realized there were no baths, the scones were tasteless, the chairs were hard, there was nothing to read, and rain prevented the husband from going out to smoke. They quickly decided to leave at five the next morning and catch the very next train: 'To think that we shall be back in dear old Chelsea tomorrow!'[197] Wrapped up with their encounter with the natural world was a lesson in how much the Victorians and Edwardians valued modern civilization. In subtle but significant ways, the attempt to connect with nature in Scotland taught visitors just what they did not wish to learn, that modernization had irreversibly distanced them from the world they sought.

Notes

[1]   Edmund Gosse, 'Journal in Scotland' (1870) MS. 2562, NLS, n.p.

[2]   S. Augustus Tipple, *A Summer Visit to Scotland* (Norwich, 1847), p. 47.

[3]   Edward Burt, quoted in A. J. Youngson, ed., *Beyond the Highland Line. Three Journals of Travel in Eighteenth-Century Scotland* (London: Collins, 1974), p. 93.

[4]   Samuel Johnson, *A Journey to the Western Islands of Scotland* Allan Wendt, ed., (Boston: Houghton Mifflin, 1965), pp. 28-9.

[5]   Marjorie Hope Nicholson, *Mountain Gloom, Mountain Glory: The Development of the Aesthetics of the Infinite* (Ithaca, NY: Cornell Univ. Press, 1959). On the new sensibilities towards landscapes see also John Barrell, *The dark side of the landscape. The rural poor in English painting 1730-1840* (New York: Cambridge Univ. Press 1980); Ann Bermingham, *Landscape and Ideology. The English Rustic Tradition 1740-1860* (Berkeley: Univ. of California Press, 1986); Andrew Hemingway, *Landscape imagery and urban culture in early nineteenth-century Britain* (Cambridge: Cambridge Univ. Press, 1992); James Holloway and Lindsay Errington, *The Discovery of Scotland: The Appreciation of Scottish Scenery through two Centuries of Painting* (Edinburgh: National Gallery of Scotland, 1978); Simon Schama, *Landscape and Memory* (New York: Alfred A Knopf, 1995); Keith Thomas, *Man and the Natural World* (New York: Oxford Univ. Press, 1983); Raymond Williams, *The Country and the City* (New York: Oxford Univ. Press, 1973).

[6]   Marjorie Morgan, *National Identities and Travel in Victorian Britain* (Houndmills: Palgrave, 2001), p. 47.

[7]   Joseph Mawman, *An Excursion to the Highlands of Scotland and the English Lakes* (London, 1805), pp. 183-84. Andrew Hemingway argues that the association between fertile landscapes and Englishness was being established by the 1820s. *Landscape imagery and urban culture*, p. 298.

[8]   Gosse, 'Journal in Scotland', n.p.

[9]   Elizabeth K. Helsinger, *Rural Scenes and National Representation* (Princeton: Princeton Univ. Press, 1997). See also Alun Howkins, 'The Discovery of Rural England' in Robert Colls and Philip Dodd, eds., *Englishness. Politics and Culture 1880-1920* (New York: Croom Helm, 1986), pp. 62-88; David Lowenthal, 'British National Identity and the English Landscape' *Rural History* 2: 2 (1991), pp. 205-30; Morgan, *National Identities and Travel*, pp. 46-82; Martin J. Weiner, *English Culture and the Decline of the Industrial Spirit 1850-1980* (New York: Penguin, 1981).

[10] Inderpal Grewal, *Home and Harem. Nation, Gender, Empire and the Cultures of Travel* (Durham: Duke Univ. Press, 1996), pp. 32-49.

[11] Chauncy Hare Townshend, *A Descriptive Tour in Scotland* (Brussels and London, 1840), p. 162.

12   Tipple, *Summer Visit to Scotland*, p. 28.

13   'Among the Lochs: Being a Narrative of some Passages in the Archdeacon's Holiday', *Blackwood's Magazine* 90 (October, 1861), p. 480.

14   Sylvan [Samuel Hobbs], *Sylvan's Pictoral Handbook to the Clyde and its Watering Places* (London, 1847), p. 26.

15   J. A. MacCulloch, *Misty Isle of Skye* (Edinburgh & London: Oliphant Anderson & Ferrier, 1905), p. 21.

16   Townshend, *Descriptive Tour*, pp. 161-62.

17   'Journal of a few days from Home in the summer of 1856 with selected poetry and songs' (1856) MS. 9233, NLS, n.p.

18   Alexander Nicholson, 'The Isle of Skye. IV- The Sea Coast' *Good Words* 16 (1875), p. 567.

19   North British Railway Co., pub., *Fort William to Mallaig* (1901), pp. 37-9.

20   'Substance of a tour through Scotland in the summer of 1836' (1836) MS. 2729, NLS, p. 90.

21   William Winter, *Over the Border* (New York: Moffat, Yard and Co, 1911), p. 159.

22   *ILN*, September 21, 1844.

23   Bruce Haley, *The Healthy Body and Victorian Culture* (Cambridge MA: Harvard Univ. Press, 1978).

24   Haley, *Healthy Body*, p. 10.

25   T. C. F. Brotchie, *Scottish Western Holiday Haunts* (Edinburgh: John Menzies, 1911), p. 38.

26   *ILN*, September 24, 1842.

27   George Anderson and Peter Anderson, *Guide to the Highlands and Islands of Scotland* (Edinburgh, 1863), p. 215.

28   Townshend, *Descriptive Tour*, p. 272.

29   Beriah Botfield, *Journal of a Tour through the Highlands of Scotland* (Norton Hall, 1830), p. 12.

30   On the Clearances, see T. M. Devine, *Clanship to Crofters' War. The social transformation of the Scottish Highlands* (New York: Manchester Univ. Press, 1994); James Hunter, *The Making of the Crofting Community* (Edinburgh: John Donald, 1976); Eric Richards, *A History of the Highland Clearances: Agrarian Transformation and the Evictions 1746-1886* (London: Croom Helm, 1982).

31   J. A. MacCulloch, *Misty Isle of Skye*, p. 133.

32   John Macculloch, *The Highlands and Western Islands of Scotland* (London, 1824), p. 3:466.

33   John Macculloch, *Highlands and Western Islands*, pp. 3:471-73.

34   John Macculloch, *Highlands and Western Islands*, pp. 3:474-76.

35   John Macculloch, *Highlands and Western Islands*, pp. 3:482-83.

36   Walter Scott, *The Lord of the Isles*, Vol. X *Poetical Works of Sir Walter Scott* (Edinburgh, 1880) Canto Third, XIV, p. 330.

37   Scott, *The Lord of the Isles*, Canto Third, XII, p. 247.

38   James Wilson, *A Voyage Round the Coasts of Scotland and the Isles* (Edinburgh, 1842), p. 1:218.

39   John Macculloch, *A Description of the Western Islands of Scotland* (London, 1819), p. 1:283.

40   Richard Ayton and William Daniell, *A Voyage Round Great Britain* (London, 1814-1825; reprint, London: Tate Gallery, 1978), p. 4:35.
41   Henry Cockburn, *Circuit Journeys* (Edinburgh, 1889), p. 126.
42   John Macculloch, *Highlands and Western Isles*, p. 3:479; Robert Buchanan, *The Land of Lorne* (London, 1871), p. 2:243.
43   J. A. MacCulloch, *Misty Isle of Skye*, p. 134.
44   Wilson, *Voyage Round the Coasts*, pp. 1:220-21.
45   John Knox [Peter Carter], *Crumbs from the Land o'Cakes* (Boston, 1851), p. 160.
46   'Substance of a Tour', p. 34.
47   J. A. MacCulloch, *Misty Isle of Skye*, p. 34.
48   Morgan, *National Identities and Travel*, pp. 56-82.
49   Chauncy Loomis, 'The Arctic Sublime' in U. C. Knoepflmacher and G. B. Tennyson, eds., *Nature and the Victorian Imagination* (Berkeley: Univ. of California Press, 1977), pp. 95-112; Francis Spufford, *I May Be Some Time. Ice and the English Imagination* (New York: St. Martin's Press, 1997). Simon Schama observes that the Romantics read mountains as judges upon human vanity, 'sabotaging' those who got above themselves. *Landscape and Memory*, pp. 459-62.
50   Alexander Smith, *Summer in Skye* (Boston, 1865), p. 172.
51   Jabez Marrat, *'Land of the Mountain and the Flood'. Scottish Scenes and Scenery Delineated* (London, 1879), p. 175.
52   Winter, *Over the Border*, p. 252.
53   William Winter, *Brown Heath and Blue Bells; Being Sketches of Scotland, With other papers* (New York: MacMillan, 1906), p. 44.
54   Winter, *Over the Border*, p. 175.
55   'The Charm of Highland Scenery' *The Spectator* 95 (September 2, 1905), pp. 314-15.
56   Wilson, *Voyage Round the Coasts*, p. 1: 122-23. For an overview of Victorian responses to science, see Peter J. Bowler, *Evolution. The History of an Idea* (Berkeley: Univ. of California Press, 1989).
57   Wilson, *Voyage Round the Coasts*, p. 1: 219.
58   On the Victorian enthusiasm for natural history, see David Elliston Allen, *The Naturalist in Britain. A Social History* (Princeton: Princeton Univ. Press, 1994).
59   Buchanan, *Land of Lorne*, p. 2:260.
60   Alexander Nicholson, 'The Isle of Skye part II. – Coiruisg' *Good Words* 16 (1875), pp. 384; 389.
61   Buchanan, *Land of Lorne*, p. 2:207.
62   Hugh Miller, *The Cruise of the Betsey* (Boston, 1858), pp. 21-2.
63   J. A. MacCulloch, *Misty Isle of Skye*, pp. 139-40.
64   See Peter Hume Brown, *Early Travellers in Scotland* (Edinburgh, 1891; reprint, Edinburgh: Mercat Press, 1978), pp. ix-x; David Inglis and Mary Holmes, 'Highland and Other Haunts. Ghosts in Scottish Tourism', *Annals of Tourism Research* 30:1 (2003), pp. 50-63.
65   J. A. MacCulloch, *Misty Isle of Skye*, p. 32.
66   George Anderson and Peter Anderson, *Guide to the Highlands and Islands of Scotland* (Edinburgh, 1863), p. 238.

67 Smith, *Summer in Skye*, p. 115; J. A. MacCulloch, *Misty Isle of Skye*, p. 235.
68 Buchanan, *Land of Lorne*, p. 2:249; Constance F. Gordon Cumming, *In the Hebrides* (London, 1883), p. 407.
69 J. A. MacCulloch, *Misty Isle of Skye*, p. 147.
70 Buchanan, *Land of Lorne*, p. 2:245.
71 Carole G. Silver, *Strange and Secret Peoples. Fairies and Victorian Consciousness* (New York: Oxford Univ. Press, 1999). On spiritualism, see Janet Oppenheim, *The Other World: Spiritualism and psychical research in England, 1850-1914* (New York: Cambridge Univ. Press, 1985).
72 John Macculloch, *Highlands and Western Islands*, 3:482. In a strikingly similar account in *The Prelude* (Book I), Wordsworth evokes the unearthly sensation of spirits (embodied by a huge black peak) chasing him in a stolen boat. Although not published until 1850, *The Prelude* was mostly completed in 1805. I do not know if Wordsworth read Macculloch in the intervening period, although it is certainly possible as Macculloch was widely known among those interested in Scotland. James Wilson, too, played with this motif. Leaving Coruisk, he looked backwards occasionally 'almost in terror, as if we felt ourselves pursued by some malignant demon, who hid himself the moment we turned around.' *Voyage Round the Coasts*, p. 224.
73 Simon Schama notes that accounts of climbing Mont Blanc were at times interpreted as demonstrations of imperial confidence over native superstition. *Landscape and Memory*, pp. 463-66.
74 John Macculloch, *Highlands and Western Islands*, p. 2:348.
75 John Macculloch, *Highlands and Western Islands*, p. 2:347.
76 J. A. MacCulloch, *Misty Isle of Skye*, p. 257.
77 J. A. MacCulloch, *Misty Isle of Skye*, pp. 142-43.
78 Silver, *Strange and Secret Peoples*, p. 45.
79 Buchanan, *Land of Lorne*, pp. 2:21-9, 259-60.
80 William Scrope, *The Art of Deer-Stalking* (New York, 1897), p. 42.
81 T. H. Holding, *Cruise of the Ospray: Canoe and Camp life in Scotland* (Newcastle-on-tyne, 1878), p. 33.
82 James Eli Adams, *Dandies and Desert Saints. Styles of Victorian Manhood* (Ithaca: Cornell Univ. Press, 1995), p. 128; Leonore Davidoff and Catherine Hall, *Family Fortunes. Men and women of the English middle class. 1780-1850* (Chicago: Univ. of Chicago Press, 1987); Peter Stearns, *Be A Man! Males in Modern Society* (New York: Holmes & Meier, 1990); John Tosh, *A Man's Place. Masculinity and the Middle-Class Home in Victorian England* (New Haven: Yale Univ. Press, 1999).
83 Stearns, *Be A Man!*, p.116. See also Haley, *Healthy Body and Victorian Culture*, pp. 23-45.
84 Peter H. Hansen, 'Albert Smith, the Alpine Club, and the Invention of Mountaineering in Mid-Victorian Britain', *Journal of British Studies* 34 (July 1995), p. 304.
85 Adams, *Dandies and Desert Saints*, pp. 9-10. See also J. A. Mangan and James Walvin, eds., *Manliness and morality: Middle-class masculinity in Britain and America 1800-1940* (Manchester: Manchester Univ. Press, 1978).

86   John M. MacKenzie, 'The imperial pioneer and hunter and the British masculine stereotype in late Victorian and Edwardian times' in Mangan and Walvin, *Manliness and morality*, pp. 176-96.

87   W. H. Maxwell, *Wanderings in the Highlands & Islands* (London, 1852), p. 1: xi.

88   See Peter Womack, *Improvement and Romance. Constructing the Myth of the Highlands* (London: MacMillan Press, 1989), esp. pp. 113-48; Malcolm Chapman, *The Gaelic Vision in Scottish Culture* (London: Croom Helm, 1978).

89   Hayden Lorimer, 'Guns, Game and the Grandee: The Cultural Politics of Deerstalking in the Scottish Highlands,' *Ecumene* 2000 7(4), p. 409.

90   John M. MacKenzie, *The Empire of Nature. Hunting, Conservation and British Imperialism.* (New York: Manchester Univ. Press, 1988), pp. 26-51; Thomas, *Man and the Natural World.*

91   *ILN*, August 16, 1862.

92   William Douglas, 'Summer Holiday' (1888) MS. 10975, NLS, p. 29.

93   Gosse, 'Journal in Scotland', n.p.

94   Adams, *Dandies and Desert Saints*, p. 111.

95   Herbert Byng Hall, *Highland Sports and Highland Quarters* (London, 1848), p. 58.

96   'A Tour in the Hebrides' (1908) ACC 7926, NLS.

97   See Charles G. Harper, *Motoring in Scotland* (London: Royal Automobile Club, 1912), p. 26.

98   R. Menzies Fergusson, *Our Trip North* (London, 1892), p. 104.

99   Philip G. Hamerton, *A Painter's Camp* (Boston, 1879), p. 70.

100   Smith, *Summer in Skye*, p. 186.

101   Holding, *Cruise of the Ospray*, p. 33.

102   Adams, *Dandies and Desert Saints*, p. 117. Adams discusses the tension between the desire for self-discipline and the attraction of a 'perpetual Saturnalia', with particular attention to Tennyson and Charles Kingsley. See pp. 107-47.

103   Hamerton, *Painter's Camp*, p. 71.

104   Maxwell, *Wanderings in the Highlands*, p. 2:304.

105   Spufford, *I May Be Some Time*, p. 26.

106   *ILN*, August, 16, 1862.

107   Ashley P. Abraham, *Rock Climbing in Skye* (London: Longmans, Green & Co., 1908), p. vii.

108   See Alexander Nicholson, 'The Isle of Skye III. Climbing in the Coolin - Scurnan-Gillian' *Good Words* 16 (1875) p. 457; Buchanan, *Land of Lorne*, p. 2:206; Adam Black and Charles Black, pub., *Black's Picturesque Tourist of Scotland* (Edinburgh, 1882), p. 515; J. A. MacCulloch, *Misty Isle of Skye*, pp. 143-45.

109   Smith, *Summer in Skye*, pp. 172-73.

110   Holding, *Cruise of the Ospray*, p. 24.

111   Buchanan, *Land of Lorne*, pp. 2:158-60.

112   Mackenzie, *Empire of Nature*, p. 24. See also Duff Hart-Davis, *Monarchs of the Glen: A History of Deer Stalking in the Scottish Highlands* (London: Jonathan Cape, 1978); Durie, *Scotland for the Holidays*, pp. 109-23; Hunter, *Making of the Crofting Community*; William Orr, *Deer Forests, Landlords and Crofters* (Edinburgh: John Donald, 1982). On grouse shooting, see Alastair

Durie, ' "Unconscious Benefactors": Grouse-shooting in Scotland, 1780-1914' *International Journal of the History of Sport* 15: 3 (Dec. 1998), pp. 57-73.

[113] Richard Ormond, *Sir Edwin Landseer*. With contributions by Joseph Rishel and Robin Hamlyn (New York: Rizzoli, 1981) p. 174.

[114] 'Red Heather,' *Memories of Sporting Days* (New York: Longmans, Green & Co., 1923).

[115] Scrope, *Art of Deer Stalking*, p. 43.

[116] *ILN*, October 21, 1843; Scrope, *Art of Deer Stalking*, pp. 97-8; 'Sixty-one,' *Twenty Years' Reminiscences of the Lews* (London, 1871), pp. 156-60; Buchanan, *Land of Lorne*, pp. 1:134-35.

[117] See Lorimer, 'Guns, Game and the Grandee', pp. 410-413; Orr, *Deer Forests, Landlords, and Crofters*, pp. 39-40.

[118] George Eyre-Todd, *Scotland: Picturesque and Traditional* (New York: Frederick A. Stokes, 1907), p. 350.

[119] Haley, *Healthy Body and Victorian Culture*, pp. 256-58.

[120] Hall, *Highland Sports*, p. 140.

[121] 'Sixty-One', *Twenty Years' Reminiscences*, pp. 270-71.

[122] Scrope, *Art of Deer Stalking*, pp. 41-2.

[123] The phrase is Peter Gay's, *The Cultivation of Hatred* (New York: Norton, 1993), p. 97.

[124] 'Tour in the Hebrides', p. 26.

[125] Scrope, *Art of Deerstalking*, p. 211.

[126] See Lorimer, 'Guns, Game and the Grandee', pp. 414-16; Mary Louise Pratt, *Imperial Eyes. Travel Writing and Transculturation* (New York: Routledge, 1992).

[127] Hall, *Highland Sports*, p. 4.

[128] Quoted in Hansen, 'Invention of Mountaineering', p. 315.

[129] See Hansen, 'Invention of Mountaineering' and 'Vertical Boundaries, National Identities: British Mountaineering on the Frontiers of Europe and the Empire, 1868-1914' *The Journal of Imperial and Commonwealth History* 24: 1 (January 1996), pp. 48-71.

[130] 'Skye. Up the Cuchullin', *The Leisure Hour* 9: 462 (November 1, 1860), p. 695.

[131] MacKenzie, 'Imperial Pioneer and Hunter', pp. 178-79.

[132] Orr, *Deer Forests, Landlords and Crofters*, pp. 119-41; Hunter, *Making of the Crofting Community*, pp. 13-183.

[133] Eyre-Todd, *Scotland: Picturesque and Traditional*, p. 1.

[134] Chapman, *Gaelic Vision in Scottish Culture*, pp. 210-11.

[135] Christopher North [John Wilson], *Recreations of Christopher North* from *The Works of John Wilson*, Prof. Ferrier, ed., vol. IX (Edinburgh, 1857), p. 53.

[136] For one example, see Hall, *Highland Sports*, pp. 74-5.

[137] James Buzard, *The Beaten Track. European Tourism, Literature, and the Ways to 'Culture'* (Oxford: Clarendon Press, 1993), p. 130. See also Chloe Chard, *Pleasure and Guilt on the Grand Tour* (New York: Manchester Univ. Press, St. Martin's Press, 1999), pp. 218-21.

[138] Holding, *Cruise of the Osprey*, pp. 42-3.

[139] Karl Baedeker, *Great Britain* (London, 1901), p. 538.

[140] James Johnson, *The Recess or Autumnal Relaxation in the Highlands and Lowlands* (London, 1834), p. 100.

[141] 'An Excursion to the English Lakes and Scotland' (1857) ACC. 8139, NLS, p. 28.

[142] Sarah Murray, *A Companion and Useful Guide to the Beauties of Scotland* William F. Laughlan, ed. (Hawick: Byways Books, 1982), pp. 84-8.

[143] Murray, *Companion and Useful Guide*, pp. 73-4.

[144] Dea Birkett, *Spinsters Abroad. Victorian Lady Explorers* (Oxford: Basil Blackwell, 1989), p. 15.

[145] Gordon Cumming, *In the Hebrides*.

[146] The literature on Victorian women travelers is growing rapidly. For a sample of some of the historiography, see Birkett, *Spinsters Abroad*; Maria H. Frawley, *A Wider Range. Travel Writing by Women in Victorian England* (Toronto: Associated University Presses, 1994); Grewal, *Home and Harem*; Susan Morgan, *Place Matters.Gendered Geography in Victorian Women's Travel Books about Southeast Asia* (New Brunswick: Rutgers Univ. Press, 1996).

[147] Mrs. John Gower, 'Illustrated Accounts of trips to France and Scotland by the family of John F. Gower' (1854,1862) ACC. 9946, NLS, n.p.

[148] 'Substance of a tour', p. 48.

[149] Willie Orr mentions several aristocratic women who stalked in the 1840s and 50s. Orr, *Deer Forests, Landlords and Crofters*, p. 29. Alma, Marchioness of Bredalbane was an enthusiastic stalker around the turn of the century, and the author of *The High Tops of Black Mount* (1907).

[150] Hall, *Highland Sports*, p. 2:92.

[151] S. Kathleen Warden, *Humorous Side-Lights on a Scotch Tour* (London, n.d.).

[152] Gosse, 'Journal in Scotland', n.p.

[153] Jacob Abbott, *A Summer in Scotland* (Dublin, 1849), p. 253.

[154] Buchanan, *Land of Lorne*, pp. 2:232-74.

[155] 'Journal of a few days from Home', n.p.

[156] Karl Baedeker, *Great Britain* (London, 1887), p. 496; Warden, *Humourous sidelights*, p. 93.

[157] John Macculloch, *Highlands and Western Islands*, p. 1:211.

[158] Wilson, *Voyage Round the Coasts*, pp. 1: 185-86.

[159] T. C. Smout, 'The Highlands and the Roots of Green Consciousness, 1750-1990', *Proceedings of the British Academy* 76(1991), pp. 240-41.

[160] John T. Reid, *Art Rambles in the Highlands and Islands of Scotland* (New York, 1878), p. 38.

[161] *Glasgow Herald*, letters to the editor, summer 1887.

[162] James Locke, *Tweed & Don, or Recollections and Reflections of an Angler* (Edinburgh, 1860), pp. 82-5.

[163] A. R. Hope Moncrieff, *Highlands & Islands of Scotland* (London: A & C Black, 1906; reprint, London: A & C Black, 1925), pp. 4-5.

[164] Gosse, 'Journal in Scotland', n.p.

[165] Michael Freeman, *Railways and the Victorian Imagination* (New Haven: Yale Univ. Press, 1999), pp. 38-55. See also Jeffrey Richards and John M. Mackenzie, *The Railway Station. A Social History* (New York: Oxford Univ. Press, 1986); Wolfgang Schivelbusch, *The Railway Journey. The Industrialization of Time*

and Space in the 19th Century (Berkeley: Univ. of California Press, 1986); Jack Simmons, *The Victorian Railway* (New York: Thames and Hudson, 1991); James Winter, *Secure from Rash Assault. Sustaining the Victorian Environment* (Berkeley: Univ. of California Press, 1999), p. 112.

166 Thomas Cook, *Cook's Scottish Tourist Official Directory* (London, 1861), p. 92.

167 *"Mountain, Moor and Loch"* Illustrated by Pen and Pencil. On the route of the West Highland Railway (London, 1895), p. 91.

168 Adam Black and Charles Black, pub., *Black's Picturesque Tourist* (Edinburgh, 1843), p. 194; Cockburn, *Circuit Journeys*, p. 300.

169 Gordon Cumming, *In the Hebrides*, pp. 420-21.

170 See a review of *Scotland for the Holidays* by George Eyre-Todd, which appeared in the *ILN*, July 20, 1912. Holloway and Errington observe that much nineteenth-century landscape painting of the Highlands can be seen as an attempt to sustain a 'myth of uncontamination'. *Discovery of Scotland*, pp. 111-12.

171 Winter, *Secure from Rash Assault*, pp. 166-83.

172 Smout, 'The Highlands and the Roots of Green Consciousness', p. 245. On the Lake Thirlwell campaign, see Winter, *Secure from Rash Assault*, pp. 176-88.

173 'The Tourist in Scotland. Roslin.' *The Leisure Hour*, (no. 449) August 2, 1860, p. 487.

174 Townshend, *Descriptive Tour*, p. 15.

175 Cuthbert Bede [Edward Bradley], *A Tour in Tartan-Land* (London, 1863), p. 239.

176 Winter, *Secure from Rash Assault*, p. 115.

177 George Anderson and Peter Anderson, *Handbook to the Highland Railway System from Perth to Forres, Keith, Inverness, and Bonar Bridge* (Edinburgh, 1865), p. 69; North British Railway Co., pub., *Fort William to Mallaig*, pp. 31-2; Anderson, *Handbook to the Highland Railway*, pp. 18-9.

178 Baedeker, *Great Britain*, (1901), p. 545.

179 *Daily Mail*, June 3, 1896.

180 W. A. Stephenson, 'A Trip to Edinburgh and Glasgow by the Polytechnic Y. M. C. I. Excursion' (1890) MS. 9234, NLS, p. 29.

181 *ILN*, August 20, 1870.

182 *ILN*, August 27, 1870; August 20, 1870.

183 Winter, *Secure from Rash Assault*, pp. 112-13.

184 *The Epistles of Peggy, Written from Scotland* (n.p., n.d.), p. 5.

185 Adam Black and Charles Black, pub. *Black's Picturesque Tourist of Scotland* (Edinburgh, 1881), p. 558.

186 *"Mountain, Moor and Loch"*, p. 13.

187 Baedeker, *Great Britain*, (1887), p. 499.

188 *"Mountain, Moor and Loch"*, p. 14.

189 *Railway Herald* quoted by John Thomas, *The West Highland Railway*, extra material by Alan J. S. Paterson (Newton Abbot: David & Charles, 1984), p. 11.

190 *"Mountain, Moor and Loch"*, p. 116.

191 See also Peter Mandler, 'Against "Englishness": English Culture and the Limits to Rural Nostalgia, 1850-1940' *Transactions of the Royal Historical Society* 6th series, 7, (1997), pp. 115-75.

192 Bermingham, *Landscape and Ideology*, pp. 157-93.

[193] Mandler, 'Against "Englishness"', p. 170.

[194] Buchanan, *Land of Lorne*, p. 2:213.

[195] Smith, *Summer in Skye*, p. 96.

[196] Alexander Nicholson, 'The Isle of Skye' *Good Words* 16 (1875), pp. 348; 346.

[197] Charles Keene, John Leech, George Du Maurier, et al., *Mr. Punch in the Highlands* (London: Educational Book Co., Ltd., 1907), pp. 84-98.

Chapter 4

'Free of one's century':
Tourism and the Scottish Past

'It is the center of the world. All else is change; this alone is stable.' Thus did Alexander Smith describe Carmyle, a village in the Clyde valley, 'where nothing has happened for the last fifty years, and where nothing will happen for fifty years to come'.[1] Though a description of a specific location, his words also express a prevalent nineteenth-century opinion about Scotland in general. In an era of rapid, continual, and sometimes unsettling change, Scotland – the Highlands in particular – seemed fixed, rooted, and constant. Indeed, tourist literature sometimes suggested that Scotland was immune to the passage of time. Scotland therefore provided a link with the past which seemed to be vanishing in the increasingly urbanized and industrialized modern world. That past, represented as available for touring, was one of Scotland's most popular tourist attractions in the nineteenth century.

Not until the late eighteenth century, David Lowenthal points out, did people differentiate the present from the past. For most of history the historical past was assumed to have been much like the present, and it therefore provided comparative lessons for contemporary society. But consequent upon the upheavals of the French Revolution, the political reform movements of the nineteenth century, and the changes wrought by industrialization, the post-1815 world came to seem disconnected from the times that had come before. The present was increasingly understood as a quantifiably different realm with a unique personality and history. The Victorians were conscious of themselves as a new society, one divided from previous centuries by railways, machines, and political change. This awareness of change, in turn, placed a new value on the past. While it no longer provided comparative lessons, the past was cherished as a heritage that authenticated and ennobled the present. Like nature, the past was an antidote to contemporary times, providing missing virtues such as rootedness, romance, the unspoiled innocence of antiquity, and the sense of continuity that came from the uninterrupted flow of history. Unlike the present, the past could be ordered, domesticated, made sense of.[2]

These qualities of the past could be found in England as much as in Scotland. But Scotland was widely considered to be a place less industrialized and less modern than England, and therefore a place where yesteryear was more accessible. Scotland offered a plethora of historic sites, ranging in period from Druidic times to the eighteenth century. One favorite in the Victorian era was Edinburgh's Old Town, described as 'Scottish history fossilized'[3]. The valley of Glencoe was the site of the 1692 'massacre'. Stirling offered several famous events, including the 1314 battle of Bannockburn. The remote island of Iona was the home of St. Columba's sixth-century monastery. Culloden Moor was the setting of the Jacobites' final defeat in 1746. Virtually every city, town, or natural landmark could boast some historic occurrence, the story of which was often dramatically retold in tourist literature.

There were escapist tendencies in tours of the Scottish past, as tourists sometimes sought to withdraw from the modern world as they journeyed through Scotland. But just as often, tourists sought not to escape from the past but to identify a sense of consecutiveness between it and the present. Scotland's role was to provide modern Britain with roots in former times. The Union allowed Scotland's past to offer a heritage that exalted the strength of Great Britain and the extent of British progress. At times Scotland's past seemed to provide a heritage for English as well as Scottish sightseers. This notion, while it promoted a sense of British national identity, also effectively marginalized the importance of Scotland's independent story. The association between Scotland and the past tended to deprecate Scotland's modern developments. Tourists could not help but notice that Scotland was not, in fact, immune to time, and they often valued the intermingling of past and present there as a sign of the seamless flow of history. But many continued to identify Scotland primarily with the past, hoping thereby to find stability in a changing world. It was therefore difficult for Scotland's national image to change along with Scotland's society and economy, an issue which has concerned many Scots in later centuries.

Historic Tourism and National Identity

English tourists were fascinated with Scottish history, often developing a vicarious Scottish patriotism during their journeys. As did Scottish tourists, they rooted for Robert Bruce at Bannockburn, idolized Mary Stuart as if she was their own queen, and hoped government troops would not cut off Charles Edward Stuart's escape. Scotland's heroes were their heroes. A female visitor in 1836 could not help feeling sorry that the soldiers at Edinburgh Castle had had their country 'wrestled from them' and had been made subject to the laws and government of another King.[4] A traveler of 1842 blamed the English for the massacre of Glencoe: 'I own I could not but feel at this moment ashamed of my country.'[5] Promoters of tourism evidently hoped that English sightseers would develop just such a kinship with their northern neighbors. They made history one of Scotland's centerpieces in an effort to emphasize Scottish differentness, educate excursionists about the country, and downplay any threat posed by Scotland's independent past. T. Holmes, an English tourist who made a quick tour of Scotland in 1874, hoped that his reflections on his travels would stimulate others to wander 'pleasantly up and down studying the history of *our* beloved country'(italics added).[6] Late in the century, 'Peggy' was shown writing home that she was 'beginning to understand the Scotchman's love of country, and I'm quite delighted to think that we English folk have some right, through the Act of Union, to regard the land north of the Border as part and parcel of a mutual heritage.'[7] As the comments of a fictionalized visitor, her words also suggest that the development of Scottish patriotism was by then a stereotype of tourism.

It was largely because of the strength of the Union in the nineteenth century and the political neutrality of Scottish history as presented by contemporary historians that English tourists were able to become so enamored of the Scottish past. With no reason to doubt the security of the Union or the stability of the crown, visitors could afford to sympathize with medieval Scottish freedom fighters or eighteenth-century pretenders to the throne. Although two of tourists' favorite moments in Scottish history, the thirteenth- and fourteenth-century Wars of Independence and the 1745-1746 Jacobite rising, centered on potentially tense issues of Scottish independence and self-determination, in the nineteenth century those topics provoked little controversy among English sightseers. Current Scottish historiography had much to do with this lack of tension. In the medieval and early modern period Scottish historians emphasized the legitimacy of Scotland's independence and demonstrated the operation of their own ancient constitution. Scholars of the Scottish Enlightenment challenged this interpretation. Their definition of 'liberty' centered on civil liberty, not Scotland's history of limited monarchy. In their eyes, Scotland had failed in the development of civil liberty, which came through the Union, not through indigenous development. Scottish history appeared to lack a 'progressive whiggish plot'[8] and thus had little to teach of constitutional development, which was the central story in nineteenth-century British academic historical writing. Stable, continuous constitutionality originated in England, not Scotland. Nor did Walter Scott, undoubtedly the source of most English tourists' knowledge of Scottish history, put forward a vigorous national Scottish past. 'By applying a sentimental Jacobite gloss to a basic Whig constitutionalism, Scott turned the Scottish past into an ideologically neutral pageant – suitable material for historical romance, but incapable of supporting a romantic nationalist historiography of either an authoritarian or liberal hue.'[9] Thus, in the nineteenth century Scottish history was presented as a loose collection of incidents with little sense of a unifying thread, which projected no particular definition of Scottish nationhood.[10] It was therefore possible for English tourists to treasure Scottish history as a series of enjoyable tales which they could even adopt as their own.

Scottish tourists were even more deeply interested in their history and retained an emotional bond with it, even though English history began to seem more relevant to an understanding of institutions, politics, and society.[11] Middle and upper-class Scots' attention to their past was manifested in their enthusiasm for heraldry, genealogy, clanship, Highland dress, Jacobitism, and stories of Scottish heroes, as well as by the sites they visited as tourists. For some, history was an inspiration for political nationalism, offering the example of a once autonomous nation that ought to be independent again.[12] For most, as Graeme Morton shows, while Scots' historical awareness was clear evidence of a strong sense of national identity, through mid-century that awareness did not push toward political nationalism. Because the Victorian state was not a centralized one, argues Morton, for much of the century the 'gap' between Scottish civil society and the British state enabled the Scottish middle class to satisfactorily combine nationalism and politics at the local level. Political nationalism was unnecessary; indeed it was anathema to a group which resisted centralization. Scots easily maintained dual identities, exhibiting pride in both Scottish independence and in the British state which they believed Scotland had joined as an equal. It was not until the state became more centralized in the late nineteenth and twentieth centuries, with the expansion of politics to a greater percentage of citizens and the involvement of the government in more and more areas of society, that political nationalism came to seem relevant to Scotland.[13]

Consequently, although Scottish history often had different meanings for English and Scottish sightseers, tourists of both nationalities shared an enthusiasm for it which made visiting historic sites a central activity of pleasure travel. Such excursions were part of the diversion from everyday life that was tourism. They were a chance to envision other times, an opportunity to place oneself in scenes where great things had happened and to imagine oneself a participant in them. In addition, the vignettes that composed the Scottish past held considerable significance for tourists. Despite the political impotence of Scottish history as a national narrative, tourists found meaning in the sites they visited. Scotland supplied several appropriate subjects for the Victorian taste for hero worship: decisive, masterful figures who provided patriotic inspiration and examples of self-sacrifice in contrast to modern commercialism and intellectual doubt. Examples included: 'The great deeds of Wallace and Bruce, the high energies of John Knox and those who acted with him in the Reformation, the sublime pertinacity of the Covenanters in the maintenance of their principles, the bold attempt of the Jacobites to restore the Stuarts to the throne of their ancestors, the genius of historians, poets, and preachers.'[14] Furthermore, the Scottish past taught tourists, both English and Scottish, of what many considered an instinctive British desire for liberty and freedom which was manifested in Scotland's struggles against English dominion. Sightseers' willingness to regard the Wars of Independence as examples of a natural *British* drive for freedom shows the extent to which they absorbed Scottish history into Britain's story. One feature of the process of nation building in the nineteenth century was the removal of sectarian divisions, which can be seen in the rehabilitation of controversial figures from the British past, such as Oliver Cromwell.[15] Telling a story of Scottish history which downplayed divisiveness was part of that effort.

Just as the fact that it was safe to travel throughout late eighteenth-century Scotland spoke to tourists of the strength of Great Britain, so did Scottish history show later visitors that the Union was a strong one. The contrast between past and present allowed them to rejoice in the political and social achievements of the united nation. Visitors frequently contrasted the calm and harmony of late eighteenth- and nineteenth-century Britain with earlier strife in Scotland. Robert Hunter was pleased that in 1837 Edinburgh Castle was only used for 'ornament' not for war. 'The period has happily passed away, when castles were considered as the strongholds of the country, and their artillery employed to pour forth death on assailing enemies.'[16] The Rev. Jabez Marrat had similar thoughts when he passed the site of a Roman wall in 1879. 'We cannot pass the spot without being reminded of the ages which have elapsed and the changes which have been wrought in the social, political, and religious aspect of the world since the time when the ancient Britons, compelled to labour by Roman captains and centurions, dug the foundations and laid the stones of the mighty rampart.'[17] At the end of a day's hunting in 1848, Herbert Byng Hall rejoiced that a countryside which had once been the site of 'bloodshed and lawless enterprise' was a place for joyous sports. 'No longer shots are fired in anger – no longer is the Highland dirk steeped in a neighbor's blood; but all, united in the bond of brotherhood, worship the same God, and honor the same sovereign.'[18]

Tales of atrocities once committed by one clan against another also evoked a sense of pride at the progress made by British society in more recent centuries. Tourists seemingly had a insatiable interest in 'the barbarity...common in those days', and tourist literature was full of bloodthirsty stories.[19] 'The associations which History furnishes of the rude manners of those turbulent and dreadful periods, strike the mind with a peculiar force. We dwell upon them for a while with horror, but turn from them with delight and gratitude that our lot is cast in more secure and peaceful times' said J. E. Bowman.[20] A tourist of 1856 was thankful he lived when he did, not in the so-called 'good old early times' when Rob Roy and the 'wild McGregors' made the Trossachs a dangerous place.[21] Discussions of some of the 'very primitive customs [that] are still observed in this part of the country', as well as the ghost stories and superstitions of Highlanders had a similar effect in demonstrating how far most features of British society had come.[22]

By the nineteenth century, the life of Mary, Queen of Scots similarly spoke of British unity and strength. To many 'The most fascinating figure in the history of Scotland is Mary Stuart....Some persons believe the best of her, and some believe the worst, but irrespective of all belief, the world is conscious of her strange allurement, her incessant, abiding charm.'[23] There were several locations associated with Mary: Linlithgow Palace, her birthplace; Edinburgh Castle, where she gave birth to her son, the future James I & VI; Stirling Castle, where she was crowned and where her son was baptized; Loch Leven Castle, where she was imprisoned, forced to abdicate, and from which she dramatically escaped; and above all, her bed chamber in the Palace of Holyroodhouse, where her secretary David Rizzio was murdered before her eyes. A visit to this room, where Rizzio's blood allegedly still stained the floor, was a highlight of many trips to Edinburgh. According to tourist Jacob Abbott it was for many people the most interesting thing they visited in Scotland.[24] Her bed reportedly remained in the same condition as when she last occupied it.[25] The immediateness of Rizzio's murder which many felt in the room made it a titillating spot; one sightseer reported a 'sensation of horror.'[26]

Britons had been fascinated by Mary Stuart ever since her death, and this long-term imaginative involvement with the Queen of Scots intensified during the nineteenth century as Victorians strove to come to terms with her place in the national identity. Between 1820 and 1892 the Royal Academy displayed fifty-six new scenes of her life. Special exhibitions were mounted across the nation. Schiller's *Maria Stuart* and theatrical versions of Scott's *The Abbott* were frequently performed, in addition to numerous new tragedies based on her life.[27] Scholar Jayne Lewis sees Mary's continued hold on the British imagination as fundamental to the creation of a coherent national history. During and after her life, Mary symbolized reoccurring threats to England's, later Great Britain's, political and psychological wholeness. She represented absolute authority, female power, Catholicism, and France. The repression of those elements through her execution was necessary to the nascent Elizabethan definition of Englishness. The 'otherness' Mary represented, however, continued to haunt British society and politics, and her image remained a factor in the popular imagination, remade by later generations to fit their particular moment in history. By the nineteenth century a strong, self-assured Britain was able to embrace Mary Stuart as part of the communal story, although efforts to do so were often far fetched. Seeking a coherent, harmonious past, Victorians downplayed the estrangement between Elizabeth and Mary, the conflict between Mary and John Knox, the antipathy between she and Darnley, even her Catholicism. By minimizing the danger Mary once posed, history could absorb that threat, and thus demonstrate the unity of

Britain's national past. The fascination with Mary also coincided with a new interest in the Stuart line.[28]

Such an interpretation also minimized the significance of political and religious upheaval in an independent Scotland. Tourist literature, which often provided its readers with considerable historical information, seldom discussed the consequences of either Mary's fabled romantic escapades, her Catholicism, or her conspiracies against the English throne. A mere footnote to the story of British constitutionalism, her tale could be recast as a tragic romance with little political repercussion. Her appeal to nineteenth-century tourists was her 'melancholy history'.[29] Locations connected with her life allowed excursionists to remember her exciting adventures and to be moved by her many misfortunes. 'As you say to yourself, these are the very fields, and this is the very lake that she saw, and here, over our heads, is the very window from which she saw them, the whole landscape assumes a melancholy expression....Poor Mary! Her memory spreads a sad and sombre atmosphere over every scene connected with her name.'[30] The death of Rizzio, mused one tourist, was no doubt a 'desolation' to Mary, 'More than perhaps the destruction of a Nation would have been.'[31] The assertion that love may have mattered more to Mary than did the nation carried the tacit comparison with Mary's contemporary, Elizabeth I, to whom the nation mattered more than love. Elizabeth was a less compelling figure to eighteenth- and nineteenth-century imaginations, but one whose political significance was more clearly recognized.

Interest in Mary Stuart's love life rather than her political significance also signals that she symbolized controversial questions about women's political power and about female desire. Women of both the eighteenth and nineteenth centuries had a particular investment in her life. Victoria, another monarch who was also a wife and mother, strongly identified with Mary. Her subjects, too, drew parallels between them, especially concerning the contradictions embodied in being a powerful woman.[32] The Queen of Scots was often presented as an exemplary woman: a devoted mother (even though separated from her child), a talented needleworker, a friend who maintained tight bonds with other women. Mary was also a vindication of women's inadmissible desires, especially for power and authority, and a transgressive figure who represented a femininity both mysterious and erotically enticing. Coming to terms with this complex figure, Lewis argues, was another way that Victorians learned to accept self-difference, thus to demonstrate their nation's strength and security.[33]

Scotland's Reformation martyrs and the Covenanters, those who held out against the reinstitution of lay patronage and the bishopric in the Church of Scotland in the 1670s and 1680s, were different sorts of heroes, who were appreciated by a large minority of tourists. To admirers of these figures, Scotland's religious history witnessed to the fact that 'North Britain' was a more pious country than was England. Those interested in the subject, who were often Evangelicals, honored Scotland's religious martyrs for their commitment to their faith and their unwillingness to betray it. Covenanters and other religious heroes symbolized a genuine godliness which their devotees believed was on the wane in the nineteenth century. They also stood for a time when Christianity was unthreatened by scientific developments, industrialization, or urbanization. Pious tourists visited St. Andrews, where George Wishart and other Reformation martyrs were executed, Greyfriars Church in Edinburgh, where the Covenant was signed; and Edinburgh's Grassmarket, the execution site of many Covenanters. As they did so, they commemorated those events and were encouraged by the memory of others' sacrifice. When he viewed the Solemn League and Covenant, Peter Carter, a Scot who lived for many years in the United States and wrote of his tour under the name 'John Knox', 'felt transported to covenanting days when religion was not a matter of custom or fashion.'[34] Jabez Marrat argued that even reformers' destruction of so much of the material culture of Catholicism, though regrettable, had its positive aspects, for it was a sign of Scots' insistence on a complete reformation of the church. Though damaging to art, reformers' thoroughness was beneficial to Protestantism, ensuring a simple worship and making ritualistic show all but impossible.[35]

Scotland's deep piety, such enthusiasts argued, was still evident. Scotland retained religious roots which were reportedly weakening elsewhere. 'The Scotch are pre-eminently a religious people – the religion of the Bible forms a part as it were of their national character.'[36] The 'simple yet impressive worship' begun when Reformers took over the Glasgow Cathedral still continued, noted Marrat.[37] Some visitors considered Scotland's strict Sabbatarianism to be evidence of the country's devoutness. Scots were said to 'attend to their external duties in Religion with much greater regularity and propriety than the English.'[38] The large crowds which attended church on Sunday, sometimes coming from long distances, impressed many tourists. Visitors also noted the attentiveness of congregations, and the devoutness with which Scots kept the Sabbath as 'a day of rest and peace'.[39] Scots argued about religious issues with more passion than did the English, travelers found, although tourists were sometimes surprised by the excitement generated by topics such as lay patronage, which were of little interest in England.[40] These were not universal sentiments, however; many non-Scots found the Scottish Sabbath 'gloomy' and believed the prohibitions of 'harmless enjoyment' did more evil than good.[41]

Iona, where St. Columba established a monastery in the sixth century from which much of pagan Scotland was converted to Christianity, was an obvious symbol of the country's historic faith connection. It was a perennially popular tourist attraction. Many visitors defined the island as a place which prompted a renewal of one's faith. This understanding owed a good deal to Samuel Johnson's nearly canonical observation that, 'That man is little to be envied, whose patriotism would not gain force upon the plain of Marathon, or whose piety would not grow warmer among the ruins of Iona.'[42] According to their memoirs, Victorian sightseers were less likely than their predecessors to quote or paraphrase Johnson as they investigated Iona, although their guidebooks usually did. Tourists sometimes created too much of a crowd on the island to foster spiritual meditation. But they were as fascinated as their eighteenth-century predecessors by the notion that Christianity spread across Scotland from a tiny island off the west coast. Iona was 'the light of the western world'.[43] Miss S. Taylor, a woman from Birmingham who spent a month and a half in Scotland in 1842, explained the island's significance: 'Lone Isle! Thou wert the Temple of the living God! & taught Earth's millions at his shrine to bow!'[44] Constance Gordon Cumming mused that 'from [Iona's] wave-beaten shores the great pure light arose, which radiating thence on every side, never waned till the whole land was Christianized, and churches and chapels were established in every corner.'[45]

The strength of character which some tourists believed enabled Scots to remain true to a pure Christianity reminds of another recurrent interpretation of Scottish history in travel literature. Scots' record of struggles against invaders, from the Romans to the English, demonstrated an instinctive love of freedom. This version of Scottish history may have had its roots in the efforts of Scottish Enlightenment historians to identify Lowland Scotland with a Teutonic notion of liberty and thus to link Scots more closely with England.[46] Eighteenth-century travelers had explained the Roman failure to occupy much of Scotland in the light of an innate desire for liberty; nineteenth-century tourist literature understood the Wars of Independence, and to some extent, the '45, in the same fashion. This vision of the past was attractive to both Scottish and English tourists, for Scotland's love of liberty was now a contribution to the Union. One of the lures Scotland held for J.E. Bowman was 'the spirit of liberty which still lingers among its mountains, and breathes in its native poetry'.[47] 'John Knox' observed that unlike the ancient Britons, 'a comparatively feeble race', the 'hardy' Picts and Scots of Scotland were never conquered.[48] Walter Scott spoke of the 'characteristic love of independence and liberty which we find [the Scots] have always displayed'.[49] T. C. F. Brotchie, author of *Scottish Western Holiday Haunts,* reminded his readers (most of whom were probably Scottish) that visitors to the seaside town of Largs tread on ground hallowed by 'men who fought and bled and died to free their country from a foreign yoke.'[50] By the early twentieth century, when Brotchie wrote, an interpretation of Scottish history as a continuous struggle for freedom against outside oppressors was taking on nationalist overtones.[51] But for much of the nineteenth century, with a secure Union and a Scottish national identity generally in support of it, English tourists could interpret this history of struggle not as a challenge, but as a sign of a natural love of freedom which many considered a defining British characteristic.

The Wars of Independence were an obvious locus of interest in Scotland's struggles for liberty. Sites associated with William Wallace were repeatedly recommended to eighteenth-century travelers, a sign both of a Scottish fascination with Wallace which grew even stronger in the nineteenth century, and of the Scottish assumption that English tourists shared that interest. So common were Wallace associations in the eighteenth century that traveler John Stoddart claimed 'The name of Wallace is attached to every spot, with which there is a bare possibility of historically connecting it.'[52] By the next century, Stirling was a favorite tourist attraction, offering the site of Wallace's 1297 victory at Stirling Bridge, Robert Bruce's victory at Bannockburn, and after 1869 the National Wallace Monument. Thomas Cook's guidebook pointed out the site of the 'great battle' of Bannockburn, but did not suggest that tourists depart from the train to visit the battlefield.[53] (Possibly because there was little to see there.[54]) The Wallace Monument attracted 4,000-5,000 visitors a day in the late 1880s. It is difficult to know the national breakdown of the visitors, however, nor how many made the trek out of reverence for Wallace and how many simply wished to see the view.[55] English tourists seldom commented on the monument.

Scottish tourists may well have been more interested in Wallace and Bruce than were English ones. Despite the anglicizing trends of much of Scottish history of the period, Wallace and Bruce still spoke to a Scottish national identity. Although it was Bruce, not Wallace, who achieved victory, and a large monument to Robert Bruce was built in front of Stirling Castle in 1877, Wallace was the eighteenth- and nineteenth-century favorite. The Victorian era saw a surge of Scottish interest in William Wallace, manifested in commemorative statues and monuments, biographies, histories, and plays. Wallace became the 'supreme patriot' to Scots, a status achievable in part because of the lack of definitive information about him. He fulfilled several symbolic meanings for Scots. Nineteenth-century historiography emphasized his great strength, portraying him as the epitome of masculine greatness. He therefore satisfied the stereotype of the brawny Scotsman vs. the effete Englishman. (To young Lucy Sherwood, visiting Bannockburn in the 1820s, it was Robert Bruce who filled that role. She described Bruce as a model of 'brave' manhood, in contrast to the 'idle and weak' Edward.[56]) Wallace was also a romantic hero who was motivated by high principles, such as the desire for Scottish independence and revenge for his wife's death, rather than political ambitions. He was a man of the people; Bruce sided with the nobility. Wallace was an outlaw; Bruce was a monarch. Wallace was a loyal Scot, Bruce an opportunist.[57]

The many commemorations of the Wars of Independence helped bolster a sense of Scottish patriotism. Visits to the battlefield of Bannockburn sometimes stirred visceral feelings of national loyalty in Scottish visitors. In 1800 John Leyden approached Bannockburn 'with such vivid emotions of patriotism, that had an Englishman presented himself I should have felt strongly inclined to knock him down.'[58] Wallace, said James Hunter, who toured parts of his 'native Caledonia' in 1834, began a series of events 'which freed his country from a foreign yoke and which has caused his memory to be revered by the people of Scotland.'[59] Scotsman Edwin Waugh nearly burst with patriotic pride when visiting the 'sacred' and 'consecrated' ground of Bannockburn in 1863. But, like many of the period, he did not consider that pride to be exclusive to Scots. Quoting Robert Burns, he insisted that the scene should arouse deep emotions in any man, not just Scots:

> Independent of my enthusiasm as a Scotchman, I have rarely met with anything in history which interests my feelings, as a man, equal with the story of Bannockburn. On the one hand, a cruel, but able, usurper, leading on the finest army in Europe, to extinguish the last spark of freedom among a greatly-daring and greatly-injured people; on the other hand, the desperate relics of a gallant nation, devoting themselves to rescue their bleeding country, or to perish with her.[60]

As Waugh's comments suggest, the idolization of Wallace in the mid-nineteenth century generally did not have an anti-English thrust. In 1834 James Johnson, himself Scottish, could not bring himself to fully sympathize with 'rebellion' against the lawful king: 'When we see a small band of patriots standing in the breach of their country's ramparts, and stemming the torrent of a foreign invasion, our feelings are wound up to the highest pitch, and we would *almost* wish rebellion success in such an unequal conflict' (italics added).[61] As the desire to be 'British' strengthened among the Scottish professional and upper classes, the symbolic meaning of the Wars of Independence was transmuted from Scottish patriotism to support for the Union. In this interpretation, the victory achieved by Wallace and Bruce ensured that Scotland entered the Union as an equal partner. Wallace inspired a deep sense of Scottish identity, but that identity was pointed towards independence within the Union. His fight for the freedom of Scotland thus inspired support for the whole of Great Britain, and was often used to rally support for Britain's nineteenth-century wars.[62]

English observers sometimes misunderstood such sentiments and interpreted Scottish patriotism as exclusive and proprietary. A *Times* editorial of 1856 criticized the plan to construct a memorial to Wallace on Abbey Craig overlooking Stirling. Scotland, said the *Times*, was 'a country manifestly in want of a grievance'. The Union, argued the paper, had brought great good fortune for Scotland, and proponents of the monument stirred up national distinctions at the expense of British patriotism, lauding their country's past rather than working to improve its current situation.[63] Yet the evidence of tourist literature suggests that this attitude was not pervasive. English sightseers went to Stirling and Bannockburn, though perhaps not in the large numbers in which they toured Mary Stuart's bedchamber or even Culloden Moor. The NBR's 'Peggy' found her newfound Scottish patriotism dimming at the sight of the Scottish flag 'flaunting' itself over the graves of her English ancestors at Bannockburn – a joke which indicates the lack of any serious tension between English and Scottish Britons at the site.[64] English interest in the Wars of Independence reflected a respect for the Scottish appreciation of national heroes who fought to secure their country's freedom from foreign domination, a particularly potent theme during the late eighteenth- and early nineteenth-century fears of a French invasion. To William Gilpin, writing in the 1770s, 'These traditional anecdotes [of Wallace], whether true or fabled, add grandeur to a scene; and the variety of these hiding places, which the Scotts [sic] have everywhere provided for Wallace in his misfortunes, show at least their gratitude and affection for one of the noblest heroes, which their own, or any other country hath produced.'[65]

Many were also willing to adopt Wallace and Bruce as their own heroes, and thus to appropriate the love of liberty to which Scottish history was believed to testify. They referred to the 'brave' Bruce and Wallace, and noted other locations associated with one or the other, such as some caves at Hawthornden where Bruce reputedly hid. Bannockburn was the 'Marathon of the North', a victory in which all Britons could take pride. Indeed, radical workers in Sheffield in 1819 marched to the tune of 'Scots Wha Hae wi' Wallace bled' as they demanded reform.[66] Touring the battlefields and monuments at Stirling, one tourist was sure that 'the people of both countries, now so happily united, will join to do homage at the shrine of him who struck for Liberty and Fatherland.'[67] A woman who toured Edinburgh Castle in 1836 was inspired by a military band playing there: 'I felt that I could have assisted in fighting the battles of any country led on by such men as Wallace, Bruce, etc. and stimulated by such soul engrossing harmony.'[68]

English tourists' vicarious Scottish nationalism was even more evident in their responses to the '45 – and equally dependent upon both the loss of political meaning attached to Scottish history and the pro-union position of nineteenth-century Scottish identity. The '45 was by far Victorian tourists' favorite moment in Scottish history, and rare was the visitor who did not express sympathy for the now-powerless House of Stuart. As American tourist William Winter commented in 1911: 'Both democracy and religion can now rejoice that the Duke of Cumberland was the victor, but, standing on that grave of valor, with every voice of romance whispering to his heart, the sympathy of the pilgrim is with the prince who was a fugitive, the cause that was lost, and the heroes who died for it – and died in vain.'[69] Sympathy with the Jacobite cause was enough of a commonplace for it to appear in 'Peggy's' account of her tour of Scotland. Going through Invergarry she felt herself to be 'a right-down, regular Jacobite.' Her father bought a glass of 'grog' for a local resident and induced him to tell them all about 'Charlie', a part of the story which played to the stereotype that Highlanders were still active Jacobites.[70]

As such examples suggest, by Victorian times the story of the Jacobites was a non-threatening tale which ultimately told of the strength of the Union, rather than the possibility of rebellion. That was not the case when English travelers began trekking north in the second half of the eighteenth century. When Richard Pococke visited Culloden Moor in 1760 he described in scathing terms the 'unsoldierlike manner' of the Highlanders, and lauded the defeat inflicted by 'our' forces against the 'enemy' Jacobites.[71] Thomas Pennant described the battlefield as the 'place that North Britain owes its present prosperity to'.[72] Before long, though, the rising was clothed in more romantic colors; by the time T. Garnett reached the Highlands in the 1790s, he described Charles Edward Stuart as 'this unfortunate man.'[73] Support for Charles Edward Stuart had been lukewarm, even in Scotland, but he was made into a glamorous figure by the tradition of the 'Bonny Highland Laddie', a physically attractive and sexually energetic figure common in Scottish popular song. The Messianic and Arthurian iconography long associated with the Stuarts also served to glorify the prince, even during the rising. Numerous histories of the '45 were published soon after its conclusion, some available in French, Spanish, and Italian.[74] The cult of the '45 quickly became an integral element in the 'Highlandism' which permeated the vision of Scotland. Once the Highlands were thoroughly subdued – a necessary prelude to the widespread adulation of the Jacobites – the achievements of Highland regiments in the wars of the eighteenth and early nineteenth centuries suggested that former Stuart supporters were now loyal to the state. Likewise, tartan-clan Highlanders showed their respect for the Hanoverian crown during George IV's 1822 visit to Scotland, an event for which Walter Scott transformed a traditional Jacobite song into a poem in support of George. At a time when the institution of kingship was under attack both inside and outside Great Britain, Jacobitism was redefined as an ideology committed to monarchy in the abstract. The dramatic story of the '45 could thus become wildly popular, and Charles Edward could be portrayed as an inspiration not only to Scots, but to the British nation.[75]

The transmutation of Jacobitism into a Hanoverian and monarchical ideology culminated with Queen Victoria, who claimed the Stuarts as her ancestors: 'I feel a sort of reverence in going over these scenes in this most beautiful country, which I am proud to call my own, where there was such devoted loyalty to the family of my ancestors – for Stuart blood is in my veins, and I am now their representative, and the people are as devoted and loyal to me as they were to that unhappy race.'[76] Following the queen's lead, her subjects could happily praise the bravery and 'mistaken loyalty' of the

Highlanders who fought for pretenders to the throne, and lament the actions of government troops in the aftermath of Culloden without compromising their loyalty to the monarch or the state. Secure in the strength of the Union, Victorians could rejoice that Charles Edward's defeat at Culloden paved the way for the consolidation of Great Britain, while also enjoying the romance of the lost cause.

Virtually any locale associated with Charles Edward was demarcated by tourist literature as sacred ground; one guidebook proclaimed that the 'whole district of the Western Highlands' was rendered interesting as the scene of his wanderings.[77] Within five pages, another pointed out four different spots where he hid and two places where his followers took cover.[78] In 1867 Peter Anderson published the first guidebook to Culloden Moor, which included a description of the battle and its aftermath, with maps detailing the course of the fighting. From the 1870s on, guidebooks regularly printed maps of the prince's routes through Scotland, as well as long accounts of his adventures, especially his flight to Skye with Flora MacDonald. The story of Charles' months of hiding in the hills and glens, protected by loyal Highlanders while government troops scoured the countryside for him, appealed to sentimental tastes. His safe passage from South Uist escorted by MacDonald was told as a romantic tale of compassion and courage. Sightseers eagerly visited key sites such as Culloden, Glenfinnan, and the Isle of Skye, although few people were motivated to follow Charles Edward's travels very closely, as they lay in difficult terrain.[79]

Not only could visitors make their way to scenes associated with Bonnie Prince Charlie, there to soak up the pathos and romance of his name, but tourist literature suggested that they might yet meet people who were loyal to his cause. Some observers affirmed that Highlanders still retained vestigial loyalty to the 'King across the water'. 'In Skye, the story of his [Charles Edward's] journeyings through the island is still preserved, for Skyemen can never forget the Prince's gratitude for their loyalty, nor the memory of their ancestor who fought and bled for his cause.'[80] Tourists' interest in Jacobites, implied J. A. MacCulloch, merely fed off the continuing fidelity of islanders, who he thus linked more closely to the eighteenth century than the early twentieth. In Skye, he observed, 'one is never far distant' from the 'age of loyalty'.[81] A guidebook of 1830 assured readers that the rock on the island of Arisaig where Charles Edward first landed in Scotland 'is still pointed out with respect.'[82] Just as the myth of Highland faithfulness to the Stuarts was a valued conservative sign during the age of the French Revolution, so was it a welcome indication to later travelers of Highlanders' and islanders' immunity to the changes of nineteenth century. In 1829 Beriah Botfield observed that Jacobites were 'a living specimen of a very fine old school, which has left little behind it but the tradition of its virtues, its talents, and its pleasantries; a school the departure of many of whose peculiarities was perhaps rendered necessary in a great measure by the spirit of the age, but of which it may be suspected not a little has been allowed to expire which might have been better worth preserving than much which has come in its place.'[83]

Scots, however, were more ambivalent towards the sacred spaces of Jacobitism than English tourists might have expected. For much of the nineteenth century nearby residents had little interest in Culloden Moor. The local *Inverness Courier* paid scant attention to the site during the first half of the century. A centenary celebration took place there in 1846, but as Colin MacArthur notes, the mood was more 'carnivalesque' than elegiac.[84] Highlanders of the early nineteenth century could not as easily put the political and social aftermath of the battle of Culloden out of their mind, linked as that outcome was with the economic transformation of the Highlands, emigration, and the Clearances. Plans were made in 1849 for a memorial cairn honoring the fallen Jacobites, but it was shelved for lack of funds by 1852. Although the idea was revived in 1858, it did yet not come to fruition.[85] When a stature honoring Flora MacDonald was erected in Inverness in 1896, it was only after a campaign of several years during which tourists had often asked why there was no memorial at her grave. Letters appeared in newspapers, 'upbraiding the descendants of Highland Jacobites for this neglect'.[86] Although Flora MacDonald quickly became a romantic heroine after the '45, her later emigration to North America and eventual return also evoked the difficulties which beset the Highlands in the late eighteenth century, memories her Skye neighbors could not forget as easily as could 'strangers'. Local ambivalence could be read as 'neglect' of her grave, necessitating outside intervention in the commemorating of Highland history.

By the time Flora MacDonald's memorial was erected, however, Jacobitism was taking on a stronger nationalist meaning for at least some Scots, as middle-class support for the Union grew less certain and support for Home Rule became more vocal. The idea of Scottish history as an ongoing struggle for liberty was to some a radical message, whose nationalist undertones began to resurface at mid-century. A commemorative cairn was eventually built at Culloden Moor in 1881. The dedication plaque, which was actually inscribed in 1858, made clear that the battle was being linked to Scottish patriotism. The cairn, said the plaque, marked 'the graves of gallant Highlanders who fought for Scotland & Prince Charlie'.[87] In 1887 Theodore Napier, an eccentric but influential nationalist of the late nineteenth century, began an annual pilgrimage to Culloden. Several neo-Jacobite organizations were founded in the 1880s and 1890s, in both England and Scotland. Their aims were varied; to some, like the writers of the Celtic Twilight, Jacobitism was a spiritual movement, a protest against utilitarianism, materialism, and commercialism. To others, support for the Stuarts was more clearly associated with Scottish autonomy. Although neo-Jacobite adherents were few, with their interpretation of the '45, they, Napier in particular, introduced a nationalist note into Scottish political discourse. For many Scots, the effect was to undo the easy consignment of Jacobitism to a colorful but neutral past. Jacobitism was 'once again an agent for change or at least an unease which contributed to a broader perspective on Scotland's future than had hitherto been taken.'[88] But this re-invigoration of the political message of Jacobitism, though an important development in Scottish nationalist discourse, was not as yet powerful enough to affect English tourists' enjoyment of their vicarious Scottish nationalism. Their ability to understand a Scottish commitment to freedom as part of a natural British instinct for liberty effaced any radicalism associated with Jacobitism in the late nineteenth century.

Scottish history as told by tourism (and by most other sources of the time) was but a delightful supplement to English history, with little independent significance. The addition of Scottish to British history strengthened the national stories of religious piety and of an instinctive drive for independence and freedom which were hallmarks of nineteenth-century Britain's sense of itself, while helping the nation to claim an integrated, non-divisive past. At the same time, this stronger national story effectively marginalized Scotland's autonomy, seeing the importance of the country's history only as it related to the British whole. As the anecdotes of Scottish history became features of the tourist circuit their context and meaning were disregarded. Meanwhile Scottish promoters of tourism, striving to advance the visibility and prestige of their country, encouraged visitors to adopt those stories as their own. Yet Scottish history remained Scottish, not British. Although they took pride in being members of a wider Union, Scots continued to ask their own questions, and seek their own answers, of their past. As time went on, their history began to teach them different lessons than it had to English fellow sightseers in the nineteenth century.

History as Geography

While tourists valued Scotland's historic attractions for the lessons available there about the meaning of Scotland's – and Britain's – past, they esteemed such locations even more highly for the opportunity to visit bygone years. Scotland's history, it often seemed, was a geographic location, a palpable, still-living entity. Travel literature implied that the past was unusually accessible in Scotland, through the landscape, the many historic buildings and locations, and an atmosphere which allowed one to forget the present. In Skye, for instance, tourists were 'free of one's century; the present wheels away into silence and remoteness.' The same wind that filled the sails of Vikings and ruffled their gold hair, might play in the hair of nineteenth-century visitors, according to Alexander Smith.[89] So ever-present was the sense of history that Herbert Byng Hall complained tourists talked of Glencoe as if they expected to arrive in time for the massacre.[90] By visiting Scotland, a culture acutely aware of the increasing pace of time could become temporarily oblivious to it. Much as immersion in nature freed business and professional men from the tyranny of the clock, engrossment in the past was a release from the oppression of the calendar. One travel writer, describing a glen near the Cuillins, affirmed that there 'the silence and the remoteness make one oblivious of time and of the lapse of history.'[91] Scotland's immunity to time modified the pervasiveness of modernization and made it more acceptable. If Scotland's past so easily came alive, then industrialization had not distanced modern society from its roots.

As the momentum of historical change altered in the nineteenth century, the importance of the past as a validation of the present became evident. The past needed to be preserved so the present would not be cut adrift from its moorings – an apparent likelihood in a time of transformation. David Brett argues that a preoccupation with the past lay at the very foundation of modernity, as the experience of continual change gave rise to its dialectical counterpoint: a fixation with the past. The past promised continuity in what seemed like an incontinuous world.[92] It also offered attractive, if imagined, counters to the perceived problems of contemporary times. In comparison with an uncertain present, the past was safe, completed, orderly. In contrast with the feared soulessness of the age of steam, the past, particularly the Middle Ages, had passion and poetry.[93] In Martin Wiener's words, by the end of the century, as doubts grew about the true consequences of progress, 'the old world had been called in to redress the balance of the new – to legitimate, to revivify, and to provide relief from the stresses of the present.'[94]

The tangibility of bygone years in Scotland alleged by tourist literature rendered that country the antithesis of the newness of the modern age. Contemporary Scotland, it often seemed, was but a thin veneer through which poked the past. Wherever one went, relics lent immediacy to history. If visitors stepped off the main streets of elegant early twentieth-century Aberdeen, said travel writer George Eyre-Todd, 'lo! the whole modern aspect and character of the place prove but skin deep; one has passed at a single step out of the twentieth century into an atmosphere of the feudal ages.'[95] Time moved so slowly at Culloden Moor that according to virtually every nineteenth-century description of the battlefield, green patches of grass still identified the graves of the fallen. The belief that the bodies of the Jacobite dead still fertilized the soil of Culloden over one hundred years after the battle symbolized the timelessness of Scotland and offered a physical link to the '45. Likewise the verdant spots and ruined huts that allegedly continued to mark the site of the Glencoe massacre erased the passage of time between 1689 and the nineteenth century. As late as 1863 *Anderson's* guidebook asserted that a cave on Eigg still contained fragments of skeletons left when a group of clansmen were secured inside and burned to death by a rival clan.[96] Whole towns might be physically unchanged for centuries; the appearance of the village of Falkland 'is now exactly that which it wore in the sixteenth century'.[97]

Because such artifacts seemingly arrested the pace of historical time, tourists in Scotland could visit other ages. As early as the 1790s, John Lettice found that '[t]he impression of antiquity' around Clackmannan 'was so strong, as almost to create a momentary illusion of our existing in other times.'[98] To visit the island of Hinba, said one travel writer, 'is to raise a section of the dead and to hold an interview with it.'[99] Numerous visitors commented on the ease with which bygone years could be conjured up. At Iona, Constance Gordon Cumming found 'it needed but a little play of fancy to pass over the intervening twelve centuries and call up visions of that old life' in the early days of monastic settlement.[100] Along Edinburgh's Royal Mile, 'The echo of our steps on the pavement seems to renew the royal pageants and martial glories of an earlier time; and we have no difficulty in imagining the windows crowded with bright ladies and sinewy burghers, to see the old monarchs with their retinue of earls and barons, and the firm warriors, whose armour bears the dint of English weapons, passing to and from the castle.'[101] Like many others, T. H. Holding, as he visited Stirling, 'could not help in fancy picturing up the long dead heroes and historical personages who once figured so prominently here, but who now only live in history.' He longed to stay until dark, the better to recreate the martial scenes which had taken place there.[102] Others found it took little imagination to catch a glimpse of Ossianic heroes, or to see the clans gathering at Glenfinnan in 1745.

Victorians were fond of historical and archeological sightseeing, an activity which grew out of their visual rather than verbal sense of the past, and one which enabled them to assert control over the calendar by playing at being members of other ages.[103] Nineteenth-century historians believed the imagination was a vital tool in their effort to uncover the highest truths about the past; the historian needed to 'resuscitate the living reality from dead facts.'[104] They thereby evoked in readers a tendency to apply their imaginations and creativity to explorations of historical locales. Imaginative interactions with the past were standard activities on journeys to Scotland and were clearly expected of tourists. Historian Peter Mandler describes Victorians' 'multi-media' approach to historic sites, whereby historic novels, history paintings, dramatic performances, and historic buildings were all staged to refer to each other.[105] Guidebooks were also key elements of this process. Those of Scotland usually contained lengthy historic narratives, drawn, when possible, from Walter Scott. Historic sites were thus more 'usable' to the tourist; already aware of the tales a historic place had to tell, visitors could unleash their imaginations once they were at the location.[106] So readily did sightseers in Scotland come upon the past, and so well prepared were they, that they often suggested those encounters were not play, but involuntary responses to the unavoidable presence of earlier years. Many travel accounts implied that previous centuries resided in a state of suspended animation, ready to return to life at the arrival of the tourist. Several visitors claimed that they 'could not help' but imagine the sight of long dead heroes, or processions of kilted warriors, or Mary Stuart fleeing Loch Leven castle.[107] Visions of Vikings 'came over' Gordon Cumming at Dunvegan.[108] As the sightseer wandered through the old apartments of Holyroodhouse, said one, 'the people of the past seem to arise up and to inhabit them again'.[109] When walking into Edinburgh's Canongate, said Winter, 'the storied figures of history walk by [the tourist's] side or come to meet him at every close and wynd'.[110]

One story which easily came alive to nineteenth-century visitors was that of Mary Stuart.[111] When Chauncy Townshend toured her rooms at Holyroodhouse, he fantasized about their return to their former splendor before his very eyes. Suddenly the small chamber appeared to be clothed with silk and tapestries. It was furnished with tapers, and set for a small banquet. He seemed to see Mary and Rizzio, to hear a noise from the adjourning chamber, and to see the queen turn pale as a man jumped into the room.[112] The '45 also readily sprang to life in tourists' imaginations. Those who visited Culloden Moor found themselves able to envision the battle with little effort, which made the events seem much less distant and more real. 'You can almost fancy the fray passing before you.'[113] At Prestonpans, too, '...the pilgrim who stands upon the veritable scene of the battle comprehends as never before the suspense, the shuddering excitement, the carnage, the panic, and the horror of that memorable episode in the Stuart Wars.'[114]

Historic locales were not difficult to find in the nineteenth century. Physical remnants of earlier times were real presences throughout much of Great Britain, as constant a feature of daily life as railways or cotton mills.[115] But England had, in John Ruskin's words, 'our new street, our new inn, our green shaven lawn, and our piece of ruin emergent from it, – a mere *specimen* of the Middle Ages put on a bit of velvet carpet'.[116] In Scotland it seemed possible to be completely overwhelmed by the past. This belief had many sources. Scotland's landscape, especially in the Highlands, was often emptier than England's and lacked many signs of modernity. Although the past was available in the heavily populated Lowland cities as well as in the Highlands, the vast empty spaces in the west and north reminded of a pre-industrial world. The widespread currency of Walter Scott's dramatizations of the Scottish past focused attention on a history that, because less familiar to English readers, was exotic and romantic. The tourist industry directed visitors to historic sites and described a country whose past was one of its most salient characteristics. Some travel literature managed to give the impression that time had stood still in Scotland since 1745 – unlike the rest of the island where time seemed to have been rushing faster and faster ever since then. For instance, the guidebook published by MacBrayne's steamship company in 1896 described the Sound of Mull by referring to an account written by Martin Martin in 1716, thereby suggesting that the west Highlands had remained essentially unchanged for 180 years.[117] Scotland's rural folk, especially those of the Highlands and islands, were usually understood to be living just as their ancestors had for generations, thus serving as living mementos of the past. *Anderson's* guidebook of 1834 advised that a 1693 description of the people of Orkney was 'probably as accurate now as it was then.'[118] Tourists' own expectations and desires also prepared them to meet the past as they traveled north.

Visits to historic attractions were important components of the Victorian adjustment to the new industrial world, operating in much the same manner that weekends in the country touring medieval churches may have helped nineteenth-century people accommodate to elements of modernity which they did not like.[119] Control over the passage of time allowed tourists to feel less displaced by change. As industrialization destroyed many of the remains of old England and created a chasm between the preindustrial world and the newness of so much of the nineteenth century, the accessibility of the past in Scotland taught that despite appearances, modern society was not disconnected from earlier times. However, it can be argued that tourism increasingly portrayed Scotland as an unchanging place of 'heritage' where the modern world might be escaped. 'Heritage' in this context, is defined as historical events which no longer have contemporary relevance, and become artifacts visited by a present no longer attached to them by any living links of political consequence.[120] It is their disconnection from real, concrete time which is the appeal of heritage sites, for they promise that something can be preserved that will not fade away. Heritage, therefore, represents security. But immunity to time also suggests an insusceptibility to the continuing forces of history. Understanding Scotland as a vast heritage site could have the effect of freezing the country in time, problemmatizing its movement into the modern age.[121] Just as eighteenth-century historians' construction of the Scottish past rendered it fascinating yet also irrelevant to the modern age, so did the idea of Scotland as 'heritage' suggest a present sterility. Critic David Lowenthal observes that an aura of antiquity in a much preserved locale signifies not historical vitality, but a dearth of innovative energy.[122] Similarly, Scotsman Robert Heron, who toured his country in the 1790s, alleged that 'monuments of antiquity' were least permanent in countries that continued to improve. It was 'where succeeding generations have degenerated from the glory, and declined from the splendor of their ancestors', or at least had advanced little, that 'works of antiquity' were preserved with pride and reverence.[123] Heron was thus pleased to see few memorials to former times as he traveled, but would surely have been saddened to see the extent to which Victorian travel writers, both Scottish and English, placed so heavy an emphasis on the past. Scotland, it has been argued, came to possess too much heritage, as, well into the twentieth century, images of the country came to depend on a series of historical symbols disconnected from any political meaning and not serving to promote a progressive understanding of the nation.[124]

Scottish promoters of tourism clearly realized the marketability of history, and they understood the celebration of it as a way to emphasize Scotland's distinctiveness. In doing so, however, they often de-emphasized Scotland's busy and creative present. While a thriving economy intrigued eighteenth-century travelers who reveled in the expansion of the British commercial spirit, Victorians sought an exotic differentness. Visitors knew of the bustling economies of Scotland's Lowland cities and included elements of them on their travel itineraries. But factories and ports could be seen at home; the availability of Scotland's history was a more valuable offering. The images presented by tourism reflected that fact. Scotland often seemed to be little more than a reservoir of the past, drinking from which refreshed tourists and refitted them for their return to the modern world, while Scotland remained stranded in time. Tourist literature often suggested that sightseers shut their eyes to features of the industrial age, the better to experience former eras. Early twentieth-century visitors to Melrose were advised that it was indeed best to see the Abbey by moonlight as followers of Walter Scott were wont to do. Only then, when the railway bridge and the modern suburban developments were less visible, could one 'seem almost to live again in the romantic times of old.'[125]

Tourists' penchant for imagining the splendors of a building which in their own era was but a ruin could stand as a metaphor for a Scotland whose greatest worth lay in the past. The crumbling walls of 'once splendid and extensive' or 'once noble' palaces and cathedrals emphasized that the glories of earlier years had vanished.[126] Beriah Botfield observed that the 'desolate grandeur' of Linlithgow, once a royal burgh, provided an idea of the attributes of an independent Scottish court – but also reminded that those days were long gone.[127] Visitors to any once-magnificent monarchical home, thought William Deane Ryland, a Cambridge student who toured Scotland in 1823, 'naturally' sought to revive the past, to imagine the beauty, mirth, and power once displayed there. 'But alas! the present forms a sad contrast to the past, the real to the imaginary scene; – as we proceed, all is silence and desolation – the bat wings its way through the roofless galleries, and weeds have sprung up in those chambers whose boast it is to have been the nursery of Princes'.[128] Only in the imagination, it seemed, did Scotland still possess the potency to built such palaces. A woman who visited Glenfinnan envisioned the gathering of the clans in 1745 through a similar lens. 'I could almost fancy, in the lonely stillness, I heard the wild notes of the pibroch and saw the waving of the tartan as the clans came winding down. But there was nothing but the lake and the watching hills, and the poor, stony waiting Prince. Our little party seemed the only spot of life in the wilderness.'[129] Her illusion had more vitality than the scene which surrounded her.

Such melancholy descriptions could be read as laments for the days of Scotland's autonomous power. As most Victorians took the Union for granted, however, they did not ask why the past witnessed to by the faded grandeur of early modern royal architecture had not sustained an independent modern nation. Nor did the tourist industry challenge them to do so. Scotland's past was not portrayed as a precursor to the country's contemporary situation, for modernity was molded by the consequences of 1707. Unable therefore to energize the present, Scottish history was reduced to a vacationland, a heritage park, for tourists. It is not surprising that the Scottish history found by tourists was selective and superficial; heritage is a construction of the present more than the past. But given the centrality of tourism in British understanding of Scotland, the triviality of the vision of Scotland's past produced by tourism had significant consequences for the development of the country's national identity.

However, sightseers' propensity to reduce Scotland to an immutable land of heritage existed alongside a contrasting desire – to observe a living present intermingled with the past. One of the attractions of Edinburgh, said Thomas Cook, quoting a Mrs. Sigourney's *Pleasant Memories of Pleasant Lands*, was the way the past there mingled with the present. One could scarcely disentangle the web of current and older associations.[130] This alternate vision of former eras attributed to them little more political consequence than did the notion of 'heritage', but did posit a connection between the past and the present. Despite many Victorians' yearning and reverence for the past, they recognized an obligation to the present.[131] The fact that Scotland was clearly part of the nineteenth century was an essential component of the past's ability to ameliorate concern about modernity, for it was through their conjunction with the contemporary age that former times witnessed to the continuity of history. Tourists seldom genuinely escaped the modern period; railroads, telegraph poles, recently constructed buildings, and other appurtenances of nineteenth-century and early twentieth-century life were often intertwined with the historic scenes they visited. The frequent injunctions to sightseers to look 'through the eyes of the imagination' were implicit recognitions that the present day was more evident at many historic locations than was the past. Scotland was fast becoming a modern place. The commercialism that often surrounded historic sites and the self-consciousness with which many visitors sought to be absorbed by the atmosphere of earlier times made these locations merely stage sets, not living presences.[132] Some tourists portrayed the nineteenth century as being more alive than were earlier years. As Cuthbert Bede gazed on Roslin Castle, he was tempted to 'throw' himself 'into the Past.' But 'the rattle of a railway train and the scream of the engine-whistle drag me back to the realities of the Present, and remind me that the Peebles railway is close at hand, and that tourists can see the sights of Roslin for one shilling.'[133] Augustus Tipple endeavored to immerse himself in former years when he visited William Douglas' grave. He fancied he heard the battle's din, and saw the triumphant Oliver Cromwell overseeing his army and the dying Douglas by 'my side'. Yet his imagination could not fully overcome more prosaic truths. 'But all this was foolish fancy, and the voices of my companions awoke me to the plain dry reality that it was dark and late, and would be later still before we reached home.' Nonetheless, he 'most certainly dreamed of battles and war that night.'[134]

As frequently as the texts of tourism counseled sightseers to ignore signs of the present they also drew attention to them, the better to witness to the continuity of history and demonstrate that no chasm divorced current from former times. 'The smart railway steamer of today travels the same 'flood' as these old Norsemen.'[135] Nineteenth-century life, suggested such guides, was but one of many layers of history in Scotland. Tourists were participants in a long march of events, which by implication would continue after them. Because each generation added something more to the scene, the present was tied to earlier ages. Sightseers could tread the same paths 'trodden by the foot of many a hero of old romance in the days of fightings and forays, Norsemen and Danes'.[136] They could sit on the same cold hearthstones where children once sat and listened to legends of witches and warlocks.[137] They could visit rooms once occupied by heroes, surrounded by walls that were mute 'witnesses' to history.

Evidence of contemporary times could be distracting to those who wished to lose themselves in romantic reveries. But by mixing the potentially threatening new with the comfortable old, visible contrasts between past and present helped to make the changes of the nineteenth century more acceptable.[138] Tourists needed Scotland to be part of the modern world, if its history was to serve this purpose. 'The profit of walking in the footsteps of the Past is perception of the value of the privilege of life in the Present', said William Winter.[139] The contrast between modern technology and medieval ruins stirred imaginations and often intensified the present's continuity with the times that had gone before. At the railway station at Lumphanan, according to George Eyre-Todd, one could throw a pebble from the train window into the base from which MacBeth made his last stand against his enemies.[140] Interminglings of the evidence of former and contemporary times provided opportunities for tourists to contemplate the differences between historic periods and those of their own. Linlithgow, where a busy rail line passed near the ruined palace where Mary Stuart was born, testified to one visitor of 1860 that the nineteenth century, not the sixteenth, was the more vital period. The palace was 'very lonely; a wreck of antique splendor, stranded beside that torrent of active life rushing hourly past on the steam road.'[141] Others, too, saw signs of progress when former and current times visibly met. The Carron Iron Works lay near Falkirk battlefield, scene of a defeat of William Wallace in 1298.[142] The disjunction between a medieval battlefield and an eighteenth-century manufactory presented two types of British pride: in the hero who epitomized the British love of liberty, and in the modern industrial skills which made Great Britain the economic leader of the world. Similarly, the furnace fires that glowed around Glasgow reminded one visitor of the beacons that must have blazed in that area in the days of Border warfare. In the nineteenth century, though, the fires told of peaceful industry, not the horrors of battle.[143] A mixture of ancient and modern buildings also made the effects of industrialization less alien, reminding viewers that the present was but another stage of history. In the resort town of Rothesay, full of 'modern villa and tenement', a ruined chapel stood as 'a solitary memorial of far-away times.'[144]

Like the 'heritage' notion of history, the vision of an intertwined past and present also depended upon the preservation of bygone years. Scotland's past remained alluring and exotic, even to those who sought continuity rather than escape. Jacob Abbott's musings at the sight of the rail line next to the ruins of Linlithgow Palace suggests the conflict many must have felt between the romance attributed to former eras and the achievements of their own.

> How strong was the contrast! The age that is past and the age that is to come visibly embodied before us, side by side; the chivalry, the wars, the superstition, the romantic sorrows and suffering of the one; the science, the energy, the industry, and the comforts and conveniences of the other; and so strong are the illusions of the imagination in such a case, that it was hard to resist the desire that the railway and all its appurtenances might disappear.[145]

Abbot was excited by the progress wrought by the 'age that is to come' and by the visible antithesis between it and that which came before. Yet a part of him yearned to wish the railway away. Many tourists found that they could do just that in Scotland. Whether they sought to flee the modern world or to experience its connectedness with former ages, Victorians' concerns about the ever-increasing pace of time, both historic and daily time, combined with the Scottish desire to call attention to the uniqueness of their country, associated Scotland with the past rather than modernity. The vibrancy and accessibility of Scotland's earlier years enabled tourists to find there the perpetuity of history which assured them of the groundedness of the modern world. Scotland's contemporary attractions, though crucial to this construction, were less important than the living spirit of former years. Scotland was the past; England represented the present and future. Scotland needed to keep earlier times alive, so the modern age could retain its historic roots. That function undervalued the necessity of progress for Scotland and would come to influence how Scots saw their own country.

Highland Traditions

One of the chief means by which tourists believed Scotland kept the past alive was through the traditions of the Highlands, particularly what was considered the historic dress of the region. Visitors to Scotland were eager to believe that well-known features of Highland life such as kilts, tartans, bagpipes, and Highland games were time-honored folkways which had remained unchanged for centuries – and were therefore tangible signs of the continuity of Scottish history. Promoters of tourism, meanwhile, saw in the popularity of Highlandism a means of claiming Scottish distinctiveness and of appealing to potential customers. Tourism was thus complicit in the 'Balmoralization' of Scotland, as practices which were of dubious historical authenticity and representative of only part of the country became symbols of the whole. In reality, by the nineteenth century many of tourists' favorite Highland traditions were artificially maintained. Sufficient evidence existed to make that fact clear to sightseers, should they choose to believe it. By electing instead to see Highland dress as evidence of Scotland's still living past, tourists demonstrated again their desire that the country remain immune to the passage of time.

Victorian tourists were less likely to engage in the detailed ethnographic work of many earlier travelers in Scotland. They were intrigued by the ways of life of ordinary Highlanders, especially the small crofters of the Western Isles. But the traditions which most interested the Victorians were not the ordinary features of daily life and work but the centerpieces of Balmoralized Scotland: kilts, tartans, bagpipes, and clans. As several historians have shown, it was only in the late eighteenth century that those elements of Highland life came to be regarded as exotic and desirable symbols of Scottishness.[146] Kilts and tartans top the list of 'invented traditions'. The kilt, known also as the 'philabeg' from the Gaelic *'feileadh beag'*, is a modern version of the *'feileadh-bhreacain'*, a long tartan cloth worn by Highland males in the sixteenth and seventeenth centuries. The wearer laid a belt on the ground and on top of it folded the plaid lengthwise into pleats, then laid down on the cloth, folded the material over the front of his body, and fastened the belt around his waist. He then had a pleated skirt below his waist and a mass of material above it which could be arranged in different ways to cover the upper body or to allow freedom of movement for his arms. Undoing the belt at night, he could wrap up in the plaid to sleep. Wealthier Highlanders, particularly clan leaders, were more likely to wear 'trews', a form of tight, close-fitting trousers, also made of tartan. The development of the modern kilt as a separate article from the plaid has been controversially attributed to Thomas Rawlinson, the owner of an iron ore furnace in Invergarry in the 1820s, who sought to make the dress of his workers more amenable to industrial occupations. Rawlinson shortened the plaids of his workmen and had a version made for himself and a business associate, MacDonnell of Glengarry, with pleats permanently stitched in. The upper portion, which came to be known simply as the 'plaid', could still be worn around the shoulders in the same manner as was the *feileadh-bhreacain*, and taken off when wet without completely undressing.[147]

All elements of Highland dress were banned under the Disarming Act of 1746. Clothing styles for Highlanders thereafter began to change, as tourists found. But the Disarming Act called attention to the kilt, plaid, and tartan as key elements of Highland culture just at the moment when the Highlands were being created as an object of fashionable attention. As soon as the proscription of Highland dress was lifted in 1782 members of both the Highland and Lowland upper and middle classes began to wear the kilt as a sign of Scottishness. (Most Highlanders, by contrast, did not have the resources in the late eighteenth century to re-outfit themselves with Highland dress.) When George IV wore the kilt during his 1822 visit to Edinburgh, he set the seal of fashionable approval on a once denigrated and outlawed costume.

Tartan underwent a similar transformation. The term 'tartan' to describe woolen cloth woven in a multi-colored striped and checked pattern dates from about 1600, although evidence for any uniformity of design by family, clan, or locality dates from the late seventeenth or early eighteenth centuries. Even then, the sett, or pattern, of fabric worn by a Highlander depended upon locality and personal preference, not upon clan identification. The association of specific tartans with individual clans as a marker of clan membership developed in the late eighteenth and early nineteenth century. The Highland regiments, recruited in the second half of the eighteenth century, wore tartan kilts as their uniforms, even during the proscription of Highland dress. In the 1790s the regiments began to differentiate themselves by tartan, which gave rise to the idea that different setts belonged to specific clans. That notion was supported by proponents of the Highlands such as Colonel David Stewart of Garth, the various Highland societies, and by an enterprising tartan manufacturing company, Wilsons of Bannockburn. The militarization of Highland dress also fostered a trend towards uniformity, spurring a search for 'authentic' histories of dress and tartans, which were sometimes invented when evidence was unavailable. George IV's 1822 Scottish visit was influential here, too. Walter Scott urged Highland chiefs to bring their clansmen to town arrayed in 'traditional' dress, causing chiefs to search for their 'own' tartans – either reviving old setts that were dying out, or purchasing newly created ones from Wilsons. The demand for tartan cloth and for specific clan setts continued after 1822, so much so that Wilsons opened a second weaving mill. As this popularity continued throughout the nineteenth century, 'Highland dress' turned into 'tartan costume', a fashionable style having little to do with its origin as practical clothes for poor peasants.[148]

Travelers of the late eighteenth and early nineteenth centuries saw clearly that kilts and tartans were no longer daily dress for ordinary folk, and many were aware there was controversy over the antiquity of the costume.[149] Samuel Johnson noted that the plaid was rarely worn in the islands; he and Boswell saw only one gentleman fully clothed in the 'ancient habit', and that man did not wear it all the time. However, Johnson asserted that the philabeg was still common.[150] In 1803 Philip Homer found that Highland dress was wearing away every hour.[151] John Carr, who in 1807 expected to find many examples of Highland dress, discovered that it was yielding, piecemeal, to southern style. Few gentlemen wore the kilt, he said, unless sporting or farming.[152] On his 1822 trip William Pearson recalled meeting only one person north of the Firth of Forth wearing a kilt – a man returning from an exhibition in Edinburgh.[153] But the 'invention of the Highlands' was taking firm hold as those travelers wrote, and was further stimulated by Victoria and Albert's taste for things Scottish. Balmoral, the royal family's home in Deeside, was built in what was deemed an 'authentic' Scots Baronial style and decorated with a profusion of tartans. The queen demonstrated in her Highland journals, published in 1868, her affection for what were becoming well-known symbols of Scotland: tartans, kilts, bagpipes, Highland games, even the Highlanders themselves. Her partiality was shared by many of her subjects, and the Balmoralization of Scotland intensified. Highland Games were revived and formalized. Bagpiping was promoted and encouraged. The modern clan societies were founded or reconstituted in the late nineteenth century; Clan MacNaughton in 1878, Clan Mackay in 1888, with more proliferating in the 1890s.[154]

Nineteenth-century sightseers, therefore, were able to believe that Highland dress was a tradition which was still very much alive. To Victorian and Edwardian tourists, a Highlander who, without giving it a second thought, still dressed as his ancestors had, was a powerful symbol of Scotland's oneness with the past. (Discussions of Highland garb focused almost exclusively on male attire.) Kilts and tartans were staples of tourist images of Scotland – and not only of the Highlands. Illustrations in guidebooks and other travel literature frequently included kilted figures. Belief in the preponderance of kilts in Scotland was a stereotype perpetuated by both Scottish guidebook authors and English tourists. *Sylvan's Pictorial Handbook to the Scenery of the Caledonian Canal*, published in Edinburgh in 1848, commented that the 'stranger' to Fort William was quickly struck by the frequency of the kilt.[155] Throughout the nineteenth century visitors continued to describe with great enthusiasm the sight of Highlanders wearing 'the garb of old Gaul'. A visitor of 1836 was excited to see soldiers of a Highland regiment on duty at Edinburgh Castle, 'attired in that most graceful of all dresses the costume of the country.'[156] C. S. Stewart, also in Scotland in the 1830s, noted that boys under ages twelve to fourteen could still be seen in the 'Highland garb' and that gentlemen sometimes wore 'the national costume' as full dress for dinner.[157] Guides at Taymouth Castle dressed in kilts in 1848. A visitor earnestly pointed out that one of the owner's aides put on trousers only once in his life – and found them so uncomfortable as he walked over the moors that he threw them away.[158] Late in the nineteenth century two sisters on a bicycle tour visited the Highland Games at Inverness: 'Kilts to the right of us, kilts to the left of us and at all we stared rudely – and wondered, trying to name the Tartans and decide the Clans; we were quite carried away with the dress!'[159]

Not only was the kilt still worn, but popular opinion asserted that it and the tartan were authentic pieces of history. T. Garnett believed Highland dress was derived from that of the ancient Romans, to which he thought it bore a considerable resemblance.[160] William Gilpin found that the sight of a Highland gentleman on horseback 'carries you back into Roman times; and presents you with the idea of Marcus Aurelius.'[161] Over one hundred years later, A. R. Hope Moncrieff called the kilt the oldest form of dress in the world.[162] Throughout the nineteenth century commentators insisted upon the antiquity of Highland dress, sometimes arguing against assertions of its comparative modernity. Soon after Victoria's first trip to Scotland, the *Illustrated London News* publicly rejected claims that Highland garb was of recent vintage. A Highland chief in full costume, the paper argued, was as accurate as possible a picture of an ancient Briton of distinction. Various elements of the usual outfit dated to the Romans, Saxons, and Elizabethans. The only reason earlier travelers had not described seeing such attire was that they could not depict it accurately.[163] In the 1880s Constance Gordon Cumming offered proof of the antiquity of the kilt 'as now worn': a sculpture on a monastery tower at Rodel, which she said was considered one of the oldest buildings in Scotland, showing Highland dress.[164]

The alleged age of such customs allowed tourists to believe the region was still intimately linked to the past. Residents of the Highlands, many visitors concluded, continued to wear the same style of clothes their ancestors had worn for centuries. Crofters lived and farmed as their forebears had. When they played the bagpipes, Highlanders performed on an instrument which originated in classical Greece or Rome, or perhaps ancient China or India, and was known in medieval England. Sports whose lineages stretched beyond modern times were played at Highland Games.[165] Just as Highlanders were sometimes viewed as the aboriginal inhabitants of Britain, their clothes might be the original national dress. The various controversies over which was the more authentic costume, kilt or trews, and how exactly specific components of the full regalia should be worn, bore witness to the emphasis on antiquity. And if indeed kilts and plaids were descendants of Roman dress, they reminded that the great age of Rome took place in part on British soil. The often encountered construction of Scots as people who had fought bravely against Rome, defending British liberty and freedom, did not interfere with the romantic notion that Highlanders copied the toga. A Roman origin for Highland dress was a link to the great empire whose legacy Britain might continue.

In fact, however, tourists' reliance on soldiers, tour guides, children, old people, and participants in Highland games as evidence for the living tradition of Highland dress really proved just the opposite, for these were exceptional cases. The excitement manifested when a tourist caught a glimpse of a kilted Scot merely demonstrated how rare the attire was. Those who looked carefully realized that Highland traditions were not caught in a time warp. The Highlands were changing and their 'ancient' practices were vanishing. Nineteenth-century commentators repeatedly informed potential tourists that the kilt was not generally worn on a daily basis in Scotland – an indication that many people believed just the opposite was true. In the 1860s Cuthbert Bede advised that the many illustrations of streets full of kilts were the product of considerable poetic license.[166] In 1906 Moncrieff warned that 'foreigners who expect to find all Scotland lit by a sunset of romance, are disappointed in the paucity of kilts and plaids as touches of human color upon the Highland scenery. The tartan, indeed, has gone out faster than some picturesque costumes of continental mountaineers.' While aristocratic patronage led to something of a revival of Highland dress, he admitted, this was true only on the edges of the Highlands. Further into the Highlands and islands, away from the affectations of aristocrats and tourists, an ordinary man 'submits to the hodden gray breeches of the Saxon for work-a-day wear.'[167]

The fact that many nonetheless continued to celebrate Highland dress as a time-honored folkway, sometimes in the face of contrary evidence, suggests a deep longing that it be so. Tourists did not passively consume Highland stereotypes; they chose to believe in them in order that Scotland might continue to play its role as a place with roots in the past. Those who were willing to admit that Highland dress was dwindling in popularity saw this development as a lamentable one. C. S. Stewart regretted 'that the people are no longer seen in their demi-savage, but picturesque dress of the kilt and tartan hose', for the 'traditional' garb was such an appropriate element in Highland scenery.[168] Later in the century, Constance Gordon Cumming bemoaned the fact that 'spreading civilization' resulted in a tendency to put away all distinctive national dress and reduce raiment to dull uniformity. She particularly noted the increase of hairnets or flowered bonnets among young women in the Highlands, rather than the more 'poetic' snood, once 'the distinguishing mark of every Highland maiden'.[169] In the 1830s, Chauncy Townshend, who was welcomed to Armadale Castle in Skye by Lord MacDonald in full Highland regalia, praised the clan chief for '[o]pposing a decided nationality to the tide of modern innovation which is fast sweeping away, together with the good old costume, all that was

characteristic in mind or manners from the inhabitants of the Highlands.'[170]
Rather than an inevitable, if unfortunate, result of the transformation of a
developing region, to Townshend the decline of the kilt was a symbol of the
destruction of that which was 'animating and glorious' in Highland
character.[171]

The disappearance of kilts, plaids, and tartans spoke of the unfortunate
consequences of modernization, for with them, argued contemporaries, went
the past and the poetry and romance associated with it. By wishing Highlanders
would continue to wear the dress which tourists considered historic and suited
to the way of life they hoped Highlanders still lived, Victorian visitors to
Scotland endeavored to preserve Highlanders' footing in the past, as a sort of
vicarious rootedness for other Britons. In so doing, tourists imposed their
own desire to ward off the passage of time upon a Scotland with very different
needs. Twentieth and twenty-first century commentators have been harshly
critical of the resulting 'tartan monster'. Their objections center on the
artificiality of the myths of Scotland at the expense of genuine Highland folk
culture, and the focus on the preservation of the past rather than exploration
of the present. As it became a hegemonic discourse which linked all things
Scottish to tartans, bagpipes, clans, and Bonnie Prince Charlie, tartanry
trivialized Scottish history and culture. Modern commentators point out that
because the popular symbols of Scotland offered no means of critiquing
existing society, they impeded the development of a realistic national self-
image and the social and political change that might flow from it. Tartanry,
many argue, hindered the growth of a progressive political nationalism.[172]
Condemnation of the romanticized and unhistorical vision of the past which
tourism helped to perpetuate is well placed. But as others have argued, a full
understanding of Balmoralization and its consequences requires an
examination of the reception of these discourses.[173] It is also necessary to
explore why such myths mattered to the tourists who helped to disseminate
them. Tourists were not empty vessels who absorbed whatever tourist literature
offered them. They responded out of their own cultural anxieties to particular
ways of viewing Scotland's past. An awareness of the dynamic relationship
between tourists' cultural background and the Scotland which was presented
to them should factor into investigations of the ways historical myths have
marked Scottish identity.

Their longing for tangible links with the past could lead English visitors
to appropriate Scotland's history for their own needs.[174] Encouraged by their
desire for a cohesive national story and by the anglicizing tendency of Scottish
historiography of the period, visitors adopted Scottish history as testifying
to the necessity of the Union and to an innate British drive for liberty.
Scottish heroes became exemplars of British virtues. Tartans could symbolize
the British empire; by the late nineteenth century the involvement of
Highland regiments in imperial wars and skirmishes prompted an identification

of tartan with 'British' bravery, reliability, and imperial pluck.[175] By wearing tartan clothes themselves – sometimes even Highland dress – English Victorians managed to usurp some of the historicity of Scotland into their own lives. Jokes about tourists who saw a Highlander at ease in his ancestral dress, only to find that he, too, was an English tourist were commonplace.[176]

The English adoption of Scottish history and culture could have adverse effects on Scottish national identity. Scottish historiography already limited the political power of Scotland's narrative; sharing that history further reduced its potential as an animating national force. Nor did the symbols which came to stand for Scotland offer much political potency. However, although these concerns became powerful ones in the twentieth century, they were less so in the nineteenth. For most of that century, middle-class Scots considered themselves equal partners within a Union in which all could take pride. The extent to which their fellow Britons borrowed Scotland's past could be seen as a sign of Scottish success in the Union. Scots, too, had a dynamic relationship with their own history, and continued to identify proudly with it. Like English visitors, Scots interpreted their history in ways that met their particular needs, which sometimes led to different understandings than those of southern sightseers. They also had access to other vehicles of national self-expression besides tartanized history. A lively native literature thrived in the weekly press in the second half of the nineteenth century, one which was not backwards-looking but which wrestled with current political and social issues.[177] By the late nineteenth century some Scots began to reinvigorate their history with nationalist discourse. Though the failure of the symbols of Scotland to genuinely reflect the country clearly troubled many people, their sense of their own culture and place in history was not stolen from Scots.

Rather, thoughtful tourists became aware that though they could continue to visit historic sites and wear kilts, Scotland might not remain grounded in the past. Scotland was modernizing and changing – possibly, many tourists believed, to the detriment of Scotland, Scots, and Great Britain. A mixture of modernity and history might help to illustrate Scotland's close connections with the past, but if nineteenth-century practices began to predominate over those of earlier centuries there would soon be no more rootedness to be found in Scotland. This was an especially urgent issue with concern to the Highlands which, even more than the rest of Scotland, represented in microcosm a window into the precivilized world. It would become apparent in the last quarter of the nineteenth century that the Highlands – and its people – might soon no longer fit that description. It was therefore all the more pressing to stem the tide of change.

Notes

[1]   Alexander Smith, *Summer in Skye* (Boston, 1865), p. 400.

[2]   David Lowenthal, *The Past is a Foreign Country* (New York: Cambridge Univ.
       Press, 1985); Charles Dellheim, *The Face of the Past. The Preservation of the
       Medieval Inheritance in Victorian England* (New York: Cambridge Univ. Press,
       1982); Jerome Buckely, *The Triumph of Time; a study of the Victorian concepts
       of time, history, progress and decadence* (Cambridge: Belknap Press of Harvard
       Univ., 1966); J. W. Burrow, 'The sense of the past' in Laurence Lerner, ed., *The
       Victorians* (London: Methuen & Co., Ltd., 1978), pp. 120-38.

[3]   Smith, *Summer in Skye*, p. 11.

[4]   'Substance of a tour through Scotland in the summer of 1836' MS. 2729,
       NLS, p. 8.

[5]   S. Taylor, 'Journal of a Tour to Scotland' (1842) MS. 8927, NLS, pp. 139-40.

[6]   T. Holmes, 'Reminiscences of a few days' Rambles in North Britain' (Bolton,
       1874), n.p.

[7]   *The Epistles of Peggy Written from Scotland* (n.p., n.d), p. 5.

[8]   Colin Kidd, *'Strange Death of Scottish History* revisited: Constructions of
       the Past in Scotland, c. 1790-1914', *The Scottish Historical Review* LXXVI,
       1: 201 (April 1977), p. 99.

[9]   Colin Kidd, 'The canon of patriotic landmarks in Scottish history', *Scotlands*
       1: (1994), p. 7.

[10]   Marinell Ash, *The Strange Death of Scottish History* (Edinburgh: The Ramsay
       Head Press, 1980); Kidd, *'Strange Death*...revisited'; Kidd, 'Canon of
       patriotic landmarks'; Colin Kidd, *Subverting Scotland's Past. Scottish whig
       historians and the creation of an Anglo-British identity, c. 1689-1830* (New
       York: Cambridge Univ. Press, 1993).

[11]   Kidd, *Subverting Scotland's Past*, pp. 209-15. See also Ash, *Strange Death*.

[12]   Ash, *Strange Death*, p. 145.

[13]   Graeme Morton, *Unionist-Nationalism. Governing Urban Scotland, 1830-1860*
       (East Linton: Tuckwell Press, 1999). On nineteenth-century Scottish
       nationalism, see also Richard J. Finlay, 'Controlling the Past: Scottish
       Historiography and Scottish Identity in the 19th and 20th Centuries' *Scottish
       Affairs* 9(Autumn 1994), pp.127-42; Michael Fry, *Patronage and Principle. A
       Political History of Modern Scotland* (Aberdeen: Aberdeen Univ. Press, 1987),
       pp. 201-22; Christopher Harvie, *Scotland & Nationalism: Scottish Society and
       Politics, 1707-1994* (New York: Routledge, 1994); Graeme Morton, 'What if?
       The Significance of Scotland's Missing Nationalism in the Nineteenth Century'
       in Dauvit Broun, R. J. Finlay and Micheal Lynch, eds., *Image and Identity. The
       Making and Re-making of Scotland Through the Ages* (Edinburgh: John Donald,
       1998), pp. 157-76.

[14]   Jabez Marrat, *'Land of the Mountain and the Flood'. Scottish Scenes and
       Scenery Delineated* (London, 1879), pp. v-vi. On hero worship, see Walter
       E. Houghton, *The Victorian Frame of Mind* (New Haven: Yale Univ. Press,
       1957), pp. 305-40.

[15]   Timothy Lang, *The Victorians and the Stuart Heritage* (New York: Cambridge
       Univ. Press, 1995).

16 Robert Hunter, *A Brief Account of a Tour Through some Parts of Scotland* (London, 1839), p. 43.
17 Marrat, '*Land of the Mountain and the Flood*,' p. 85.
18 Herbert Byng Hall, *Highland Sports and Highland Quarters* (London, 1848), pp. 114-15.
19 George Anderson and Peter Anderson, *Guide to the Highlands and Islands of Scotland* (London, 1834), p. 85.
20 J. E. Bowman, *The Highlands and Islands: A 19ᵗʰ Century Tour*, introduction by Elaine M. E. Barry (New York: Hippocreme Books, 1986), p. 64.
21 'A Journal of a few days from Home in the summer of 1856 with selected poetry and songs' MS. 9233, NLS, n.p.
22 Catherine Sinclair, *Sketches and Stories of Scotland and the Scotch and Shetland and the Shetlanders* (London, n.d.), p. 331.
23 William Winter, *Over the Border* (New York: Moffat, Yard and Co., 1911), p. 51.
24 Jacob Abbott, *A Summer in Scotland* (Dublin, 1849), p. 140. Many Victorian tourists enjoyed telling the story of a traveling soap salesman who toured Holyrood. Upon being told of the antiquity of the stains of Rizzio's blood, he assured the crowd that his stain remover could take care of the problem, and proceeded to attempt to scrub the spots away, to the great consternation of the tour guide. See Adam Black and Charles Black, pub., *Black's Picturesque Tourist of Scotland* (Edinburgh, 1852), p. 27.
25 *Black's Picturesque Tourist* (1852), p. 26.
26 Mrs. John F. Gower, 'Illustrated Accounts of trips to France and Scotland by the family of John F. Gower' (1854, 1862) ACC. 9946, NLS, n.p.
27 Jayne E. Lewis, *Mary Queen of Scots. Romance and Nation* (New York: Routledge, 1998), p. 173. See also Helen Smailes and Duncan Thomson, *The Queen's Image* (Edinburgh: Scottish National Portrait Gallery, 1987).
28 Lewis, *Mary, Queen of Scots.*
29 Winter, *Over the Border*, p. 62.
30 Abbott, *Summer in Scotland*, p. 167.
31 'Substance of a tour', p. 17
32 Lewis, *Mary, Queen of Scots*, pp. 171-73.
33 Lewis, *Mary, Queen of Scots*, pp. 180-81.
34 John Knox [Peter Carter], *Crumbs from the Land o' Cakes* (Boston, 1851), p. 58.
35 Marrat, *Land of the Mountain and the Flood*, p. 110.
36 Knox, *Crumbs*, p. 18.
37 Marrat, *Land of the Mountain and the Flood*, p. 71.
38 Clement Mansfield Ingleby, 'Journal of a tour to Scotland' (1842) MS. 8926, NLS, p. 84.
39 Taylor, 'Journal', pp. 50-51.
40 Marjorie Morgan, *National Identities and Travel in Victorian Britain* (Houndmills: Palgrave, 2001), pp. 103-7.
41 'Journal of a few days from Home', n.p.
42 Samuel Johnson, *A Journey to the Western Islands of Scotland*, Peter Levi, ed., (New York: Penguin, 1984), p. 141.

43   Adam Black and Charles Black, pub., *Black's Picturesque Tourist of Scotland* (Edinburgh, 1843), p. 274.

44   Taylor, 'Journal', pp. 166-67.

45   Constance F. Gordon Cumming, *In the Hebrides* (London, 1883), p. 77.

46   See Kidd, *Subverting Scotland's Past* and Murray G. H. Pittock, *Celtic Identity and the British Image* (Manchester: Manchester Univ. Press, 1999), pp. 54-60.

47   Bowman, *The Highlands and Islands*, p. 3.

48   Knox, *Crumbs*, p. 40.

49   Walter Scott, *Tales of a Grandfather* (Philadelphia, 1836), p. 276.

50   T. C. F. Brotchie, *Scottish Western Holiday Haunts* (Edinburgh: John Menzies, 1911), p. 19.

51   See Murray G. H. Pittock, *The Invention of Scotland. The Stuart Myth and the Scottish Identity, 1638 to the Present* (New York: Routledge, 1991), pp. 127-33.

52   John Stoddart, *Remarks on Local Scenery & Manners in Scotland during the Years 1799 and 1800* (London, 1801), p. 1:163.

53   Thomas Cook, *Cook's Scottish Tourist Official Directory* (London, 1861), p. 48.

54   Alastair Durie, *Scotland for the Holidays. Tourism in Scotland, c.1780-1939* (East Linton: Tuckwell Press, 2003), p. 99.

55   Graeme Morton, 'The Most Efficacious Patriot: The Heritage of William Wallace in Nineteenth-Century Scotland' *Scottish Historical Review*, LXXVII, 2: 204 (October 1998), pp. 246-47.

56   Lucy Elizabeth Sherwood, Journal of Lucy Elizabeth Sherwood, (1826-1827) ACC. 8679, NLS, Sep. 24.

57   Morton, 'The Most Efficacious Patriot'.

58   John Leyden, *Journal of a Tour in the Highlands and Western Islands of Scotland in 1800* James Sinton, ed. (Edinburgh: William Blackwood & Sons, 1903), p. 6.

59   James Hunter, 'Journal Through Clydesdale and parts of the Western Highlands' (1834) MS. 1776, NLS, pp. 3, 5-6.

60   Robert Burns to the Earl of Buchan, quoted by Edwin Waugh, *Fourteen Days in Scotland* (Manchester, 1863), pp. 58-9.

61   James Johnson, *The Recess, or Autumnal Relaxation in the Highlands and Lowlands* (London, 1834), p. 44.

62   Morton, *Unionist-Nationalism*; Marinell Ash, 'William Wallace and Robert the Bruce. The life and death of a national myth' in Raphael Samuel and Paul Thompson, eds., *The Myths We Live By* (New York: Routledge, 1990), pp. 82-94; Morton, 'The Most Efficacious Patriot', p. 249.

63   *Times*, (London), Dec. 4, 1856. See also *ILN*, October 29, 1853 for a criticism of the National Association for the Vindication of Scottish Rights.

64   *Epistles of Peggy*, p. 23.

65   William Gilpin, *Observations on the Highlands of Scotland* (London, 1789; reprint, with an introduction by Sutherland Lyall, Richmond, England: The Richmond Publishing, 1973), p. 2:73.

66   Linda Colley, *Britons. Forging the Nation, 1707-1837* (New Haven: Yale Univ. Press, 1992), p. 338.

67   'Journal of a few days', n.p.

68   'Substance of a tour', pp. 14-15.

69   Winter, *Over the Border*, p. 153.

70   *Epistles of Peggy*, p. 9.

71   Richard Pococke, *Tours in Scotland, 1747, 1750, 1760* Daniel William Kemp, ed., (Edinburgh, 1887), pp. 105-8.

72   Thomas Pennant, *A Tour in Scotland MDCCLXIX* (London, 1790), p. 1:176.

73   T. Garnett, *Observations on a Tour through the Highlands and Part of the Western Isles of Scotland* (London, 1800), p. 2:30.

74   T. M. Devine, *Clanship to Crofters' War. The social transformation of the Scottish Highlands* (New York: Manchester Univ. Press, 1994), pp. 88-91; Pittock, *Invention of Scotland*. On support for the Stuarts, see Devine, *Clanship to Crofters' War*, pp. 19-31; Bruce Lenman, *The Jacobite Risings in Britain 1689-1746* (London: Methuen, 1980); Michael Lynch, *Scotland. A New History* (London: Pimlico, 1991), p. 336; Frank McLynn, *The Jacobites* (London: Routledge and Kegan Paul, 1985). Murray Pittock argues that historians have marginalized the importance of the '45 and that Charles Edward's army was a much more national Scottish force than has been recognized. *The Myth of the Jacobite Clans* (Edinburgh: Edinburgh Univ. Press, 1995).

75   Devine, *Clanship to Crofters' War*, pp. 88-91; Pittock, *Invention of Scotland*, pp. 88-90.

76   Victoria, Queen of Great Britain, *Leaves from the Journal of Our Life in the Highlands. 1848-1861* Arthur Helps, ed. (London, 1868), p. 288. See Richard J. Finlay, 'Queen Victoria and the Cult of Scottish Monarchy', in Edward J. Cowan and Richard J. Finlay, eds., *Scottish History. The Power of the Past* (Edinburgh: Edinburgh Univ. Press, 2002), pp. 209-24.

77   'Sylvan' [Samuel Hobbs], *Sylvan's Pictorial Handbook to the Scenery of the Caledonian Canal, the Isle of Staffa, etc.* (Edinburgh, 1848), p. 97.

78   Thomas Murray & Son, pub., *Murray's Scottish Tourist* (Glasgow 1868), pp. 88-92.

79   John R. Gold and Margaret M. Gold, 'Representing Culloden: Social Memory, Battlefield Heritage, and Landscapes of Regret' in Stephen P. Hanna and Vincent J. Del Casino, Jr., eds., *Mapping Tourism* (Minneapolis: Univ. of Minnesota Press, 2003), p. 125.

80   J. A. MacCulloch, *Misty Isle of Skye* (Edinburgh: Oliphant Anderson & Ferrier, 1905), p. 304.

81   J. A. MacCulloch, *Misty Isle of Skye*, p. 62.

82   *Scottish Tourist and Itinerary or A Guide to the Scenery and Antiquities of Scotland and the Western Islands* (Edinburgh, 1830), p. 261.

83   Beriah Botfield, *Journal of a Tour through the Highlands of Scotland* (Norton Hall, 1830), p. 178.

84   Colin McArthur, 'Culloden: A Pre-Emptive Strike', *Scottish Affairs* 9 (Autumn 1994), p. 106.

85   MacArthur, 'Culloden: A Pre-Emptive Strike', p. 106. See also Gold and Gold, 'Representing Culloden', and David McCrone, Angela Morris, Richard Kiely, *Scotland-The Brand. The Making of Scottish Heritage* (Edinburgh: Edinburgh Univ. Press, 1995), pp. 191-95.

86   Quoted by MacArthur, 'Culloden: A Pre-Emptive Strike', p. 113.

87   Quoted by Gold and Gold, 'Representing Culloden', p. 120.
88   Pittock, *Invention of Scotland*, p. 126.
89   Smith, *Summer in Skye*, pp. 124; 91.
90   Hall, *Highland Sports*, p. 190.
91   J. A. MacCulloch, *Misty Isle of Skye*, pp. 99-100.
92   David Brett, *The Construction of Heritage* (Cork: Cork Univ. Press, 1996). See also Dellheim, *Face of the Past*; Lowenthal, *Past is a Foreign Country.*
93   See Dellheim, *Face of the Past;* Mark Girouard, *The Return of Camelot: Chivalry and the English Gentleman* (New Haven: Yale Univ. Press, 1981); A. D. Culler, *The Victorian Mirror of History* (New Haven: Yale Univ. Press, 1985).
94   Martin J. Weiner, *English Culture and the Decline of the Industrial Spirit* (New York: Penguin, 1981), p. 45.
95   George Eyre-Todd, *Scotland: Picturesque and Traditional* (New York: Frederick A. Stokes, 1907), p. 198.
96   George Anderson and Peter Anderson, *Guide to the Highlands and Islands of Scotland* (Edinburgh, 1863), p. 219.
97   Botfield, *Journal*, p. 29.
98   John Lettice, *Letters on a Tour through various parts of Scotland in the year 1792* (London, 1794), p. 470.
99   'A Visit to Hinba', *Cornhill Magazine* 41:242 (February, 1880), p. 172.
100 Gordon Cumming, *In the Hebrides*, p. 97.
101 Marrat, *Land of the Mountain and the Flood*, p. 11.
102 T. H. Holding, *Cruise of the Ospray: Canoe and Camp life in Scotland* (Newcastle-on-tyne, 1878), pp. 32-3.
103 Dellheim, *Face of the Past*, pp. 39-45.
104 Rosemary Jann, *The Art and Science of Victorian History* (Columbus: Ohio State Univ. Press, 1985), p. xiii.
105 Peter Mandler, ' "The Wand of Fancy": The Historical Imagination of the Victorian Tourist' in Marius Kwint, Christopher Breward and Jeremy Aynsley, eds., *Material Memories* (New York: Berg, 1999), pp. 125-41.
106 Mandler, 'The Wand of Fancy'.
107 Bowman, *Highlands and Islands*, p. 38; Holding, *Cruise of the Ospray*, p. 32.
108 Gordon Cumming, *In the Hebrides*, p. 318.
109 'Journal of a few days', n.p.
110 Winter, *Over the Border*, p. 35.
111 Lewis, *Mary, Queen of Scots*, pp. 204-7.
112 Chauncy Hare Townshend, *A Descriptive Tour in Scotland* (Brussels, 1840), pp. 374-5.
113 Journal of a tour of Scotland made by an Englishman in 1850, MS. 17957, NLS, April 1.
114 Winter, *Over the Border*, p. 81.
115 Dellheim, *Face of the Past*, p. 37.
116 Quoted by Culler, *Victorian Mirror of History*, p. 181.
117 David MacBrayne's Royal Mail Steamers, pub., *Summer Tours in Scotland* (Glasgow, 1896), pp. 92-3.
118 Anderson, *Highlands and Islands* (1834), p. 632.
119 Dellheim, *Face of the Past*, pp. 1-31, 179-81.

120 Pittock, *The Myth of the Jacobite Clans*, p. 7.
121 Brett, *Construction of Heritage;* John Urry, *The Tourist Gaze: Leisure and Travel in Contemporary Societies* (New York: Sage Publications, 1990), pp. 104-34. See also McCrone, Morris, Kiely, *Scotland the Brand.*
122 Lowenthal, *Past is a Foreign Country*, p. 243.
123 Robert Heron, *Observations made in a Journey through the Western Counties of Scotland in the autumn of 1792* (Perth, 1793), pp. 1:379-80.
124 McCrone, Morris, Kiely, *Scotland – the Brand*, p. 5. See also Tom Nairn, *The Break-Up of Britain* (London: NLB, 1977) and Craig Beveridge and Ronald Turnbull, *The Eclipse of Scottish Culture* (Edinburgh: Polygon, 1989).
125 Charles G. Harper, *Motoring in Scotland* (London: Royal Automobile Club, 1912), p. 24.
126 Botfield, *Journal*, p. 29; Elizabeth Isabella Spence, *Sketches of the Present Manners, Customs, and Scenery of Scotland* (London, 1811), 2:19.
127 Botfield, *Journal*, p. 13.
128 William Deane Ryland, 'Journal of a tour in Scotland during the long Vacation of 1823', ACC. 8801, NLS, 22 Aug.
129 *Over the Border: or a Rossendale Lady's Impressions of Scotland* (Haslingden, 1869), p. 47.
130 Cook, *Scottish Tourist Official Directory*, p. 42.
131 Buckely, *The Triumph of Time*, pp. 117-36.
132 Lowenthal, *Past is a Foreign Country*, p. 50.
133 Cuthbert Bede [Edward Bradley], *A Tour in Tartan-Land* (London, 1863), pp. 405-6.
134 S. Augustus Tipple, *A Summer Visit to Scotland* (Norwich, 1847), pp. 39-40.
135 Brotchie, *Holiday Haunts*, p. 62.
136 'Notes of a Wanderer in Skye', *Temple Bar*, vol. 69 (Sept.-Dec. 1883), p. 88.
137 Brotchie, *Holiday Haunts*, pp. 66-7.
138 Dellheim, *Face of the Past.*
139 Winter, *Over the Border*, p. 260.
140 Eyre-Todd, *Scotland: Picturesque and Traditional*, p. 220.
141 'The Tourist in Scotland. A Roofless Palace', *Leisure Hour*, 451 (Aug. 16, 1860) p. 523.
142 *Black's Picturesque Tourist of Scotland* (1843), pp. 160-66.
143 *Rossendale Lady's Impressions*, p. 25.
144 Brotchie, *Holiday Haunts*, pp. 12, 16.
145 Abbott, *Summer in Scotland*, pp. 163-64.
146 See Robert Clyde, *From Rebel to Hero. The Image of the Highlander, 1745-1830* (East Linton: Tuckwell Press, 1995); Hugh Trevor-Roper, 'The Invention of Tradition: The Highland Tradition of Scotland', in Eric Hobsbawn and Terence Ranger, eds., *The Invention of Tradition* (New York: Cambridge Univ. Press, 1983), pp. 15-41; Charles Withers, 'The Historical Creation of the Scottish Highlands' in Ian Donnachie and Christopher Whatley, eds., *The Manufacture of Scottish History* (Edinburgh: Polygon, 1992), pp. 143-56; Peter Womack, *Improvement and Romance. Constructing the Myth of the Highlands* (London: MacMillan Press, 1989).

[147] Hugh Cheape, *Tartan. The Highland Habit* (Edinburgh: National Museums of Scotland, 1991); John Telfer Dunbar, *History of Highland Dress* (London: Oliver & Boyd, 1962); Trevor-Roper, 'The Invention of Tradition'.

[148] Cheape, *Tartan*, pp. 52. See also Womack, *Improvement and Romance*, pp. 47-8. On the history of tartan, see Cheape, *Tartan*, pp. 13-20 and Dunbar, *History of Highland Dress.*

[149] The debate over the authenticity of the kilt as a 'genuine' national dress began in the *Edinburgh Magazine* in 1785. Womack, *Improvement and Romance*, p. 48.

[150] Johnson, *Journey to the Western Islands*, pp. 113-14.

[151] Philip B. Homer, *Observations on a Short Tour Made in the Summer of 1803 to the Western Highlands of Scotland* (London, 1804), p. 161.

[152] John Carr, *Caledonian Sketches, or a Tour through Scotland in 1807* (London, 1809), pp. 265-66.

[153] William Pearson, *Papers, Letters, & Journal of William Pearson*, ed. by his wife (London, 1863), p. 264.

[154] Lynch, *Scotland*, p. 356.

[155] 'Sylvan', *Pictorial Handbook to the Scenery of the Caledonian Canal*, p. 45.

[156] 'Substance of a tour', p. 8.

[157] C. S. Stewart, *Sketches of Society in Great Britain and Ireland* (Philadelphia, 1834), pp. 2:158, 2:202.

[158] 'Diary of a visit to Edinburgh and Perthshire' (1848), ACC. 8442, NLS, September, 16.

[159] S. Kathleen Warden, *Humorous Side-Lights on a Scotch Tour* (London, n.d.), pp. 195-96.

[160] Garnett, *Observations*, p. 2:88.

[161] Gilpin, *Observations*, p. 2:138.

[162] A. R. Hope Moncrieff, *Highlands & Islands of Scotland* (London: A & C Black, 1906; reprint, London: A & C Black, 1925), p. 22.

[163] *ILN*, October 8, 1842, October 15, 1842.

[164] Gordon Cumming, *In the Hebrides*, p. 270.

[165] On Highland Games, see Grant Jarvie, *Highland Games. The Making of the Myth* (Edinburgh: Edinburgh Univ. Press, 1991).

[166] Bede, *Tour in Tartan-Land*, pp. 50-51.

[167] Moncrieff, *Highlands and Islands*, p. 19.

[168] Stewart, *Sketches of Society*, pp. 2:157-58.

[169] Gordon Cumming, *In the Hebrides*, pp. 126-28.

[170] Townshend, *Descriptive Tour*, p. 189.

[171] Townshend, *Descriptive Tour*, p. 190.

[172] Nairn, *Break-Up of Britain*. The discussion over tartanry is nicely summarized by McCrone, Morris, Kiely, *Scotland-the Brand*, pp. 50-56.

[173] Beveridge and Turnbull, *The Eclipse of Scottish Culture*. See also McCrone, Morris, Kiely, *Scotland – the Brand*, pp. 61-72.

[174] On the appropriative effects of tourism, see Donald Horne, *The Great Museum: the Re-presentation of History* (London: Pluto Press, 1984); Trevor R. Pringle, 'The privation of history: Landseer, Victoria and the Highland myth' in Denis

Cosgrove and Stephen Daniels, eds., *The Iconography of Landscape* (New York: Cambridge Univ. Press, 1988), pp. 142-61.

[175] Pittock, *Myth of the Jacobite Clans*, p. 120.

[176] A couple of examples are in Joseph Pennell and Elizabeth Robins Pennell, *Our Journey to the Hebrides* (New York, 1889), p. 112, and James Locke, *Tweed and Don or Recollections and Reflections of an Angler* (Edinburgh, 1860), p. 113.

[177] William Donaldson, *Popular Literature in Victorian Scotland* (Aberdeen: Aberdeen Univ. Press, 1986).

Chapter 5

'A Fountain of Renovating Life':
Tourists and Highlanders

On her 1826 Scottish trip, Lucy Sherwood was delighted with everything she saw, 'but chiefly the Highlanders who please me extremely.'[1] A tourist of 1829 was glad to find that taking an east coast route to Inverness provided many opportunities of observing 'the customs and manners of the natives'.[2] A guidebook of the 1840s recommended that tourists spend a few days in Oban, as the neighborhood 'cannot be surpassed for specimens of Highland scenery, life and manners.'[3] As these travel writers testified, the people who lived in the Highlands and Western Isles, especially the small tenant farmers or crofters, were central to the area's attraction. Highlanders and islanders were compelling figures to Britons throughout the history of tourism in Scotland, chiefly because of their isolated situation and comparatively recent introduction to 'civilization'. If the Highlands were the true Scotland, the rural folk who lived there retained the undiluted essence of Scottishness. Eighteenth-century visitors were deeply curious about both Highlanders and Lowlanders, both of whom seemed strikingly different from the English. As the Lowlands grew more integrated into British society and culture, Victorian tourists focused their interest on denizens of the Western Highlands and islands. To most Victorian and Edwardian sightseers, from both England and the Lowlands, Highlanders were historical artifacts who lived just as their ancestors had and therefore preserved an ancient rural way of life in a rapidly changing world. Stopping in a 'black house' to meet the inhabitants and view their living conditions was a regular occasion on many tours. By 1906 tourists evinced enough interest in Highlanders for A. R. Hope Moncrieff to complain about the 'Cockney tourists who get the length of Skye to stare at the children's bare legs and to sniff at the peat fires, such admiration as they are capable of being directed by tourist tickets and guide-books'.[4]

It was inescapable public knowledge that poverty and poor living conditions were widespread in the Highlands. In fact, much of the curiosity about Gaels was stimulated by recurrent controversies over land distribution in the area, including the extensive emigration of the late eighteenth century, the clearances of the late eighteenth and early nineteenth centuries, and the Land War of the 1880s. Many tourists simply blocked local inhabitants out of their minds, the better to enjoy the scenery which remained the chief lure of the Highlands. Others found the popular construction of Highlanders, which offered up Gaels' simple ways of life as antidotes to urbanization, industrialization, racial degeneration, rural depopulation, and gender transgressions, too compelling to ignore. This was especially true in the late nineteenth and early twentieth centuries. But because this rendition of Highlanders centered on the contributions they made, through their very existence, to the wider British nation, the lenses through which visitors viewed these fellow citizens mitigated most humanitarian anxieties about their situation.

Throughout the period under discussion, tourism allowed sightseers to develop a sense of mastery over these unfamiliar and exotic people. After touring the Highlands and observing local residents, visitors were eager to assert their knowledge of Gaels by using their travel accounts and letters home to pen what they considered authoritative characterizations of the people they had seen. Guidebooks, too, were sources of knowledge, as most provided descriptions of Highlanders and their customs. The subjugating power of the tourist gaze, alongside the tendency to situate crofters' significance in their usefulness for the wider British community, effectively erased Highlanders' autonomy. However, in the late nineteenth century, even as tourism to the Highlands and Hebrides was on the rise, crofters (small tenant farmers) of the region presented an alternative image of themselves through their well-publicized dispute over land control, often known as the Crofters' War or Land War. In the process, they challenged the authority of racial and gendered understandings of themselves. The confluence of tourism and the land dispute provides a rare opportunity to investigate the interaction between the crofters' self-identity and the meanings of the Highlands imposed by others. The active contestation of the idea of the Highlander seen in the discourse surrounding the Crofters' War is testimony to the crucial significance attached to interpretations of crofters in the late Victorian period.

A Folk Community

Interest in Gaels was as carefully ritualized as was the appreciation of landscape, making clear their roles as members of a folk culture who, through their closeness to nature and their racial heritage, offered a contrast to the rational, mechanical, and progress-obsessed world from which tourists came.[5] To those travelers who ventured to the Highlands in the late eighteenth century, Gaels were aliens, as exotic and foreign as South Sea islanders. Perceptions of the men and women of the Highlands and islands in the late eighteenth and early nineteenth centuries were strongly marked by the belief that these fellow Britons had fairly recently been a violent people under the sway of feudalism. They were outside the law and spoke an outlandish language. They were the 'Indians of Scotland'.[6] The 'savagery' of the not-too-distant past was intriguing, rather than repulsive. The many stories of violence and clan warfare which tourists so enjoyed illustrated the extent to which clansmen were 'natural' soldiers, possessing a raw and untamed energy not to be found in commercial society. Assertions that clansmen were not randomly destructive, but possessed a distinctive code of ethics and honor marked them as noble savages. Stories of Highlanders' continued devotion to their chiefs even in contemporary times indicated that enough vestiges of the old ways survived to make the Gaels a distinctive people. Just as importantly, the present-day lack of violence was evidence that the British state and the inevitable cycle of civilization were making themselves known.[7]

This process of change continued to be regarded as one of the exciting things about a visit to the Highlands. There, '...they who were once thieves, vagabonds, and half-starved for want of comfortable lodging, food, and clothing, are now as industrious, pious, and charitable perhaps as any in the kingdom.'[8] By the 1790s, though visitors continued to be fascinated by Highlanders' 'barbarous' past, they commented mostly on Gaels' simple and primitive virtues.[9] As would later travelers, those of the first phase of tourism constructed Highlanders as exemplars of the pastoral idylls of the poets. Because secluded from the world, they were contented, religious, unaffected, and hospitable. Nonetheless, the shocking poverty of the region also told many tourists that the pastoral life 'is wholly destitute of those Arcadian delights which have been described to it by the wanton imaginations and 'seething brains' of the poets.'[10] Though they regretted that Highland distinctiveness would be lost when the former clansmen and women grew more assimilated into modern ways – no longer did the Highlands form a nation and a people[11]– the changes that were taking place were for the greater good of the region, and of the nation as a whole.

> To lament that they neither possess the peculiar virtues, nor enjoy the peculiar happiness, which belong to a low or early stage of civilization, is to regret the progress of civilization. To desire that to these, they should unite all the virtues and blessings which arise from improvement, is to wish for what the world never yet saw; to grieve that we cannot at the same instant possess the promise of spring and the performance of autumn.[12]

Nineteenth-century tourists, especially those later in the century, were not sure that change in the Highlands was for the better. Victorians were less interested in Highlanders as former clansmen who were being introduced to the ways of modern life, than as peasants who preserved unchanged the ways of their forefathers. As such, Highlanders secured rural traditions in an urbanized and industrial society – and hopefully would continue to do so. Both because they were members of a natural and organic society, and because they were Celts, the denizens of the Highlands and islands could potentially enrich and renew the wider nation. Were Highlanders to adopt modern ways they would no longer retain the country values threatened by industrial society, a threat which seemed more real in the nineteenth than eighteenth century. Even in the late Victorian and Edwardian periods, a hundred years after earlier visitors asserted that the Highlands were in the midst of the transition to the modern world, tourists preferred to believed that the region was still only on the cusp of change. They thus affirmed again that time stood still there.

Aside from these differences in visitors' attitudes towards change in the Highlands, perceptions of the people whose land they traversed were generally consistent throughout the period. These observations were often based on scanty evidence. Mid- and late-Victorian tourists were less likely than their predecessors to actually *study* Highland ways of life. Their comments were less anthropological in tone than those of late eighteenth-century travelers, who understood one of their roles to be that of collecting evidence about 'primitive' ways of life. Victorians, whose tours were often rushed and concentrated primarily on landscape and historical monuments, had fewer occasions for investigations of indigenous culture. Because of the infrequency of substantive contact between Highlanders and visitors, the men and women described in travelers' accounts were often imaginary beings, created as much out of tourists' expectations and desires as out of any precise investigations.

Central to tourists' understanding of Highlanders was the belief that they lived in the same manner as had generations of their ancestors. As members of a folk community, believed observers of the late eighteenth and nineteenth centuries, Gaels still possessed the beliefs and customs of some of the ancient inhabitants of Britain as well as those of other early cultures. In the Western Isles, according to Ada Goodrich-Freer, who visited several of the Hebrides in 1894, 'one may yet study, as perhaps in few other places in Europe, something of the childhood of the world.'[13] Traditions and ways of life allegedly linked inhabitants of the Highlands and Western Isles to ancient Greeks and Romans, Native Americans, Arabs, Vikings, islanders of the South Seas, and the Ten Tribes of Israel. Malcolm Ferguson, a late nineteenth-century visitor to Skye, commented that 'to a stranger from the far south, the scene presented to his gaze on board the steamer [to Portree] – the people, dress, language, and general appearance – seemed quite unique, stirring and interesting, and apt to make him fancy that he had been suddenly transported to some far off region of the world.'[14] Constance Gordon Cumming, who considered herself an authority on world cultures, echoed a common motif when she likened the religious sensibilities and practices of the Hebrideans to the early Christian church and to the 'wild song of the Paharis' in the Himalayas.[15] Many visitors were especially interested in Highland agricultural techniques. J. A. MacCulloch believed the Hebrideans' farming practices descended directly from the 'primitive land tenure which was once common all over Europe'.[16] Gordon Cumming asserted that to visitors from the mainland, 'the primitive agricultural implements in common use [on Skye], were objects of wonder and of interest, and many a time we halted to watch the patient toilers at their slow and weary work.'[17] From the time of James Boswell, tourists had compared the quern or handmill of the Hebrides to those used by the ancient Romans.[18] In 1902 Goodrich-Freer noted its resemblance to those of the ancient near East as well.[19]

Tourists believed that Highlanders retained pagan superstitions. One visitor concluded that the 'curious mixture of religion and superstition' in the Hebrides gave her an idea of what life must have been like in the days when Christianity was first superimposed on paganism.[20] Another affirmed that in the Highlands one could find 'early pagan instincts and memories still uneradicated.'[21] Throughout the late eighteenth and nineteenth centuries, tourists detailed the credulity of Highlanders and their own experiences of observing or hearing of superstitious practices, such as belief in fairies or witchcraft, charms with curative power, or the conviction that seals could transform themselves into humans and should not be killed.[22] Central to tourists' interest in Gaelic superstitions was the conviction that such practices were quickly dying out in the face of education and greater contact with the outside world. Although visitors continued to report that superstition was 'fast wearing away', late into the Victorian period others still asserted that many old beliefs remained.[23] Tourists also disagreed about whether or not the persistence of such irrationality was a welcome development. In the 1770s Thomas Pennant had endeavored to preserve information about Highlanders' 'ancient customs and superstitions' in order to teach the later 'unshackled and enlightened mind the difference between the pure ceremonies of religion and the wild and anile flights of superstition'.[24] Late Victorian tourists, some of them no doubt influenced by the new interests in folklore and spiritualism, made note of regional folk beliefs in order to preserve ancient practices from oblivion.[25] Although nineteenth-century travelers welcomed the spread of education, they also lamented the loss of the irrational. Chauncy Hare Townshend was skeptical about a story related to him of a woman who was cured of evil spirits with water from a holy well, but he considered it 'pleasant to find a bit of credulity left upon earth; and where should the misty twilight of old imagination linger more fitly than amongst these wild and unworldly regions?'[26] Part of the purpose of Ada Goodrich-Freer's journeys to the Hebrides in the 1890s was to undertake investigations into the 'second sight' for the Society for Psychical Research.[27]

According to visitors, Highlanders' customs and beliefs were outward and visible signs that theirs was an old culture, one whose people were still part of the Golden Age. As portrayed in tourist literature and the popular press, Gaels were simple, untutored, innately virtuous folk. Innumerable discussions characterized the men and women of the Highlands and islands as 'brave', 'courteous,' 'kind', 'God-fearing', 'honest', 'cheerful', 'hospitable', 'candid', 'good', 'sensible', 'intelligent', 'noble-minded'. Although their indigence might suggest otherwise, Highlanders were content, even happy. They knew nothing of ambition, greed, or jealousy. Having no access to the luxuries of life, they did not pine for them, thus their ignorance kept them at peace. 'Happy crofter, who knows nothing of *sturm and drang*, and has enough to live on of simple food, and has learned contentment apart from ease and luxury.'[28] Despite what might appear to be the miserable condition of their dwellings, there was no reason for visitors to feel sorry for the inhabitants even of 'primitive Highland bothies', for they were quite cheerful and satisfied.[29] Their serenity led tourist Frances Murray to wonder 'whether the thousand artificial necessities and endless and varied appliances of modern civilization, are a benefit or otherwise to our race.'[30] Tourists stereotyped Highlanders as generous and hospitable, even when they had little to give. Local residents offered visitors refreshments and sometimes a place to change wet clothes, and accepted little or no recompense. Even the poorest Gael, travelers claimed, was courteous, well-bred, and dignified. 'Every Highlander is a gentleman, and in the poorest homes, under the roughest circumstances, we never met with anything less than a courtesy, kindliness and what I can only call a *savoir faire* which one misses in many a drawing room of the rich and great.'[31] Goodrich-Freer believed that this good breeding and self-assurance, which was 'largely inherent', also derived from the fact that chiefs had once lived on close terms with their clansmen, and many Highlanders had had relations in the 'higher ranks'.[32]

Highlanders allegedly possessed a natural, untutored virtue. Even in the days of clan violence, some commentators alleged, clansmen maintained a strict honesty amongst themselves. The foremost example of this innate integrity was Highlanders' and islanders' unwillingness to turn in Charles Edward Stuart after Culloden despite the massive reward offered by the government.[33] Discussants claimed that crime was nearly unknown in the Highlands and islands, and the moral standard there was the highest in Britain.[34] There was little need for prisons in the Highlands.[35] 'The people here are "dull as ditchwater". All are moral and straightforward.'[36] Malcolm Ferguson could not recollect seeing a tipsy person during his rambles through Skye in the 1880s, and 'very rarely' heard cursing or strong language.[37] The deep religiosity attributed to Scots in general was especially marked in the Highlands, thought some observers. Though uneducated, alleged David Stewart of Garth, Highlanders were well instructed in a knowledge of the scriptures, and their faith was founded on the simple principles of Christianity, not on denominational guidelines.[38] Goodrich-Freer found Highlanders to be religious by 'temperament'; 'they are a worshipping, God-fearing people'.[39] Tourists delightedly described scenes of family worship reminiscent of 'A Cotter's Saturday Night', the 'pretty' sight of Highlanders in their best clothes heading off to church on Sunday morning, and the large crowds who turned out for the annual Gaelic communion services.

Primitive, untouched, and untainted by modern values and ways of life, crofters were creatures of the state of nature. That state, according to many, was the source of their purity, contentment, and morality. Living hand in hand with nature, Highlanders' ears were 'ever close to the beatings of her heart', as could be seen by their capacity for friendship, their appreciation of the environment, and in their gift of the second sight.[40] They had a natural affinity for music and poetry. 'Song is with them as with the wild birds of their native woods and wilds, an instinct, an inspiration.'[41] They were healthy and long-lived; steamer passengers enroute from Raasay to the Portree cattle market, said Ferguson, were mostly 'big, strong, healthy, hardy-looking men'.[42] And, according to visitors, they had access to all the bounty of the natural world: ash trees and birches danced beside their homes, soft mosses covered their roofs, mountain burns provided trout, the sea offered lobsters and oysters. There was pure water, good food (if sometimes sparse), and healthy exercise.[43] Alexander Nicholson likened several places on Skye to 'the very picture of a Happy Valley, sequestered from all the world, the home of innocence and peace.'[44]

It was partly by protecting Highlanders from outside influences that nature made them what they were. Mountains and rough seas safeguarded Highlanders and islanders from sordid civilization, enabling them to maintain their instinctive characteristics. Many tourists also argued that it was the uniqueness of the Highland landscape which made the residents of the region a distinctive people. 'It is the daily contemplation of scenes where nature is displayed in sublime and awful forms, that produces the melancholy turn of thought, deep undercurrent of feeling, and romantic enthusiasm, which distinguish the Highland character; with that energy of soul which sustains the Gael in the hour of danger and of death.'[45] The idea that their constant exposure to magnificent scenery elevated and expanded the mind of the Highlander is found frequently in tourist literature. Gordon Cumming believed that the terrain which surrounded them helped explain why 'these children of the Mist are so dreamy and unpractical as compared with their Anglo-Saxon neighbors.'[46] Stewart noted that the 'poetical propensity of the Highlanders' was the 'natural result of their situation'.[47] Alexander Smith commented that the harshness of the environment made the Celt 'the most melancholy of men', as well as superstitious and poetic, for it constantly reminded him of his mortality.[48]

The understanding of Highlanders as 'nature-taught'[49] was part of a long tradition dating at least to Martin Martin's accounts of Skye in 1703 and it owed much to the traditions of pastoral poetry, as well as Enlightenment and Romantic belief in the virtues to be found in the state of nature. The motif took on new importance in the late nineteenth century as social ills seemingly proliferated and reformers offered proof of the decaying consequences of urban life within three generations. The contrast expressed by many tourists between Highlanders' ways of life and contemporaneous accounts of the slums of Outcast London reflected and expressed middle-class doubts about the equation of industrialism with progress. The morality attributed to Highlanders, even though they lived in unsanitary one-room houses, compared favorably to the vices believed to be rampant in overcrowded urban slums.[50] Ferguson compared the sobriety and clean language found on Skye to 'the shocking scenes, and the outrageous and blasphemous swearing often heard in some of the streets of our large cities, which makes one actually shudder.'[51] Tourists credited Highlanders with glowing good health; they were large, robust, and hardy, a contrast to the puniness of urban factory workers. A writer of 1886 described 'healthy' crofting children with 'chubby and brown' cheeks and legs and the 'clear blue of heaven in their eyes', who spent autumn days helping their father with the harvest.[52] Crofters' oft-described self-respect was the antithesis of the slovenliness and lack of pride often attributed to slum dwellers. Likewise, Highlanders' regard for the social hierarchy distinguished them from urban workers who were increasingly crossing borders and disputing their place in the late nineteenth century. Commentators stressed the 'respectability' and 'decency' of Gaels, indeed often of Scots in general. Highland servants were courteous and devoted, said one writer, rendering service as one would offer kindness to a friend.[53] They did not resent their 'superiors', a point Queen Victoria often mentioned in praise of her Highland servants and tenants. The generosity of Highlanders who offered food and drink to weary travelers, even those who just wanted to view the inside of their homes, could be interpreted as appropriate displays of deference towards their social betters.

The men and women of the Highlands and Western Isles thus became necessary counters to the ills of urban life. Throughout the late eighteenth and nineteenth centuries, commentators on the Highlands argued that it was essential for the health of the nation as a whole to retain a rural population and rural virtues. To those eighteenth- and early nineteenth-century observers who were opposed to widespread emigration from the Highlands, this argument rested largely on the economic and social importance of retaining a large population, especially one which served the nation so well through the military.[54] When necessary, Highlanders could fill the nation's military ranks, send laborers south, even colonize Britain's distant possessions, all with the virtues of a 'loyal and well-principled race.'[55] As time went on, and concern about the consequences of commercial and industrial life grew stronger, writers emphasized the importance of preserving an agrarian population in order to retain the morality considered to be inherent in country life. 'In a country where the natural tendencies to city life are so great, it is for the advantage of the community to have a rural population attracted by favorable circumstances to the country.'[56] By definition, Highlanders could not preserve the rural essence of 'Englishness' which many historians argue was increasingly considered endangered in the late nineteenth century.[57] But the traits attributed to them were similar to those associated with the rural south, and contemporaries clearly believed Highlanders, too, could play a role in the conservation of those important qualities derived from country life. The *Illustrated London News* opined in 1888 that, 'Far from the smoke of the city...by seashore and in Highland glen, the blood grows pure and the race grows strong. And assuredly depth and strength of character, and stamina of physique are the growing wants of Britain in these days of political enfranchisement and of crowded cities.'[58] To the Napier Commission, the Parliamentary commission charged with investigating conditions in the Highlands in the wake of the Crofters' War, the north was a fit place for the nurturing of qualities threatened by industrial society:

> The crofting and cottar population of the Highlands and islands, small though it be, is a nursery of good workers and good citizens for the whole empire. In this respect the stock is exceptionally valuable. By sound physical constitution, native intelligence, and good moral training, it is particularly fitted to recruit the people of our industrial centres, who without such help from wholesome sources in rural districts, would degenerate under the influences of bad lodging, unhealthy occupations, and enervating habits. It cannot be indifferent to the whole nation, constituted as the nation now is, to possess within its borders a people, hardy, skilful, intelligent, and prolific, as an everflowing fountain of renovating life.[59]

Nor was the life of Highland crofters a foil only to life in urban slums; some Victorian tourists claimed to find such an existence more appealing than the stresses of the middle-class world. It was attractive, said J. A. MacCulloch, to those weary of 'the many unnatural ways of modern life, and who sigh for Wordsworth's plain living and high thinking.'[60] Her visit to the island of Mingulay seemed more 'real' to Goodrich-Freer than her usual existence.[61] When the sun sank in the Hebrides, described a columnist for the *Illustrated London News*, 'the simple crofter hamlet by the shore will sink to rest. And the weary and the disappointed, soiled with the dust of the far-off city, striving all their lives after what they will never win, have forgotten that sweet bread may be earned on the cornlands and fair fish caught in the sea, that there is music for listening here by the murmuring brooks, and rest in the setting of the sun.'[62]

Yet while their significance to British society lay in their alleged perpetuation of a community and values threatened by industrialization, the dire poverty of crofters made them ambiguous figures. Few visitors failed to record their astonishment at the destitution they encountered in the Highlands.

The typical Highland and island home was the 'black house,' a small structure of rough stone and turf and a thatched heather roof pegged to a few timbers, with no paved floor, ceiling, windows, or chimney. This was usually shared with the family cow, whose quarters were only partially separated from the human living space.[63] Descriptions of the 'most wretched' cottages, the indigenous squalor and lethargy, the 'hovels', 'too wretched to be even picturesque', and the 'very present sight of poverty and desolation' were commonplaces of tourist literature.[64] Despite what they had heard of Highland indigence, many Victorian sightseers were unprepared for what they found. To W. W. Nevin, an American writing in 1881, the living conditions of Highlanders were a misery and degradation perhaps unequalled in any civilized land.[65] Also writing in the 1880s, Joseph and Elizabeth Robins Pennell could not believe that people lived in such a manner in the nineteenth century; nothing had changed, they said, from the time of Thomas Pennant.[66] Goodrich-Freer spoke of the 'ever present sight of poverty and desolation'.[67] Groups of children hoping to sell shells, interesting rocks, or drinks of milk often met tourists at famous attractions, another indication of local indigence. This happened particularly frequently at Iona, where 'the spectacle of [the children's] poverty and wretchedness, their eagerness to sell their little treasures, the roughness with which they were repulsed and their looks of mournful disappointment' gave Jacob Abbott more pain than the ruins brought him pleasure.[68]

Such conditions were an implicit indictment of the moral standards of Highlanders, and the discourse about them was liberally sprinkled with pejorative references to them as 'simple', 'primitive', and 'naturally lazy', often within the same texts that honored their goodness and simplicity. A large element of public opinion in England and the Lowlands regarded Highlanders as an inferior people, whose shortcomings were evident in their living standards. Contempt towards Highlanders was particularly strong during the potato famine of the 1840s and 50s, during which Lowland newspapers published numerous editorials and letters to the editor critical of Gaels.[69] Witnessing the poverty of the Highlands afforded a lesson in the importance of the moral value of hard work, as well as an opportunity for the 'subtle pleasures' of 'sympathy, moral scrutiny and paternalistic rebuke' on the part of tourists.[70] Plenty of food was available to Highlanders, said critics, if they would only exert the energy to fish for it. Rarely did they make the best use of their land, seldom rotating crops or using manure. Mothers did not wash their children. Those who worked on steamers or in inns were prone to procrastination. They were overly fond of whisky. Although he admitted that not all crofters' problems were their own fault, James Wilson alleged that Highlanders' dark, moist, dirty dwellings were surely their own free choice; as evidence he noted that for many years islanders had refused to walk on the roads in Skye, claiming the hard surface wore their shoes and bruised their feet.[71] No amount of advice, Malcolm Ferguson said, could convince Hebrideans to deviate from the 'primitive' methods of farming they had practiced for generations.[72] In sum, 'Highlanders have not yet come to appreciate the true dignity of ordinary labor.'[73] Such arguments turned against Highlanders the very devotion to tradition for which they were frequently lauded, lambasting them for refusing to accept the benefits of progress. Gaels, tourists seemed to argue, should accept enough of the advances of modernization to demonstrate that they met modern standards of virtue – and to keep from embarrassing the nation – but not enough to endanger their status as historic artifacts.

In other ways, too, the qualities for which outsiders praised Highlanders could be used to disparage them. Tourists valued Gaels' primitiveness, but condescended to them as members of a backwards society. Crofters' 'simplicity' suggested a lack of knowledge about the wider world, which could be charming, but could also translate as 'ignorance'. The argument that their virtue was 'natural' and unlearned implicitly denigrated their intellectuality, as did their preservation of old superstitions. In the early nineteenth century, John Carr argued that Highlanders were motivated by 'a powerful moral sense, more than by reflection and education.'[74] Their supposed love of nature, tourists believed, was not the same thing as an aesthetic appreciation of landscape, which 'uncivilized' Highlanders had not yet developed.

Defenders of Highlanders, however, claimed they were neither ignorant nor idle. Some visitors argued that the effects of Calvinism's emphasis on education were seen in the Highlands and islands. Goodrich-Freer wrote at length of the excellent schools on several of the Hebridean islands and of the 'extreme intelligence' and 'intense desire for education and for self-improvement of every kind' which she found among islanders, including women, at the turn of the nineteenth century.[75] Many commentators noted the mental sharpness of Highlanders with whom they spoke.[76] The alleged indolence of Gaels, many observers claimed, was due to their situation, not their character. Those who left Scotland showed themselves to be productive and energetic workers in other countries. The perception of idleness arose in part from a lack of understanding of crofters' work patterns; spells of busyness alternated with times when there was little that needed to be done. Fishermen lying asleep in the sun may have been out all night working.[77] Sympathizers also attributed poverty to the great difficulty of reaping subsistence from the Highland geography; their continual effort to keep going ennobled Hebrideans in Gordon Cumming's eyes.[78]

The equivocal meanings read onto Highlanders are particularly evident in discussions of gender. As spontaneous children of nature, they exhibited gender roles which were undefiled by commercial and industrial society and compared favorably to other segments of British society. Men were 'big, strong, healthy, hardy-looking'[79]; young women possessed an unaffected grace and beauty. Such images, Murray Pittock notes, were at odds with the reality that Highlanders were often undernourished and undersized,[80] but corresponded with the perception that they lived much of their lives outdoors, engaging in what tourists considered healthy physical exercise rather than enervating factory work, business enterprises, or the silly pursuit of fashion.

The vital masculinity of Highland males was manifested in their daily pursuits as fishermen, farmers, and soldiers. Their ability to survive in the often harsh environment in which they lived rendered Highland men hardy and tough in many tourists' eyes. Highlanders and islanders effortlessly traversed territory which English visitors would find formidable.[81] As discussed in Chapter 3, the stamina of Highland ghillies was often contrasted with the lack of endurance of the upper-class hunters and stalkers who hired them. S. Augustus Tipple remarked on the 'great height and muscular power' of the 'Highland mountaineers, in reference to whose extraordinary and daring feats of strength many wonderful legends exist.'[82] Edmund Gosse considered the fishermen of Lewis to be 'handsome giants', 'a fine race of men'.[83] Those travelers who ventured as far as the Shetland Islands or St. Kilda considered the cliff climbing engaged in by men of those islands to be the epitome of Highlanders' manliness. Island males rappelled down the steep cliffs to reach bird nests situated on ledges and crevices alongside the cliff face, an activity requiring strength, courage, and 'steely nerves.'[84] The physical abilities attributed to male Highlanders became particularly well-known, even to those who never set foot in Scotland, through the exploits of the Highland military regiments. Indeed, Highlanders first impressed themselves upon British consciousness as warriors.[85] With their distinctive kilted uniforms, Highland regiments were a visible feature of Continental and imperial wars throughout the late eighteenth and nineteenth centuries, ever since they were first used on a large scale in the Seven Years' War. David Stewart of Garth's *Sketches of the Character, Manners and Present State of the Highlanders of Scotland: with details of the Military Service of the Highland Regiments*, first published in 1821, did much to disseminate belief in Highlanders' talent for war. According to Stewart, the harsh living conditions of the area imparted a toughness which strengthened Highlanders' bodies and enabled them to sustain privation.[86] They deemed courage the highest virtue, and believed in loyalty to chief, clan, and country. As Peter Womack points out, the army was considered the home of the Highland essence in the late eighteenth century. Clans were widely understood to be military regiments and the chief was conceived of as a commander, a belief which helped to further the notion of Highlanders as paragons of masculine vigor.[87]

Corresponding to the rugged masculinity of male Highlanders was the beauty of younger women, among whom tourists detected a natural purity, healthiness, and modesty not to be found among more sophisticated communities or among the urban working class. Perceptions of younger Highland women owed much to the Romantic tradition which identified women with nature; both were fertile and nurturing and existed to lead sensitive males to a higher self.[88] Gaelic women were believed to fulfill this ideal especially well. It was something of a staple of male travelers' reminiscences of Scotland to recount an unexpected meeting in a lonely locale with either a solitary lassie or a small group of attractive women, who were perhaps too shy to speak. Sometimes the author compared these young women to Wordsworth's 'The Highland Girl', or described them as 'nymphs', 'fairies', or 'kelpies', devices which reminded of their symbolic power as representatives of nature. A striking young woman who Townshend saw from the Broadford steamer possessed 'the nobility of nature'.[89] Their beauty, physical competence, uncovered hair, and skirts which were often shorter than those worn by middle-class urban women made Highland women erotic attractions to many male tourists. Townshend, for instance, pointed out the 'extreme luxuriance' of the hair of Skye women, and wondered if it might be better for English women, too, to bare their heads.[90] The fact that, according to their texts, these men had only brief interactions, if any, with the women they admired, added a sense of mystery which intensified the eroticism. Seeking shelter in a shepherd's hut on Uist during a downpour on a hunting trip, Robert Buchanan was greeted by a beautiful, other-worldly woman who possessed a 'strange whiteness and purity'. Although he knew her to be the shepherd's daughter-in-law, he referred to her as 'Bonnie Kilmeny', the title character in a James Hogg poem who was transported by spirits to the other world.[91]

It was their naturalness which made Highlanders exemplars of ideal masculinity and femininity, but that same naturalness could be used to denigrate them and the validity of their gender identifications. Looked at strictly within a male symbolic context, the comparison between Lowland/ English males and those of the north and west of Scotland represented Highland males as possessing 'an unrestrained masculine sexuality'.[92] However, within a different set of symbols, their construction as 'natural' beings, as well as their supposed emotional spontaneity, apparent laziness, and willingness to let women do heavy work feminized Gaelic men in middle-class eyes.[93] The elegiac mode of commemoration with which the Ossianic poems surrounded ancient Highland warriors negated their physical abilities. So did public exhibits of the 'savage Highlander' within controlled environments, which effectively rendered him tame.[94] The 15,000 Atholl Highlanders in full battle gear who welcomed Victoria and Albert to Dunkeld in 1842 were described by the press as 'the warlike sons of the mountain'.[95] But they were present only for purposes of display, to create atmosphere, not to utilize their prowess. The very existence of Highland regiments suggested that the potency of the Highlander was under the authority of the state. 'The

Celtic spirit is valorized, but only in the context of Anglo-Saxon discipline and military technology.'[96] The famed virility of the Highlander was thus neutralized. The containment of his military skill suggested the power of civilization to control that which was once wild.

Similarly, by rendering Highland women as part of the scenery open to the male gaze, the association between women and nature testified to their ultimate powerlessness and the superior status of civilized male tourists. At the same time, women's naturalness could be as unattractive as it was attractive. In a time when delicacy and fragility were the epitome of middle-class standards of beauty, tourists frequently described women, like men, as 'strong', 'hardy', 'sturdy', and 'robust'. The 'unwomanly' physical labor they engaged in shocked visitors. Tourists considered older Highland women far less handsome than youthful ones, a result of the work expected of them. Indoors without chimneys or windows, or outdoors cutting and carrying peat and tending to animals, women became withered and anemic, their skin stained with peat, their eyes bleared with smoke, their bodies 'prematurely aged with hardship'.[97] Beauty was indicative of women's virtue in the nineteenth century, symbolizing effective control over their moral and physical natures.[98] Crofting women could not possess for long the sort of beauty protected by the comfortable lives of middle- and upper-class Victorian women. Few travelers blamed female Highlanders for their coarse looks, but discussions of the toll taken by their ways of life reminded of social and economic barriers between locals and visitors. J. A. MacCulloch saw two women with ropes across their chests pulling a harrow across a field.[99] Women carried heavy baskets of peat on their backs across steep hillsides. In the eighteenth century women occasionally rowed male travelers across rivers, or carried them on their backs through streams, practices travel writers described as evidence of 'barbarism' and the 'primitive customs of the people'.[100] The practice common to women and girls in rural Scotland of going without shoes was shocking and disagreeable to most tourists. Although they struggled to remember that bare feet were but a custom of the society, the habit also suggested a lapse of moral control. Such images pointed out the unenlightened character of preindustrial societies and made evident the benefits of modern civilization.

The various meanings attached to Highlanders depended on their remaining untouched by time and social change. This was a fragile construction and had been even in the eighteenth century. Malcolm Chapman demonstrates that the very notion of Highlanders as the embodiment of the 'folk' connoted a culture vanishing in the path of spreading modernization.[101] The idea that the Highlands were in the midst of a transition out of a traditional society was a well-established staple of tourist rhetoric, dating from the late eighteenth century. It was a central theme of Stewart of Garth's analysis of Highland character in the early 1820s. He believed that 'much of the romance and chivalry of the Highland character is gone. The voice of the bard has long been silent, and poetry, tradition and song, are vanishing away.'[102] As concern about the direction of modern society intensified in the late nineteenth century, the need to arrest Highlanders' passage to modernity was made manifest just as threats to the cultural understanding of them became increasingly evident. Discussions of Highland society began to emphasize the extent to which it had not changed, rather than to laud the spread of progress and civilization. Highlanders came to be symbols of stability who were frozen in time. In Pittock's words, Highlanders (and other Celts) became 'something to look back on, to memorialize under the drifting gaze of social change'.[103] Guidebooks, too, endeavored to demonstrate the unchangeability of Highland society. The descriptions of the life of Skye islanders in Anderson's *Guide* were virtually word for word the same in the 1834 and 1863 editions. Though few tourists were likely to compare the sources, the authors nonetheless suggested that the intervening thirty years, which brought dramatic change to social, economic, and political life in areas more closely tied to the metropolis, had no similar effect in the Highlands.

Victorians were well aware that the Highlands and islands were changing, but often admitted it only grudgingly or with trepidation. Goodrich-Freer noted sadly that on Skye 'there are electric light and Tottenham Court Road furniture, and the exorbitant, even worse, the pretentious and incompetent innkeeper, with other blessings of civilization'.[104] Nearly all the young people spoke English, one could easily obtain the *Times*, there were telegraphs and plenty of shops.[105] Living conditions, said some, were less picturesque than formerly; by the turn of the century residents of Eriskay were importing corrugated iron for their roofs, and new and more modern cottages were being built for the tenants at Invergarry.[106] Young people at Lochgoilhead self-consciously tried to look and sound English.[107] Alexander Smith commented in the 1860s that the younger generation of Highlanders were not like their elders; they were more knowledgeable, had fewer prejudices, and were more amenable to advice. In a few years, he was sure, better sheep would be produced and finer wool sent forth – but Skye would have become tame, would have lost its human character.[108]

Several late nineteenth-century commentators worried that the coming of progress was likely to weaken the distinctive Highland character, which was Gaels' most valuable contribution to the British community. The Highlander was 'slowly moving into another day.' 'He is a remnant of an old state of society which existed throughout England as well as Scotland – a state that has disappeared, as it must disappear also around him'.[109] The process was similar to that taking place among the 'decaying races of North America', the 'Europeanized peoples of India', and the 'gin-sodden tribes of Western Africa'.[110] As J. A. MacCulloch mourned, 'we cannot but feel that the race is one which, in its present surroundings is enfeebled and dying....Habits of procrastination denote a feeble vitality and the customary submission to fate suggests that the fires of energy are burning low.[111] According to many observers the reason for the imminent moral decline of Highlanders lay in an attack upon the ancient purity of the folk by corrupting and alien values. Highlanders thrived best when they were secluded from outsiders. This argument was in part a castigation of tourists, especially English ones, for their ignorance of native culture and their introduction of commercial values to the islands. 'Wherever the great or little Sassenach comes, he leaves a dirty trail like the slime of a snake. He it is who abuses the people for their laziness, points sneeringly at their poor houses, spits scorn on their wretchedly cultivated scraps of land; and he it is who, introducing the noble goad of greed, turns the ragged domestic virtues into well-dressed prostitutes, heartless and eager for hire.'[112] J. F. Campbell, one of the premier folklorists of the Highlands who published a major study of the lore of Scottish Gaeldom in 1860, lamented that 'Railways, roads, newspapers, and tourists are slowly but surely doing their accustomed work. They are driving out romance.'[113] Others lay the source of the infection at the feet of landlords, themselves influenced by commercial values, arguing that the old Highland virtues had been the product of genuine personal relationships between classes which no longer existed. This was Stewart's argument in the early nineteenth century, and it was echoed by later writers. Highlanders' 'spirit and independence' was gone, according to a late Victorian observer, replaced with 'a fear and awe of their proprietors which no previous generation exhibited.'[114]

An equally serious threat was the general crisis of rural depopulation believed by late Victorians to be edging towards the Highlands. Poverty and land shortages, some fretted, would lead to emigration, either overseas or to the cities. In 1882 Donald H. MacFarlane, an Irish nationalist MP and Highlander by birth who was a vocal champion of crofters, argued that they were being pushed off the land and 'going into the slums of the towns to breathe foul air, to drink vile drink and to inhale demoralization from corrupt surroundings'.[115] A writer in the *Illustrated London News* in 1888 was distressed that young Highland men were 'making the mistake' of seeking their fortunes and were 'crowding in to the cities to degenerate into pale faced clerks and puny shopkeepers' instead of 'enjoying the simple, honest life of their fathers.'[116]

Thus while the vision of crofters as children of nature provided the comforting hope that their rural virtues might yet revitalize urban society, it also implied that this prospect was not certain. This disturbing possibility was mitigated by the Celt/Anglo-Saxon dichotomy that crofters represented in addition to the country/city juxtaposition. Throughout the nineteenth century many writers on the Highlands emphasized that inhabitants of the Highlands and Western Isles were 'the comparatively pure and unmixed descendants of the aboriginal Celts'.[117] Hebrideans were considered to be particularly genuine examples of Celts, having mixed less with other populations. Late in the nineteenth century J. A. MacCulloch insisted that 'when we think of Skye, it must inevitably be as of an island of the Celts governed by Celtic ideals from first to last.'[118] Interpreting Highlanders' characteristics as racial in origin held out hope that these qualities would not disintegrate under changing social or environmental conditions. Observers commonly reported that despite the 'lamentable' alterations in the crofters' ways of life, they had not lost their 'instinctive' deference, courtesy, self-respect, or spirituality.[119] 'Treated and looked upon like foxes as mere vermin that interfere with sport, discouraged and thwarted in every direction, these people, notwithstanding their poverty and the hardships of their lot, have maintained unimpaired the noblest attributes of their race.'[120] Despite the influx of civilization to the Highlands, said Alexander Smith, the 'old descent and breeding are still visible through all modern disguises'.[121]

Racial and environmental interpretations of Highland crofters sat easily next to each other in nineteenth-century literature of the Highlands, often intertwined in the same author's text. Most discussions of Scottish Celts' surroundings implied that it was their inborn virtues that allowed them to rise above their poverty, an idea which could be interpreted in biological terms. Although the term 'race' was used loosely by most Victorians, not always connoting biological determinism, belief in the absoluteness of the racial differences between Anglo-Saxons and Celts was intrinsic to Victorian culture. This categorization interpreted crofters in much the same way as did the environmental construction. Celts were natural, pure, intuitive, and sentimental, all of which contrasted with the materialistic, practical, scientific, and factual Anglo-Saxon. Many of the characteristics which would come to define Celts were already in place earlier in the century, but Matthew Arnold's *The Study of Celtic Literature* (first published in 1867), which in turn owed much to Ernest Renan's *Poesie des Races Celtiques* (1860), cemented the understanding of the race. Renan and Arnold located Celts in opposition to the modern world, finding that they lacked the discipline and drive for action necessary for economic, political, or even artistic success, but possessed strong capacities for emotion, sensibility, religion, and the minor arts. Both cloaked Celts in nostalgia; Renan looked at them with a longing for the emotionality he believed his intellect deprived him of, Arnold for the 'sweetness and light' missing from the Anglo-Saxon Philistine. To the British public Arnold's interpretation of Celts took on the status of established fact, coloring, for instance, the way nineteenth-century folklorists understood Highlanders.[122]

It was their contrast to the industrial age which Arnold, Renan, and many others found attractive – and necessary – about Celts, but, as was true with the environmental construction, the qualities which rendered them different could also be used against them. The attributes praised in Celts were the same ones often used to justify women's exclusion from economic and political power. As applied to Ireland, as L. P. Curtis shows, the traits popularly ascribed to Celts usually translated into racial inferiority and backwardness.[123] Some observers absolved crofters from any connection to the Irish by arguing that Highlanders were primarily Scandinavian, not Celtic, or at least that the 'upper ranks' were mainly of Scandinavian origin.[124] One late Victorian writer argued that Hebrideans rarely demonstrated the physical characteristics of Celts.[125] More commonly, Western Highlanders and islanders were considered to belong to a different subdivision of Celts than did the Irish. Ethnologist John Beddoe's 'index of nigrescence', a formula which calculated the level of Africanoid elements in a given people and thus their ancestral connection to primitive man, gave Ireland a 'nigrescence' rating of 65 percent, compared to 41 percent for the Highlands and 29 percent for the Bristol area.[126] The occasional writer might refer to the 'invincible Celtic slovenliness' of Highlanders or the *Times* might characterize western islanders as 'pure Celts' who displayed the typical traits of shrewdness, laziness, disregard for veracity, lack of ambition, and rebellion against civilization.[127] Nonetheless, it seems that in general Western Highlanders, although clearly regarded as inferior to Anglo-Saxons, were considered good Celts. They were mostly Protestant, had generally accepted the fundamental notions of the English constitution, and had historically demonstrated courage and love of independence. And as the Napier Commission report noted, because crofters possessed some property (livestock, boats, agricultural implements), they were equipped to become 'substantial occupiers' of small holdings.[128]

Such distinctions made possible a positive interpretation of the crofters' racial background, with particular value placed on their corresponding feminine construction. Like women, Hebrideans retained the moral and spiritual qualities threatened by the world of business, competition, and mechanization, thus providing a counter-effect to those distressing trends of the modern world. And just as women were to preserve the spiritual health of the family while men faced the potentially corrupting forces of capitalism, so could Celts maintain for the nation those vanishing qualities of poetry, a sense of the past, emotion, and strong moral fiber. So suggested Arnold who argued that the English were 'imperiled' by the Philistinism of the middle class and could be saved by the feminine qualities of Celts: 'Now, then, is the moment for the greater delicacy and spirituality of the Celtic peoples who are blended with us, if it be but wisely directed, to make itself prized and honored.'[129]

By attributing crofters' ability to serve as a fountain of renovating life to their Celtic blood, such arguments allowed for a flirtation with a sentimental Scottish distinctiveness without compromising England's dominant role in the Union. To some commentators, particularly those associated with the

'Celtic Twilight', the Celtic connection assumed new importance in the late nineteenth century in the face of fears of the impending decline of the Anglo-Saxon race. Moncrieff quoted Fiona MacLeod [William Sharp] on this point:

> [W]e, what is left of the Celtic races, of the Celtic genius, may permeate the greater race of which we are a vital part, so that with this emotion, Celtic love of duty, and Celtic spirituality, a nation greater than any the world has seen may issue, a nation refined and strengthened by the wise relinquishings and steadfast ideals of Celt and Saxon, united in a common fatherland, and in singleness of pride and faith'.[130]

According to Pittock, the idea of 'Celtic Darwinism' suggested that Celts 'though unfitted to territorial identity, had left a kind of hereditary cultural imprint on British society which helped give it a gentler, more sympathetic and feminine dimension.'[131] Themselves less fit than Anglo-Saxons, Celts might not survive indefinitely, but their contribution to British character would. An emphasis on the fusion of Celtic and Saxon blood also served to distinguish English from German character, a politically attractive concept after 1871.[132] Grant Allen argued in a *Fortnightly Review* article in 1880 that in blood the English were 'preponderantly if not overwhelmingly Kymric and Gaelic'. Differing from Arnold in his assessment of the Celtic contribution to the English inheritance, Allen maintained that it was the Celtic element in the English that was dynamic and energetic and had done much to differentiate the national character from that of the 'slow and ponderous continental Teutons'.[133]

This appreciation of Celtic blood did not seek to provide a strategy for autonomy or self-sufficiency. Indeed, the gender construction which defined Celts implicitly demanded the paternalism of outsiders. Arnold's qualification that the race's qualities must be 'wisely directed' was indicative. He praised the Celtic spirit in its 'blended form', imprisoned in the British domestic body, and his assertion that England 'owned' the Celts and wanted to 'know' them made clear their position in the British hierarchy.[134] While an environmental reading of islanders posited outsiders as dangerous, the feminizing racial interpretation made their practical and rational abilities necessary to the child-like Celts. To many visitors, Highlanders' poverty was evidence of their impracticality. J. A. MacCulloch observed: 'Crofters...are not always alive to what is best for them. They are affected deeply by sentimental reasons, they do not always exercise forethought, and they too often seize upon a present good (which is easily obtained) to avoid the trouble involved in obtaining a future greater good.'[135] According to the Marquis of Lorne, himself a Highland landowner, the land shortage of which crofters complained was the result of the lack of foresight of 'an ignorant and warm-hearted people', who needed the influence of the landlord or some other outside force to restrain them.[136]

In this manner, the rendition of Highlanders as female served to uphold the necessity of the 'male' Anglo-Saxon world, reminding visitors from England and the Lowlands of their superiority. Highlanders were at once idealized and denigrated, the objects both of nostalgia for the past and contempt for pre-modern societies. Together, the environmental and racial understandings of inhabitants of the Highlands and Western Isles in the nineteenth century invested them with a symbolism which counteracted and reflected the difficulties facing British society and culture towards the turn of the century. These perceptions of Highlanders were, of course, stereotypes which often had little to do with the reality of Gaels' lives. Travel writers occasionally pointed this out, but to little avail. In the 1820s, John Macculloch, in a volume published as letters to Walter Scott, commented that many characteristics attributed to Highlanders had long ago faded away. Travelers would be disappointed, he continued, if they expected to be greeted in Iona or Skye by a gifted seer, or to find every cottage resounding with the songs of Ossian.[137] Nearly one hundred years later, A. R. Hope Moncrieff maintained that Highland character was 'exaggerated into a caricature as like the original as is the rigid Highlander of a snuff shop.'[138] On the other hand, in his popular *A Summer in Skye* of 1865, Alexander Smith maintained that although the 'Highlander of Sir Walter... is to a large extent an ideal being', Highlanders did indeed possess many of the qualities popularly ascribed to them.[139] These archetypes clearly mattered to tourists and to the wider British public. Highlanders became plastic figures to be shaped according to the needs of outside observers, with little ability to speak for themselves – until the 1880s. By that time, changes in the region enabled crofters to attempt to make their own voices heard over the discourse which surrounded them.

Contesting the Image of the Highlander

As one of the 'must-see' attractions of the Highlands, the men and women who lived there were made into living museum pieces by tourists. They were flesh and blood examples of another culture and an earlier way of life. Rarely appearing by name or as individuals, crofters were reduced to symbols which stood as one of the noteworthy sights of the region. The definition of Highlanders as members of a folk culture positioned them as subjects to be scientifically and rationally studied, particularly as interest in both folklore and ethnography increased in the late nineteenth century.[140] Victorians were accustomed to the display of members of other cultures, such as African tribesmen or Australian aborigines, in theatres, exhibition halls, museums, and zoos.[141] The Highlands became another venue where one could observe the daily lives of a little-known people. Tourists sometimes encouraged Highlanders, especially children, to perform a Gaelic song or prayer, and occasionally rewarded them with a small tip.[142] Mrs. Beecroft and her daughter, visiting Scotland in the 1830s, 'amused themselves' by talking to 'the natives' because they enjoyed hearing the almost undecipherable accents.[143] The structures of tourism created a distance between the tourist as spectator and the Highlander as display or object, a distance furthered by social and economic differences between them as well as by the language barrier.[144]

As part of the effort to learn more about Highlanders and their social and cultural milieu, tourists sometimes visited Highlanders' homes. On occasion they were invited to do so by local residents who offered shelter from rain or cold. In many other instances, however, sightseers simply dropped in, sometimes to discover that their 'hosts' could not speak English. Tourists described how they 'walked into' or 'went into' a nearby black house or other dwelling, apparently uninvited. Sightseer Mrs. John F. Gower defined Highland dwellings as simply one of the available tourist attractions when she chose to visit some 'cottages or shelings [sic] as they are called, and have some conversation with their inhabitants' instead of going to Dunstaffage Castle with her family.[145] When a Highland woman invited a party of tourists at Lochearnhead to take shelter from the rain in her home, one of the group 'took the liberty' of 'reconnoitering' a little, as she had not previously seen the inside of a Highland residence.[146] 'Guests' were generally complimentary towards the Highlanders whose homes they viewed, if not towards the conditions of the dwellings, and claimed to have been hospitably received. Mrs. Gower found the residents of the homes she visited to be 'very intelligent and communicative'. When her family returned, they all went to one of the 'shielings' and partook of bannocks made especially for them, served with butter and milk.[147] The woman who was invited into a cottage at Lochearnhead reflected that 'it was a very delightful visit to me and must be to all reflective minds to see the distinctions of society laid aside for awhile and the reins given to the common feeling of humanity.'[148] However, such meetings also reinforced the class and ethnic hierarchies which differentiated tourists and Highlanders. Sightseers' insistence that Highlanders were pleased that they came to call evoked stereotypes of the innate hospitality of the Gaels but also of their natural deference to their superiors, for many travel writers implied that residents were honored by a visit from someone of a higher class. Highlanders, said tourists, rushed to brush off chairs for their unexpected callers and offered food. 'It would have done your heart good to have witnessed the gratification felt by this poor honest industrious family' commented one visitor.[149]

Women sightseers were more likely than men to enter Highland dwellings. In 1836 a male tourist asked a female member of his party to talk with a family whose 'Highland hut' he noticed, which she considered a 'delightful' way to spend a few minutes.[150] Queen Victoria was fond of paying visits to homes of those who lived near Balmoral. As the frequent conduit of encounters with 'natives', women remained within the domestic sphere, while staking a claim to help inform their society about Highland conditions and thus to participate in the shaping of social attitudes. This was especially true of women like Constance Gordon Cumming whose book on the Hebrides was but one of several travel accounts she wrote with an ethnographic focus, such as *At Home in Fiji* (1882) and *From the Hebrides to the Himalayas* (1876). Women who did not publish their travel accounts evidently did not seek the same kind of cultural capital as did Gordon Cumming, Sarah Murray, or Ada Goodrich-Freer, but by writing to friends and sharing their impressions with family members they nonetheless constituted themselves as knowledgeable, possessing opinions worth hearing. The popular feminization of Celts may also have made it particularly important for female tourists to differentiate themselves by demonstrating their authority over Highlanders, which could be done by bestowing a visit upon them and by defining them through writing.[151] By criticizing living conditions or childrearing practices they asserted their superior social and ethnic standing, as well as their ability to help determine standards of civilization.[152]

Some tourists evinced a genuine intellectual curiosity, as when Edmund Gosse struck up a conversation aboard the steamer to Stornoway with a minister from Lewis who taught him a great deal about Highland culture.[153] But in most cases the structure surrounding meetings between residents and visitors, and the limited nature of such encounters, meant that tourists' 'observations' of Highlanders rested more on preconceived expectations than on sustained encounters with the objects of their discussions. Although few tourists resisted the opportunity provided by travel writing to declaim upon the character of Highlanders, even fewer reached their conclusions after anything but very brief contact with local residents. Gordon Cumming's idyllic portraits of rural life are based almost entirely on supposition, although she supplemented her opinions with a reading of transcripts from the Napier Commission interviews. Her rendition of a picturesque black house and the inhabitants' contentment is full of qualifiers: 'apparently' the 'kindly-looking old crone' rejoiced in the peat smoke that filled the room. 'Possibly' the family owned a loom. 'Probably' a baby slept in a cradle at her side.[154] When a 'whole-hearted son of the Isles' accused her of misinterpreting the sensitivity and thoughtfulness she attributed to Highlanders, Gordon Cumming stood by her comments, affirming that she wrote of the people as they seemed to her.[155] Similarly, Ada Goodrich-Freer's opinions were based on extensive reading in the nineteenth-century works about Highlanders, and mamy of her comments were plagiarized from a Hebridean folklorist, Father Allan MacDonald.[156] Some travel writers knowingly and purposefully retained certain stereotypes. The editor of an 1883 source noted that he had never heard Highlanders use the accent often ascribed to them, in which 'p' was substituted for 'b', as in 'poat.' But if it pleased Lowlanders to believe this, he continued, it did Highlanders no harm. He used the style in his book.[157]

Yet while tourism and its objectifying gaze turned crofters into 'living signs of themselves',[158] the image of the Highlander – as of other Celts – was actively contested in the late nineteenth century through the Crofters' War and the discourse surrounding it. Highlanders had long expressed their hostility to landowning policies by means both of open opposition to evictions and by less overt actions such as sheep stealing, mutilations, and emigration.[159] The events of the 1880s were more flagrant, proactive, and successful manifestations of a long continuity of protest, one which had seldom before moved out of what James C. Scott calls the 'hidden transcript' into the realm of public consciousness.[160] In the 1880s Highlanders made this 'transcript' more accessible by putting forward a representation of themselves which in many ways defied the authoritative stereotypes of the region. But because the crofters based their stand in part on their own readings of the dominant discourse, it was possible for tourists and would-be tourists to construe events in the northwest as affirmations of the long-established symbolic meaning of the area. Their tendency to do so, in the face of alternative interpretations, attests to the importance attached to understandings of the crofters and the strength of tourism's images. Whether explicitly stated or not, much of the public discussion about the men and women of the Highlands in the late nineteenth century was a direct response to the Crofters' War, an attempt to ensure it did not destroy the accepted constructions.

Scottish crofting communities were created out of the revolution in land use which took place in the Highlands in the late eighteenth century. Clan chiefs' conversion of much of their land to large-scale pastoral farms entailed a massive relocation of the Highland population. Inhabitants of inland areas were moved, often forcibly, to coastal regions. There they received individual smallholdings, or crofts, of one or two acres of arable land, rather than the traditional communal townships of the Highlands. These crofts, often located on marginal land, were not expected to provide a full living for a family; they were to be supplemented by fishing and the newly-developing kelp industry. Those enterprises, however, proved far less useful for crofters than expected. The Clearances, which in the nineteenth century sometimes involved forced emigration, were a ruthless violation of the values of clanship and a profound 'cultural trauma' for the Gaelic world.[161] Although Highlanders did frequently protest the Clearances, they were powerless to mount any concerted opposition, and most removals took place without physical resistance. What defiance occurred was intermittent and localized, a reaction of desperation. As an assertive, sustained, and coordinated response to landowning policy, the Crofters' War therefore stands out as unique in the nineteenth-century Highland experience. A number of factors contributed to crofters' new ability to take the initiative against landowners. A period of relative prosperity in the 1860s and 70s raised expectations which were dashed by poor harvests, a potato blight, and meager fishing seasons in the early 1880s. Contemporaneous events in Ireland provided a model for action. A public conscience which was more sympathetic than ever to accounts of poverty in the Highlands made it difficult for the government to aid landlords. The growth of Celtic societies in Scotland and the support of second generation Highland emigrants in the Lowlands also helped raise the level of awareness and encourage active resistance among crofters. Greater literacy consequent upon the Scottish Education Act of 1872 likely increased political awareness in the north. Radical newspapers did the same, especially *The Highlander*, founded in 1873 by John Murdoch, who had grown up in the Hebrides and was involved in Irish nationalist politics in Dublin in the 1850s and 60s.

In 1882, tenants in the east coast district of Skye known as the Braes staged a rent strike to regain grazing rights on a nearby hill which had been leased to a sheep farmer in 1865. As the strike went on, mobs accosted sheriff officers charged with serving summons of removal to strikers. At the April 'Battle of the Braes' police supported by 50 fellow officers from Glasgow managed to arrest five men, but several lawmen were injured by a large crowd of crofters armed with stones and large sticks. In the following years similar events took place across the Highlands and Hebrides: rent strikes, the occupation of sheep and deer farms, the destruction of fences, the deforcement of sheriffs, and the mutilation and killing of stock. While action was sporadic and confined to certain areas, mainly on the islands of Skye and Lewis, disturbances seemed serious enough that the government sent troops on several occasions to protect sheriff officers serving eviction notices or collecting rents. Most famously, in the fall of 1884 Gladstone's government sent 300 Royal Marines to Skye when eviction notices were to be presented. They remained until the following June, but the troops' stay on the island was peaceful.[162] In the summer of 1886 a detachment of police accompanied by marines landed on the island of Tiree to arrest crofters who had occupied land from which tenants had been cut off 30 or 40 years earlier. That fall another contingent of police and Royal Marines was sent to Skye, this time by Lord Salisbury's Conservative administration, to collect unpaid taxes.

These events were widely publicized. In November 1884 at the height of the dispute on Skye, 16 newspaper reporters and two artists covered events on the island.[163] The *Illustrated London News* provided numerous illustrations of events in the Hebrides, including two front-page sketches of riots on Lewis in 1888.[164] While readers of *The Nineteenth Century, Blackwood's, The Saturday Review, The Contemporary Review*, and most British newspapers debated events in the Western Isles, sympathizers in southern cities founded the Highland Land Law Reform Association, a political movement which soon had branches across the Highlands and Hebrides. Taking its cue from the Irish Land League, the HLLRA called for fair rents, security of tenure, compensation for improvement, and redistribution of land. In 1883 the government established a Royal Commission under the leadership of Sir Francis Napier, a Scottish landowner and former diplomat known for his interest in public health, education, and poverty. The Napier Commission was charged with investigating conditions in crofting regions and recommending improvements. Although the eventual legislation ignored most of their proposals, the Commission's recognition of crofters' claims was a symbolic victory. Based on the Irish Land Act, the Crofters' Holdings Act of 1886 guaranteed the 'Three Fs' (fair rent, free sale, and fixity of tenure) and established a commission to decide upon fair rents. However, because little was done to enlarge land holdings, which was actually the crux of the problem in Scotland, occasional disturbances continued for a few more years. In the winter of 1887-1888 several land raids, some quite bloody, took place on Lewis, this time led by landless cottars who were not being helped by the Crofters' Act. A company of the Royal Scots was dispatched to the scene.

There is some evidence that the agrarian conflict discouraged travelers from venturing to the Western Isles. A visitor, Malcolm Ferguson, reported that Skye hotelkeepers were finding 1882 the 'dullest' season ever experienced. 'Not a few' parties from London and the south had written asking if it was safe to visit. The shooting preserve at Glendale, located near some of the most notorious scenes of unrest, remained unrented that year.[165] Yet Ferguson's observations do not demonstrate a serious or long-lasting decline in tourism. Indeed, the expansion of tourism which took place across Scotland in the last quarter of the nineteenth century was also felt on Skye, the center of the land dispute. So crowded was the island when Joseph and Elizabeth Robins Pennell visited in 1888, that the only available space in the popular Sligachan Inn was the drawing room.[166] Many of these sightseers may simply have overlooked the dispute. The Pennells asserted that most of those who toured Skye intentionally ignored the plight of crofters. Among the 'immaculately dressed young ladies and young Oxford men' at Sligachan, the talk was all of 'hotels and lochs and glens and travels' with not a world about the inhabitants of the island.[167] An 1883 article in *Temple Bar* describing winter at the same locale reinforced such tendencies. The anonymous author began by announcing his/her intention of 'forgetting for the moment the agitation which is still going on between the crofters and their lairds'.[168]

Victorian travelers were hardly unique in rejecting the possible intrusion of current events on their vacations. As Maria Frawley points out, by representing the people they encountered as either radically different from themselves or as absent, travelers preserved the contrasts that made travel exciting.[169] It was not difficult to ignore crofters if one chose, for the main sites of the land dispute, even those on Skye, were in territory rarely visited by tourists. Despite the fascination with Highlanders, the ritual of tourism in the Highlands focused primarily on encounters with an allegedly wild and empty landscape, a manner of viewing the region which effectively wrote natives off the land. The treatment of the journey to the Quirang, a striking rock formation on the northern peninsula of Skye, in M. J. B. Baddeley's *The Highlands of Scotland* provides an instructive example. While the route was not heavily populated, it passed by several valleys 'in which are more than one "bothy" hamlet, occupied by the real *aborigines.*' The guide emphasized that this section of the route 'presents absolutely no feature of interest', an assertion which encouraged tourists to ignore local residents and hurry on to more intriguing attractions.[170] Such comments were the ultimate means of authority over crofters; their very existence could be dismissed and the meaning of the island could lie in its scenic significance for tourists, not its life-sustaining role for natives.

However, the Crofters' War aroused other tourists' curiosity about denizens of the Highlands and islands and their living conditions. Even those who chose to overlook the disturbances could not help but be aware of them and the defiance crofters thereby posed to the dominant construction of themselves in popular culture. One possible reading of the land dispute posited Highlanders not as symbols of stability, but as yet one more threat to the social order. In the light of these events, crofters showed themselves as active, assertive, violent, and public, rather than passive, contented, and deferential. They were armed with cudgels, sticks, and possibly firearms. They attacked police and sheriff-officers, in 1882 forcing a sheriff-officer to burn the summons he was required to present and threatening his life. They knocked police to the ground and injured some with stones.[171] They insisted that they did not want the 'gratuitous advice' of landlords.[172] Rent strikes proliferated in the northwest of Scotland in 1885-1886 and acts of terrorism, such as the destruction of fences and dykes, the burning of peat and hay stacks, and the cutting of telegraph wires, took place in several communities. A spokesman for Highland landlords in 1886 claimed that Skye was 'in a state of anarchy'.[173] It would seem that time, in the form of the rejection of social deference, had indeed encroached upon the Western Isles, undercutting both the environmental and the racial explanations of Highland character. If isolated rural districts like this could so openly turn violent, it might be difficult to see country life as the solution to urban ills. If Hebrideans were to emulate the Irish, then the possibility of the Celt as the spiritual infusion of the nation was denied. Women's active and sometimes violent participation in the dispute raised questions about the gender construction of Celts. Women had long played a central role in acts of defiance against landlords and were at the forefront of the disputes of the late nineteenth-century, shrieking curses at officers of the law, throwing stones, and helping to knock officials to the ground. They sometimes offered more determined resistance than did men.[174] The examples provided by sympathetic reporter Alexander MacKenzie of 'Amazons' 'with their hair down and streaming loosely in the breeze,' armed, and 'uttering the most violent gestures and imprecations, hurling forth the most terrible vows of vengeance against the enemy' symbolized forcefully the lack of social order in the Hebrides.[175]

The land dispute can also be seen as part of a re-masculinization of Celts in the late nineteenth century, which though centered in Ireland and expressed most cogently by W. B. Yeats, was also experienced in Scotland. Radical newspaper editor John Murdoch encouraged crofters to be less quiet and submissive[176] and with their aggression, violence, and self-assurance, crofters disputed feminized images of themselves. Their declarations that they did not need the paternalism of landlords were statements of manly independence. Likewise, the vision of townships as replacements for tenantry in the Highlands could be considered a masculine one. Inspired by W. F. Skene's argument in *Celtic Scotland* (1880) that Anglo-Saxon ideas of private ownership of property had been superimposed on a Celtic agrarian society of communal property, many supporters of crofters favored the creation of townships, basing their arguments in part on the male tacksmen and tenants who had once been the chief's warriors and now needed a chance to rediscover that warrior spirit.[177]

The crofters' opposition to the rights of property owners was one of many late Victorian assaults on aristocratic influence. To MacKenzie, editor of the *Celtic Magazine,* whose best-selling *History of the Highland Clearances* (1883) was a passionate inventory of the wrongs done to crofters, the land war was a 'social revolution'.[178] Supporters of the Highlanders such as Joseph and Elizabeth Robins Pennell placed the blame squarely on slaveholding landlords.[179] Their warning to owners was as ominous as any posed by crofters: 'Let the laird make hay while the sun shines, for the day is coming when the storms, forever brooding over the Isle of Mists, will break forth with a violence he has never felt before, and he and his kind will be swept away from off the face of the land.'[180] There was considerable public sympathy for crofters, especially in Radical circles, and Gladstone's early tentativeness in dealing with the dispute can be attributed in part to a hesitation to offend the Liberal Party's left wing.[181] Many of those who defended landlords sought to maintain a 'traditional' rural paternalism which was being threatened throughout Britain with the nationwide restructuring of agriculture resulting from the depression.[182] The *Saturday Review* asserted that the landlords were integral to the well-being of the Highlands, having brought improvements to the region in recent years. The problems of the crofters would be solved with the 'gentle remedies' of proprietors, not with 'revolutionary legislation.'[183] But in spite of the partisan issues linked with reactions to the land war, the symbolic significance attached to the crofters cut across political lines, and Highlanders' defiance of that symbolism was potentially a cause for distress even amongst those for whom the land question had little personal or political relevance.

Although the land dispute challenged outsiders' sense of knowledge about crofters, in the final analysis the Crofter's War caused barely a ripple in the longstanding stereotypes of islanders. The reason for this, and the cause of the success of the movement, lies in the second possible interpretation of events in the Highland and islands. Because Gaels relied on the 'public transcript' of power relations in the Highlands in order to object to them, their challenge to the dominant discourse also had the effect of reinforcing the sentimental impressions of tourists. Although protestors openly and sometimes violently confronted the authority of landlords, they posed only a slight physical threat. Their motivation, they said, was not to overthrow landlords, but to reclaim what was theirs. As they and their defenders saw it, Highland tenants possessed a hereditary right to land occupied for three generations. Consequently owners, not crofters, were breaking tradition. In this view, islanders upheld past values, a sign perhaps of their rootedness in former times.[184] Their use of poetry and songs as a form of protest seemed to be more evidence of their links with earlier times, given their reputation for a natural gift of music.[185] Champions of crofters believed that they demonstrated their 'natural' deference by absolving landlords from blame, placing it instead upon the hired factors who managed the estates. MacKenzie quoted an address from a group of tenants: 'We, your humble petitioners, believe that none of the grievances mentioned were known to our late good and famous proprietor, being an absentee, in whom we might place our confidence had he been present to hear and grant our request.'[186] Even the violence could be rendered acceptable, for its objective was the protection of domesticity, an appropriate and non-threatening use of masculinity.

That protesters played on the dominant understanding of Highlanders, intentionally or not, does not negate the forcefulness of their stand. Malcolm Chapman argues that as a marginalized people, Highlanders have had difficulty finding a voice independent of the prevailing discourse.[187] That discourse could carry more than one meaning. Crofters' demonstration of their own adherence to the accepted perception of Highlanders was a subtle but radical indictment of the failings of landlords and was thus grounds for violence. This strategy also enabled commentators on the Highlands to assure readers and tourists that the popular myths of life in the region were yet valid, which they did with striking energy. Visitors stressed that islanders' innate respect for the social hierarchy was still strong. On the island of Lewis, at least, there was nothing personal in the attacks on landlords, said Goodrich-Freer; they were spoken of with 'unfailing respect'.[188] Other observers agreed that in spite of recent antagonism, 'the deep seated feeling of real allegiance to old blood, the hereditary owners of the soil, happily still exists'.[189] Lord Napier confirmed this with his remembrance of crofters' interactions with landlords on the investigating Commission: 'Indeed, one of the pleasing features of the inquiry was the trusting expression with which the Highland witness would occasionally turn to these gentlemen, endeared to the poor by hereditary associations and personal benevolence. In that touching attitude, in which familiarity and respect were curiously blended, you saw that the patriarchal sentiment was not then extinguished in the crofters' heart.'[190] Assurances that crofters were 'far too wise...to make their local grievances, as some Irishmen do, the occasion of a vain conflict with the forces of the United Kingdom' and that in most cases they respected the government forces which were sent to the Hebrides, helped to mitigate the images of militancy among Highlanders.[191] Many commentators asserted that the land dispute was not actually the doing of the crofters, who were variously seen to be unduly influenced by 'professional agitators' and 'pernicious communistic doctrine', or too simple and ignorant truly to understand the issues.[192] Because Highlanders were construed as fundamentally child-like, they could not be held accountable for their actions, though they must be taught to do right. Absolving crofters from responsibility made possible a continuing belief in their innate social respect. A factor on Skye was quoted as saying in 1884 that 'If it were not that the people themselves are essentially a good, and on the whole a sensible people, the condition of Skye just now would be that of simple anarchy.'[193]

The consistency with which so many tourists continued to see rural destitution as picturesque and cozy, despite evidence to the contrary, also served to undercut the seriousness of the complaints voiced by protesters. The tradition of 'picturesque poverty' was well established by the late Victorian period, having been frequently used by landscape artists and travel writers of the eighteenth and nineteenth centuries to distance audiences from the harsh realities of rural life. As a technique for conceptualizing landscape, the picturesque encouraged observers to consider scenes of country life as aesthetic objects. The peasants who frequently appeared in the foregrounds of picturesque paintings or narrative descriptions had no social meaning or reality, they were but figures in a landscape.[194] As such, the difficulties of their lives could be downplayed. This narrative device can be found throughout the tourist literature of late eighteenth- and nineteenth-century Scotland. A guidebook of 1827, for instance, suggested that near Killin 'the habitations of the natives, though mean, are prettily grouped along the sides of the hill.'[195] Tourists were thus advised to concentrate on the pictorial effect of the structures, not the trials faced by those who lived there. Queen Victoria's description of the scenery around the hunting lodge of Alt-na-Guithasach operated in a similar fashion to focus attention on the loveliness of the location, not the labor being performed. 'The scenery is beautiful there, so wild and grand – real severe Highland scenery, with trees in the hollow…It was so picturesque – the boat, the net, and the people in their kilts in the water and on the shore.'[196] Lucy Sherwood considered the sight of a dozen women and girls pulling up potatoes one of the prettiest sights she had seen in a long time.[197]

Such a means of perceiving poverty and hard work, combined with the Highlands' role in the popular imagination, diminished the effectiveness of visitors' oft-expressed distress over Hebridean social conditions. By interpreting the many homes vacated by emigrating crofters as contributions to the general melancholy and mystery of the islands, travel literature effectively mediated any indignation readers might feel towards their plight.[198] In spite of genuine humanitarian concern among the British public over their hardships, which was a key factor in the success of the Crofters' War, the indigence of Highlanders was a crucial ingredient in the image of them, the more so as concern about the effects of urban life intensified. Most of the key texts of the late nineteenth-century Highlands asked readers to interpret poverty as central to the city/country and progress/tradition dichotomies within which Gaels' meaning lay. Tourist literature presented the black houses as a sign of the crofters' commendable lack of greed and their contentment with their lot in life. Gordon Cumming believed that the hardships suffered by the people of Skye were evidence of their capacity for endurance and hard work; they would consider it weakness to complain.[199] J. A. MacCulloch argued that although the Skye homes seemed the very 'abomination of desolation', visitors forgot just how dear they were to the inhabitants: 'The crofter is contented with it; he is not overdriven with work; the work is congenial; he is a son of the soil; he can turn to many other occupations; and, compared with the lot of slum-dwellers in town, his is a pleasant one.'[200]

Such arguments asked that economic conditions in the Highlands be accepted because of the contribution made by crofters to the jaded modern world. As important as the social and political concerns raised by protesting islanders was their role as preservers of British core values, a role which the authors of tourist literature sought to retain. For example, Malcolm Ferguson's description of Glendale ignored the knowledge that the area was one of the most notorious scenes of unrest, presenting instead an idyllic picture of rural contentment and peace. Milch cows browsed among the blooming heather, collies roamed the hills, women descended from the moor with creels of peat on their backs. It was a 'most interesting, unique, and picturesque landscape picture'.[201] The ire directed against the Pennells when they denied that crofters were contented with their lot, and denounced fellow tourists for labeling as 'picturesque' conditions they would find appalling outside of Britain, points to the deep significance invested in the figure of the crofter in the late nineteenth-century public consciousness.[202]

Such images and interpretations suggest that far from impeding tourism to the Highlands and islands in the late nineteenth century, the Crofters' War was a vital piece of it. The dispute called attention to the crofters, allowing them to be represented in a manner useful to contemporary concerns and fears. In turn, the widely agreed upon myths of the Highlands which were disseminated through tourism and the popular press shaped the terms of the debate over land policy there. With its acknowledgement of tenants' rights for those who occupied land, transformation of tenant-landlord relations, and influence upon later government policy to enable crofters to buy their own land, the Crofters' Act signaled a retreat from doctrines of *laissez faire*. Yet the popular rhetoric surrounding the dispute suggests that the Crofters' Holding Act was motivated as much by the belief in the importance of Highlanders' role as a 'fountain of renovating life' as by concern to ameliorate their economic condition or to strike a blow against the power of landlords. Chapman argues that the legislation of the 1880s was predicated upon crofters' sentimental love of the land and upon the perceived need to keep them on it. The effect was the economic marginalization of Highlanders. 'The crofting laws have in a sense operated to keep the crofter in precisely that idealist half-world to which Arnold blithely consigned him, economically and politically irrelevant'.[203] In parliamentary debate in 1884, the Home Secretary, William Harcourt, praised the Highlanders' 'passionate devotion to the soil' and urged that a way be found to enable them to remain on the land.[204] The Napier Commission report noted the importance of taking action on behalf of a group of people 'which does possess…in ordinary times, conditions of welfare and happiness unknown to some orders of the people, for instance to the poorer sort of rural day labourers in England, or to those who depend on casual employment in the cities.'[205]

Thus while crofters did successfully assert themselves to improve their economic situation, their challenge to the prevailing image of the Highlander was short lived. The land disputes of the late nineteenth century ironically proved to be a welcome sign that the Highlands and Hebrides were not yet part of the modern age. Crofters could not compete with tourism's power to define the meaning of a people and a place. As George Eyre-Todd said in 1907, the publicity created by the Skye crofters had evoked a great deal of curiosity about their lives: 'Nor is this curiosity without its reward; for dwellings and people alike, speech and circumstances, manners and ways of living, remain as picturesque and full of interest as can well be imagined, and forever afterwards a hint of peat-reak in the air will have power to bring back many a scene of simple charm to the mind of him who has once wandered in Skye.'[206]

Notes

1　Lucy Elizabeth Sherwood, 'Journal of Lucy Elizabeth Sherwood' (1826-1827) ACC. 8679, NLS, Sep. 27.

2　'Journal of a Tour through Some Parts of Scotland' (1829) MS. 3529, NLS, pp. 37-8.

3　'Sylvan' [Samuel Hobbs], *Sylvan's Pictoral Handbook to the scenery of the Caledonian Canal, the Isle of Staffa, etc.* (Edinburgh, 1848), pp. 25-6.

4　A. R. Hope Moncrieff, *Highlands and Islands of Scotland* (London: A & C Black, 1906; reprint, London: A & C Black, 1925), p. 142.

5　On folk culture, see Hermann Bausinger, *Folk Culture in a World of Technology*, Elke Dettmer, trans., (Bloomington: Indiana Univ. Press, 1990). Hayden Lorimer discusses efforts to preserve Highland folk culture in the twentieth century in 'Ways of seeing the Scottish Highlands: marginality, authenticity and the curious case of the Hebridean blackhouse' in *Journal of Historical Geography* 25: 4 (1999), pp. 517-33.

6　John Leyden, *Journal of a Tour in the Highlands and Western Islands of Scotland in 1800* James Sinton, ed., (Edinburgh: William Blackwood & Sons, 1903), p. 252.

7　See Robert Clyde, *From Rebel to Hero. The Image of the Highlander, 1745-1830* (East Linton: Tuckwell Press, 1995); Peter Womack, *Improvement and Romance. Constructing the Myth of the Highlands* (London: MacMillan Press, 1989).

8　Robert Heron, *Observations made in a Journey through the Western Counties of Scotland in the autumn of 1792* (Perth, 1793), p. 1:220.

9　T. Garnett, *Observations on a Tour through the Highlands and Part of the Western Isles of Scotland* (London, 1800), p. 1:215.

10　Joseph Mawman, *An Excursion to the Highlands of Scotland and the English Lakes* (London, 1805), pp. 135-36.

11　Beriah Botfield, *Journal of a Tour through the Highlands of Scotland* (Norton Hall, 1830), p. xii.

12　John Macculloch, *The Highlands and Western Islands of Scotland* (London, 1824), pp. 1:8-9.

13　Ada Goodrich-Freer, *Outer Isles* (Westminster: Archibald Constable & Co., 1902), p. 275. For more on Goodrich-Freer, a controversial figure who used several different names, see John L. Campbell and Trevor H. Hall, *Strange Things* (London: Routledge & Kegan Paul, 1968).

14　Malcolm Ferguson, *Rambles in Skye* (Glasgow, 1885), p. 6.

15　Constance F. Gordon Cumming, *In the Hebrides* (London, 1883), pp. 124-26.

16　J.A. MacCulloch, *The Misty Isle of Skye* (Edinburgh & London: Oliphant, Anderson & Ferrier, 1905), p. 211.

17　Gordon Cumming, *In the Hebrides*, p. 144.

18　James Boswell, *Journal of a Tour to the Hebrides with Samuel Johnson, LL.D.* Alan Wendt, ed. (Boston: Houghton Mifflin, 1965), p. 256; 'Notes of a Wanderer in Skye', *Temple Bar* 69 (Sep. – Dec. 1883), p. 81.

19　Goodrich-Freer, *Outer Isles*, p. 200.

20　Goodrich-Freer, *Outer Isles*, p. 230.

21　J. A. MacCulloch, *Misty Isle of Skye*, p. 198.

22   Gordon Cumming, *In the Hebrides*, pp. 255-58; R. Menzies Ferguson, *Our Trip North* (London, 1892), pp. 134-36; 189.

23   Garnett, *Observations*, p. 118.

24   Thomas Pennant, *A Tour in Scotland MDCCLXIX* (London, 1790), p. 1:109.

25   Malcolm Chapman, *The Gaelic Vision in Scottish Culture* (London: Croom Helm, 1978), pp. 114-15.

26   Chauncy Hare Townshend, *A Descriptive Tour in Scotland* (Brussels, 1840), pp. 53-4.

27   Campbell and Hall, *Strange Things*.

28   J. A. MacCulloch, *Misty Isle of Skye*, pp. 223-24.

29   Herbert Byng Hall, *Highland Sports and Highland Quarters* (London, 1848), p. 171.

30   Frances Murray, *Summer in the Hebrides* (Glasgow, 1887), p. 43.

31   Goodrich-Freer, *Outer Isles*, p. 16.

32   Goodrich-Freer, *Outer Isles*, pp. 84-5.

33   David Stewart of Garth, *Sketches of the Character, Manners and Present State of the Highlanders of Scotland: with details of the Military Service of the Highland Regiments* (Edinburgh, 1822; reprint, Edinburgh: John Donald, 1977), pp. 1:35-6; M. Ferguson, *Rambles*, p. 156.

34   J. A. Cameron, 'Storm Clouds in the Highlands', *The Nineteenth Century* 16 (September 1884), p. 385.

35   Moncrieff, *Highlands and Islands*, p. 17.

36   W. H. Maxwell, *Wanderings in the Highlands & Islands* (London, 1852), pp. 1:25-6.

37   M. Ferguson, *Rambles*, p. 127.

38   Stewart, *Sketches*, pp. 2:219, 1:101-4.

39   Goodrich-Freer, *Outer Isles*, p. 94.

40   Goodrich-Freer, *Outer Isles*, p. 426.

41   'Nether Lochaber', 'Winter Night with the Highland Crofters', *Good Words* 30 (1889), p. 113.

42   M. Ferguson, *Rambles*, p. 5.

43   Alexander Smith, *A Summer in Skye* (Boston, 1865), p. 318.

44   Alexander Nicholson, 'The Isle of Skye IV. The Sea Coast', *Good Words* 16 (1875), p. 567.

45   *The Scottish Tourist and Itinerary or a Guide to the Scenery and Antiquities of Scotland and the Western Islands* (Edinburgh, 1827), p. 200.

46   Gordon Cumming, *In the Hebrides*, p. 289.

47   Stewart, *Sketches*, p. 1:94.

48   Smith, *Summer in Skye*, pp. 171-72.

49   Gordon Cumming, *In the Hebrides*, pp. 286-87.

50   On fears of the moral degeneration of urban slum dwellers, see Gertrude Himmelfarb, *Poverty and Compassion: The Moral Imagination of the late Victorians* (New York: Knopf, 1991). On concern over the health of the urban poor, see Ellen Ross, *Love and Toil. Motherhood in Outcast London* (New York: Oxford Univ. Press, 1993).

51   M. Ferguson, *Rambles*, p. 127.

52   *ILN*, Oct. 2, 1886.

53   Mrs. Fleming Jenkin, 'Highland Crofters', *Good Words* 26 (1885), p. 504.

54   See Garnett, *Observations*, pp. 296-97.
55   Stewart, *Sketches*, p. 1:231.
56   Marquis of Lorne, 'The Highland Land Agitation', *Contemporary Review* 46 (Dec. 1884), p. 836.
57   See Alun Howkins, 'The Discovery of Rural England' in Robert Colls and Philip Dodd, eds., *Englishness: Politics and Culture 1880-1920* (New York: Croom Helm, 1986), pp. 62-88; Martin J. Wiener, *English Culture and the Decline of the Industrial Spirit* (New York: Penguin, 1981). For a counter argument, see Peter Mandler, 'Against "Englishness": English Culture and the Limits to Rural Nostalgia, 1850-1940', *Transactions of the Royal Historical Society* 6th series, 7 (1997), pp. 155-75.
58   *ILN*, Feb. 4, 1888.
59   *Report of Her Majesty's Commissioners of Inquiry into the Conditions of the Crofters and Cottars in the Highlands and Islands of Scotland*, Parliamentary Papers, sessional vols. XXXII-XXXVI (1884), p. 110.
60   J. A. MacCulloch, *Misty Isle of Skye*, p. 207.
61   Goodrich-Freer, *In the Hebrides*, p. 402.
62   *ILN*, October, 2, 1886.
63   T. C. Smout, *A Century of the Scottish People 1830-1950* (London: Fontana, 1986), p. 11.
64   'Skye: From the top of Cuchullin' Part II, *The Leisure Hour* 9 (8 November, 1860), p. 715; John Rae, 'The Crofter Problem', *The Contemporary Review* 47 (February 1885), p. 197; 'Notes of a Wanderer', p. 79; Goodrich-Freer, *Outer Isles*, p. 301.
65   W. W. Nevin, *Vignettes of Travel* (Philadelphia, 1881), pp. 230-32.
66   Joseph Pennell and Elizabeth Robins Pennell, *Our Journey to the Hebrides* (New York, 1889), p. 137.
67   Goodrich-Freer, *Outer Isles*, p. 301.
68   Jacob Abbott, *A Summer in Scotland* (Dublin, 1859), p. 218.
69   Krisztina Fenyo, *Contempt, Sympathy and Romance. Lowland Perceptions of the Highlands and the Clearances During the Famine Years, 1845-1855* (East Linton: Tuckwell Press, 2000).
70   Fraser MacDonald, 'St. Kilda and the Sublime', *Ecumene* 8 (2): 2001, p. 161.
71   James Wilson, *A Voyage Round the Coasts of Scotland and the Isles* (Edinburgh, 1842), pp. 1: 432-33.
72   M. Ferguson, *Rambles*, pp. 8-9.
73   Duke of Argyll [G. D. Campbell], 'A Corrected Picture of the Highlands', *The Nineteenth Century* XCII: 16, (Nov. 1884), p. 692. See also MacDonald, 'St. Kilda and the Sublime'.
74   John Carr, *Caledonian Sketches, or a Tour through Scotland in 1807* (London, 1809), pp. 258-59.
75   Goodrich-Freer, *Outer Isles*, p. 56.
76   See, for instance, R. M. Fergusson, *Our Trip North*, pp. 73-4; S. Taylor, 'Journal of a Tour to Scotland' (1842) MS. 8927, NLS, p. 271.
77   Goodrich-Freer, *Outer Isles*, p. 123-24.
78   Gordon Cumming, *In the Hebrides*, pp. 139, 145.
79   M. Ferguson, *Rambles*, p. 5.

[80]   Murray G. H. Pittock, *Celtic Identity and the British Image* (New York: Manchester Univ. Press, 1999), p. 39.

[81]   Christopher North [John Wilson], *Recreations of Christopher North* vol. IX, in Prof. Ferrier, ed., *The Works of John Wilson* (Edinburgh, 1857), pp. 53-4.

[82]   S. Augustus Tipple, *A Summer Visit to Scotland* (Norwich, 1847), p. 56.

[83]   Edmund Gosse, 'Journal in Scotland' (1876) MS. 2562, NLS, n.p.

[84]   Maxwell, *Wanderings*, pp. 1: 248-50; Wilson, *Voyage Round the Coasts*, pp. 2:50-3.

[85]   Womack, *Improvement and Romance*, p. 27.

[86]   Stewart, *Sketches*, pp. 1:44-5.

[87]   Womack, *Improvement and Romance*, pp. 45, 39. See also Clyde, *From Rebel to Hero*, pp. 150-80.

[88]   Inderpal Grewal, *Home and Harem. Nation, Gender, Empire and the Cultures of Travel* (Durham: Duke Univ. Press, 1996), p. 33.

[89]   Townshend, *Descriptive Tour*, p. 230.

[90]   Townshend, *Descriptive Tour*, pp. 230-31.

[91]   Robert Buchanan, *The Land of Lorne* (London, 1871), pp. 2:127-30.

[92]   Chapman, *Gaelic Vision*, p. 210.

[93]   See Chapman, *Gaelic Vision*, pp. 81-112; Pittock, *Celtic Identity*, pp. 61-74.

[94]   Pittock, *Celtic Identity*, pp. 61-3.

[95]   *ILN*, Sep. 3, 1842.

[96]   Pittock, *Celtic Identity*, pp. 44.

[97]   Goodrich-Freer, *Outer Isles*, p. 90.

[98]   Grewal, *Home and Harem*, p. 40. On Victorian perceptions of women in 'savage' societies, see Cynthia Eagle Russett, *Sexual Science. The Victorian Construction of Womanhood* (Cambridge, MA: Harvard Univ. Press, 1989), pp. 54-7. Marjorie Morgan also discusses travelers' perceptions of women's physical labor. *National Identities and Travel in Victorian Britain* (Houndmills: Palgrave, 2001), pp. 180-81.

[99]   J. A. MacCulloch, *Misty Isle of Skye*, p. 202.

[100]   John Stoddart, *Remarks on Local Scenery & Manners in Scotland during the Year1799 and 1800* (London, 1801), p. 254; Richard Ayton and William Daniell, *A Voyage Round Great Britain* (London, 1814-1825, reprint; London: Tate Gallery, 1978), p. 4:6.

[101]   Chapman, *Gaelic Vision*, pp. 113-38. See also Bausinger, *Folk Culture*.

[102]   Stewart, *Sketches*, p. 1:121.

[103]   Pittock, *Celtic Identity*, p. 37.

[104]   Goodrich-Freer, *Outer Isles*, p. 389.

[105]   Alexander Nicholson, 'The Isle of Skye', *Good Words* 16 (1875), p. 349.

[106]   Goodrich-Freer, *Outer Isles*, p. 198; John T. Reid, *Art Rambles in the Highlands and Islands of Scotland* (New York, 1878), pp. 86-7.

[107]   'Among the Hills', *Temple Bar* 27 (November 1869), pp. 94-5.

[108]   Smith, *Summer in Skye*, p. 307.

[109]   Lorne, 'Highland Land Agitation', p. 829.

[110]   Goodrich-Freer, *Outer Isles*, p. 319.

[111]   J. A. MacCulloch, *Misty Isle of Skye*, p. 201

[112]   Robert Buchanan, quoted in Goodrich-Freer, *Outer Isles*, pp. 316-19.

[113]   Quoted in Chapman, *Gaelic Vision*, p. 117.

[114] Rae, 'Crofter Problem', p. 190.

[115] *Times*, 16 Oct. 1882.

[116] *ILN*, Feb. 4. 1888.

[117] Robert Chambers, *The Picture of Scotland* (Edinburgh, 1827), p. 1:17.

[118] J. A. MacCulloch, *Misty Isle of Skye*, pp. 195-96.

[119] Goodrich-Freer, *Outer Isles*, pp. 29-30; Gordon Cumming, *In the Hebrides*, pp. 145-46; Jenkin, 'Highland Crofters', p. 504; J. A. MacCulloch, *Misty Isle of Skye*, p. 198.

[120] Cameron, 'Storm Clouds', p. 385.

[121] Smith, *Summer in Skye*, pp. 130-31.

[122] Matthew Arnold, *The Study of Celtic Literature* (1905, reprint; Port Washington, NY: Kennikat Press, 1970); Chapman, *Gaelic Vision*, pp. 81-112, 134; Pittock, *Celtic Identity*, pp. 67-71.

[123] Chapman, *Gaelic Vision*, pp. 107-8; L. P. Curtis, Jr., *Anglo-Saxons and Celts* (Bridgeport, CT: Conference on British Studies, 1968). See also Pittock, *Celtic Identity*, pp. 25-33.

[124] Lorne, 'Highland Land Agitation', p. 834; George Anderson and Peter Anderson, *Guide to the Highlands and Islands of Scotland* (London, 1834), p. 4.

[125] Lorne, 'Highland Land Agitation', p. 834.

[126] Curtis, *Anglo-Saxons and Celts*, pp. 21, 72, 136; John Beddoe, *The Races of Britain* (London, 1885), p. 245.

[127] Jenkin, 'Highland Crofters', 503; *Times*, Jan. 30, 1883. See also Morgan's discussion of English travelers' perceptions of Celts. *National Identities*, pp. 211-14.

[128] Report of Her Majesty's Commissioners, p. 109.

[129] Arnold, *Celtic Literature*, p. x. See also Pittock, *Celtic Identity*, pp. 65-7.

[130] Moncrieff, *Highlands and Islands*, p. 231.

[131] Pittock, *Celtic Identity*, p. 71.

[132] Michael Banton, *The Idea of Race* (Boulder, CO: Westview Press, 1977), p. 59.

[133] Quoted in Michael Biddiss, ed., *Images of Race* (New York: Holmes & Meier, 1979), pp. 239, 255.

[134] Chapman, *Gaelic Vision*, pp. 107-8; Pittock, *Celtic Identity*, pp. 67, 65.

[135] J. A. MacCulloch, *Misty Isle of Skye*, p. 226.

[136] Lorne, 'Highland Land Agitation', p. 831.

[137] John Macculloch, *Highlands and Western Islands*, p.1:8.

[138] Moncrieff, *Highlands and Islands*, p. 18.

[139] Smith, *Summer in Skye*, p. 129.

[140] On the growing interest in folklore, see Chapman, *Gaelic Vision*, pp. 113-38.

[141] Richard D. Altick, *The Shows of London* (Cambridge, MA: Belknap Press of Harvard Univ. Press, 1978); Barbara Kirshenblatt-Gimblett, *Destination Culture. Tourism, Museums, and Heritage* (Berkeley: Univ. of California Press, 1998), pp. 35-47.

[142] Abbott, *Summer in Scotland*, p. 170; 'Diary of a visit to Edinburgh and Perthshire' (1848) ACC. 8442, NLS, Sept. 16.

[143] Mrs. & Miss Beecroft, 'Mrs. and Miss Beecroft's Third Tour to Scotland' (1833) MS. 1674, NLS, pp. 20, 23.

[144] See Grewal, *Home and Harem*, p. 91.

[145] Mrs. John F. Gower, 'Illustrated Accounts of trips to France and Scotland by the family of John F. Gower' (1854, 1862) ACC. 9946, NLS, n.p.

[146] 'Substance of a tour through Scotland in the summer of 1836' MS. 2729, NLS, pp. 63-4.

[147] Gower, 'Illustrated Accounts', n.p.

[148] 'Substance of a tour', p. 6.

[149] 'Substance of a tour', p. 99.

[150] 'Substance of a tour', pp. 98-100.

[151] See Maria H. Frawley, *A Wider Range. Travel Writing by Women in Victorian England* (Cranbury, NJ: Associated University Presses, 1994), pp. 22-31, 114-24; Sara Mills, 'Knowledge, Gender, and Empire' in Alison Blunt, Gillian Rose, eds., *Writing Women and Space. Colonial and Postcolonial Geographies* (New York: The Guilford Press, 1994), pp. 40-42.

[152] For an example of such criticism, see 'Substance of a Tour', pp. 109-12.

[153] Gosse, 'Journal', n.p.

[154] Gordon Cumming, *In the Hebrides*, p. 130.

[155] Gordon Cumming, *In the Hebrides*, pp. 186-87.

[156] Campbell and Hall, *Strange Things*.

[157] Aliquis [C. G. Dawson], *Rambles in the Highlands and Islands of Scotland* (Glasgow, 1883), pp. 23-4.

[158] Kirshenblatt-Gimblett, *Destination Culture*, p. 18

[159] T. M. Devine, *Clanship to Crofters' War. The Social Transformation of the Scottish Highlands* (New York: Manchester Univ. Press, 1994); Eric Richards, *A History of the Highland Clearances: Agrarian Transformation and the evictions 1746-1886* (London: Croom Helm, 1982); Eric Richards, 'How Tame were the Highlanders During the Clearances?' *Scottish Studies* 17:1 (1973), pp. 35-50.

[160] James C. Scott, *Domination and the Arts of Resistance: Hidden Transcripts* (New Haven: Yale Univ. Press, 1990).

[161] Devine, *Clanship to Crofters' War*, p. 41.

[162] On the creation of the crofting community and the Crofters' War, see Ian Bradley, ' "Having and Holding": The Highland Land War of the 1880s', *History Today* 37 (December 1987), pp. 23-8; Devine, *Clanship to Crofters' War*; James Hunter, *The Making of the Crofting Community* (Edinburgh: John Donald, 1976); Richards, *Highland Clearances*.

[163] Devine, *Clanship to Crofters' War*, p. 219.

[164] *ILN*, Jan. 21, 1888.

[165] M. Ferguson, *Rambles*, p. 36.

[166] Pennell, *Journey to the Hebrides*, p. 160.

[167] Pennell, *Journey to the Hebrides*, p. 160.

[168] 'Skye', *Temple Bar* 68 (June 1883), p. 276.

[169] Frawley, *A Wider Range*, p. 124.

[170] M. J. B. Baddeley, *The Highlands of Scotland* (London, 1881), p. 216.

[171] *Times*, 10 Nov. 1884; Alexander MacKenzie, *The History of the Highland Clearances* (Inverness, 1883; reprint, with an introduction by John Prebble, 1979, Edinburgh: Mercat Press, 1997), pp. 458, 430-33.

[172] *Times*, 11 Nov. 1884.

173   Quoted in Richards, *Highland Clearances*, p. 485.
174   Devine, *Clanship to Crofters' War*, p. 210, MacKenzie, *Highland Clearances*, pp. 429, 462, 492.
175   MacKenzie, *Highland Clearances*, pp. 491, 429.
176   John Shaw, 'Land, people and nation: historicist voices in the Highland land campaign, c. 1850-1883' in Eugenio F. Biagini, ed., *Citizenship and community. Liberals, radicals and collective identities in the British Isles, 1865-1931* (New York: Cambridge Univ. Press, 1996), p. 309.
177   Pittock, *Celtic Identity*, pp. 74-86.
178   MacKenzie, *Highland Clearances*, p. 407.
179   Pennell, *Journey to the Hebrides*, p. 124.
180   Pennell, *Journey to the Hebrides*, pp. 157-58.
181   Hunter, *Crofting Community*, p. 151.
182   See Alun Howkins, *Reshaping Rural England: A Social History 1850-1925* (London: Harper Collins Academic, 1991).
183   *Saturday Review*, 3 May 1884.
184   Hunter, *Crofting Community*, pp. 156-57.
185   Shaw, 'Historicist Voices', p. 318.
186   MacKenzie, *Highland Clearances*, p. 419.
187   Chapman, *Gaelic Vision*, p. 108. On the intentionality of the vision which crofters put forward, see also Shaw, 'Historicist voices'.
188   Goodrich-Freer, *Outer Isles*, p. 336.
189   Gordon Cumming, *In the Hebrides*, pp. 145-46.
190   Lord Napier and Ettrick [Sir Francis Napier], 'The Highland Crofters: A Vindication of the Report of the Crofters' Commission', *The Nineteenth Century* 17 (March 1885), p. 452.
191   *ILN*, Dec. 10, 1887.
192   Argyll, 'Corrected Picture', p. 682; M. Ferguson, *Rambles*, pp. 120-22.
193   Cameron, 'Storm Clouds', p. 379.
194   Ann Bermingham, *Landscape and Ideology. The English Rustic Tradition 1740-1860* (Berkeley: Univ. of California Press, 1986), pp. 72-83; William H. A. Williams, 'Putting Paddy in the Picture' (paper presented at Snapshots from Abroad: A conference on American and British Travel Writers and Writing, Minneapolis, MN, November, 1997), p. 3. See also John Barrell, *The Dark Side of the Landscape. The rural poor in English painting, 1730-1840* (New York: Cambridge Univ. Press, 1980).
195   *The Scottish Tourist and Itinerary or a Guide to the Scenery and Antiquities of Scotland and the Western Islands* (Edinburgh, 1827), p. 88.
196   Victoria, Queen of Great Britain. *Victoria in the Highlands: The Personal Journal of Her Majesty Queen Victoria*, David Duff, ed. (London: Muller, 1968), pp. 112-13.
197   Sherwood, 'Journal', Oct. 13.
198   J. A. MacCulloch, *Misty Isle of Skye*, pp. 17-18; William Keddie, *Maclure & MacDonald's Series of Illustrated Guides to the Western Highlands of Scotland* (Glasgow, n.d.), p. 39.
199   Gordon Cumming, *In the Hebrides*, p. 145.
200   J. A. MacCulloch, *Misty Isle of Skye*, p. 223.
201   M. Ferguson, *Rambles*, pp. 32-3.

[202] Pennell, *Journey to the Hebrides*, pp. 146, v-xv; Moncrieff, *Highlands and Islands*, pp. 143-44.

[203] Chapman, *Gaelic Vision*, p. 230. See also Richards, *Highland Clearances*, pp. 499-501, who argues that the Crofters' Act 'exerted a profoundly conservative force upon the community' (p. 500).

[204] *Times*, 15 Nov., 1884.

[205] Quoted in Richards, *Highland Clearances*, p. 492.

[206] George Eyre-Todd, *Scotland Picturesque and Traditional* (New York: Frederick A. Stokes, 1907), p. 314.

Postscript

The author of *Bonnie Scotland*, a 1916 guidebook, noted that the Highlands were the epitome of all the most popular tourist countries: the mountains of Switzerland, the lakes of Italy, the Rhine river of Germany, the cataracts of Norway, the scenery of Heidelberg, the air of Baden, the waters of Vichy, the cure of Marienbad.[1] That anonymous travel writer was one of many tourists of the period who likened Scottish scenery to that of famous vistas on the Continent. Such comparisons asserted the cultural worth of Scotland's landscapes, but they also remind us that many eighteenth- and nineteenth-century Britons were well traveled in Europe. Scotland was not the only place to view sublime scenery, remember a fascinating history, and witness a quaint folk culture. But while many individual attractions on the Continent were similar to those in Scotland, and travel there shared the goal of revivifying and refreshing the traveler, for British tourists the Continent had a very different cultural significance. Europe offered cultural accreditation and the chance to demonstrate one's Romantic spirit by identifying with such passionate souls as Byron.[2] This book argues that for English and Scottish sightseers, Scotland's unique value lay in the vision it presented of their own nation. The Continent was inescapably foreign, a fact of which travelers were constantly reminded by passport checks, customs agents, foreign languages, and unfamiliar currencies.[3] Scotland, however, was British, which meant that visitors could claim Scotland's virtues as their own. If, as the tourist ritual of Scotland promised, that country retained the romance, poetry, spirituality, and human goodness attributed to the premodern world, then those essential qualities were still British ones. The might of nature still reigned, a welcome reminder of human humility. The past was still present, demonstrating that modernity had not separated Britain from its preindustrial roots. And human beings were still uncorrupted by a utilitarian, soulless society. To those Britons of the nineteenth century who felt various degrees of unease over the directions in which industrialization, urbanization, and political change were leading modern society, Scotland seemed to be unaffected by those movements, a 'fact' which offered hope for the nation's soul. The foreignness of the Continent, experienced by travelers not only through border crossings but by encounters with unfamiliar material goods, foods and drink, rituals, landscapes, and religion, worked in a variety of ways to deepen Britons' sense of national belonging, as Marjorie Morgan argues. But Europe could not witness to the continuing vitality of those qualities which seemed essential to Britain's spiritual, social, and cultural health – and might be disappearing. Scotland could.

The 'Scotland' imagined by eighteenth- and nineteenth-century travelers was the product less of any objective reality of the country, than of the preconceptions, longings, and cultural concerns which they brought with them. Despite the frequent assertions of tourists both then and now that they wish to see 'real' life, they usually do not. Instead they are in search of a culturally created ideal of an attraction, one which often has a strong emotional and personal significance. In examining the particulars of the tourist vision of Scotland in the eighteenth and nineteenth centuries, how it was sustained, and what it meant to those who sought it, this study treats tourist stereotypes as reflections of the collective desires and apprehensions of the contemporary middle classes about what their society was and could be. False though those commonplaces of tourism often are, and frequently harmful to those places they are believed to represent, they matter deeply to those who accept and search for them. The reasons why they are valued so intensely are an intriguing window into the worldview of the visitors themselves. In the late eighteenth century, I have argued, ideas of Scotland reflected excitement about the newly-formed Great Britain, and pride in the way that country was becoming a contributing member of the Union. In the nineteenth century, uncertainty about the consequences of industrialization found expression in a vision of Scotland which, as a place seemingly untouched by change, offered sanctuary from the transitoriness that often seemed to underlie modern life. The many images which contributed to this understanding of Scotland appealed to Scots as well as visitors, both because Scots, too, experienced anxiety about the many transformations of the era, and because those visions provided a distinctive identity for their nation. As Great Britain became an ever more industrial, urban society, the representation of Scotland became less so, the better to counter the mundaneness of daily life. Consequently many Britons' conception of Scotland grew more and more out of step with that region's actual concerns.

Today, however, Scots are seeking new ways to represent themselves. Their efforts, examples of which are evident in the methods by which the Scottish Tourist Board, 'VisitScotland', endeavors to attract visitors, illustrate both changing cultural concerns in the twenty-first century, and the pervasiveness of well-established tourist stereotypes. Tourism is now one of Scotland's most important industries, its centrality to the nation's economy underscored by its oversight by government agencies and Parliamentary ministers. Scotland competes for tourists in a world market, and the high financial stakes of modern tourism results in careful attempts to manage the images designed to attract visitors, which are often conceived by professional 'branding consultants'. Yet because even official representations of the nation must appeal to both the nation's sense of itself and the desires of potential tourists, those images continue to reflect the culture's collective consciousness.

As such, the official website of the Scottish Tourist Board, www.VisitScotland.com, provides one means of exploring twenty-first century Scottish national identity, and its role in the British imagination. Although 'gateways' are provided for Americans and several different European nationals, the British site is of more interest here. In some respects the website suggests a return to the late eighteenth-century vision of Scotland as progressive and modern. It showcases a post-devolution nation which is self-confident and forward-looking. This is most evident in VisitScotland.com's emphasis on contemporary, not historic Scotland. The images which first appear on the site are not of kilted clansmen or ruined castles, but of attractive scenery, world-class golf courses, and renowned arts festivals. Victorian 'tartanry' is not to be found. The site emphasizes the 'lively, cosmopolitan entertainment of the towns and cities', the 'wealth of artistic and cultural activities', 'some of the best cuisine in the world.'[4] Although Scottish pride in 'icons' like kilts, tartans, bagpipes, and clans is asserted, potential visitors are also reminded that 'there's no single element that defines the country.'[5] VisitScotland.com's narrative of Scottish history has a clear nationalist slant, which, by downplaying the importance of the Union of Parliaments, emphasizes native abilities and accomplishments. The interspersing of photographs of Highland castles with those of modern buildings asserts that today's Scotland is not a heritage park.

A promotional campaign designed to entice young adults to Scotland on weekend getaways is explicitly anti-tartanry. Of Edinburgh, the campaign's website says, 'Castle. Blah, blah, blah. World's largest arts festival. Yada, yada, yada. Think you know what Edinburgh is about? Ok – so the big stone building and the street theatre are pretty difficult to miss. But what about the real Edinburgh, lurking not so far away from the more obvious parts?'[6] This anti-touristic advertising, which also appeals to the MTV generation's desire to differentiate themselves from older travelers, continues the well-established tradition of envisioning journeys to Scotland as departures from one's ordinary life. 'Scotland is the place for a city break from the usual'. Rather than a break from the modern world, however, trips to Scotland are shown as trips to that which is youthful, trendy, and sophisticated. The 'real' Edinburgh promised to young people is 'the manicured neatness of the New Town', the galleries of modern art, the excellent shopping, the abundant and sophisticated bars and restaurants, and the challenging exercise facilities. Similar sentiments are expressed about Scotland's other cities.[7] Frank McAveety, Scotland's tourism minister, praised the campaign as a 'great example of the image we should be promoting of Scotland – modern, vibrant, fun, exciting and welcoming.'[8]

McAveety's proposed vision of Scotland is revealing both of Scots' sense of themselves, and of his perception of what images will attract visitors, which is, after all, the ultimate goal of VisitScotland. The absence of tartanry suggests that in the opinion of the tourist board, an opinion presumably supported by market research, 'Balmoralized' Scotland is no longer enticing, at least not to the most desirable tourists. True, representations of Scotland as the home of clans and bagpipes are so well established and so prominent in other tourist advertising that it may not be necessary for VisitScotland to include them. They may also be 'old news', too well established in British culture to attract much attention. Nonetheless, those visions were once very attractive to English travelers. The belief that they no longer are may say something about upper- and middle-class British culture. Perhaps an increasingly post-modern, post-Christian Britain no longer has such a stake in a Scotland which preserves the traditions, values, and 'authenticity' of the past. In an age of world travel, perhaps, the multi-cultural, multi-ethnic society which Great Britain is becoming no longer finds Scotland the most appropriate source of societal and cultural roots.

If that is so, however, another element of the current representation of Scotland suggests that twenty-first century Britons still long to witness the limits of industrialization. 'Twenty-somethings' are advised that 'the great outdoors is also seriously close to these great cities. So you can decide to spend the day taking in galleries and culture. Or you can career down a mountain on a bike, kayak along the shores of a loch, or hit the surf.'[9] The nineteenth-century impression of the Highlands as untouched and possibly untouchable by humans echoes strongly in VisitScotland.com's discussions of 'Active Scotland' and 'Wild Scotland'. Information about these visions of Scotland feature much more prominently on the tourist board's websites than do discussions of Scottish history or symbols, on both the general site and the one directed towards young adults. The Western Isles, it is alleged, are 'one of the last real wildernesses', 'full of rare and iconic species'.[10] In Scotland, one can grow close to nature, whether through seeking and observing wildlife, or participating in outdoor activities ranging from golf and fishing to snowboarding and whitewater rafting. Hunting may be out of style in modern Britain, and the physical challenge of the Scottish environment is no longer geared specifically to men. Yet danger still lurks, in 'extreme sports' and in the vagaries of the Scottish weather. Just as the need for a guide pointed to the risks of the landscape to Victorians, today's visitors are encouraged to use 'professional wildlife operators to release the full potential of your wildlife experience in a safe and controlled environment.' Wildlife watchers are thus subtly reminded that on their own, they might not be safe. Those who choose to go their own way are advised to be prepared for any eventuality, especially a sudden weather shift.[11]

There are subtle differences between the vision of nature which lured Victorians to the Highlands and that presented by VisitScotland.com. Although descriptions of the environment as 'rare' and 'unique' serve both to highlight Scottish distinctiveness and to remind of the fragility of nature in the industrial world, it is difficult in the twenty-first century to assert that humans cannot transform nature there, or that signs of modernity are not evident. Rather, the Highlands are envisioned as a place where humans live in harmony with the natural world. 'Scotland is blessed with some of the most precious and special natural environments in the world, environments that have evolved through a long partnership between people and nature.'[12] To an age even more dominant over nature than the Victorians, this image is a powerful one. Tourism officials stated in June 2004 that wildlife tourism had increased 34 percent in the previous four years, and continued expansion was expected. Ironically, perhaps, they attributed the increase in part to recent natural history television shows and to the ways in which technology facilitates wildlife watching.[13] Nonetheless, the popularity of Scotland as a wildlife destination serves much the same role as the stern and bleak images of Loch Scavaig did to Victorians. It reassures modern culture that nature still has power, that we have not yet erased its force. Journeys to the wild, even quick ones made in automobiles and boats, restore a sense of the equilibrium between humans and the natural world which much of daily life does not possess.

The promotion of 'wild Scotland' works because it resonates with the interests and needs of the audience to which it is directed. Despite the efforts of tourist boards and promoters to control how a particular destination is imagined, ultimately the traveler, responding out of his or her cultural and social environment, is just as crucial in determining the meaning of any attraction. Just as Victorians found that there were limits to their ability to influence the meaning of Scotland, VisitScotland cannot exert complete authority over the way visitors see the nation. The organization confessed to feeling 'slightly nervous' in the winter of 2003 when Edinburgh crime novelist Ian Rankin announced plans to write a travel book exposing the dark side of life in Scotland, with photographs of such places as mortuaries, cemeteries, and abandoned mining works. A spokesman for VisitScotland cautioned, 'We always have to be careful that we present the right image to visitors or we could put them off. I'm not sure how many people would be drawn to mortuaries....Scotland has a new image with its new parliament and new investment. We are cleaning up the place and we should present that as a positive thing.'[14] Yet since 2000 enough people have been drawn to 'alternative' Edinburgh to sustain regular walking tours through some of the city's seedier areas based on Rankin's books about the cynical Inspector John Rebus. The tours include stops at a city morgue and a local police station. The tour guide finds that participants enjoy seeing another side of Edinburgh, 'not just the Royal Mile, the pipers and the festival madness.'[15] Interest has also been expressed in *Trainspotting* tours, based on the novel and movie detailing the Edinburgh drug scene in the 1980s.[16]

Nor is the Scottish Tourist Board likely to erase tartanry from the image of Scotland. They may be right that a more up-to-date vision of Scotland is likely to attract greater numbers of contemporary British visitors. But tartan kitsch still sells across Scotland, and many advertisements aimed at tourists are very similar to those of the nineteenth century. Research commissioned by the Scottish Executive in 2004 found that worldwide, although people have a positive image of Scotland, it is one still rooted in history or myth. Scotland continues to be associated with 'kilts, the Loch Ness Monster, whisky and mountains'.[17] This may be especially true in the United States, where many Scottish-Americans' sense of ethnic identity is tied to their belief in the importance of supposed Highland traditions.[18] McAveety, Scotland's tourism minister, interpreted the findings about the prevalence of tartanry as motivation for stronger efforts to modernize Scotland's image. If, however, the tartan and shortbread tin image of Scotland continues to resonate with those he hopes to attract to Scotland, he may have a difficult task.

Notes

[1] *"Bonnie Scotland": A Comprehensive Guide and Reference Book to Scotland* (London: The Photocrom Co., 1916), p. 5.

[2] James Buzard, *The Beaten Track. European Tourism, Literature, and the Ways to 'Culture' 1800-1918* (Oxford: Clarendon Press, 1993).

[3] Marjorie Morgan, *National Identities and Travel in Victorian Britain*, (Houndsmills: Palgrave, 2002), pp. 25-31.

[4] www.visitscotland.com/sightsandactives, visited on August 8, 2004.

[5] www.visitscotland.com/aboutScotland, visited on August 8, 2004.

[6] www.MyvisitScotland.com/citypages/edinburgh/citylife/citylife, visited on August 10, 2004.

[7] Ibid.

[8] Sam Halstead, 'Tourism bid to lure MTV generation', *Edinburgh Evening News*, April 2, 2004, [http://news.scotsman.com, visited on July 7, 2004.]

[9] www.myvisitscotland.com, visited on August 10, 2004.

[10] www.wildlife.visitscotland.com/unique, visited on August 8, 2004.

[11] www.wildlife.visitScotland.com/faq, visited on August 8, 2004.

[12] www.visitscotland.com/aboutscotland/explorebymap/features/naturalheritage, visited on August 8, 2004.

[13] James Reynolds, 'Scotland's wild side brings an upsurge in tourism,' *The Scotsman*, June 26, 2004, [http://news.scotsman.com, visited on July 6, 2004].

[14] Jason Allardyce, 'Never mind castles, check out crime scenes,' *The Scotsman*, Feb. 9, 2003, [http://news.scotsman.com, visited on July 7, 2004]. See also www.rebustours.com.

[15] Allardyce, 'Never mind castles'. See also www.rebustours.com.

[16] Rhiannon Edward, 'Organiser of tour features the Trainspotting trail,' *The Scotsman*, June 5, 2004, [http://news.scotsman.com, visited on July 7, 2004].

[17] Andrew Denholm, 'Scotland still seen as land of Nessie,' *The Scotsman*, July 2, 2004, [http://news.scotsman.com, visited on July 7, 2004].

[18] See Celeste Ray, *Highland Heritage. Scottish Americans in the American South* (Chapel Hill: Univ. of North Carolina Press, 2001).

Bibliography

Primary Sources

Newspapers and Periodicals

Cook's Excursionist and Tourist Advertiser. Thomas Cook, pub., London, 1851-1902.
Daily Mail. London, 1896-1912.
Glasgow Herald. Glasgow, 1820-1918.
Illustrated London News. London, 1842-1918.
Times. London, 1795-1914.
The Scotsman. Edinburgh, 1820-1918, 2003-2004.

Guidebooks

An Account of the Principal Pleasure Tours in Scotland. Edinburgh, 1819, 1821.
Anderson, George and Peter Anderson. *Guide to the Highlands and Islands of Scotland.* London, 1834.
—. *Guide to the Highlands and Islands of Scotland.* Edinburgh, 1851,1863.
—. *Handbook to the Highland Railway System from Perth to Forres, Keith, Inverness, and Bonar Bridge.* Edinburgh, 1865.
—. *Handbook to the Highland Railway System and the Sutherland Railway.* Edinburgh: John Menzies, 1900.
Baddeley, M. J. B. *The Highlands of Scotland.* London, 1881.
Baedeker, Karl. *Great Britain.* London, 1887, 1901.
Black, Adam and Charles Black, pub. *Black's Picturesque Tourist of Scotland.* Edinburgh, 1840, 1843, 1852, 1857, 1865, 1881, 1882.
—. *Black's Guide to Scotland.* London: Adam & Charles Black, 1902.
"Bonnie Scotland": A Comprehensive Guide and Reference Book to Scotland. London: The Photocrom Co., Ltd. 1916.
Bradshaw's Descriptive Guide to the Caledonian Railway. London, 1848.
Brotchie, T. C. F. *Scottish Western Holiday Haunts.* Edinburgh: John Menzies, 1911.
Caledonian and London & Northwestern Railways, pub. *Summer Tours in Scotland and England.* 1893.
Chambers, Robert. *The Picture of Scotland.* 2 vols. Edinburgh, 1827.
'The Charm of Highland Scenery.' *The Spectator* 95 (Sept. 2, 1905), pp. 314-15.
Cook, Thomas. *Handbook of a Trip to Scotland.* Leicester, 1846.
—. *Cook's Scottish Tourist: A Handbook of Cheap Excursions and Tours in Scotland.* Leicester, 1858.
—. *Cook's Scottish Tourist Official Directory.* London, 1861.
—. *Cook's Scottish Tourist.* London, 1870.
—. *Cook's Tourist Handbook of Scotland.* London, 1895.

David MacBrayne's Royal Mail Steamers, pub. *Summer Tours in Scotland*. Glasgow, 1885, 1893, 1896, 1905.

Denholm, James. *The History of the City of Glasgow. To which is added a sketch of a Tour to Loch Lomond and the Falls of the Clyde*. Glasgow, 1798.

A Description of the Most Remarkable Highways and whole known fairs and Mercats in Scotland. Edinburgh, 1711.

Duncan, James. *The Scotch Itinerary, Containing the Roads through Scotland, on a New Plan*. Glasgow, 1805.

The Gazetteer of Scotland. Dundee, 1803.

Guide to all the Watering and Sea Bathing Places. London, n.d.

Glasgow and Ayrshire Railway Co., pub. *Guide to Glasgow and Ayrshire Railway*. Glasgow, 1841.

Harper, Charles G. *Motoring in Scotland*. London: Royal Automobile Club, 1912.

Heron, Robert. *Scotland Described: or a Topographical Description of all the Counties of Scotland*. Edinburgh, 1797.

—. *Scotland Delineated: or a Geographical Description of every Shire in Scotland*. Edinburgh, 1799.

Highland Railway Co., pub. *The Highland Railway Programme to Tourist, Weekend, Day and Half Day Excursion Arrangements*. 1910.

Keddie, William. *Maclure & MacDonald's Illustrated Guides to the Highlands*. Glasgow, n.d.

Kincaid, Alexander. *The History of Edinburgh. From the Earliest Accounts to the Present Time*. Edinburgh, 1787.

'The Land o' Burns.' *Harper's New Monthly Magazine* 59 (1879), pp. 180-191.

Lizars, W. H., pub. *Lizars' Scottish Tourist*. Edinburgh, 1850.

London and Northwestern Railway Co., pub. *Where to Spend the Holidays*. London, 1906.

Lumsden, James & Son, pub. *Steam Boat Companion and Stranger's Guide to the Western Islands and Highlands of Scotland*. Glasgow, 1825, 1828, 1831.

Macintyre, Donald. *Guide to Prince Charlie's Country*. Fort William, 1859.

McPhun, W. R., pub. *The Scottish Tourist's Steamboat Pocket Guide*. Glasgow, 1835.

Marrat, Jabez. *'Land of the Mountain and the Flood'. Scottish Scenes and Scenery Delineated*. London, 1879.

Meason, George. *The Official Guide to the North Western Railway*. London, 1859.

M'Nayr, James. *A Guide from Glasgow to Some of the most Remarkable Scenes in the Highlands of Scotland and to the Falls of Clyde*. Glasgow, 1797.

Moncrieff, A. R. Hope. *Bonnie Scotland*. London: A & C Black, 1904. Reprint, London: A & C Black, 1912.

—. *Highlands & Islands of Scotland*. London: A & C Black, 1906. Reprint, London, A & C Black, 1925.

"Mountain, Moor, and Loch." illustrated by Pen and Pencil. On the route of the West Highland Railway. London, 1895.

Murray, John, pub. *Handbook for Travellers in Scotland*. London, 1868, 1875.

Murray, Thomas & Son, pub. *Murray's Handbooks for Scotland, No. 10, The Perthshire Highlands*. Glasgow, 1852.

—. *Murray's Scottish Tourist*. Glasgow, 1868.

North British Railway Co., pub. *Fort William to Mallaig*. 1901.

—. *Pleasure Sails on the Firth of Clyde.* 1917.

The New Picture of Scotland. 2 vols. Perth, 1807.

Rhind, William, ed. *The Scottish Tourist; Being a Guide to the Picturesque Scenery and Antiquities of Scotland.* Edinburgh, 1845.

—. *The Scottish Tourist's Portable Guide to the Great Highland Tour.* Edinburgh, n.d.

—. *The Scottish Tourist's Portable Guide to the Principal Steamboat Tours.* Edinburgh, n.d.

Scotland Delineated, or a Geographical Description of every shire in Scotland. Edinburgh, 1791.

The Scottish Tourist and Itinerary or A Guide to the Scenery and Antiquities of Scotland and the Western Islands. Edinburgh, 1827, 1830, 1834.

A Sketch of the Most Remarkable Scenery near Callander of Monteath. Stirling, 1808.

Souvenir of Scotland: Its Cities, Lakes, and Mountains. London, Edinburgh, New York, 1889.

'Sylvan' [Samuel Hobbs]. *Sylvan's Pictorial Handbook to the Clyde and its Watering Places.* London, 1847.

—. *Sylvan's Pictorial Handbook to the scenery of the Caledonian Canal, the Isle of Staffa, etc.* Edinburgh, 1848.

The Tourists' Handy Guide to Scotland. Edinburgh, 1884.

The Traveller's Guide through Scotland and its Islands. Edinburgh, London, 1814.

The Traveller's Guide, or a Topographical Description of Scotland. Edinburgh, 1798.

Wilson's Guide to the Scott Country and Fife Summer Resorts by the North British Railway. Glasgow: Wilson Publishing Co., 1915.

Diaries, Journals, and Travel Accounts

Abbott, Jacob. *A Summer in Scotland.* Dublin, 1849.

Abraham, Ashley P. *Rock-Climbing in Skye.* London: Longmans, Green & Co., 1908.

Account of a tour in Scotland. (1845) ACC 8087, NLS.

Aliquis [C. G. Dawson]. *Rambles in the Highlands and Islands of Scotland.* Glasgow, 1883.

'Among the Hills.' *Temple Bar* (November 1869), pp. 88-102.

'Among the Lochs: Being a Narrative of some Passages in the Archdeacon's Holiday.' *Blackwood's Magazine* 90(October, 1861), pp. 479-98.

Argyll, Duke of [G. D. Campbell]. 'A Corrected Picture of the Highlands.' *The Nineteenth Century* XCIII:16 (Nov. 1884), pp. 681-701.

Ayton, Richard and William Daniell. *A Voyage Round Great Britain.* London, 1814-1825. Reprint, London: Tate Gallery, 1978.

Barr, Amelia. 'Spin-Drift from the Hebrides.' *Lippincott's Magazine* Vol. 6 (New Series), (Oct. 1883), pp. 337-49.

Bede, Cuthbert [Edward Bradley]. *A Tour in Tartan-Land.* London, 1863.

Beecroft, Mrs. & Miss. 'Mrs. and Miss Beecroft's Third Tour to Scotland.' (1833) MS. 1674, NLS.

Boswell, James. *Journal of a Tour to the Hebrides with Samuel Johnson, LL.D.* Alan Wendt, ed. Boston: Houghton, 1965.

—. *The Journal of a Tour to the Hebrides.* Peter Levi, ed. New York: Penguin, 1984.

Botfield, Beriah. *Journal of a Tour through the Highlands of Scotland.* Norton Hall, 1830.

Bowman, J. E. *The Highlands and Islands: A 19th Century Tour.* introduction by Elaine M. E. Barry. New York: Hippocreme Books, 1986.

Bristed, John. *Anthzplanomenoz, or a Pedestrian Tour through part of the Highlands of Scotland in 1801.* 2 vols. London, 1803.

Buchanan, Rev. John Lane. *Travels in the Western Hebrides.* London, 1793.

Buchanan, Robert. *The Land of Lorne.* 2 vols. London, 1871.

Cameron, J. A. 'Storm-Clouds in the Highlands.' *Nineteenth Century* 16 (Sep. 1884), pp. 379-95.

Carlyle, Alexander. *Journal of a Tour to the North of Scotland.* introduction by Richard B. Sher. Aberdeen: Aberdeen Center for Scottish Studies, 1982.

Carr, John. *Caledonian Sketches, or a Tour through Scotland in 1807.* London, 1809.

'Carr's Caledonian Sketches.' *Quarterly Review* (February, 1809), pp. 178-93.

Cobbett, William. *Cobbett's Tour in Scotland.* Daniel Green, ed. Aberdeen: Aberdeen Univ. Press, 1984.

Cockburn, Henry. *Circuit Journeys.* Edinburgh, 1889.

Combe, William. *The Tour of Doctor Prosody in Search of the Antique and Picturesque, through Scotland, the Hebrides, the Orkney and Shetland Islands.* London, 1821.

Cordiner, Charles. *Antiquities and Scenery of the North of Scotland in a series of letters to Thomas Pennant, Esq.* London, 1780.

Dalgleish, W. Scott. 'The Coast Scenery of Scotland.' *Good Words* 33 (1829), pp. 310-15.

Defoe, Daniel. *A Tour Through the Whole Island of Great Britain.* Vol. 2. introduction by G. D. H. Cole and D. C. Browning. New York: Everyman's Library, Dutton, 1962.

'Diary of a visit to Edinburgh and Perthshire.' (1848) ACC. 8442, NLS.

Douglas, William. 'Summer Holiday.' (1888) MS. 10975, NLS.

The Epistles of Peggy Written from Scotland. n.p., n.d.

Eyre-Todd, George. *Scotland: Picturesque and Traditional.* New York: Frederick A. Stokes, 1907.

'An Excursion to the English Lakes and Scotland.' (1857) ACC. 8139, NLS.

Ferguson, Malcolm. *Rambles in Skye.* Glasgow, 1885.

Fergusson, R. Menzies. *Our Trip North.* London, 1892.

'A Fortnight's Cruise in the "Ailsa."' (1892) MS. 9231, NLS.

Garnett, T. *Observations on a Tour through the Highlands and Part of the Western Isles of Scotland.* 2 vols. London, 1800.

Gaskell, Catherine Milnes. 'My Stay in the Highlands.' *The Nineteenth Century* (August 1893), pp. 230-47.

Gilpin, William. *Observations on the Highlands of Scotland.* London, 1789. Reprint, with an introduction by Sutherland Lyall, Richmond, England: The Richmond Publishing Co., 1973.

Goodrich-Freer, Ada. *Outer Isles.* Westminster: Archibald Constable & Co., 1902.

Gordon Cumming, Constance F. *From the Hebrides to the Himalayas.* 2 vols. London, 1876.

—. *In the Hebrides.* London, 1883.

Gosse, Edmund. 'Journal in Scotland.' (1876) MS. 2562, NLS.

Gower, Mrs. John F. 'Illustrated Accounts of trips to France and Scotland by the family of John F. Gower.' (1854, 1862) ACC. 9946, NLS.

Hamerton, Philip Gilbert. *A Painter's Camp.* Boston, 1879.

Hall, Herbert Byng. *Highland Sports and Highland Quarters.* London, 1848.

Heron, Robert. *Observations made in a Journey through the Western Counties of Scotland in the autumn of 1792.* Perth, 1793.

Holding, T. H. *Cruise of the Ospray: Canoe and Camp life in Scotland.* Newcastle-on-tyne, 1878.

Holmes, T. *Reminiscences of a few days Rambles in North Britain.* Bolton, 1874.

Homer, Philip B. *Observations on a Short Tour Made in the Summer of 1803 to the Western Highlands of Scotland.* London, 1804.

Howel, James. *A Perfect Description of the People and Country of Scotland.* London, 1649. Reprint, Edinburgh, 1900.

Hunter, James. 'Journal Through Clydesdale and parts of the Western Highlands.' (1834) MS. 2776, NLS.

Hunter, Robert. *A Brief Account of a Tour Through some Parts of Scotland.* London, 1839.

Ingleby, Clement Mansfield. 'Journal of a tour to Scotland.' (1842) MS. 8926, NLS.

'An Islesman.' 'The Crofters II. Their Condition and Prospects.' *Blackwood's Edinburgh Magazine* (Oct. 1889), pp. 527-41.

James, Thomas L. 'A Summer Tour in the Scottish Highlands.' *The Cosmopolitan,* (October, 1896), pp. 571-81.

Jenkin, Mrs. Fleming. 'Highland Crofters.' *Good Words* 26 (1885), pp. 502-8.

John English's Travels Through Scotland. London, n. d.

Johnson, James. *The Recess, or Autumnal Relaxation in the Highlands and Lowlands.* London, 1834.

Johnson, Samuel. *A Journey to the Western Islands of Scotland.* Alan Wendt, ed. Boston: Houghton Mifflin, 1965.

—. *A Journey to the Western Islands of Scotland.* Peter Levi, ed. New York: Penguin, 1984.

'A Journal of a few days from Home in the summer of 1856 with selected poetry and songs.' (1856) MS. 9233, NLS.

'Journal of a tour of Scotland made by an Englishman in 1850.' (1850) MS. 17957, NLS.

'Journal of a Tour through Some parts of Scotland.' (1829) MS. 3529, NLS.

'A Journey to Scotland.' (1790) MS. 15905, NLS.

Keats, John. *Letters from a Walking Tour.* Jack Stillinger, ed. New York: The Grolier Club, 1995.

Knox, John. *A Tour Through the Highlands of Scotland and the Hebride Islands in 1786.* London, 1787. Reprint, Edinburgh, James Thin, 1975.

Knox, John [Peter Carter]. *Crumbs from the Land o' Cakes.* Boston, 1851.

'A Lady.' *A Journey to the Highlands of Scotland with Occasional Remarks on Dr. Johnson's Tour.* London, 1776.

'The Land o' Burns.' *Harper's New Monthly Magazine* 59 (1879), pp. 180-191.

Lettice, John. *Letters on a Tour through various parts of Scotland in the Year 1792.* London, 1794.

Leyden, John. *Journal of a Tour in the Highlands and Western Islands of Scotland in 1800.* James Sinton, ed. Edinburgh: William Blackwood & Sons, 1903.

Locke, James. *Tweed and Don or Recollections and Reflections of an Angler.* Edinburgh, 1860.

Lorne, Marquis of. 'The Highland Land Agitation.' *Contemporary Review* 46 (Dec. 1884), pp. 827-37.

MacCulloch, J. A. *The Misty Isle of Skye.* Edinburgh & London: Oliphant Anderson & Ferrier, 1905.

Macculloch, John. *A Description of the Western Islands of Scotland.* 3 vols. London, 1819.

—. *The Highlands and Western Islands of Scotland.* 4 vols. London, 1824.

MacLeod, Reginald. 'The Crofters: How to Benefit Them.' *Blackwood's Edinburgh Magazine* 139:846 (April 1886), pp. 559-63.

—. 'The Crofters I. The Crofter Commission.' *Blackwood's Edinburgh Magazine* 146:888(Oct. 1889), pp. 517-26.

Martin, Martin. *A Description of the Western Islands of Scotland.* London, 1716. Reprint, Edinburgh: Mercat Press, 1970.

Mawman, Joseph. *An Excursion to the Highlands of Scotland and the English Lakes.* London, 1805.

Maxwell, W. H. *Wanderings in the Highlands & Islands.* 2 vols. London, 1852.

Miller, Hugh. *The Cruise of the Betsey.* Boston, 1858.

Murray, Frances. *Summer in the Hebrides.* Glasgow, 1887.

Murray, Sarah. *A Companion and Useful Guide to the Beauties of Scotland.* William F. Laughlan, ed. Hawick: Byways Books, 1982.

Napier and Ettrick, Lord [Sir Francis Napier]. 'The Highland Crofters: A Vindication of the Report of the Crofter's Commission.' *Nineteenth Century* 17 (March 1885), pp. 437-63.

'Nether Lochaber.' 'A Winter Night with the Highland Crofters.' *Good Words* 30 (1889) part I, pp. 30-35, Part II, pp. 112-17.

Nevin, W. W. *Vignettes of Travel.* Philadelphia, 1881.

Newte, Thomas [William Thomson]. *A Tour in England and Scotland in 1785.* London, 1788.

Nicholson, Alexander. 'The Isle of Skye.' *Good Words* 16 (1875), part I, pp. 344-50, Part II, 'Coiruisg', pp. 384-92, Part III, 'Climbing in the Coolin - Scur-nan-Gillean, pp. 457-62, Part IV, 'The Sea Coast', pp. 561-68.

North, Christopher [John Wilson]. *Recreations of Christopher North* from *The Works of John Wilson.* Prof. Ferrier, ed. vol. IX., Edinburgh, 1857.

The Northern Excursion: or the Highland Village. Glasgow, 1818.

'Notes of a Wanderer in Skye.' *Temple Bar* 69 (Sept-Dec. 1883), pp. 75-92.

'An old Highlander.' 'Home Truths on the Crofter Agitation.' *Blackwood's Edinburgh Magazine* 138:837 (July 1885), pp. 92-100.

Over the Border: or a Rossendale Lady's Impressions of Scotland. Haslingden, 1869.

Parker, Miss. *A Tour in Scotland in 1863.* London: The Roxburghe Club, 1984.

Pennell, Joseph and Elizabeth Robins Pennell. *Our Journey to the Hebrides.* New York, 1889.

Pennell, Elizabeth Robins. 'Our Journey to the Hebrides.' *Harper's New Monthly Magazine.* 77 'First Paper.'(September, 1888), pp. 489-503, 'Second Paper.' (October, 1888), 'Third Paper.' (November, 1888).

Pennant, Thomas. *A Tour in Scotland MDCCLXIX.* London, 1790.

Pearson, William. *Papers, Letters & Journal of William Pearson.* ed. by his wife. London, 1863.

Pococke, Richard. *Tours in Scotland, 1747, 1750, 1760.* Daniel William Kemp, ed. Edinburgh, 1887.

Rae, John. 'The Crofter Problem.' *The Contemporary Review* 47 (Feb. 1885), pp. 185-201.

'Red Heather.' *Memories of Sporting Days.* New York: Longmans, Green & Co., 1923.

Reid, John T. *Art Rambles in the Highlands and Islands of Scotland.* New York, 1878.

Ryland, William Deane. 'Journal of a tour in Scotland during the long Vacation of 1823.' (1823) ACC. 8801, NLS.

Selwyn, Elizabeth. *Journal of Excursions Through the Most Interesting Parts of England, Wales, & Scotland.* London, 1823.

[Shaw, Stebbing]. *A Tour, in 1787, from London to the Western Highlands of Scotland.* London, n.d.

'Skye.' *Temple Bar* 68 (May-Aug. 1883), pp. 276-79.

Sherwood, Lucy Elizabeth. 'Journal of Lucy Elizabeth Sherwood. Visit to Glasgow, Edinburgh'. (1826-1827), ACC. 8679, NLS.

Sinclair, Catherine. *Sketches and Stories of Scotland and the Scotch and Shetland and the Shetlanders.* London, n.d.

'Sixty-one'. *Twenty years' Reminiscences of the Lews.* London, 1871.

Smith, Alexander. *A Summer in Skye.* Boston, 1865.

Smith, Rev. C. Lesingham. *Excursions Through the Highlands and Isles of Scotland in 1835 and 1836.* London, 1837.

Spence, Elizabeth Isabella. *Sketches of the Present Manners, Customs, and Scenery of Scotland.* London, 1811.

Spencer, Frederick Charles. *Journal of a Tour to Scotland.* Oxford, 1816.

Stephenson, W. A. 'A Trip to Edinburgh and Glasgow by the Polytechnic Y. M. C. I. Excursion.' (1890) MS. 9234, NLS.

Stewart, David. *Sketches of the Character, Manners and Present State of the Highlanders of Scotland; with details of the Military Service of the Highland Regiments.* 2 vols. Edinburgh, 1822. Reprint, Edinburgh: John Donald, 1977.

Stewart, C. S. *Sketches of Society in Great Britain and Ireland.* 2 vols. Philadelphia, 1834.

Stoddart, John. *Remarks on Local Scenery & Manners in Scotland during the Year 1799 and 1800.* vol 1. London, 1801.

'Substance of a tour through Scotland in the summer of 1836.' MS. 2729, NLS.

Taylor, S. 'Journal of a Tour to Scotland.' (1842) MS. 8927, NLS.

'Three Days in the Highlands.' *Blackwood's Magazine* 90(August 1861), pp. 256-66.

Tipple, S. Augustus. *A Summer Visit to Scotland.* Norwich, 1847.

Tonna, Mary Ann. *What Aunty Saw in Scotland.* London, 1855.

'A Tour in the Hebrides.' (1908) ACC. 7926, NLS.

Townshend, Chauncy Hare. *A Descriptive Tour in Scotland.* Brussels, 1840.

'The Tourist in Scotland.' *The Leisure Hour.* vol. 9 (July 19 - Nov. 8, 1860).

'A Trip to Scotland.' *Fraser's Magazine.* (January, 1856), pp. 39-44.

Victoria, Queen of Great Britain. *Leaves from the Journal of Our Life in the Highlands. 1848-1861.* Arthur Helps, ed. London, 1868.

—. *Victoria in the Highlands: The Personal Journal of Her Majesty Queen Victoria.* David Duff, ed. London: Muller, 1968.

'A Visit to Hinba.' *Cornhill Magazine* 41:242 (February, 1880), pp. 171-80.

Warden, S. Kathleen. *Humorous Side-Lights on a Scotch Tour.* London, n.d.

Watson, Jean Logan. *The Grand Highland Tour.* Edinburgh, 1875.

Waugh, Edwin. *Fourteen Days in Scotland.* Manchester, 1863.

Wilson, James. *A Voyage Round the Coasts of Scotland and the Isles.* 2 vols. Edinburgh, 1842.

Winter, William. *Brown Heath and Blue Bells; Being Sketches of Scotland. With other papers.* New York: MacMillan, 1906.

—. *Over the Border.* New York: Moffat, Yard and Co., 1911.

Wordsworth, Dorothy. *Recollections of a Tour Made in Scotland in 1803.* J. C. Shairp, ed. Edinburgh, 1874. Reprint, New York: AMS Press, 1973.

Yates, Edmund. 'Letters to Joseph, no. II' *Temple Bar* vol. 18 (November, 1866), pp. 414-23.

Youngson, A. J. ed. *Beyond the Highland Line: Journals of Travel in Eighteenth Century Scotland.* London: Collins, 1974.

Other

Arnold, Matthew. *The Study of Celtic Literature.* 1905. Reprint, Port Washington, NY: Kennikat Press, 1970.

Beddoe, John. *The Races of Britain.* London, 1885.

Black, William. *Macleod of Dare.* New York, 1879.

—. *In Far Lochaber.* New York, 1888.

Burke, Edmund. 'A Philosophical Enquiry into the Origin of our ideas of the Sublime and the Beautiful.' In vol. I of *The Works of the Right Honorable Edmund Burke.* London, 1801.

Keene, Charles, John Leech, George Du Maurier, et al. *Mr. Punch in the Highlands.* London: Educational Book Co., Ltd., 1907.

Keene, Charles, George Du Maurier, W. Ralston. *Mr. Punch's Scottish Humor.* London: Educational Book Co., Ltd., 1907.

MacKenzie, Alexander. *The History of the Highland Clearances.* Inverness, 1883. Reprint, with an introduction by John Prebble, 1979, Edinburgh: Mercat Press, 1997.

Macpherson, James. *The Poems of Ossian.* New York, 1835.

Report of Her Majesty's Commissioners of Inquiry into the Conditions of the Crofters and Cottars in the Highlands and Islands of Scotland. Parliamentary Papers, sessional vols. XXXII-XXXVI (1884), pp. 1-111.

Scott, Walter. *Tales of a Grandfather.* Philadelphia, 1836.

—. *The Lady of the Lake*. Vol. VIII of *Poetical Works of Sir Walter Scott*. Edinburgh, 1880.

—. *The Lord of the Isles*. Vol. X of *Poetical Works of Sir Walter Scott*. Edinburgh, 1880.

—. *Waverley; or 'Tis Sixty Years Since*. Claire Lamont, ed. Oxford: Clarendon Press, 1981.

Scrope, William. *The Art of Deer-Stalking*. New York, 1897.

Smollett, Tobias. *The Expedition of Humphry Clinker*. London: Oxford Univ. Press, 1960.

Stevenson, Robert Louis. *Kidnapped*. New York: Prestige Books, 1967.

Timetables from the Caledonia Railway Co. (1847-1907) BR/TT(S)/55, the Highland Railway Co. (1884-1910) BR/TT(S)/60, and the North British Railway Co. (1853-1917) BR/TT(S)/53. SRO.

Timetables from the London & North Western and Caledonian Railway Co. (1893) RAIL/ 410/1365. PRO.

Posters issued by the Caledonian Railway Co. (1911, 1915-1919) BR/CAL/4/156, 160. SRO.

Short history of tourist arrangements of the London and Northwestern Railway Co. RAIL/410/1365. PRO.

Program of tourist arrangements of the London and Northwestern Railway Co. (1863, 1866, 1876) RAIL/1015/1.48A, 48B, RAIL/410/1359. PRO.

Secondary Sources

Adams, James Eli. *Dandies and Desert Saints. Styles of Victorian Manhood*. Ithaca: Cornell Univ. Press, 1995.

Allen, David Elliston. *The Naturalist in Britain. A Social History*. Princeton: Princeton Univ. Press, 1994.

Altick, Richard D. *The Shows of London*. Cambridge, MA: Balknap Press of Harvard Univ. Press, 1978.

Anderson, James. *Sir Walter Scott and History*. Edinburgh: The Edina Press, 1981.

Andrews, Malcolm. *The Search for the Picturesque. Landscape Aesthetics and Tourism in Britain 1760-1800*. Stanford: Stanford Univ. Press, 1989.

The Art of Paul Sandby. New Haven: Yale Center for British Art, 1985.

Ash, Marinell. *The Strange Death of Scottish History*. Edinburgh: The Ramsay Head Press, 1980.

—. 'William Wallace and Robert the Bruce. The life and death of a national myth.' in Raphael Samuel and Paul Thompson, eds. *The Myths We Live By*. New York: Routledge, 1990, pp. 83-94.

Baines, Paul. 'Ossianic Geographies: Fingalian Figures on the Scottish Tour, 1760-1830.' *Scotlands* 4.1 (1997), pp. 44-61.

Banton, Michael. *The Idea of Race*. Boulder, CO: Westview Press, 1977.

Barrell, John. *The Idea of Landscape and the Sense of Place*. Cambridge: Cambridge Univ. Press, 1972.

—. *The dark side of the landscape. The rural poor in English painting 1730-1840*. New York: Cambridge Univ. Press, 1980.

Bausinger, Hermann. *Folk Culture in a World of Technology*. Elke Dettmer, trans. Bloomington: Indiana Univ. Press, 1990.

Bermingham, Ann. *Landscape and Ideology. The English Rustic Tradition 1740-1860*. Berkeley: Univ. of California Press, 1986.

Bernard, Paul P. *Rush to the Alps: The Evolution of Vacationing in Switzerland*. Boulder: East European Quarterly, 1978.

Beveridge, Craig and Ronald Turnball. *The Eclipse of Scottish Culture*. Edinburgh: Polygon, 1989.

Biddiss, Michael, ed. *Images of Race*. New York: Holmes & Meier, 1979.

Birkett, Dea. *Spinsters Abroad. Victorian Lady Explorers*. Oxford: Basil Blackwell, 1989.

Bowler, Peter J. *Evolution. The History of an Idea*. Berkeley: Univ. of California Press, 1989.

Bradley, Ian.' "Having and Holding": The Highland Land War of the 1880's.' *History Today* 37(December 1987), pp. 23-8.

Bray, Elizabeth. *The Discovery of the Hebrides. Voyages to the Western Isles. 1745-1883*. London: Collins, 1986.

Brendon, Piers. *Thomas Cook.150 Years of Popular Tourism*. London: Secker & Warburg, 1991.

Brett, David. *The Construction of Heritage*. Cork: Cork Univ. Press, 1996.

Broun, Dauvit, R. J. Finlay and Michael Lynch, eds. *Image and Identity. The Making and Re-making of Scotland Through the Ages*. Edinburgh: John Donald, 1998.

Brown, David. *Walter Scott and the Historical Imagination*. Boston: Routledge & Kegan Paul, 1979.

Brown, Mary Ellen. *Burns and Tradition*. London: Macmillan, 1984.

Brown, P. Hume. *Early Travellers in Scotland*. Edinburgh, 1891. Reprint, Edinburgh: Mercat Press, 1978.

Buckley, Jerome. *The Triumph of Time; a study of the Victorian concepts of time, history, progress and decadence*. Cambridge, MA: Belknap Press of Harvard Univ. Press, 1966.

Burke, Peter. *Popular Culture in Early Modern Europe*. New York: New York Univ. Press, 1978.

Burrow, J. W. 'The Sense of the past', in Laurence Lerner, ed., *The Victorians*. London: Methuen & Co., Ltd., 1978, pp. 120-38.

—. *A Liberal Descent. Victorian historians and the English past*. New York: Cambridge Univ. Press, 1981.

Butler, R. W. *The Tourist Industry in the Highlands and Islands*. Ph.D. diss., Univ. of Glasgow, 1973.

—. 'Evolution of Tourism in the Scottish Highlands,' *Annals of Tourism Research* 12(1985), pp. 371-91.

Buzard, James. *The Beaten Track. European Tourism, Literature, and the Ways to 'Culture' 1800-1918*. Oxford: Clarendon Press, 1993.

—. 'Translation and Tourism: Scott's *Waverley* and the Rendering of Culture.' *Yale Journal of Criticism* 8, no. 2 (Fall, 1995), pp. 31-59.

Campbell, John L. and Trevor H. Hall. *Strange Things*. London: Routledge & Kegan Paul, 1968.

Cannadine, David. *Decline and Fall of the British Aristocracy*. New Haven: Yale Univ. Press, 1990.

Chapman, Malcolm. *The Gaelic Vision in Scottish Culture*. London: Croom Helm, 1978.

Chard, Chloe. *Pleasure and Guilt on the Grand Tour. Travel writing and imaginative geography 1600-1830*. New York: Manchester Univ. Press, St. Martin's Press, 1999.

Cheape, Hugh. *Tartan. The Highland Habit*. Edinburgh: National Museums of Scotland, 1991.

Checkland, Olive and Sydney Checkland. *Industry and Ethos: Scotland 1832-1914*. Edinburgh: Edinburgh Univ. Press, 1984.

Clyde, Robert. *From Rebel to Hero. The Image of the Highlander,1745-1830*. East Linton: Tuckwell Press, 1995.

Colley, Linda. *Britons. Forging the Nation, 1707-1837*. New Haven: Yale Univ. Press, 1992.

Cooper, Derek. *Road to the Isles: Travellers in the Hebrides 1770-1914*. Boston: Routledge & Kegan Paul, 1979.

Cosgrove, Denis E. *Social Formation and Symbolic Landscape*. London: Croom Helm, 1984.

Culler, Dwight. *Victorian Mirror of History*. New Haven: Yale Univ. Press, 1985.

Curtis, L. P. Jr. *Anglo-Saxons and Celts*. Bridgeport, CT: Conference on British Studies, 1968.

Davidoff, Leonore and Catherine Hall. *Family Fortunes. Men and women of the English middle class, 1780-1850*. Chicago: Univ. of Chicago Press, 1987.

Daiches, David. *The Paradox of Scottish Culture: The Eighteenth-Century Experience*. New York: Oxford Univ. Press, 1964.

—. *Glasgow*. New York: Granada, 1982.

Dellheim, Charles. *The face of the past. The preservation of the medieval inheritance in Victorian England*. New York: Cambridge Univ. Press, 1982.

Devine, T. M. *Clanship to Crofters' War. The social transformation of the Scottish Highlands*. New York: Manchester Univ. Press, 1994.

Donaldson, William. *Popular Literature in Victorian Scotland*. Aberdeen: Aberdeen Univ. Press, 1986.

Dunbar, John Telfer. *History of Highland Dress*. London: Oliver & Boyd, 1962.

Durie, Alastair J. ' "From Agreeable to Fashionable"; the Development of Coastal Tourism in Nineteenth Century East Lothian.' article manuscript supplied by the author.

—. 'Tourism in Victorian Scotland: The Case of Abbotsford.' *Scottish Economic & Social History* 2 (1992), pp. 42-54.

—. ' "Unconscious Benefactors": Grouse-shooting in Scotland, 1780-1914.' *The International Journal of the History of Sport* 15: 3 (Dec. 1998), pp. 57-73.

—. *Scotland for the Holidays. Tourism in Scotland c. 1780-1939*. East Linton: Tuckwell Press, 2003.

Fabricant, Carole. 'The Literature of Domestic Tourism and the Public Consumption of Private Property' in Felicity Nussbaum and Laura Brown, eds. *The New Eighteenth Century. Theory, Politics, English Literature*. New York: Methuen, 1987, pp. 254-75.

Feifer, Maxine. *Tourism in History: From Imperial Rome to the Present*. New York: Stein and Day, 1985.

Fenyo, Krisztina. *Contempt, Sympathy and Romance. Lowland Perceptions of the Highlands and the Clearances During the Famine Years, 1845-1855*. East Linton: Tuckwell Press, 2000.

Finley, Gerald. *Turner and George IV in Edinburgh.* Edinburgh: Tate Gallery in association with Edinburgh Univ. Press, 1981.

Finley, Richard J. 'Controlling the Past: Scottish Historiography and Scottish Identity in the 19th and 20th Centuries.' *Scottish Affairs* 9 (Autumn 1994), pp. 127-42.

—. 'Queen Victoria and the Cult of Scottish Monarchy', in Edward J. Cowan and Richard J. Finlay, eds. *Scottish History. The Power of the Past.* Edinburgh: Edinburgh Univ. Press, 2002, pp. 209-24.

Frawley, Maria H. *A Wider Range. Travel Writing by Women in Victorian England.* Toronto: Associated University Presses, 1994.

Freeman, Michael. *Railways and the Victorian Imagination.* New Haven: Yale Univ. Press, 1999.

Fry, Michael. *Patronage and Principle: A Political History of Modern Scotland.* Aberdeen: Aberdeen Univ. Press, 1987.

Fussell, Paul. *Abroad: British Literary Travelling Between the Wars.* New York: Oxford Univ. Press, 1980.

—. *Norton Book of Travel.* New York: Norton, 1987.

Gaskill, Howard, ed. *Ossian Revisited.* Edinburgh: Edinburgh Univ. Press, 1991.

Gaull, Marilyn. *English Romanticism: The Human Context.* New York: Norton, 1988.

Girouard, Mark. *The Return to Camelot: Chivalry and the English Gentleman.* New Haven: Yale Univ. Press, 1981.

—. *Life in the English Country House.* New York: Methuen, 1987.

Glendening, John. *The High Road. Romantic Tourism, Scotland and Literature, 1720-1820.* New York: St. Martin's, 1997.

Gold, John R., and Margaret M. Gold. *Imagining Scotland. Tradition, Representation and Promotion in Scottish Tourism since 1750.* Aldershot: Scolar Press, 1995.

—. 'Representing Culloden: Social Memory, Battlefield Heritage, and Landscapes of Regret.' in Stephen P. Hanna and Vincent J. Del Casino Jr., eds. *Mapping Tourism.* Minneapolis: Univ. of Minnesota Press, 2003, pp. 108-31.

Grenier, Katherine Haldane. 'Tourism and the Idea of the Skye Crofter: Nature, Race, Gender and the Late Nineteenth-Century Highland Identity.' *Victorians Institute Journal* 25 (1997), pp. 105-32.

Grewal, Inderpal. *Home and Harem. Nation, Gender, Empire and the Cultures of Travel* Durham, NC: Duke Univ. Press, 1996.

Hagglund, Elizabeth. 'Tourists and Travellers: Women's Non-Fictional Writing about Scotland 1770-1830.' Ph.D. diss., Univ. of Birmingham, 2000.

Haldane, Katherine J. 'Imagining Scotland: Tourist Images of Scotland, 1770-1914.' Ph.D. diss., Univ. of Virginia, 1990.

—. '"No human foot comes here": Victorian Tourists and the Isle of Skye.' *Nineteenth Century Studies* 10 (1996), pp. 69-92.

Haley, Bruce. *The Healthy Body and Victorian Culture.* Cambridge, MA: Harvard Univ. Press, 1978.

Hansen, Peter H. 'Albert Smith, the Alpine club, and the Invention of Mountaineering in Mid-Victorian Britain.' *Journal of British Studies* 34 (July 1995), pp. 300-324.

—. 'Vertical Boundaries, National Identities: British Mountaineering on the Frontiers of Europe and the Empire, 1868-1914.' *The Journal of Imperial and Commonwealth History* 24:1 (January 1996), pp. 48-71.

Hart, Francis Russell. *The Scottish Novel: From Smollett to Spark.* Cambridge, MA: Harvard Univ. Press, 1978.

Hart-Davis, Duff. *Monarchs of the Glen: A History of Deer Stalking in the Scottish Highlands.* London: Jonathan Cape, 1978.

Harvie, Christopher. *Scotland & Nationalism: Scottish Society and Politics 1707-1994.* New York: Routledge, 1994.

—. 'Scott and the image of Scotland.' in Raphael Samuel, ed. *Patriotism: The Making and Unmaking of British National Identity.* vol. II. *Minorities and Outsiders.* New York: Routledge, 1989, pp. 173-91.

Hayden, Donald E. *Wordsworth's Travels in Scotland.* Tulsa, OK: Univ. of Tulsa Press, 1985.

Hayden, John O., ed. *Scott, the Critical Heritage.* London: Routledge & Kegan Paul, 1970.

Hechter, Michael. *Internal Colonialism: The Celtic Fringe in British National Development 1536-1966.* Berkeley: Univ. of California Press, 1975.

Helsinger, Elizabeth K. *Rural Scenes and National Representation.* Princeton: Princeton Univ. Press, 1997.

Hemingway, Andrew. *Landscape imagery and urban culture in early nineteenth-century Britain.* Cambridge: Cambridge Univ. Press, 1992.

Hillhouse, James. *The Waverley Novels and their Critics.* New York: Octagon Books, 1970.

Himmelfarb, Gertrude. *Poverty and Compassion: The Moral Imagination of the late Victorians.* New York: Knopf, 1991.

Holloway, James and Lindsay Errington. *The Discovery of Scotland: The Appreciation of Scottish Scenery through two Centuries of Painting.* Edinburgh: National Gallery of Scotland, 1978.

Holt, Richard. *Sport and the British.* Oxford: Clarendon Press, 1989.

Hook, Andrew. 'Scotland and Romanticism: The International Scene.' in Andrew Hook, ed. *The History of Scottish Literature.* vol. 2. Aberdeen: Aberdeen Univ. Press, 1987, pp. 307-21.

Horne, Donald. *The Great Museum: The Re-presentation of History.* London: Pluto Press, 1984.

Houghton, Walter. *The Victorian Frame of Mind.* New Haven: Yale Univ. Press, 1957.

Howkins, Alun. 'The Discovery of Rural England.' in Robert Colls and Philip Dodd, eds. *Englishness: Politics and Culture 1880-1920.* New York: Croom Helm, 1986. pp. 62-88.

—. *Reshaping Rural England: A Social History 1850-1925.* London: Harper Collins Academic, 1991.

Hunt, Margaret. 'Racism, Imperialism, and the Traveler's Gaze in Eighteenth-Century England.' *Journal of British Studies* 32: 4 (October 1993), pp. 333-57.

Hunter, James. *The Making of the Crofting Community.* Edinburgh: John Donald, 1976.

—. *On the Other Side of Sorrow. Nature and People in the Scottish Highlands.* Edinburgh: Mainstream Publishing, 1995.

Inglis, David and Mary Holmes. 'Highland and Other Haunts. Ghosts in Scottish Tourism.' *Annals of Tourism Research* 30:1 (2003), pp. 50-63.

Irwin, David. 'A "Picturesque" Experience: The Hermitage at Dunkeld.' *The Connoisseur*, 187(Nov. 1974), pp. 196-202.

—. 'Three Foaming Cataracts. The Falls of Clyde.' *Country Life* 161 (May 5, 1977), pp. 1166-168.

Jann, Rosemary. *The Art and Science of Victorian History.* Columbus: Ohio State Univ. Press, 1985.

Jarvie, Grant. *Highland Games. The Making of the Myth.* Edinburgh: Edinburgh Univ. Press, 1991.

Jenkyns, Richard. *The Victorians and Ancient Greece.* Cambridge, MA: Harvard Univ. Press, 1980.

Johnson, Edgar. *Sir Walter Scott: The Great Unknown.* 2 vols. New York: Macmillan, 1970.

Kidd, Colin. *Subverting Scotland's Past. Scottish whig historians and the creation of an Anglo-British identity, 1689-c.1830.* New York: Cambridge Univ. Press, 1993.

—. 'The canon of patriotic landmarks in Scottish history.' *Scotlands* 1: (1994), pp. 1-17.

—. 'Gaelic Antiquity and National Identity in Enlightenment Ireland and Scotland'. *English Historical Review* 109: 434 (Nov. 1994), pp. 1197-214.

—. '*The Strange Death of Scottish History* revisited: Constructions of the Past in Scotland, c. 1790-1914.' *The Scottish Historical Review* LXXVA, 1: 201 (April 1997), pp. 86-102.

Kirshenblatt-Gimblett, Barbara. *Destination Culture. Tourism, Museums, and Heritage.* Berkeley: Univ. of California Press, 1998.

Lang, Timothy. *The Victorians and the Stuart Heritage. Interpretations of a discordant past.* New York: Cambridge Univ. Press, 1995.

Langford, Paul. *A Polite and Commercial People. England 1727-1783.* New York: Oxford, 1992.

Lears. T. J. Jackson. *No Place of Grace: Antimodernism and the Transformation of American Culture 1880-1920.* New York: Pantheon Books, 1981.

Leed, Eric J. *The Mind of the Traveler. From Gilgamesh to Global Tourism.* New York: BasicBooks, 1991.

Lenman, Bruce. *The Jacobite Risings in Britain 1689-1746.* London: Methuen, 1980.

—. *Integration, Enlightenment, and Industrialization: Scotland 1746-1832.* London: Edward Arnold, 1981.

Lewis, Jayne E. *Mary Queen of Scots. Romance and Nation.* New York: Routledge, 1998.

Lindsay, Maurice. *History of Scottish Literature.* London: Robert Hale, 1977.

Lennie, Campbell. *Landseer: The Victorian Paragon.* London: Hamish Hamilton, 1976.

Loomis, Chauncy. 'The Arctic Sublime' in U. C. Knoepflmacher and G. B. Tennyson, eds., *Nature and the Victorian Imagination.* Berkeley: Univ. of California Press, 1977.

Lorimer, Hayden. 'Guns, Game and the Grandee: The Cultural Politics of Deerstalking in the Scottish Highlands.' *Ecumene* 2000 7(4), pp. 403-31.

—. 'Ways of seeing the Scottish Highlands: marginality, authenticity and the curious case of the Hebridean blackhouse.' *Journal of Historical Geography* 25: 4(1999), pp. 517-33.

Low, Donald A. ed. *Critical Essays on Robert Burns*. Boston: Routledge & Kegan Paul, 1975.

Lowenthal, David. *The Past is a Foreign Country*. New York: Cambridge Univ. Press, 1985.

—. 'British National Identity and the English Landscape.' *Rural History* 2: 2 (1991), pp. 205-30.

Lynch, Michael. *Scotland. A New History*. London: Pimlico, 1991.

MacArthur, Mairi. 'Blasted Heaths and Hills of Mist. The Highlands and Islands through travellers' eyes.' *Scottish Affairs* 3 (Spring, 1993), pp. 23-31.

McArthur, Colin. 'Culloden: A Pre-Emptive Strike.' *Scottish Affairs* 9 (Autumn 1994), pp. 97-125.

MacCannell, Dean. *The Tourist. A New Theory of the Leisure Class*. New York: Schoken Books, 1976.

Maclean, James N. M. and Basil Skinner. *The Royal Visit of 1822*. Edinburgh: Edinburgh Univ. Press, 1972.

McCoy, Drew R. *The Elusive Republic. Political Economy in Jeffersonian America*. Chapel Hill: Univ. of North Carolina Press, for the Institute of Early American History and Culture, Williamsburg, VA, 1980.

McCrone, David, Angela Morris, Richard Kiely. *Scotland – The Brand. The Making of Scottish Heritage*. Edinburgh: Edinburgh Univ. Press, 1995.

MacDonald, Fraser. 'St. Kilda and the Sublime.' *Ecumene* 2001 8(2), pp. 151-74.

MacDonald, Sharon. *Reimagining Culture. Histories, Identities and the Gaelic Renaissance*. New York: Berg, 1997.

Mackenzie, John M. *The Empire of Nature. Hunting, Conservation and British Imperialism*. New York: Manchester Univ. Press, 1988.

—. 'The imperial pioneer and hunter and the British masculine stereotype in late Victorian and Edwardian times.' in Mangan and Walvin, *Manliness and morality*, pp. 176-96.

McLynn, Frank. *The Jacobites*. London: Routledge and Kegan Paul, 1985.

McPherson, Bruce. *Between Two Worlds: Victorian Ambivalence about Progress*. Washington, DC: Univ. Press of America, 1983.

Mandler, Peter. 'Against "Englishness": English Culture and the Limits to Rural Nostalgia, 1850-1940.' *Transactions of the Royal Historical Society* 6th series 7 (1997), pp. 155-75.

—. ' "In the Olden Time" : Romantic history and English national identity, 1820-50' in Laurence Brockliss and David Eastwood, eds. *A Union of multiple identities. The British Isles, c. 1750-c.1850*. New York: Manchester University Press, 1997, pp. 78-92.

—. ' "The Wand of Fancy": The Historical Imagination of the Victorian Tourist.' in Marius Kwint, Christopher Brewarda and Jeremy Aynsley, eds. *Material Memories*. New York: Berg, 1999, pp. 125-41.

Mangan, J. A. and James Walvin, eds. *Manliness and morality: Middle-class masculinity in Britain and America 1800-1940*. Manchester: Manchester Univ. Press, 1978.

Mills, Sara. 'Knowledge, Gender and Empire' in Alison Blunt, Gillian Rose, eds. *Writing Women and Space. Colonial and Postcolonial Geographies.* New York: The Guilford Press, 1994, pp. 29-50.

Mingay, G. E., ed. *The Victorian Countryside.* 2 vols. London: Routledge & Kegan Paul, 1981.

Mitchell, Arthur. *List of Travels and Tours in Scotland 1296-1900.* Edinburgh, 1902.

Mitchell, W. J. T., ed. *Landscape and Power.* Chicago: Univ. of Chicago Press, 1994.

Mitchison, Rosalind. *A History of Scotland.* New York: Routledge, 1970.

Moir, Esther. *The Discovery of Britain.* London: Routledge & Kegan Paul, 1964.

Monk, Samuel. *The Sublime.* Ann Arbor: Univ. of Michigan Press, 1960.

Morgan, Marjorie. *National Identities and Travel in Victorian Britain.* Houndsmills: Palgrave, 2001.

Morgan, Susan. *Place Matters. Gendered Geography in Victorian Women's Travel Books about Southeast Asia.* New Brunswick: Rutgers Univ. Press, 1996.

Morton, Graeme. 'The Most Efficacious Patriot: The Heritage of William Wallace in Nineteenth-Century Scotland.' *The Scottish Historical Review* LXXVII, 2: 204 (October 1998), pp. 224-51.

—. 'What if? The Significance of Scotland's Missing Nationalism in the Nineteenth Century.' in Dauvit Broun, R. J. Finlay and Michael Lynch, eds. *Image and Identity. The Making of Scotland Through the Ages.* Edinburgh: John Donald, 1998, pp. 157-76.

—. *Unionist Nationalism. Governing Urban Scotland, 1830-1860.* East Linton: Tuckwell Press, 1999.

Muir, Edwin. *Scott and Scotland: The Predicament of the Scottish Writer.* Edinburgh: Polygon Books, 1982.

Nairn, Tom. *The Break-Up of Britain.* London: NLB, 1977.

Newman, Gerald. *The Rise of English Nationalism.* New York: St. Martin's, 1987.

Nicholson, Marjorie Hope. *Mountain Gloom, Mountain Glory: The Development of the Aesthetics of the Infinite.* Ithaca, NY: Cornell Univ. Press, 1959.

O'Connor, Maura. *The Romance of Italy and the English Political Imagination.* New York: St. Martin's, 1998.

Ormond, Richard. *Sir Edwin Landseer.* New York: Rizzoli, 1981.

Orr, Willie. *Deer Forests, Landlords, and Crofters.* Edinburgh: John Donald, 1982.

Ousby, Ian. *The Englishman's England. Taste, travel and the rise of tourism.* New York: Cambridge, 1990.

Paterson, Alan J. S. *The Golden Years of the Clyde Steamers.* Newton Abbot: David & Charles, 1969.

Piggott, Stuart. *Ancient Britons and the Antiquarian Imagination.* New York: Thames and Hudson, 1989.

Pittock, Murray G. H. *The Invention of Scotland. The Stuart Myth and the Scottish Identity, 1638 to the Present.* New York: Routledge, 1991.

—. *The Myth of the Jacobite Clans.* Edinburgh: Edinburgh Univ. Press, 1995.

—. *Celtic Identity and the British Image.* New York: Manchester Univ. Press, 1999.

—. 'The Jacobite Cult' in Edward J. Cowan and Richard J. Finlay, eds. *Scottish History. The Power of the Past.* Edinburgh: Edinburgh Univ. Press, 2002, pp. 191-208.

Pocock, Douglas C. D. ed. *Humanistic Geography and Literature: Essays on the Experience of Place.* London: Croom Helm, 1981.

Pratt, Mary Louise. *Imperial Eyes. Travel Writing and Transculturation.* New York: Routledge, 1992.

Pringle, Trevor R. 'The privation of history: Landseer, Victoria and the Highland myth' in Denis Cosgrove and Stephen Daniels, eds. *The iconography of landscape.* New York: Cambridge Univ. Press, 1988, pp. 142-61.

Pudney, John. *The Thomas Cook Story.* London: Michael Joseph, 1953.

Ray, Celeste. *Highland Heritage. Scottish Americans in the American South.* Chapel Hill: Univ. of North Carolina Press, 2001.

Richards, Eric. 'How Tame were the Highlanders During the Clearances?' *Scottish Studies* 17:1 (1973), pp. 35-50.

—. *A History of the Highland Clearances: Agrarian Transformation and the Evictions 1746-1886.* London: Croom Helm, 1982.

—. 'Scotland and the Uses of the Atlantic Empire' in Bernard Bailyn and Phillip D. Morgan, eds. *Strangers within the Realm: Cultural Margins of the First British Empire.* Chapel Hill: Univ. of North Carolina Press, 1991, pp. 67-114.

Richards, Jeffrey and John M. MacKenzie. *The Railway Station. A Social History.* New York: Oxford Univ. Press, 1986.

Robertson, C. J. A. *The Origins of the Scottish Railway System 1772-1844.* Edinburgh: John Donald, 1983.

Ross, Ellen. *Love and Toil. Motherhood in Outcast London.* New York: Oxford Univ. Press, 1993.

Ross, Ian. 'A Bluestocking over the Border: Mrs. Elizabeth Montague's Aesthetic Adventures in Scotland, 1766.' *Huntington Library Quarterly: A Journal for the History and Interpretation of English and American Civilization* 28(1965), pp. 213-33.

Russett, Cynthia Eagle. *Sexual Science: The Victorian Construction of Womanhood.* Cambridge, Harvard Univ. Press, 1989.

Said, Edward. *Orientalism.* New York: Vintage Books, 1979.

—. *Culture and Imperialism.* New York: Vintage Books, 1994.

Schama, Simon. *Landscape and Memory.* New York: Alfred A. Knopf, 1995.

Schivelbusch, Wolfgang. *The Railway Journey. The Industrialization of Time and Space in the 19th Century.* Berkeley: Univ. of California Press, 1986.

Schmitt, Peter J. *Back to Nature. The Arcadian Myth in Urban America.* Baltimore: Johns Hopkins Univ. Press, 1990.

Scott, James C. *Domination and the Arts of Resistance: Hidden Transcripts.* New Haven: Yale Univ. Press, 1990.

Sears, John F. *Sacred Places. American Tourist Attractions in the Nineteenth Century.* New York: Oxford Univ. Press, 1989.

Shaw, John. 'Land, people and nation: historicist voices in the Highland land campaign, c. 1850-1883.' in Eugenio F. Biagini, ed. *Citizenship and community. Liberals, radicals and collective identities in the British Isles, 1865-1931.* New York: Cambridge Univ. Press, 1996, pp. 305-24.

Silver, Carole G. *Strange and Secret Peoples. Fairies and Victorian Consciousness.* New York: Oxford Univ. Press, 1999.

Simmons, Jack. 'Railways, Hotels, and Tourism in Great Britain, 1830-1914.' *Journal of Contemporary History* 19 (1984), pp. 201-22.

—. *The Victorian Railway.* New York: Thames and Hudson, 1991.

Smailes, Helen and Duncan Thomson. *The Queen's Image.* Edinburgh: Scottish National Portrait Gallery, 1987.

Smart, J. S. *James Macpherson: An Episode in Literature.* London, 1905. Reprint, New York, AMS Press, 1973.

Smiles, Sam. *The Image of Antiquity. Ancient Britain and the Romantic Imagination.* New Haven: Yale Univ. Press, 1994.

Smout, Christopher. 'Tours in the Scottish Highlands from the eighteenth to the twentieth centuries.' *Northern Scotland* 5(1983), pp. 99-121.

Smout, T. C. *A History of the Scottish People 1560-1830.* London: Fontana Press, 1972.

—. *A Century of the Scottish People 1830-1950.* London: Fontana Press, 1987.

—. 'The Highlands and the Roots of Green Consciousness, 1750-1990.' *Proceedings of the British Academy* 76 (1991), pp. 237-64.

Spufford, Francis. *I May Be Some Time. Ice and the English Imagination.* New York: St. Martin's Press, 1997.

Stafford, Barbara Maria. *Voyage Into Substance: Art, Science, Nature and the Illustrated Travel Account, 1760-1840.* Cambridge, MA: MIT Press, 1984.

Stearns, Peter. *Be A Man! Males in Modern Society.* New York: Holmes & Meier, 1990.

Stowe, William W. *Going Abroad. European Travel in Nineteenth-Century American Culture.* Princeton: Princeton Univ. Press, 1994.

Swinglehurst, Edmund. *Cook's Tours: The Story of Popular Travel.* Poole, Dorset: Blandford Press, 1982.

Thomas, John. *A Regional History of the Railways of Great Britain, vol. VI Scotland: The Lowlands and the Borders.* 1971. Revised and enlarged by Alan J. S. Paterson. Newton Abbot: David & Charles, 1984.

—. *The West Highland Railway.* 1965. extra material by Alan J. S. Paterson. Newton Abbot: David & Charles, 1984.

Thomas, Keith. *Man and the Natural World.* New York: Oxford Univ. Press, 1983.

Thomson, Derick S. ed. *The Companion to Gaelic Scotland.* Oxford: Basil Blackwell, 1983.

Thompson, F. M. L. *The Rise of Respectable Society.* Cambridge, MA: Harvard Univ. Press, 1988.

—. 'Victorian England: The Horse-Drawn Society' in Richard M. Golden, ed. *Social History of Western Civilization.* Vol. II. New York: St. Martin's 1992, pp. 159-70.

Tinniswood, Adrian. *A History of Country House Visiting. Five Centuries of Tourism and Taste.* Cambridge: Basil Blackwell and the National Trust, 1989.

Tosh, John. *A Man's Place. Masculinity and the Middle-Class Home in Victorian England.* New Haven: Yale Univ. Press, 1999.

Trevor-Roper, Hugh. 'The Invention of Tradition: The Highland Tradition of Scotland.' in Eric Hobsbawm and Terence Ranger, eds. *The Invention of Tradition.* New York: Cambridge Univ. Press, 1983, pp. 15-41.

Trinder, Barrie. *The Making of the Industrial Landscape*. London: Phoenix Giant, 1997.

Trumpener, Katie. *Bardic Nationalism. The Romantic Novel and the British Empire*. Princeton: Princeton Univ. Press, 1997.

Turner, Victor and Edith Turner. *Image and Pilgrimage in Christian Culture*. New York: Columbia Univ. Press, 1978.

Urry, John. *The Tourist Gaze: Leisure and Travel in Contemporary Societies*. New York: Sage Publications, 1990.

Utz, Hans. 'A Genevan's Journey to the Hebrides in 1807: An Anti-Johnsonian Venture.' *Studies in Scottish Literature* 27(1992), pp. 47-71.

Vamplew, Wray. 'Railways and the Scottish Transport System in the Nineteenth Century.' *The Journal of Transport History* 1:3 (February, 1972), pp. 133-45.

Walker, Eric G. *Scott's Fiction and the Picturesque*. Salzburg: Institute fur Anglistik & Amerikansitik, Universitat Salzburg, 1982.

Weiner, Martin J. 'England is the Country: Modernization and the National Self-Image.' *Albion* I (1971), pp.198-211.

—. *English Culture and the Decline of the Industrial Spirit 1850-1980*. New York: Penguin, 1981.

Winter, James. *Secure from Rash Assault. Sustaining the Victorian Environment*. Berkeley: Univ. of Calif. Press, 1999.

Withers, Charles E. *Gaelic in Scotland 1689-1981. The Geographical History of a Language*. Edinburgh: John Donald, 1984.

—. 'The Historical Creation of the Scottish Highlands.' in Ian Donnachie and Christopher Watley, eds. *The Manufacture of Scottish History*. Edinburgh: Polygon, 1992, pp. 143-56.

—. 'Picturing Highland landscapes: George Washington Wilson and the photography of the Scottish Highlands.' *Landscape Research* 19:2 (1994), pp. 68-79.

—. 'Authorizing landscape: "authority", naming and the Ordnance Survey's mapping of the Scottish Highlands in the nineteenth century'. *Journal of Historical Geography* 26: 4 (2000), pp. 532-54.

Withey, Lynne. *Grand Tours and Cook's Tours*. New York: William Morrow, 1997.

Williams, Raymond. *The Country and The City*. New York: Oxford Univ. Press, 1973.

—. *Culture & Society: 1780-1950*. New York: Columbia Univ. Press, 1983.

Williams, William H. A. 'Putting Paddy in the Picture.' Paper presented at Snapshots from Abroad: A conference on American and British Travel Writers and Writing, Minneapolis, MN, November, 1997.

—. 'Blow, Bugle, Blow: Romantic Tourism and the Echoes of Killarney.' in S. Henriquez, ed. *Travel Essentials. Collected Essays on Travel Writing*. Las Palmas de Gran Canaria: Chandlon Inn Press, 1998, pp. 133-47.

—. 'Into the West: Landscape and the Imperial Imagination in Connemara, 1820-1870.' *New Hibernia Review* 2: 1 (Spring 1998), pp. 69-90.

Womack, Peter. *Improvement and Romance. Constructing the Myth of the Highlands*. London: MacMillan Press, 1989.

Youngson, A. J. *After the Forty-Five. The Economic Impact on the Scottish Highlands*. Edinburgh: Edinburgh Univ. Press, 1973.

—. *The Making of Classical Edinburgh*. Edinburgh: Edinburgh Univ. Press, 1966.

Index

(references to illustrations are in **bold**)